# Preface

THE aim in this anthology is simply to portray a number of explorers in action, either at critical moments in their journeys or when displaying their individual qualities conspicuously. Within this general scheme, I then looked for readable passages dealing as far as possible with complete incidents in a convenient length. Sea voyages and mountaineering expeditions have in general been excluded. The wide range has made it possible to achieve variety and to avoid overlapping. The choice is not put forward as a comprehensive survey; the absence of well-known names does not imply any criticism of them or of their achievements.

I have made no attempt to edit the texts extensively, as this book is intended, not for the specialist, but for the general reader. To assist him I have on occasion modernized the spelling or amended the punctuation. Omissions have been shown in the usual manner. If the place-names are not those in present use, the modern forms are indicated. Each place can therefore be found on a good modern atlas. The introductory notes before the extracts are intended only to place them in their context; they are neither complete biographies nor excerpts from a history of exploration. Footnotes have also been kept to a minimum. The maps are designed to indicate the area with which each extract deals and to enable it to be located on an atlas.

In compiling this anthology I have benefited much from access to the comprehensive library of the Royal Geographical Society. This lightened the task considerably. The greater part of the African extracts were chosen by Mrs. Dorothy Middleton, who also contributed the introductory notes, as well as those on Isabella Bird and Wilfred Thesiger. Miss Alison Usher prepared the typescript efficiently, and Miss Wendy Gross, of Messrs. Cassell's editorial department, checked many references and names.

I am also indebted to the Council of the Hakluyt Society for generous permission to quote freely from its publications. The publications of the Society are in themselves a gigantic anthology of exploration, and those who wish to read further should certainly consult their volumes.                                    G.R.C.

# THE EXPLORERS

## Great Adventurers Tell
## Their Own Stories of Discovery

COMPILED AND EDITED BY

## G. R. CRONE

INTRODUCTION BY

## SERGE A. KORFF

*President, The Explorers Club*

THOMAS Y. CROWELL COMPANY

*New York • Established 1834*

# Contents

# NORTH AMERICA

# SOUTH AMERICA

# AUSTRALIA

# POLAR REGIONS

# List of Maps

The editor wishes to acknowledge the kindness of those authors and publishers from whose work the various extracts in this book have, with their permission, been taken.

# Introduction to the American Edition
## by Serge A. Korff

PROFESSOR OF PHYSICS, NEW YORK UNIVERSITY

PRESIDENT, THE EXPLORERS CLUB

EXPLORATION and explorers always seem romantic. We picture a lone man—or, at most, a small band—heroically winning past obstacles to a noble goal.

Yet this emphasis on romantic adventure only incites the fury of the professional explorer and his colleagues. The explorer himself is chagrined that a trivial incident is played up while the significant part of his work is overlooked. Meanwhile, his friends and professional equals denounce him as a faker, a publicity hound, or, what may be worse, a bungler.

To the experts, adventures demonstrate incompetence. Someone goofed. A properly run expedition will have very few adventures. But if ignorance or bravado leads an explorer to annoy a native or an animal, or violate a safety rule, or neglect maintenance of his equipment, or misjudge his supplies . . . then an adventure may result. And all the expedition's skill may be called upon to extricate the goofer from disaster while productive duties are laid aside.

Yet exploration, by definition, requires men to live and work in strange, usually hostile, territory. The most careful plans cannot foresee every difficulty. The most conscientious attention to detail cannot always forestall the unexpected. And, to ordinary citizens at home, the mere fact of travel into unfamiliar corners of the world is itself an adventure.

In this book, the author has selected excerpts from the actual accounts written by various explorers. Here we can relive adventures, ranging from attacks by natives to lonely treks across harsh desert. But more important is the revealing glimpse into the explorers' thoughts and hopes which we get by reading their own words.

The merits of any exploration must be judged in the light of the problems of the day in which it was carried out, and in the light of the means then available. The tools have changed remarkably, especially in the last half-century. Air transport in particular has made a substantial change in what can be done. Yet it has not necessarily made things easier or less dangerous. The explorer flying through a severe storm is just as much at the mercy of the elements as his predecessor was in an old sailing ship. He can starve to death today if a helicopter engine fails over some remote area, just as he might have starved if bearers had deserted an overland expedition.

The great boon of air transport is its reduction of travel time between home and base. By sailing ship the trip from England to India took months. So did the voyage from New England to Antarctica. Today the explorer reaches his base in hours. In some cases, the entire expedition—men, supplies, and even housing—can be airlifted. Certain types of aircraft also speed the exploration itself. They make possible effective scouting for the best routes and airdropped supplies to field parties.

Yet some of the most important exploration must still be done the old-fashioned way. To make the recent measurements of ice thickness on the Antarctic continent—measurements which have completely changed our ideas of the physical geography of this part of the globe —men had to slog overland, often with just as great physical difficulty as did Scott and Amundsen half a century ago. While air transport has added a new and useful tool, it has not supplanted men on foot, and the accounts of the treks of Sir Vivian Fuchs and Sir Edmund Hillary are well worth reading.

Modern transport has made possible larger expeditions. This increase in manpower is essential today, for many of the simple problems that could be handled by one man unaided have now been solved. Some of the large expeditions are staffed by a whole group of specialized experts: anthropologists, archeologists, botanists, cosmic-ray physicists, glaciologists, seismologists, zoologists. Still, the skillful individual often determines the value of the entire expedition. It is the small field parties, consisting of one man or a very few, that go out from the main base and bring back the major discoveries that contribute to man's knowledge of the world. All the aids of modern science and technology are useful tools, but good science is practiced today by men, just as it was centuries ago.

# Introduction

THE figure of the explorer occupies a more prominent place in British history than perhaps that of any other country. For this there are sufficient reasons in the course of British overseas expansion and settlement. In the popular mind, the explorer is a tough and dedicated character, who pushes out into the 'blanks on the map', with little regard to personal safety, and after a series of startling and hair-raising incidents returns to civilization with a rough map of the hitherto unknown country and stories of strange peoples. This limited application of the term is largely a product of the nineteenth century, when western civilization was pouring out over the globe. It is founded upon popular images, such as Edward John Eyre plodding obstinately across the sands of central Australia, or of Franklin's men struggling to escape southwards from the Arctic wastes. It is in fact against the Polar regions that this image of the explorer is most clearly focused. As L. P. Kirwan has shown, the recent development of this conception owes much to the manœuvres of the great newspaper proprietor, eager to feed the appetite for sensation of his millions of readers. To the expert, an expedition which meets with accidents, however 'heroic' and sensational, is a failure, if they reveal bad planning or foolhardiness. To the news-paperman, an expedition, however important its scientific results, which can release no 'human' story, is a dead loss, as explorers have found to their cost. Since the first war, another impulse has rein-forced increasingly the urge to explore. Dissatisfied with many aspects of modern life, with its increasing emphasis upon the machine and upon material rewards, explorers have deliberately sought conditions in which they can pit their physical and spiritual resources against the forces of nature at its most pitiless, for their own personal satisfaction. This is not, of course, an entirely new phenomenon; to go no further back than the early days of this century, it was un-doubtedly the driving force behind Ernest Shackleton's unsurpassed feats in the Antarctic. It is this movement which has also transformed mountaineering from the rather leisurely recreation of Victorian gentlemen into the exacting and testing pursuit it is today. This was certainly one of the most powerful springs of action in 'Gino' Watkin's character and has animated many of his successors in this field. Allied to it in many instances is the spirit of inquiry, in its highest manifestation a dedication to science. This is the spirit which impelled Scott and his companions to drag with them a collection of geological specimens on the closing stages of their last journey, or Fuchs to carry out a series of geophysical soundings on his Antarctic crossing. One cannot but feel that much of the energy and high spirits which formerly found an outlet in so-called 'colonial' wars and overseas administration is now harnessed to the cause of exploration.

But exploration is customarily and historically applied in a much wider sense, and has certainly not been limited to uninhabited regions previously untraversed by man, such as the summit of Mount Everest, the Greenland ice sheet, or the great empty desert of southern Arabia. If 'revelation' is substituted for 'exploration', the position is clearer, in the sense of the first revelation of a region— its physical features and the ways of its inhabitants—to the traveller's own countrymen. From this point of view the region may have been 'explored' several times in history, and from different angles. Central Asia has been explored by the Hellenic armies of Alexander the Great, by Chinese administrators and pilgrims, by the politico-scientific travellers of the nineteenth century, among many others. Central Africa had been explored in part by Arab slavers before the days of Livingstone and Stanley, and some would argue that Irish monks or Norse adventurers had preceded the sixteenth-century explorers of North America.

After each great wave of expansion, such areas have frequently lapsed into oblivion as far as the outside world is concerned, to be rediscovered by a new generation impelled by fresh motives and with a different outlook. Often it has been a matter of the explorer breaking into, as it were, a closed system, cultural or political. Once this opening was made good, a wide area for travel almost automatically presented itself. The autocracy of the Mongol Khans, maintaining order and an internal system of communications, opened the way for European friar or merchant, a William of Rubruquis or a Marco Polo, to Karakoram or Cambaluc, the capital of an almost mythical Cathay. Within twenty years of the Portuguese fleet appearing off Cochin and seizing the nerve centre of the great maritime trading organism built up on the Indian Ocean and the regularity of the monsoon, Portuguese traders and missionaries were in the Moluccas and seeking entry into the empire of China. After some hard fighting and bloody massacres, the Aztec empire in Mexico and the Inca lands in South America were open to the Spaniards—but the course of events in the great, monotonous tropical forests of the Amazon basin was vastly different. Apart from natural hindrances, in fact, the lack of a pre-existing political or social unity was often the great obstacle confronting the explorer. The rivalry of Iroquois and Hurons set a problem for the explorers of North America just as the militant sects of Islam bedevilled the traveller in the East, or, on a minor scale, the local hostilities and xenophobia of the numerous tribes of the New Guinea interior hampered the work of the Australian administrative officers. It is easy, also, to overlook the strain which the food demands of even a relatively small expedition placed upon economies which were barely above the subsistence line, or had been dislocated by a series of bad harvests.

Another factor of considerable importance was the readiness or otherwise of the potential traveller to understand and adopt the outlook and travel techniques of the peoples in whose lands they proposed to wander, a reluctance summed up in one traveller's report: 'their habits are filthy and customs they have none.' The French Canadian *coureur de bois* had no inhibitions against adopting the methods of the North American Indians, while his English contemporaries of the Hudson's Bay Company slept the 'long sleep by the frozen sea'. The best example of this is the revolution in Polar travel effected by Nansen when he boldly abandoned conventional methods and applied to similar environments techniques evolved over the years by the Eskimo, following out in this respect the largely unappreciated innovations of Dr. John Rae fifty years earlier. (Vilhjalmur Steffanson, the great protagonist of 'living off the land', holds that the Game Laws of England were a contributory factor in the inability of naval Arctic expeditions to maintain themselves on local resources.) It is difficult not to share the repugnance of Captain

Scott against one extreme manifestation of it—the slaughtering and eating of the sledge dogs in an emergency, though this embargo did not apply, curiously enough, to ponies.

But nothing which has been said above in explanation of the success or failure of explorers diminishes in any degree the quality or the splendour of their achievements. In the long run it is nothing greater or lesser than personality, a factor which it is perhaps easy to overlook or underrate, if they are regarded as little more than figures operating under the strains and stresses of their day and age. Hernando Cortés, Fridtjof Nansen, David Livingstone, Alexander von Humboldt, would have been great men in any age or profession, indeed many later made names for themselves in other paths of life. Their common characteristic was an unquenchable curiosity and the power and will to indulge it.

If these men are regarded, as with few exceptions they must be, as primarily the advance guard of expanding cultures, it is perhaps idle to inquire into the particular motives which inspired them, since they are as varied as those of all the other actors on the stage of history—the lust for power and an unshakable belief in the Christian religion as he understood it, of Cortés, the restless, self-destructive energy of Burton, the sympathetic humanity and determination of David Livingstone, the sense of duty of James Cook, the loyalty to naval tradition of Robert Falcon Scott, the almost mystical sense of destiny of Christopher Columbus, the intense desire to know of Alexander von Humboldt, the indomitable high spirits of Mary Kingsley in pursuit of anthropological oddities, even the desire for notoriety of Frederick Cook. Others, like Cabeza da Vaca, had the role of explorer thrust upon them. As to conduct when in action, the basic characteristics common to them all are obvious: a clear-cut idea of what they were attempting and the determination, courage and adaptability to changing circumstances required to carry it out. But each have possessed some special ingredient or ingredients of their own, to which their achievements owe their special flavour or the degree of success attained. The ruthlessness of Stanley or Cortés is set against the sympathetic feeling towards the native peoples of Meriwether Lewis, David Livingstone or Wilfred Thesiger and many another; the self-centred individualism of Richard

Burton or Aurel Stein against the inspired leadership of Ernest Shackleton or Robert Falcon Scott. But to carry such an analysis too far would result in a biographical sketch of each individual explorer. However, one more perhaps deserves notice: ingenuity in meeting a crisis—as displayed by Cortés and his bridge, Mawson and his ladder, even Samuel Baker breaking in oxen for riding when other means of transport failed.

As to the power of their narratives, we hope this anthology will speak for them; but whatever their prose style—Elizabethan, Johnsonian, or the more relaxed style of the present, there is never any doubt about what they were doing or what they thought about their surroundings.

Their narratives are arranged here first by continents and then chronologically. In reading each section it will help to keep certain general considerations in mind. This is perhaps hardest in the case of Asia. To isolate even a few out of the manifold phases in her 'exploration' is well nigh impossible; the story is almost as much one of the 'exploration' of her civilizations as of her mountains and plains. Mongol supremacy and the spread of Moslem culture afforded opportunities which were put to good use by medieval Christian and Arab travellers: Tudor expansion took British merchants to every port of note from the Persian Gulf to Japan; in the nineteenth century it was the Celestial Empire, the vast mountains and the harsh interior which drew men from the West. And for the last century at least, particularly for the British, there has been the strange, almost unaccountable attraction of Arabia.

With Africa, the course of events since the Renaissance has been simpler, but in no way of lesser interest; nearly four centuries of skirmishing and trading along the coasts—sought after rather as stages on the route to India than for their intrinsic value; then little more than one century of penetration inland in every direction, with all the international political manœuvring which followed in its wake, but often dictated also by that philanthropic idealism which is now too commonly decried.

In North America exploration followed well-marked stages: the revelation of the south-west by the Spaniards, ancillary to their conquest of Mexico; the opening-up of the great river basins of the

St. Lawrence and the Mississippi by the French in the north; the pioneering of routes to the Pacific Ocean and the North-West by French and British fur-trappers and traders, and finally the great surge of occupation and settlement from the Alleghenies across the Plains and the Rockies to the Pacific, which irrevocably shaped the destiny of the continent. The story is less integrated in South America; the establishment of European control on the coastal margins and the uplands of the north and west and the penetration along the great Amazon river and its tributaries, followed by the piecemeal exploration of the interior, largely anonymous and still incomplete. A somewhat similar pattern is revealed by Australia; the completion of the coastal surveys by the opening years of the nineteenth century; the exploration of the great Murray-Darling river system, and finally the penetration of the vast interior, hostile to man and yet continually luring him on. The course of polar exploration has shown rather different features. The penetration of the Arctic was attempted in the sixteenth century by the Dutch and English as a move against Portugal and Spain, but the North-East and North-West Passages were not achieved until the end of the nineteenth century. Since then science and international politics have supplied the main motives. The latter also dominate the Antarctic scene, where exploration began with the object of proving or disproving the existence of a great, hypothetical Southern continent, and has continued to probe the last great unknown area on the earth's surface and to determine its position in the physics of the globe. The bitter, storm-swept Antarctic plateau, without human or natural life, is a unique testing ground for spiritual and material values, and until recently it has been almost a British preserve. As a commentator has recently remarked: 'The British public remains obstinately obsessed with snowy wastes. The idea of a million square miles of ice, with no one in it but oneself and a few friends of the same sex, exerts a strange fascination on the Englishman.'

In the past it has sometimes been fashionable to mock at the conventional figure of the explorer, with his concern over tedious details of the march or the absence of creature comforts, but modern geography, and all its political and social bearings, rests firmly upon his achievements. And yet today, even in these islands there are areas in which literally the scientist is ignorant of the natural processes at work. The Humboldts or Darwins of the future, and their humbler colleagues, will never be at a loss for new fields to explore.

'Ever since Almighty God commanded Adam to subdue the earth, there have not wanted in all ages some heroicall spirits which, in obedience to that high mandate, either from manifest reason alluring them, or by secret instinct inforcing them thereunto, have expended their wealth, imployed their times, and adventured their persons to finde out the true circuit thereof.'

Francis Drake, the younger

# ASIA

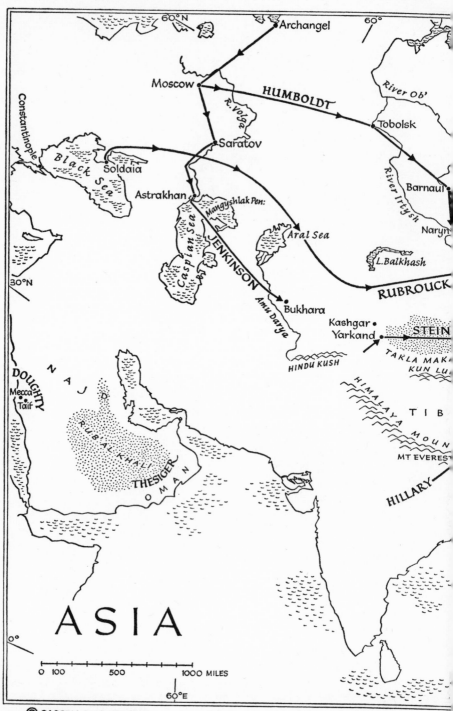

ASIA

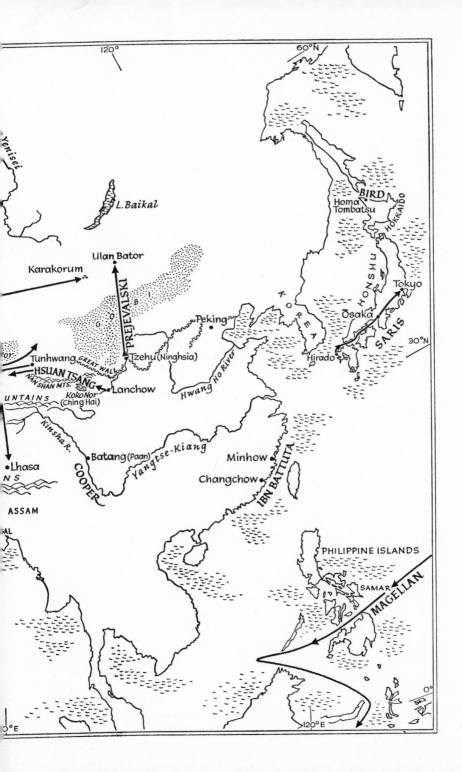

# Hsuan-tsang
## 603–664

UNDER the Tang dynasty, China embarked upon one of her periods of expansion westwards into Central Asia. The way was thus open for Buddhist scholars, anxious to re-establish contact with India, the birthplace of their religion. One of the most famous of these travelling scholars was Hsuan-tsang, 'The Master of the Law', who wished to collect and bring back to China the sacred books of the Buddha. Setting out from Lanchow (Kaolan) near the western end of the Great Wall, he journeyed along the trade route which ran by the foot of the Nan Shan mountains and the South Gobi and Takla Makan desert to Yarkand and Kashgar, and thence southwards through the Pamirs and the Hindu Kush to Peshawar and the great plains of Northern India. Hsuan-tsang was warmly welcomed by the rulers of the territories through which he passed, and provided with escorts. After travelling as far as Bengal and Assam and visiting many holy sites, he successfully reached China by a somewhat more northerly route, with a most valuable collection of sacred writings. Subsequent travellers have borne enthusiastic testimony to the accuracy of his descriptions and to his remarkable intellectual powers (see p. 59). This extract, from a biography by his disciple Hwui-lih, describes his experiences in the Southern Gobi.

(see p. 59)

\*     \*     \*

And now, alone and deserted, he traversed the sandy waste (the Gobi); his only means of observing the way being the heaps of bones and the horse-dung, and so on; thus slowly and cautiously advancing, he suddenly saw a body of troops amounting to several hundreds covering the sandy plain; sometimes they advanced and sometimes they halted. The soldiers were clad in fur and felt. And now the appearance of camels and horses, and the glittering of standards and lances met his view; then suddenly fresh forms and figures changing into a thousand shapes appeared, sometimes at an immense distance and then close at hand, and then they dissolved into nothing.

3

The Master of the Law when he first beheld the sight thought they were robbers, but when he saw them come near and vanish, he knew that they were the hallucinations of demons. Again, he heard in the void sounds of voices crying out, 'Do not fear! do not fear!' On this he composed himself, and having pushed on eighty li or so, he saw the first watch-tower [Chinese frontier post]. Fearing lest the lookouts should see him, he concealed himself in a hollow of sand until night; then going on west of the tower, he saw the water; and going down, he drank and washed his hands. Then as he was filling his water vessel with water an arrow whistled past him and just grazed his knee, and in a moment another arrow. Knowing then that he was discovered, he cried with a loud voice, 'I am a priest come from the capital; do not shoot me!' Then he led his horse towards the tower, whilst the men on guard opening the gate came out; after looking at him they saw that he was indeed a priest, and so they entered in together to see the commander of the guardhouse whose name was Wang-siang. Wang, having ordered the fire to be well lit for the purpose of inspecting the Master, said: 'This is no priest of our country of Ho-si, he is indeed one from the capital.' Then he asked him about his object in travelling.

The Master of the Law replied, 'Captain! have you not heard men of Lanchow talk about a priest named Hsuan-tsang, who was about to proceed to the country of the Brahmans to seek for the Law?' He answered, 'I have heard that Hsuan-tsang has returned already to the East. Why have you come here?' The Master of the Law then took him to his horse and showed him various places on which were written his name and familiar title. On this the other was convinced. He then said, 'Sir, the western road is dangerous and long, you cannot succeed in your plan. But I have no fault to find with you. I myself am a man of Tunhwang and I will conduct you there.'

When the morning came, the Master of the Law having taken some food, Siang sent a man to fill his water-vessel, and providing him with some cakes made of flour, he himself conducted him for ten li or so [about four miles], and then he said, 'From this point, sir, the road goes straight on to the fourth watch-tower; the man there is a good-hearted person; moreover, he is a near relation of mine. His family name is Wang, his private name is Pi-lung. When you

4

come to see him you can say that I have sent you to him.' Then, with tearful salutations, they parted.

Having gone on till night he came to the fourth watch-tower, and fearing lest he should be detained, he purposed to get some water quietly, and to go on. Coming to the water, and scarcely there, there came an arrow flying towards him; turning round he called out as before, and went forward to the tower. Then the men coming down, he entered the building. The officer of the tower having spoken to him, he answered, 'I purpose going to India, and my way is in this direction. Wang-siang, the officer of the first tower, has commissioned me to meet you.' Hearing this he was much pleased, and detained him for the night; moreover, he gave him a great leather bottle for water, and fodder for his horse. Then conducting him by his side he said, 'You had better not, sir, go towards the fifth tower, for the men there are rude and violent, and some mishap may befall you. About a hundred li [30 miles] from this is the Yema spring, where you can replenish your supply of water.'

Having gone from this he forthwith entered on the Mokia Yen desert,[1] which is about eight hundred li in extent. The old name of it is Shaho. There are no birds overhead and no beasts below; there is neither water nor herb to be found.

After going a hundred li or so, he lost his way, and searching for the fountain called Yema he could not find it to get water from. Then when he was going to drink from the pipe of his water-vessel, because of its weight it slipped from his hands, and the water was wasted; thus, a supply enough for a thousand li was lost in a moment. Then again because of the winding character of the road, he did not know which way to follow it. At length, purposing to return eastward to the fourth watch-tower, after going ten li, he thought thus within himself, 'I made a vow at the first that if I did not succeed in reaching India I would never return a step to the East; what then am I now doing here? It is better to die in the attempt to go to the West than to live by returning to the East.' Then turning his bridle he invoked Kwan-Yin, and proceeded in a north-west direction.

At this time, in all four directions, the view was boundless; there were no traces either of man or horse, and in the night the demons

1 The Takla Makan desert.

and goblins raised fire-lights as many as the stars; in the daytime the driving wind blew the sand before it as in the season of rain. But notwithstanding all this his heart was unaffected by fear; but he suffered from want of water and was so parched with thirst that he could no longer go forward. Thus for four nights and five days not a drop of water had he to wet his throat or mouth; his stomach was racked with a burning heat and he was well-nigh thoroughly exhausted. And now not being able to advance he lay down to rest on the sands, invoking Kwan-Yin without intermission, although worn out with sufferings. And as he addressed the Bodhisattva, he said, 'Hsuan-tsang in adventuring this journey does not seek for riches or worldy profit, he desires not to acquire fame, but only for the sake of the highest religious truth does his heart long to find the true Law. I know that the Bodhisattva lovingly regards all living creatures to deliver them from misery! Will not mine, bitter as they are, come to his knowledge!'

Thus he prayed with earnest heart and without cessation the while, till the middle of the fifth night, when suddenly a cool wind fanned his body, cold and refreshing as a bath of icy water. His eyes forthwith recovered their power of sight and his horse had strength to get up. His body being thus refreshed, he lay still and fell asleep for a little while. Whilst he slept thus he had a dream, and in his sleep he thought he saw a mighty spiritual being, several chang in height, holding in his hand a halberd used for signalling, who spake thus: 'Why are you still sleeping and not pressing on with all your might?'

The Master of the Law, rousing himself from slumber, pushed on for ten li, when his horse suddenly started off another way and could not be brought back or turned. Having gone some li in the new direction, he saw all at once several acres of green grass; getting off his horse, he let him graze; when leaving the grass, purposing to resume his journey, about ten paces off he came to a pool of water, sweet, and bright as a mirror; dismounting again, he drank without stint, and so his body and vital powers were restored once more, and both man and horse obtained refreshment and ease.

Having bivouacked near the grass and fountain of water for a day, on the day following he filled his water-vessel and cut some

6

grass, and proceeded onward. After two days more they got out of the desert and arrived at I-gu. The myriads of dangers and difficulties through which he passed cannot be recounted in detail.

*The Life of Hsuan-tsang.* By Hwui-lih. Ed. by S. Beal, 1888.

# William of Rubrouck
## fl. 1255

AFTER the establishment of Mongol rule under the Great Khan
and his successors in China and Central Asia, rumours circulated
through Christendom regarding his religion and his alleged willingness to adopt the Christian faith. To test these reports and to win a
powerful supporter to his side, the Pope during the thirteenth
century despatched several envoys to the Khan's court. Travel was
made easier by the fact that the Khan's writ ran throughout immense
areas, and this facilitated the progress of accredited envoys. Among
the latter was William of Rubrouck (Guillaume Rubruquis) a monk
from Flanders. In 1253, he set out from the Crimea crossing the
Volga river and the plains of Southern Russia, whence after an
astonishing and painful journey of four months across the continent he reached the headquarters of Manga Khan at Karakorum.

Here William was surprised to find Armenian priests, French
jewellers and Chinese merchants among the foreigners in the Khan's
entourage. His mission however met with little success; the Khan
refused to attend Mass, but instigated a religious discussion between
Christians, Moslems and Buddhists, and despatched the Friar on his
homeward journey with an evasive message to St. Louis: 'Through
the might of the eternal king, the whole world will be united in joy
and peace.' Friar William is the first to report the paper money,
block printing and the written characters of the Chinese.

*   *   *

We arrived then in Soldaia[1] on the 12th of the calends of June
(May 21st), and there had preceded us certain merchants of Constantinople who had said that envoys from the Holy Land were
coming who wished to go to Sartach.[2] I had, however, publicly
preached on Palm Sunday (April 12th) in Saint Sophia that I was not
an envoy, neither yours nor anyone's, but that I was going among
these unbelievers according to the rule of our order. So when I

[1] Sudak, a Black Sea port in the Crimea.
[2] A minor Tartar khan, son of Batu.

arrived these said merchants cautioned me to speak guardedly, for they had said that I was an envoy, and if I said I was not an envoy I would not be allowed to pass. So I spoke in the following way to the captains of the city, or rather to the substitutes of the captains, for the captains had gone to Baatu during the winter bearing the tribute, and had not yet returned: 'We have heard say in the Holy Land that your Lord Sartach is a Christian, and greatly were the Christians rejoiced thereat, and chiefly so the most Christian lord the King of the French, who has come thither on a pilgrimage and is fighting against the Saracens to wrench the holy places from out their hands. It is for this I wish to go to Sartach, and carry to him the letters of the lord king, in which he admonisheth him of the weal of all Christendom.' And they received us right favourably, and gave us lodgings in the episcopal church. And the bishop of this church had been to Sartach, and he told me much good of Sartach, which I later on did not discover myself.

Then they gave us the choice whether we would have carts with oxen to carry our effects, or sumpter horses. And the merchants of Constantinople advised me to take carts, and that I should buy the regular covered carts such as the Ruthenians carry their furs in, and in these I could put such of our things as I would not wish to unload every day; should I take horses it would be necessary to unload them at each stopping-place and to load other horses; and furthermore I should be able to ride more slowly following the gait of the oxen. Then I accepted their advice, unfortunately, however, for I was two months on the way to Sartach, which I might have travelled in one had I gone with horses.

I had brought with me from Constantinople, on the advice of merchants, fruits, muscadel wine and dainty biscuits to present to the first captains (of the Tartars), so that my way might be made easier, for among them no one is looked upon in a proper way who comes with empty hands. All these things I put in one of the carts, since I had not found the captains of the city, and I was told they would be most acceptable to Sartach if I could carry them to him that far. We set out on our journey about the calends of June (1st June) with our four covered carts and two others which were lent us by them and in which was carried bedding to sleep on at night. And they

9

gave us also five horses to ride, for us five persons, myself, and my companion Friar Bartholomew of Cremona, and Gosset the bearer of the presents, and Homo Dei the dragoman, and the boy Nicholas whom I had bought at Constantinople by means of your charity. They gave us also two men who drove the carts and looked after the oxen and horses. . . .

There opened a valley which came from out high mountains in the south-east, and there amidst the mountains was visible another big sea,[1] and a river came through that valley from that sea into the first one, and there blows nearly continuously such a wind through that valley that persons cross it with great danger, lest the wind should carry them into the sea. So we crossed this valley, following a northerly direction towards great mountains[2] covered with deep snow which then covered the ground. On the feast of Saint Nicholas (6th December) we began greatly accelerating our speed, for we already found no one, only those *iams*, that is to say those men who are stationed a day apart to look after ambassadors, for in many places in the mountains the road is narrow and the grazing bad, so that from dawn to night we would cover the distance of two *iams*, thus making of two days one, and we travelled more by night than by day. It was extremely cold, so we turned our sheepskins with the wool outside.

On the second Sunday in Advent (13th December) in the evening, while we were passing through a certain place amidst most terrible rocks, our guide sent me word begging me to say some prayers, by which the devils could be put to flight, for in this gorge devils were wont suddenly to bear men off, and no one could tell what they might do. Sometimes they seized the horse and left the rider, sometimes they tore out the man's bowels and left the body on the horse, and many such things happened there frequently. So we chanted in a loud voice 'Credo in unum Deum,' when by the mercy of God the whole of our company passed through. From that time they began asking me to write cards [texts] for them to carry on their

[1] Rubruquis was now east of Lake Balkash. The lake he mentions here is the Ebi Nor.
[2] The Tarbagatay mountains, Kazakhstan.

10

heads, and I would say to them, 'I will teach you a phrase to carry in your hearts, which will save your souls and your bodies for all eternity.' But always when I wanted to teach them, my interpreter failed me. I used to write for them, however, the '*Credo in Deum*' and the '*Pater noster*,' saying, 'What is here written is what one must believe of God, and the prayer by which one asks of God whatever is needful for man; so believe firmly that this writing is so, though you cannot understand it, and pray God to do for you what is written in this prayer, which He taught from His own mouth to His friends, and I hope that He will save you.' I could do no more, for it was very dangerous, not to say impossible, to speak on questions of the faith through such an interpreter, for he did not know how.

Cathay is on the ocean. And master William told me that he had himself seen the envoys of certain people called Caule[1] and Manse who live on islands; the sea around freezes in winter, so that at that time the Tartars can make raids thither; and they had offered (them) thirty-two thousand tumen of iascot a year, if they would only leave them in peace. A tumen is a number containing ten thousand.

The common money of Cathay is a paper of cotton, in length and breadth a palm, and on it they stamp lines like those on the seal of Mangu. The Cathayans write with a brush such as painters paint with, and they make in one figure the several letters containing a whole word. The Tebet write as we do, and have characters quite like ours. The Tanguts write from right to left like the Arabs, but they repeat the lines running upwards; the Igur, as previously said, write up and down.

On Pentecost day (31st May) Mangu Khan[2] called me before him, and also the Tuin with whom I had discussed; but before I went in, the interpreter, master William's son, said to me that we should have to go back to our country, and that I must not raise any objection, for he understood that it was a settled matter. When I came before

[1]Perhaps Koreans.
[2] Mangu Khan, the Mongol ruler, was a grandson of the great Chengiz Khan. His court, where this interview took place, was then at Karakoram, south of Lake Baikal.

the Khan, I had to bend the knees, and so did the Tuin[1] beside me with his interpreter. Then the Khan said to me, 'Tell me the truth, whether you said the other day, when I sent my secretaries to you, that I was a Tuin.' I replied, 'My Lord, I did not say that: I will tell you what I said, if it pleases you.' Then I repeated to him what I had said, and he replied, 'I thought full well that you did not say it, for you should not have said it; but your interpreter translated badly.' And he held out toward me the staff on which he leaned, saying, 'Fear not.' And I, smiling, said in an undertone, 'If I had been afraid, I should not have come here.' He asked the interpreter what I had said, and he repeated it to him. After that he began confiding to me his creed. 'We Moal,' he said, 'believe that there is only one God, by whom we live and by whom we die, and for whom we have an upright heart.' Then I said, 'May it be so, for without His grace this cannot be.' He asked what I had said; the interpreter told him. Then he added, 'But as God gives us the different fingers of the hand, so he gives to men divers ways. God gives you the Scriptures, and you Christians keep them not. You do not find in them, for example, that one should find fault with another, do you?' 'No, my lord,' I said; 'but I told you from the first that I did not want to wrangle with anyone.' 'I do not intend to say it,' he said, 'for you. Likewise you do not find that a man should depart from justice for money.' 'No, my lord,' I said. 'And truly I came not to these parts to obtain money; on the contrary I have refused what has been offered me.' And there was a secretary present who bore witness that I had refused an iascot and silken cloths. 'I do not say it,' he said, 'for you. God gave you therefore the Scriptures, and you do not keep them; He gave us diviners, we do what they tell us, and we live in peace.'

[1] Probably a Buddhist priest.

*The Journey of William of Rubrouck to the Eastern Parts of the World, 1253–55.* Trsl. & ed. by W. W. Rockhill, 1900. Hakluyt Soc., 2nd. ser., vol. 4.

# Ibn Battuta
## A.D. 1304-1377

DURING the later Middle Ages, the spread of the Muhammadan religion, culture and commerce established a great zone extending from the Western Sudan to China within which travel was relatively safe for the followers of the Prophet. Among Moslems the desire to travel was also stimulated by the annual pilgrimage, or Haj, to the holy city of Mecca. Ibn Battuta, born in Tangier, turned these opportunities to good account. Animated by a keen and intelligent interest in persons and places, he became what might be described as a professional traveller, supporting himself in turn as a Qadi, or judge, envoy, scholar or merchant as occasion arose. In this manner, he travelled throughout the Moslem world, and compiled a most valuable account of the countries, peoples, and cultures with which he came in contact. The extract describes his journey in China, and is one of the few accounts of the country from this period by a non-Chinese writer. His description of the organization of travel is of particular interest.

\*     \*     \*

China is the safest and best regulated of countries for a traveller. A man may go by himself a nine months' journey, carrying with him large sums of money without any fear on that account. The system by which they ensure his safety is as follows. At every post-station in their country they have a hostelry controlled by an officer who is stationed there with a company of horsemen and foot soldiers. After sunset or later in the evening the officer visits the hostelry with his clerk, registers the names of all travellers staying there for the night, seals up the list, and locks them into the hostelry. After sunrise he returns with his clerk, calls each person by name, and writes a detailed description of them on the list. He then sends a man with them to conduct them to the next post-station and bring back a clearance certificate from the controller there to the effect that all these persons have arrived at that station. If the guide does not produce this document, he is held responsible for them. This is the

13

practice at every station in their country from Sin as-Sin [Canton] to Khan-Baliq.[1] In these hostelries there is everything that the traveller requires in the way of provisions, especially fowls and geese. Sheep, on the other hand, are scarce with them.

To return to the account of our journey. The first city which we reached after our sea voyage was the city of Zaytun.[2] Now, although *zaytun* means 'olives', there are no olives in this city, nor indeed in all the lands of the Chinese nor in India; it is simply a name which has been given to the place. Zaytun is an immense city. In it are woven the damask silk and satin fabrics which go by its name, and which are superior to the fabrics of Khansa and Khan-Baliq. The port of Zaytun is one of the largest in the world, or perhaps the very largest. I saw in it about a hundred large junks; as for small junks, they could not be counted for multitude. It is formed by a large inlet of the sea which penetrates the land to the point where it unites with the great river. In this city, as in all Chinese towns, a man will have a fruit garden and a field with his house set in the middle of it, just as in the town of Sijilmasa in our own country.[3] For this reason their towns are extensive. The Muslims live in a town apart from the others.

On the day that I reached Zaytun I saw there the amir who had come to India as an envoy with the present to the sultan, and who afterwards travelled with our party and was shipwrecked on the junk. He greeted me and introduced me to the controller of the customs and saw that I was given good apartments. I received visits from the *qādi* of the Muslims (the '*sheikh al-Islam*') and the principal merchants. Amongst the latter was Sharaf ad-Din of Tabriz, one of the merchants from whom I had borrowed at the time of my arrival in India, and the one who had treated me most fairly. He knew the Koran by heart and used to recite it constantly. These merchants, living as they do in a land of infidels, are overjoyed when a Muslim comes to them. They say 'He had come from the land of Islam,' and they make him the recipient of the tithes on their properties,

[1] Peking; a frequent form of the name is Cambaluc.
[2] This great port is generally accepted to be Tsinkiang (Chuanchow) in Fukien.
[3] Now a ruined site, near Tafilelt, southern Morocco.

so that he becomes as rich as themselves. There was living at Zaytun, amongst other eminent sheikhs, Burhan ad-Din of Kazarun, who has a hermitage outside the town, and it is to him that the merchants pay the sums they vow to Sheikh Abu Ishaq of Kazarun.

When the controller of the customs learned my story he wrote to the Khan, who is their Emperor, to inform him of my arrival on a mission from the king of India. I asked him to send with me someone to conduct me to the district of Sin (Sin as-Sin), which they call Sin-kalan, so that I might see that district which is in his province in the interval before the arrival of the Khan's reply. He granted my request and sent one of his officers to conduct me. I sailed up the river on a vessel resembling the war galleys in our country, except that in this the rowers plied their oars standing upright, their place being in the centre of the vessel, while the passengers were at the forepart and the stern. They spread over the ship awnings made from a plant which grows in their country, resembling but different from flax, and finer than hemp (perhaps grass-cloth). We sailed up this river for twenty-seven days. Every day we used to tie up about noon by a village where we could buy what we needed and pray the noon prayers, then in the evenings we went ashore at another village and so on, until we reached the city of Sin-kalan [Canton].

Porcelain is manufactured there as well as at Zaytun, and hereabouts the river of the 'Water of Life' flows into the sea, so they call the place 'The Meeting of the Waters'. Sin-kalan is a city of the first rank, in regard to size and the quality of its bazaar, from which porcelain is exported to all parts of China, to India, and to Yemen. In the centre of this city there is an enormous temple with nine portals inside each of which there is a portico with benches where the inmates of the temple sit. Between the second and third portals there is a place containing chambers which are occupied by the blind and crippled. Each of the occupants receives subsistence and clothing from the endowment of the temple. There are similar establishments between all the portals. In the interior there is a hospital for the sick and a kitchen for cooking food, and it has a staff of doctors and servitors. I was told that aged persons who are incapacitated from gaining their livelihood receive subsistence and clothing at this temple, likewise orphans and destitute widows. This temple was built by one of their kings, who moreover endowed it with the revenues of this city and the villages and fruit gardens belonging to it. The portrait of this king is painted in the temple we have described, and they worship it.

In one of the quarters of this city is the Muhammadan town, where the Muslims have their cathedral mosque, hospice and bazaar. They have also a *qādi* and a sheikh, for in every one of the cities of China there must always be a 'Sheikh al-Islam', to whom all matters concerning the Muslims are referred, and a *qādi* to decide legal cases between them. My quarters were in the house of Awhad ad-Din of Sinjar, one of their principal men, of excellent character and immensely wealthy. I stayed with him for fourteen days during which gifts were poured upon me one after the other from the *qādi* and other Muslims. Every day they made a new entertainment to which they came in beautifully appointed boats, bringing musicians with them. Beyond the city of Sin-kalan there is no other city, either infidel or Muslim. It is sixty days' journey, so I was told, from there to the Rampart of Gog and Magog,[1] the intervening territory being occupied by nomadic infidels, who eat men when they get hold of them. On that account no one ever crosses their country or visits it, and I did not find in Sinkalan anyone who had himself seen the Rampart or even seen anyone who had seen it.

A few days after my return to Zaytun, the Khan's order arrived with instructions to convey me to his capital with all honour and dignity, by water if I preferred, otherwise by land. I chose to sail up the river, so they made ready for me a fine vessel of the sort that is designed for the use of governors. The governor sent his staff with us, and he, and likewise the *qādi* and the Muslim merchants, sent us large quantities of provisions. We travelled as state guests, eating our midday meal at one village and our evening meals at another. After ten days' journey we reached Qanjanfu,[2] a large and beautiful city set in a broad plain and surrounded by fruit gardens, which gave the place the look of the Ghuta at Damascus.

One day as I was staying at Qanjanfu, a very large vessel came in, belonging to one of their most respected doctors. I was asked if he

[1] This mythical wall, located near Darbent on the Caspian, was later confused with the Great Wall of China.
[2] Identified by Gibb as most probably Minhow (Foochow).

might see me, and he was announced as 'Mawlana (Our master i.e. The reverend) Qiwam ad-Din of Ceuta.' His name roused my interest, and when he came in and we fell to conversation after the usual greetings, it struck me that I knew him. I kept looking at him intently and at last he said, 'I see you are looking at me as if you knew me.' So I said to him, 'Where do you come from?' He replied, 'From Ceuta.' 'And I,' said I, 'from Tangier.' Whereupon he broke into fresh greetings to me, and wept until I wept in sympathy with him. I then said to him, 'Did you go to India?' He replied, 'Yes, I went to the capital, Delhi.' Then when he told me that, I remembered him and said, 'Are you al-Bushri?' and he replied, 'Yes.' I remembered he had come to Delhi with his mother's brother, Abu-'l-Qasim of Murcia, as a beardless youth and a very clever student. I had spoken of him to the sultan of India, who gave him three thousand dinars and invited him to stay at his court, but he refused, as he was set on going to China, where he prospered exceedingly and acquired enormous wealth. He told me that he had about fifty white slaves and as many slave-girls, and presented me with two of each along with many other gifts. I met his brother in after years in the Negro lands[1]—what a distance lies between them!

[1] The western Sudan.

*Ibn Battuta: Travels in Asia and Africa 1325–54.* Edited by H. A. R. Gibb, Routledge and Kegan Paul, 1929.

# Anthony Jenkinson
## died 1611

FIRST attracted to the Arctic by the hope of establishing a route to the Far East which would not be menaced by the Portuguese or Spaniards, the Tudor pioneers concentrated on rounding Asia by the North-East Passage. This brought them into contact with the autocratic state of Muscovy, with which they established trade relations. Sir Richard Chancellor obtained in 1555 the monopoly of the White Sea trade from the Grand Duke Ivan, and three years later Anthony Jenkinson with the support of Ivan journeyed southwards from Moscow to investigate possibilities in Central Asia. From Kazan he descended the Volga by boat to Astrakhan. There he embarked on the Caspian Sea and reached Mangishlak on its eastern shores. Joining a camel caravan for Central Asia he passed up the Amu Darya (he calls it the Ardock). After an adventurous journey, as described below, he reached the great trading centre of Bukhara, the first Englishman to do so. Here he abandoned any hopes of reaching Cathay. His experiences had shown the obstacles to establishing trade relations with Central Asia: the northerly route was too circuitous and hazardous, and in Asia the caravans were subject to exactions by local chieftains and robber bands. A few years later, an anonymous English merchant attempted once more to take the eastern road from Persia but failed to get far. English hopes were then concentrated upon Persia, where Anthony Jenkinson again did good service.

★    ★    ★

The 26th day of November (1558), we departed from the towne of Urgence, and having travailed by the river Oxus[1] a hundred mile, we passed over another great river called Ardock where we paid a certaine pety custome. This river Ardock is great and very swift, falling out of the foresaid Oxus, and passing about a thousand mile to the northward, it then consumeth itselfe in the ground, and passing

[1] Jenkinson's Oxus and Ardock were one and the same river, now known as the Amu Darya. Urgence was near the modern Urgench.

under the same about five hundred mile, issueth out againe, and falleth into the lake of Kitay [the Aral Sea], as I have before declared.

The 7th of December following, we arrived at a castle called Kait, subject to a soltan called Saramet Soltan, who meant to have robbed all the Christians in the caravan, had it not bene for feare of his brother the king of Urgence, as we were informed by one of his chiefest counsellers, who willed us to make him a present which he tooke and delivered; besides, we paid at the said castle for custom, of every camel one red hide of Russia, beside pety gifts to his officers.

Thus proceeding in our journey, the tenth day at night being at rest and our watch set, there came unto us foure horsemen which we tooke as spies, from whom wee tooke their weapons and bound them and having well examined them, they confessed that they had seene the tract of many horsemen, and no footing of camels, and gave us to understand that there were rovers and theeves abroade; for there travaile few people that are true and peaceable in that countrey, but in companie of caravan, where there be many camels, and hoof-marks new without camels were to be doubted. Whereupon we consulted and determined amongst our selves, and sent a poste to the said Soltan of Kayte who immediately came himselfe with three hundred men and mette these foure suspected men which we sent unto him, and examined them so streightly and threatned them in such sort that they confessed there was a banished Prince with forty men three daies journey forward, who lay in wait to destroy us, if he could, and that they themselves were of his companie.

The soltan therefore understanding that the theeves were not many, appointed us eighty men well armed with a captaine to goe with us and conduct us in our way. And the soltan himselfe returned backe againe, taking the foure theeves with him. These souldiers travailed with us two dayes, consuming much of our victuals. And the 3rd day in the morning very earely they set out before our caravan, and having ranged the wilderness for the space of foure houres, they mette us, comming towards us as fast as their horse could runne, and declared that they had founde the tract of horses not farre from us, perceiving well that we should meete with enemies, and therefore willed us to appoint our selves for them, and asked us what wee would give them to conduct us further, or els they would returne.

To whom we offered as we thought good, but they refused our offer and would have more, and so we not agreeing they departed from us and went back to their soltan, who (as wee conjectured) was privie to the conspiracie.

But they being gone, certaine Tartars of our companie called holy men, (because they had bene at Mecca) caused the whole caravan to stay, and would make their prayers, and devine howe wee should prosper in our journey and whether we should meet with any ill company or no? To which our whole caravan did agree. And they tooke certaine sheepe and killed them, and tooke the blade bones of the same, and first sodde [boiled or soaked] them, and then burnt them, and tooke of the blood of the said sheepe, and mingled it with the powder of the saide bones, and wrote certaine characters with the saide blood, using many other ceremonies and wordes, and by the same devined and found that wee shoulde meete with enemies and theeves (to our great trouble) but should overcome them, to which sorcerie I and my companie gave no credit, but we found it true, for within three houres after that the souldiers departed from us, which was the 15th day of December; in the morning we escried farre off divers horsemen which made towards us, and we (perceiving them to be rovers) gathered ourselves together, being forty of us wel appointed and able to fight, and we made our prayers together every one after his lawe, professing to live and die one with another, and so prepared ourselves.

When the theeves were nigh unto us, we perceived them to be in number thirty-seven men well armed, and appointed with bowes, arrowes and swords, and the captaine a prince banished from his countrey. They willed us to yeelde ourselves or els to be slaine, but wee defied them, wherewith they shotte at us all at once, and we at them very hotly, and so continued our fight from morning until two houres within night, divers men, horse and camels being wounded and slaine on both partes; and had it not bene for four hand-gunnes which I and my companie had and used, we had been overcome and destroyed, for the theeves were better armed and were also better archers then we. But after wee had slaine divers of their men and horses with our gunnes, they durst not approach so nigh, which caused them to come to a truce with us untill the next morning, which we accepted, and encamped ourselves upon a hill and made the fashion of a castle, walling it about with packes of wares, and laide our horses and camels within the same to save them from the shotte of arrowes; and the theeves also incamped within an arrowe shotte of us, but they were betwixt us and the water, which was to our great discomfort because neither we nor our camels had drunke in two days before.

Thus keeping good watch, when halfe the night was spent, the Prince of the theeves sent a messenger halfe way unto us requiring to talke with our captaine, (in their tongue, the caravan basha) who answered the messenger, 'I will not depart from my companie to goe into the halfe way to talke with thee, but if that thy Prince with all his companie will sweare by our lawe to keepe the truce, then will I send a man to talke with thee, or els not.' Which the prince understanding as well himselfe as his company, swore so loude that we might all heare. And then we sent one of our company (reputed a holy man) to talke with the same messenger. The message was pronounced aloude in this order, 'Our prince demaundeth of the caravan basha, and of all you that be Bussarmans, (that is to say circumcized) not desiring your bloods, that you deliver into his hands as many Caphars, that is, unbeleevers (meaning us the Christians) as are among you with their goods, and in so doing, hee will suffer you to depart with your goods in quietnesse, and on the contrary, you shall be handled with no lesse cruelty then the Caphars, if hee overcome you, as he doubteth not.' To the which our caravan basha answered, that he had no Christians in his company nor other strangers, but two Turkes which were of their law, and although hee had, hee would rather die then deliver them, and that we were not afraide of his threatnings, and that should he know when day appeared. And so passing in talke, the theeves (contrary to their othe) carried our holy man away to their prince, crying with a lowde voyce in token of victory, 'Allah! Allah!'

Wherewith we were much discomforted, fearing that the holy man would betray us; but he being cruelly handled and much examined, would not to death confesse any thing which was to us prejudiciall, neither touching us, nor yet what men they had slaine and wounded of ours the day before. When the night was spent, in the morning we prepared our selves to battel againe, which the theeves perceiving, required to fall to agreement and asked much of us. And to be briefe, the most part of our companie being loth to go to battel againe, and having little to loose, and safeconduct to passe, we were compelled to agree, and to give the theeves twenty ninths (that is to say) twenty times nine severall things, and a camell to carry away the same, which being received, the theeves departed into the wilderness to their old habitation, and we went on our way forward. And that night came to the river Oxus, where we refreshed ourselves, having bene three dayes without water and drinke, and tarried there all the next day, making mery with our slaine horses and camels, and then departed from that place, and for feare of meeting with the said theeves againe or such like, we left the high way which went along the said river, and passed through a wildernes of sand, and travelled four dayes in the same before we came to water, and then came to a wel, the water being very brackish, and we then as before were in neede of water and of other victuals, being forced to kill our horses and camels to eate.

In this wildernes also we had almost fallen into the handes of theeves, for one night being at rest there came certaine scoutes, and caried away certaine of our men which lay a litle separated from the caravan, wherewith there was a great shoute and crie, and we immediately laded our camels and departed being about midnight and very darke, and drove sore till we came to the river Oxus againe, and then we feared nothing being walled with the said river, and whether it was for that we had gotten the water, or for that the same theeves were far from us when the scoutes discovered us, we knowe not, but we escaped that danger. So upon the 23rd day of December wee arrived at the citie of Boghar [Bukhara] in the lande of Bactria.

'The voyage of Master Anthony Jenkinson' in Richard Hakluyt's *Principal Navigations*, vol. I. (Dent edition).

# John Saris
# died 1646

IN 1598, William Adams, shipbuilder and navigator, arrived in Japan in the first Dutch ship to touch there. The next English visitor was John Saris from the Moluccas in 1611. With the aid of Adams he established commercial relations with the Emperor on behalf of the East India Company, as described in the extract. From Hirado Saris went by sea to Ōsaka and thence by land to Surunga, where he was received by the Emperor, and on to Tokyo. Diplomatically, Saris was successful but in the event all western merchants save the Dutch were excluded from Japan, until the arrival of the American Commodore Perry in 1853. Saris was a keen observer with a vivid style, and his picture of Japan was substantially that of most Europeans for two centuries. He set out for home the same year, but William Adams, happy with his Japanese wife, settled permanently in Japan.

*     *     *

We were rowed through, and amongst divers islands all which, or the most part of them, were well inhabited, and divers proper towns built upon them; whereof one called Fuccate[1] hath a very strong castle built of freestone, but no ordnance nor soldiers therein. It hath a ditch about five fathom deep and twice as broad round about it, with a drawbridge, kept all in very good repair. I did land and dine there in the town, the tide and wind so strong against us as that we could not pass. The town seemed to be as great as London is within the walls, very well built, and even, so as you may see from the one end of the street to the other. The place exceedingly peopled, very civil and courteous, only that at our landing, and being here in Fuccate and so through the whole country withersoever we came, the boys, children, and worser sort of idle people would gather about and follow along after us, crying, 'Core, Core, Cocore, ware,' that is to say, 'You Coreans with false hearts,' wondering, hoping, hollowing and making such a noise about us that we could scarcely

[1] Hakata, in northern Kiūshiū.

hear one another speak, sometimes throwing stones at us (but that not in many towns) yet the clamour and crying after us was everywhere alike, none reproving them for it. The best advice that I can give those who hereafter shall arrive there is that they pass on without regarding those idle rabblements, and in so doing, they shall find their ears only troubled with the noise.

All along this coast and so up to Osaca[1] we found women divers that lived with their household and family in boats upon the water, as in Holland they do the like. These women would catch fish by diving, which by net and lines they missed, and that in eight fathom depth; their eyes by continual diving do grow as red as blood, whereby you may know a diving woman from all other women.

We were two days rowing from Firando[3] to Fuccate. About eight or ten leagues on this side the straits of Xeminaseque (Shimonoseki), we found a great town where there lay in a dock a junk of eight hundred or a thousand tons of burden, sheathed all with iron, with a guard appointed to keep her from firing and treachery. She was built in a very homely fashion, much like that which describeth Noah Ark unto us. The naturals told us that she served to transport soldiers into any of the islands if rebellion or war should happen.

We found nothing extraordinary after we had passed the straits of Xeminaseque until we came unto Osaca, where we arrived the twenty-seventh day of August. Our galley could not come near the town by six miles, where another smaller vessel met us, wherein came the good man or host of the house where we lay in Osaca and brought a banquet with him of wine and salt fruits to entertain me. The boat having a fast made to the masthead was drawn by men, as our barques are from London westward.

We found Osaca to be a very great town, as great as London within the walls, with many fair timber bridges of a great height, serving to pass over a river there as wide as the Thames at London. Some fair houses we found there, but not many. It is one of the chief seaports of all Japan having a castle in it, marvellous large and strong, with very deep trenches about it, and many drawbridges with gates plated with iron. The castle is built all of freestone without any filling

[1] Ōsaka.
[2] Hirado, where Adams had his headquarters.

24

in the inward part with trumpery, as they reported unto me. The stones are great, of an excellent quarry, and are cut so exactly to fit the place where they are laid that no mortar is used, but only earth cast between to fill up void crevices if any be. In this castle did dwell at our being there the son of Tiquasamma ( Tai Kô sama), who being an infant at the time of his father's decease, was left to the government and education of four, whereof Ogoshosamma (Iyeyasu), the now Emperor, was one and chief....

The eight and twentieth day at night, having left musters and prices of our commodities with our host, we parted from Osaca by barque towards Fushimi, where we arrived the nine and twentieth at night.

We found here a garrison of three thousand soldiers maintained by the Emperor to keep Miaco and Osaca in subjection....

The captain-general of this garrison we met two days after we had met his first troop (having still in the meantime met with some of these companies as we passed along, sometimes one league, sometimes two leagues distant one from another). He marched in very great state, beyond that the others did (for the second troop was more richly set out in their arms than the first, and the third than the second, and so still every one better than the other, until it came unto this the last and best of all). He hunted and hawked all the way, having his own hounds and hawks along with him, the hawks being hooded and lured as ours are. His horses for his own saddle being six in number, richly trapped. Their horses are not tall, but of the size of our middling nags, short and well trusted, small headed and very full of mettle, in my opinion far excelling the Spanish jennet in pride and stomach. He had his paladin carried before him, the inside of crimson velvet, and six men appointed to carry it, two at a time.

Such good order was taken for the passing and providing for of these three thousand soldiers that no man either travelling or inhabiting upon the way where they lodged was any way injured by them, but cheerfully entertained them as other their guests because they paid for what they took, as all other men did—every town and village upon the way being well fitted with cooks and victualling houses where they might at an instant have what they needed, and diet themselves from a penny English a meal to two shillings a meal.

The thirtieth (August) we were furnished with nineteen horse at the Emperor's charge to carry up our King's presents and those that attended me to Surunga (Suruga).

I had a palladin appointed for me, and a spare horse led by, to ride when I pleased, very well set out. Six men appointed to carry my palladin in plain and even ground. But where the country grew hilly, ten men were allowed me thereto. The guardian whom King Foyn sent along with us did from time to time and place to place by warrant take up these men and horses to serve our turns, as the postmasters do here in England, as also lodging at night. According to the custom of the country I had a slave appointed to run with a pike before me.

Thus we travelled until the sixth of September before we got to Surunga, each day fifteen or sixteen leagues of three miles to a league as we guessed it. The way for the most part is wonderful even, and where it meeteth with mountain passage is cut through. This way is the sand and gravel; it is divided into leagues, and at every league's end are two small hills, viz. of either side of the way one, and upon every one of them a fair pine-tree trimmed round in fashion of an arbor. These marks are placed upon the way to the end that the Hackney men, and those which let out horses to hire, should not make men pay more than their due, which is about threepence a league. The road is exceedingly travelled, full of people. Ever and anon you meet with farms and country houses, with villages, and often with great towns, with ferries over fresh rivers, and many Futtakeasse or Fotoquis, which are their temples, situate in groves and most pleasantest places for delight of the whole country. The priests that tend thereupon dwelling about the same, as our Friars in old time planted themselves here in England.

When we approached any town we saw crosses with the dead bodies of those who had been crucified thereupon; for crucifying is here an ordinary punishment for most malefactors. Coming near Surunga, where the Emperor's court is, we saw a scaffold with the heads of divers (which had been executed) placed thereupon, and by

26

were divers crosses with the dead corpses of those which had been executed remaining still upon them, and the pieces of others, which after their execution had been hewn again and again by the trial of their cattans [swords]. All which caused a most unsavoury passage to us, that to enter into Surunga must needs pass by them. This city of Surunga[1] is full as big as London, with all the suburbs. The handicrafts men we found dwelling in the outward parts and skirts of the town, because those that are of the better sort dwell in the inward part of the city, and will not be annoyed with the rapping, knocking, and other disturbance that artificers cannot be without.

The 6th September we arrived at Surunga in the morning very early. . . .

And towards noon [12th] departed for Edo to the young king's court, the Emperor furnishing me with nineteen horse and six men for my pallankeene, which were changed at every six mile or ten mile, as we shifted horses, and if it were any hills in the way ten men to the pallenkeene.

The fourteenth September I arrived at Edo[2], a city much greater than Surunga, far fairer buildings, and made a very glorious appearance unto us; the ridge-tiles and corner-tiles richly gilded, the posts of their doors gilded and varnished. Glass windows they have none, but great windows of board, opening in leaves, well set out with painting, as in Holland. There is a cawsey which goeth through the chief street of the town; underneath this cawsey runneth a river; at every fifty paces there is a well-head, fitted very substantially of freestone, with buckets for the neighbours to fetch water, and for danger of fire. This street is as broad as any of our streets in England.

[1] Surunga (Suruga) is the name of a province on the south-east coast of Honshiu. The city is Shizuoka.
[2] Edo (Yedo) is the modern Tokyo.

*The Voyage of Captain John Saris to Japan, 1613.* Edited by Sir Ernest M. Satow. Hakluyt Soc., 2nd. ser. v. 5. 1900.

# Alexander von Humboldt
## 1769-1859

A MORE detailed account of Humboldt's researches in South America and of his contributions to geography in general is given later in this book. His other important journey was to Central Asia in 1829, made at the request of the Russian government, who wished him to investigate the mineralogical resources. With his companion, G. Stein, Humboldt crossed the Urals to Tobolsk on the Irtysh, traversed the Siberian plain to Barnaul on the Ob', and reached the Chinese frontier at Naryn. The scientific results were of considerable value, Humboldt incidentally foretelling correctly the discovery of diamonds in the Ural mountains. Humboldt did not himself write a detailed account of the journeys. The following is one of his letters addressed to his brother William, Prussian ambassador in Rome.

*   *   *

*Barnaul on the Ob, on the Northern Slopes of the Altai, 4th August, 1829.*

I take every opportunity, my dear brother, to send you a few lines on the happy course of my journey. You will know from my letter from Tobolsk (if letters do not go astray over such distances) that we had resolutely determined to visit the most important section of the Altai, an excursion of 2833 versts, 1400 of which (the distance from Berlin to St. Petersburg) we have happily completed. One journeys, or rather flies, through these monotonous grassy plains of Siberia as though over the sea, a true voyage on land in which we cover 240 to 280 versts in a day. We suffered little between Tobolsk and Tara, but much in Kainsk and the Boraba steppe—from heat, dust and yellow flies (a particular species). The plague on the Orinoco is hardly worse and although the thermometer only stands at 24–24½° Réaumur in the shade, one suffers much from the heat through the contact with the cold nights (7–8°R., even 5°). In the little town of Kainsk we experienced some alarms, since for two days we had to traverse a district in which cattle disease made it difficult to obtain horses (we need twenty-five to thirty) and in which many

28

men were dying from the so-called 'fire blisters'. This is a Siberian plague, a typhus which, lacking medical attention, ends fatally within five days of the appearance of a small burning patch. As regards its infectiousness there was, as usual, much doubt and argument. After many consultations with a doctor, who had never heard of Berlin, we decided not to turn back, to put the servants inside the waggons out of contact with the drivers (Siberian peasants), to enter no hut, and to fetch water from the wells ourselves.

On July 19th we first sighted the majestic River Ob, and crossed it at Berski.[1] We found much sickness in the villages, where in one day sometimes four or five persons died. But, travelling day and night, on the morning of July 20th, we reached the banks of the meandering Ob near the Altai mountain town of Barnaul (as far to the east of Berlin as Caracas is to the west!), safe and sound. A storm from the Kirgiz steppes to the SSW raged for seventeen hours. There were waves like those of the sea on the Ob and to cross was unthinkable. We had to bivouack all night on the banks. Blazing fires in the forest reminding me of the Orinoco. It blew and rained by turns. All in all a benefit, for we were now free of mosquitoes. At two in the morning we were able to cross the Ob, and here in Barnaul, where eight thousand marks of silver were melted and the Intendent of the Province of Tomsk brought together a fine collection of Chinese, Mongolian and Tibetan manuscripts, we spent two agreeable and quiet days. Unfortunately, the great and all too good care of the Government for our safety daily increases our escort. The Governor-General of Tobolsk has not only provided us with his adjutant and four Cossacks, this evening suddenly appeared the Commandant General of Tomsk with his suite who are to accompany us for fifteen hundred versts along the line of frontier fortifications to Omsk itself. We leave here tonight for the beautiful Koliwan Lake,[2] the 'Snake Mountains' (stopping at the Altai silver mines and Ust-Kamenogorsk) thence up the Irtysh to the Chinese frontier post of Naryn[3] in Chinese Mongolia. Thus we shall have seen in one

[1] Berdsk, south of Novosibirsk.
[2] Kolyvan lake is approximately two hundred miles south of Barnaul and the Snake mountains are near Zmyeinogorsk, thirty miles further south.
[3] Now in the Soviet republic of Tuva near the boundary with Outer Mongolia.

summer a great, great stretch of Northern Asia—the Urals, Altai and the Orenburg[1] salt mines. The vegetation has now, since we have penetrated three thousand five hundred versts from the Urals south-eastwards into Asia, at last become by degrees Siberian; thus the banks of the Ob, for unfortunately the trees alone characterize a country, resemble as a whole the Havel and the Tegel lake.[2] About the greater animals, I note only that large tigers, striped very like the Bengal tiger, not merely show themselves in these northern latitudes near Irkutsk, but that for some years, when there are tiger shoots in Chinese Mongolia, three or four have been shot here in the Altai, attacking horsemen. We have seen the skins of two of these displaced animals. The existence of these beasts in such northerly latitudes is very, very remarkable.

[1] Now known as Chkalov.
[2] Humboldt's family home in Germany.

*Alexander von Humboldt, 1769–1859. Werke, Briefe, Selbstzeugnisse.* Ed. by L. Sroka. Hamburg, K. Wesemayer, 1959. Trsl. by G.R.C.

# Évariste Régis Huc
## 1813-1860

By the mid-nineteenth century, European rivalries in China were coming to a head. The Chinese authorities still adhered to their policy of excluding foreigners, but breaches were being made in this prohibition. The British fought the war of 1842 to extend their trading privileges. The French mission saw its work destroyed and its adherents scattered. The Lazarist Fathers Huc and Gabet, working hard in Tartary to rally their dispersed followers and acquiring a sound knowledge of the Chinese and Mongol languages, determined to make the long journey westwards to the Tibetan capital of Lhasa, the centre of Chinese Buddhism. Dressed as lamas, and profiting from their wide knowledge of local customs and languages (they acquired Tibetan on their journey), they set out in 1844. Moving westwards approximately along the line of the Great Wall and the Hwang Ho, they reached the southern shores of the lake Koko Nor, where they eventually joined the annual caravan to Lhasa. The extract pictures vividly this great assembly on its way to the west and south-west. After a hard journey across the bitter barren plateau of north-eastern Tibet, the Fathers finally reached Lhasa, the first Europeans to do so from the east. Though they were hospitably received, national prejudices proved too strong, and they were returned under escort to China. Huc's cultivated and sympathetic narrative, sometimes excited and exaggerated, is a wonderful storehouse of information on ninteenth-century China.

★　　★　　★

The march and the movements of the caravan were effected with much order and precision, especially on setting out. Usually we started two or three hours before dawn each day, to be able to camp about midday and to give the animals time to graze. Reveille was announced by a cannon shot; immediately everyone rose, fires were lit in all the tents, and while some loaded the baggage animals, others boiled soup and prepared buttered tea. After some cupfuls had been hastily swallowed and handfuls of tsamba eaten, the tents were struck. A second cannon shot was the signal to start. Experienced horsemen, charged with directing the caravan, took the lead. They were followed by the long files of camels; then came the yaks, in troops of two or three hundreds, in the charge of several lakto. The horsemen had no fixed places; they came and went in all directions, guided solely by caprice. The plaintive cries of the camels, the grunting of the yaks, the neighs of the horses, the shouts and noisy songs of the travellers, the thin whistles with which the lakto urged on the baggage animals, and above all the innumerable bells hanging from the necks of yaks and camels—all these produced an immense, indescribable concert, which far from being fatiguing, appeared on the contrary to inspire everyone with courage and energy.

The caravan advanced in this fashion across the desert by troops and platoons, stopping every day in plain, valley or on the mountain side, and improvising out of its numerous tents, of varied shapes and colours, towns and villages which vanished the next morning to reappear an instant later in an entirely different form. How astonishing for these vast and silent deserts to witness at every turn the passage of so great and so noisy a multitude! Watching all these travelling tents, these many troops, and these men, by turns herdsmen and warriors, it was impossible not to recall constantly the march of the Israelites across the solitudes of Madian in search of the Promised Land.

Leaving the shores of the Blue Sea [Koko Nor] we struck westwards, inclining perhaps slightly to the south. The first days of the march were nothing but poetry; everything went as we wished, the weather was magnificent, the track was good and easy, the water limpid, and pasture rich and abundant. As for brigands, no one gave them a thought. At night the cold indeed made itself felt, but this inconvenience was overcome by sleeping in fur clothing. We fell at last to asking ourselves what was so terrible about this celebrated journey through Tibet. It appeared to us impossible to travel in a more comfortable and agreeable fashion. Alas, this enchantment was not to last long!

Six days after our start we had to cross the Pouhain-Gol, a river which, rising at the foot of the Nan Shan mountains, flows into the Blue Sea. It is not very deep, but since it is divided into twelve branches very near to each other it occupies a space of about one league. We had the misfortune to arrive at the first arm of the Pouhain-Gol long before dawn; the water was frozen, but not thick enough for the ice to serve us as a bridge. The horses, the first to reach it, were frightened and dared not advance. They halted on the banks, giving the yaks time to overtake them. Soon the whole caravan was re-united at one spot. It would be impossible to describe the disorder and confusion which reigned in the centre of this immense mob, wrapped in the shades of night. At last several riders urged on their horses, and broke through the ice at several places. At once the caravan rushed pell-mell into the river. The animals jostled each other, splashing the water everywhere; the ice cracked and the men yelled; it was a frightful uproar. Having crossed the first arm, the manœuvre began again at the second, then at the third, and so on. When day broke, the 'holy embassy' was still wallowing in the water. At last very chilled and weary in body and mind, we were fortunate to have the twelve branches of the Pouhain-Gol behind us, and to find ourselves on dry land. But all our fanciful notions had vanished, and we were coming to find this method of travel altogether hateful.

Yet everyone appeared jubilant. The crossing of the Pouhain-Gol was declared to have been admirably executed. One man alone had broken limbs, only two yaks had been drowned. As for what had been lost or stolen during this disorder, there was no reckoning.

When the caravan resumed its usual march, it was a really laughable sight. Men and animals were almost loaded down with icicles. The horses proceeded sadly, much embarrassed by their tails, which hung in one piece, stiff and motionless, as though made of lead and not of hair. The camels had the long hair on their limbs laden with wonderful icicles, which jangled harmoniously. It was plain however that these pretty ornaments were little to their liking; from time to time they tried to shake them off by stamping heavily on the ground. The yaks were truly caricatures; it would be impossible to imagine a more comical sight. They walked with their legs straddled, struggling painfully under enormous loads of icicles which hung from their bellies almost to the ground. The poor brutes were so shapeless, so covered with ice, that they appeared to have been dipped in sugar candy. . . .

On November 15th, we left the magnificent plain of Koko Nor and arrived among the Mongols of Tsaidam. Immediately after the crossing of the river of that name, the appearance of the country changes immediately. Nature is mournful and wild; the land, dry and stony, seems to support with difficulty a few dried-up bushes, impregnated with salt. The dull and melancholy hue of this forlorn tract seems to have influenced the character of its people, who all display a melancholy air. . . .

The crossing of the Bayan Buta was only a trial run. Some days later, the Chuga mountain put all our strength and courage to a much more severe test. The march became long and painful; the cannon shot, the usual signal for departure, was heard an hour after midnight. Tea was made with melted snow, and a good meal of tsamba, seasoned with a garlic clove chopped finely, followed and then we set out. When the great caravan began to unwind itself, the sky was clear and the brilliant moon made the great carpet of snow, which completely covered the country, sparkle. The Chuga on the side by which we approached was not steep, and we were able to reach the summit as dawn was breaking. Soon the sky was covered by cloud, and the wind blew with ever increasing force. The further side was so deep in snow that the animals sunk up to their bellies. They advanced tumbling and sprawling in the snow and often ended by pitching into chasms from which they could not be extricated. Several perished in this way. We marched against so strong and icy a wind that breathing was sometimes impossible, and despite our fur clothing, we feared to die at any moment from the cold. At last, to avoid the snow flurries which the wind continually dashed in our teeth, we followed the example of several other travellers who were mounted back to front on their horses, allowing them to follow their instinct. When we arrived at the foot of the mountain and, out of the wind, could look about us, we saw more than one frozen face. M. Gabet's ears and nose were frostbitten, and our skins were cracked or burnt by the cold.

The caravan halted at the foot of the mountain and each went to find shelter among the labyrinth of gorges. Worn out by hunger and with numbed limbs, we needed a hostelry with a good fire, a well-

furnished table and a warm bed to restore us but the Chuga is far
from having all the comforts of the Alps; the Buddhist monks have
not yet thought of establishing themselves there to rescue unfortunate travellers. We were obliged therefore to pitch our tent in
the snow and to go to look for dung. It was a pitiful sight to see this
crowd wandering everywhere and burrowing hopefully in the snow
in the hope of finding a few old yak droppings. After a long and
painful search, we had just sufficient to melt three large pieces of ice
which we were obliged to hack from a near-by pool. Our fire not
being large enough to boil soup, we had to content ourselves with
dipping our tsamba in the lukewarm water and swallowing it
hurriedly before it froze in our fingers. That was all the supper we
had after this terrible journey. We finally rolled ourselves in our
goatskins and coverings, and awaited, cowering in a corner of the
tent, the cannon shot which would cause us continue our impressions
of travel. . . .

It was at Chuga that our long succession of miseries really began.
Snow, wind and cold attacked us with a fury that grew daily. The
deserts of Tibet are, without dispute, the most terrible country
imaginable. As the land rose continuously, the vegetation diminished
as we advanced, and the intensity of the cold was frightful. Then
death began to strip the miserable caravan. The lack of water and
grazing promptly reduced the strength of the animals. Every day
we had to abandon baggage animals which could no longer proceed.
The turn of the men came a little later. The appearance of the route
foreshadowed a very sad future for us. For several days we journeyed
as through the excavations of a vast graveyard. Human bones and the
carcasses of animals, met with at every step, served to warn us in that
murderous land and surrounded by savage nature that the caravans
which had preceded us had met with no kinder a fate than ours.

*Souvenirs d'un Voyage dans la Tartarie, le Thibet et la Chine, 1844–6.*
2nd ed. 2 vols. Paris 1853. Trsl. by G.R.C.

# Isabella Bird Bishop
## 1831-1904

ISABELLA LUCY BIRD was born in 1831 of a prosperous middle-class family with a powerful tradition of service to God and the community. She suffered from ill-health and was advised to travel as a remedy for her severe headaches, insomnia and diseased spine. Her travels included journeys of increasing range: she visited Hawaii and the American West in 1873, Japan and Malaya in 1878. In 1881 she married Dr. John Bishop and on his death in 1886 resumed her wanderings, in India, Persia, China, Korea and Morocco. Isabella was highly observant and practical, an excellent horsewoman and a pioneer photographer. The extract below is from her *Unbeaten Tracks in Japan* when, suffering from her ills and afraid to accept Dr. Bishop's first proposal lest she should be 'an invalid wife', she took refuge among the huts of the aborigines (the 'Hairy Ainu') of Japan, as related below. She was something of a celebrity in her adopted home of Edinburgh, and died there in the midst of preparations for a journey to China.

★    ★    ★

I am in the lonely Aino land, and I think that the most interesting of my travelling experiences has been the living for three days and two nights in an Aino hut, and seeing and sharing the daily life of complete savages who go on with their ordinary occupations just as if I were not among them. I found yesterday a most fatiguing and over exciting day, as everything was new and interesting, even the extracting from men who have few if any ideas in common with me, all I could extract concerning their religion and customs, and that through an interpreter. I got up at six this morning to write out my notes, and have been writing for five hours, and there is shortly the prospect of another savage seance. The distractions, as you can imagine, are many. At this moment a savage is taking a cup of *sake* by the fire in the centre of the floor. He salutes me by extending his hands and waving them towards his face, and then dips a rod in the *sake*, and makes six libations to the god—an upright piece of wood

36

with a fringe of shavings planted in the floor of the room. Then he waves the cup several times towards himself, makes other libations to the fire, and drinks. Ten other men and women are sitting along each side of the fire-hole, the chief's wife is cooking, the men are apathetically contemplating the preparation of their food; and the other women, who are never idle, are splitting the bark of which they make their clothes. I occupy the guest seat—a raised platform at one end of the fire with the skin of a black bear thrown over it.

I have reserved all I have to say about the Ainos till I had been actually among them, and I hope you will have patience to read to the end. Ito is very greedy and self-indulgent, and whimpered very much about coming to Biratori at all—one would have thought he was going to the stake. He actually borrowed for himself a sleeping-mat and *futons*[1], and has brought a chicken, onions, potatoes, French beans, Japanese sauce, tea, rice, a kettle, a stewpan, and a ricepan, while I contented myself with a cold fowl and potatoes.

We took three horses and a mounted Aino guide, and found a beaten track the whole way. It turns into the forest at once on leaving Sarufuto,[2] and goes through forest the entire distance with an abundance of reedy grass higher than my hat on horseback along it, and as it is only twelve inches broad and much overgrown, the horses were constantly pushing through leafage soaking from a night's rain, and I was soon wet up to my shoulders. The forest trees are almost solely the *Ailanthus glandulosus* and the *Zelkowa keaki*, often matted together with a white-flowered trailer of the hydrangea genus. The undergrowth is simply hideous, consisting mainly of coarse reedy grass, monstrous docks, the large-leaved *Polyfonum cuspidatum*, several umbelliferous plants, and a 'ragweed' which, like most of its gawky fellows, grows from five to six feet high. The forest is dark and very silent, threaded by this narrow path, and by others as narrow, made by the hunters in search of game. The 'main road' sometimes plunges into deep bogs, at others is roughly cor-duroyed by the roots of trees, and frequently hangs over the edge of abrupt and much-worn declivities, in going up one of which the baggage-horse rolled down a bank fully thirty feet high and nearly

[1] Padded cotton quilts.
[2] Sarufutsu, in northern Hokkaido.

37

all the tea was lost. At another the guide's pack-saddle lost its balance and man, horse and saddle went over the slope, pots, pans and packages flying after them. At another time my horse sank up to his chest in a very bad bog, and as he was totally unable to extricate himself, I was obliged to scramble upon his neck and jump to terra firma over his ears.

There is something very gloomy in the solitude of this silent land, with its beast-haunted forests, its great patches of pasture, the resort of wild animals which haunt the lower regions in search of food when the snow drives them down from the mountains, and its narrow track, indicating the single file in which the savages of the interior walk with their bare, noiseless feet. Reaching the Sarufu-togawa, a river with a treacherous bottom, in which Mr. Von Siebold[1] and his horse came to grief, I hailed an Aino boy who took me up the stream in a 'dug-out', and after that we passed through Biroka, Saruba, and Mina, all purely Aino villages situated among small patches of millet, tobacco, and pumpkins, so choked with weeds that it was doubtful whether they were crops. I was much surprised with the extreme neatness and cleanliness outside the houses: 'model villages' they are in these respects, with no litter lying in sight anywhere, nothing indeed but dog troughs, hollowed out of logs, like 'dug-outs', for the numerous yellow dogs which are a feature of Aino life. There are neither puddles nor heaps, but the houses, all trim and in good repair, rise clean out of the sandy soil.

Biratori, the largest of the Aino settlements in this region, is very prettily situated among forests and mountains on rising ground with a very sinuous river winding at its feet and a wooded height above. A lonelier place could scarcely be found. As we passed among the houses the yellow dogs barked, the women looked shy and smiled, and the men made their graceful salutation. We stopped at the chief's house where, of course, we were unexpected guests; but Shinondi, his nephew, and two other men came out, saluted us, and with most hospitable intent helped Ito to unload the horses. Indeed their eager hospitality created quite a commotion, one running hither and the other thither in their anxiety to welcome a stranger. It is a

[1] Philip F. B. von Siebold, German naturalist, travelled extensively in Japan during the years 1822–30 and 1859–62.

large house, the room being thirty-five by twenty-five and the roof twenty feet high; but you enter by an ante-chamber in which are kept the millet-mill and other articles. There is a doorway in this but the inside is pretty dark and Shinondi, taking my hand, raised the reed curtain bound with hide which concealed the entrance into the actual house, and leading me into it retired a footstep, extended his arms, waved his hands inwards three times, and then stroked his beard several times, after which he indicated by a sweep of his hand and a beautiful smile that the house and all it contained were mine. An aged woman, the chief's mother, who was splitting bark by the fire, waved her hands also. She is the queen-regnant of the house.

Again taking my hand, Shinondi led me to the place of honour at the head of the fire, a rude, movable platform six feet long by four broad and a foot high on which he laid an ornamental mat, apologizing for not having at that moment a bearskin wherewith to cover it. The baggage was speedily brought in by several willing pairs of hands, some reed mats fifteen feet long were laid down upon the very coarse ones which covered the whole floor, and when they saw Ito putting up my stretcher they hung a fine mat along the rough wall to conceal it, and suspended another on the beams of the roof for a canopy. The alacrity and instinctive hospitality with which these men rushed about to make things comfortable were very fascinating, though comfort is a word misapplied in an Aino hut. The women only did what the men told them.

They offered food at once, but I told them that I had brought my own and would only ask leave to cook it on their fire. I need not have brought any cups, for they have many lacquer bowls, and Shinondi brought me on a lacquer tray a bowl of water from one of their four wells. They said that Benri, the chief, would wish me to make his house my own for as long as I cared to stay, and I must excuse them in all things in which their ways were different from my own. Shinondi and four others in the village speak tolerable Japanese, and this of course is the medium of communication. Ito has exerted himself nobly as an interpreter, and has entered into my wishes with a cordiality and intelligence which have been perfectly invaluable; and though he did growl at Mr. Von Siebold's injunctions regarding politeness, he has carried them out to my satisfaction, and even admits that the mountain Ainos are better than he expected: 'but,' he added, 'they have learned their politeness from the Japanese!' They have never seen a foreign woman, and only three foreign men, but there is neither crowding nor staring as among the Japanese, possibly in part from apathy and want of intelligence. For three days they have kept up their graceful and kindly hospitality, going on with their ordinary life and occupations, and though I have lived among them in this room by day and night, there has been nothing which in any way could offend the most fastidious sense of delicacy.

*Unbeaten Tracks in Japan.* By Isabella Bird. 1880. Vol. 2.

# Thomas Thornville Cooper
## 1839-1878

AFTER the convention of 1860, the Chinese Government permitted some Europeans to visit the interior, as diplomats, travellers or merchants. Thenceforward, knowledge of China expanded considerably. English travellers showed particular interest in the head-water regions of the Yangtse Kiang, since it was hoped to establish a trade route from Shanghai up the Yangtse and across Northern Burma to India. The extract which follows is from the narrative of a remarkable journey by an English traveller who went alone, save for two Chinese companions, on an attempt to reach Burma. Despite slender means and local hostility, he came near to pulling off the gamble. Arriving at Batang in Sikiang from the east, he pushed on to the Kinsha river (the upper course of the Yangtse Kiang) but was ultimately turned back at Atuntze. He tells his story vividly and with much humour—on one occasion he discovered too late that he had gone through a marriage ceremony with a Tibetan girl. Fearless, physically strong, obstinate, with a proper concept of the Englishman's place in the world, but no scholar, he may stand as a representative of the numerous half-forgotten travellers who sustained British prestige in the nineteenth century. The incidents related below took place in June 1868.

*      *      *

Our position was apparently becoming hopeless. Hungering and without a prospect of food, we ran the risk of losing our way, for the bewildering yak-tracks rendered it impossible to distinguish the right path. Yet neither my brave Philip nor the boy Low-dzung even hinted at turning back.

I had observed, when holding the conference with the soldier at the foot of the Boundary mountain, a gigantic range of snowy mountains running almost due N. and S., rearing their white peaks and ridges far above the surrounding mountains, and at once recognized them for the range described to me by Father Desgodins in Batang as forming the right bank of the Lan-tsan river, and according to my Chinese map the road to Yunnan led along the left bank. These mountains were now visible, towering above us on the right, a lesser range only intervening, which I concluded formed the left bank of the Lan-tsan. As long as I could keep them in view I had little fear of actually losing myself, and we carefully followed the broadest track.

About noon we came to a large wooden bridge, spanning a stream of considerable size, flowing to the SE., marked in the Chinese map as a tributary of the Kin-sha-kiang.[1] Its waters were vermilion coloured, so in the absence of any name assigned to it by the Chinese, I named it the Vermilion River. Having crossed to the right bank, we followed the stream for several miles along its course, between lofty hills rising on either hand, at an angle of 75 or 80°.

We were slowly proceeding, sullen and indifferent to everything but the desire of reaching the next station, when the whistling of a bullet within a few feet of me, simultaneously with the report of a gun, quickly roused all my faculties. In the direction of the report a large party of men appeared, high up, near the mouth of a cave on the opposite bank of the stream. I had scarcely time to make the observation when we were greeted with a volley; we were evidently out of range of the matchlocks, but several balls dropped amongst us, and one hit Philip's mule which resented the liberty by throwing up its heels and depositing him on the ground; following up their volley with frightful yells the banditti, as they evidently were, charged down the mountain towards us.

I confess that for a moment or two I felt very much like making a bolt, but a moment's reflection showed me that I could not do so without losing my baggage animals, and I determined to fight for it; so, dismounting, I made a barrier of the body of my mule Jacob, an example quickly followed by Philip and Low-dzung. In this order we waited until the robbers got within a hundred yards of us when, laying my double Enfield over Jacob's back, I took a steady aim at them and pulled trigger. If a thunderbolt had fallen amongst the band it could not have created greater consternation. I distinctly saw the splinters fly from the wooden stock of one fellow's matchlock, and another scoundrel threw up his arms, evidently hit, but not

[1] The Kinsha or upper Yangtse Kiang.

so severely as to prevent him following his companions uphill at double quick time. I thought I would just give them a further proof of the power of my weapon, and waited until they had got away three or four hundred yards, when sighting at seven hundred yards, I fired and struck the mountain some distance above them; this made them stop for a second or two, when again taking heart of grace they hurried on, and reaching their cave dashed in pell-mell like so many rats down a sewer.

My delight at the result of this engagement was slightly dashed by the thought that I had probably mortally wounded one of the robbers, in which case it was not at all improbable that I should be followed and shot from behind a tree or rock; however, by this time the constant expectation of coming to grief had settled down into a dogged indifference that I had felt once before in my life, when in a gale of wind in the Southern ocean. The ship in which I was the only passenger sprang a leak; for several days the water, despite the crew's exertions, kept gaining on the pumps, and as the truth gradually forced itself upon us that our sinking was merely a question of time, we grew perfectly indifferent, eating and sleeping as though nothing unusual had occurred, only the quiet and serious expression of all countenances spoke of the absence of hope in our hearts. Thus it was with our little party now. We kept on doggedly, much oppressed with the excessive heat, and in the evening reached the station of Jessundee, consisting of two musk hunters' cabins in one of which we found shelter for ourselves and animals, and above all a kindly welcome from the hunter. Our host was very poor; a long run of ill luck had left him without musk to buy powder, and to add to his misfortune his wife had died a few days before, leaving to his care four small children. The poor fellow was heart-broken and seemed like ourselves, reduced to the last extremity; his chief article of subsistence was a sort of creeper growing on the mountain; but he possessed two she-goats, and the milk from these he divided between Philip and myself, giving us each about half a pint. This with a couple of hard-boiled eggs served us for supper, and was the first food we had tasted for forty-eight hours. Low-dzung shared the host's tsamba, and I added a present of brick tea; for this the gratitude of the hunter knew no bounds; he would

43

have killed one of his goats for us, but this I would not permit. I was glad, however, when I saw him lop off several large branches from a walnut tree growing near his cabin and give them to my starved cattle; the poor brutes looked at the glossy green leaves for a moment or two as if they doubted their own eyesight, and then fell to on them, crunching up the branches, some of which were an inch in diameter, as if they were straws.

The aspect of the country was extremely dreary; bare limestone mountains rose abruptly everywhere around us in chaotic confusion; no cultivation was visible, but in some places patches of withered scrub clothed the mountain-sides, affording cover to numbers of pheasants and tragopans—occasionally the summit of some more than usually lofty peak covered with forest would stand out in bold relief to the surrounding barrenness, and in such places as these the hunters stalked the musk deer.

After a watchful night, for we still dreaded the banditti in the neighbourhood, who as the hunter informed us with a laugh were brother sportsmen, we continued the march, our host's son, a lad of ten years acting as guide, to the village of Tsali, where we were told provisions could be had in plenty. From the hunter's cabin our road gradually led us upwards until we entered a finely wooded country; we passed several houses but the inhabitants were either abroad or disinclined to admit us, for every house was locked, and but for the barking of watch-dogs all was perfectly still.

About ten o'clock we came across a large flock of sheep. The sight of them made our mouths water; and, on coming up with three or four men in charge of them, we at once entered into negotiations for the purchase of a lamb; but the fellows treated the request with scorn, and told us to be off. So Philip threw them three rupees and, bending down, without further ceremony, lifted a nice young lamb on to the front of his saddle. The owners picked up the rupees, apparently quite indifferent; and we continued on our way rejoicing.

Shortly after noon we stopped at a road-side house, and were at once admitted by a woman who turned out to be the only person at home. Philip immediately prepared to kill our lamb, while I attended to the boiling of the two eggs which the woman gave me. It seemed as if, with the prospect of a good meal, all our cares had vanished;

and I was sitting, patiently waiting for the eggs to boil, when suddenly I heard an agonizing cry of, 'Mr. Copper! come quick, sir.' Rushing to the door, I saw Philip, with bared arms, a knife in one hand, and holding on to the lamb with the other; while a stalwart lama was trying to drag it away from him.

On seeing me the lama dropped his hold of the lamb and commenced yelling at me in a frantic manner. As soon as he stopped to recover breath, Low-dzung informed me that the fellow claimed the lamb, and insisted on its being given up. This I refused to do, saying I was starving, and had paid three times its value, but as 1 did not wish to have a row I would give three rupees more.

During the altercation numbers of men, armed with matchlocks and the long Tibetan knife, seemed to spring from the ground and, while I was in the act of taking the rupees from my pocket, a fellow suddenly pinioned my arms from behind. An elderly virago of huge proportions planted herself in front, and commenced a furious assault on me with a cudgel, aiming vigorous blows at my head, which I avoided only by moving my head from side to side, thus allowing the blows to fall upon my shoulders. The giant who held me almost made me frantic by yelling in my ears; and I was decidedly getting badly used, when Philip at last abandoned our precious lamb, and came to my rescue. Having got my rifle, he pointed it at my captor's head, causing him to let go his hold when, turning sharply round, I stretched him on the ground by a well-planted blow on the nose, receiving at the same instant a frightful blow from the female fury behind me, which laid my head open, and for a second it seemed to bring all the stars into my eyes. She was about to repeat the dose when, with the little remaining strength I possessed, I poked her in the stomach and stretched her alongside her assistant in the fray.

Low-dzung, whom until now I had always looked upon as rather soft, had, during the encounter, with wonderful sagacity, replaced the packs which we had unloaded to rest our animals; and the moment I was free both Philip and myself mounted and rode off; not before, however, both men and lama had disappeared, together with the lamb. Thus, in the place of a meal, I got a severe beating and, what was worse than all, in my haste to be off, forgot the eggs which the good woman of the house had given me.

Hurrying away as quick as possible from the scene of the disaster, and followed by the screams and curses of the terrible female, we continued our march for the village of Tsali, about ten miles distant, fearing every moment that some of the armed men who had so suddenly appeared on the scene might quietly pot us from behind some rock or tree. Nothing happened, however, and towards sundown we reached the village situated in the centre of one of those plateaux so common in Tibet.

*Travels of a Pioneer in Commerce.* By T. T. Cooper, 1871.

# Nikolai Mikailovich Prejevalski
## 1839-1888

It was inevitable that Russians should figure among the European explorers who furnished their governments with geographical, political and military intelligence on Central Asia. France, from Indo-China, vied with Britain for control of the Yangtse valley and Southern China, and in the west sought to oust British influence from Persia and the Arabian peninsula. Britain was also constantly casting anxious glances at Tibet and Afghanistan in Russia's shadow. Elsewhere, Russia countered French and British activities in South China by improving her position in the north, and was actively opposed to British influence in Persia. Amid these conflicting pressures, the Celestial Empire maintained for decades a precarious balance, aided in the long run by Russia's domestic troubles, by the British Government's dislike of a 'forward' policy and the rise of Japan. In these circumstances, explorers were often frustrated by political expediency—throughout the latter half of the nineteenth century Lhasa was closed to foreigners—but in the new century, the *Entente Cordiale* and the understanding with Russia eased the tension. The greatest Russian explorer, perhaps the greatest European explorer of Central Asia was Nikolai Mikailovich Prejevalski; he traversed eastern Central Asia from north-eastern Mongolia to the Kunlun, providing the first exact account of the Gobi and of the northern ramparts of the Tibetan plateau. He failed however to obtain permission to enter Lhasa. Prejevalski was a tough traveller of many interests. ('Prejevalski's Horse', a species of wild horse, and the wild camel were discovered by him). His narratives are matter-of-fact and avoid sensationalism. The incidents below occurred when he returned across the Ala Shan range and the Gobi in 1877.

★    ★    ★

It was on the morning of the 13th July; the summits of the mountains [Ala Shan] were enveloped in mist, a sure indication of rain. Towards midday, however, it became perfectly clear and gave every promise of a fine day, when, three hours later, all of a sudden clouds began to settle on the mountains and the rain poured down in buckets. Our tent was soon soaked through and we dug small trenches to drain off the water which made its way into the interior. This continued for an hour without showing any signs of abatement, although the sky did not look threatening. The rainfall was so great that it was more than could be absorbed by the soil or retained on the steep slopes of the mountains; the consequence was that streams formed in every cleft and gorge, even falling from the precipitous cliffs, and uniting in the principal ravine where our tent happened to be pitched, descended in an impetuous torrent with terrific roar and speed. Dull echoes high up in the mountains warned us of its approach, and in a few minutes the deep bed of our ravine was inundated with a turbid, coffee-coloured stream, carrying with it rocks and heaps of smaller fragments, while it dashed with such violence against the sides that the very ground trembled as though with the shock of an earthquake. Above the roar of the waters we could hear the clash of great boulders as they met in their headlong course. From the loose banks and from the upper parts of the defile whole masses of smaller stones were detached by the force of the current and thrown up on either side of the channel, whilst trees were torn up by their roots and rent into splinters.

In the meanwhile the rain continued with undiminished violence and the torrent kept ever swelling. The deep bed of the ravine was soon choked with stones, mud, and fallen timber, which forced the water out of its channel on to higher ground. Barely twenty feet from our tent rushed the torrent, destroying everything in its course. Another minute, another foot of water, and our collections, the fruit of our expedition, were irrevocably gone! The flood had been so sudden that we had not a chance of rescuing them; all we could have done would have been to save our own lives by climbing on the nearest rocks. The disaster was so unexpected, the ruin so imminent that a feeling of apathy took possession of me, and although face to face with so terrible a misfortune I could not realize it.

Fortune, however, again befriended us. Before our tent was a small projecting ledge of rock upon which the waves threw up stones which soon formed a breakwater, and this saved us. Towards evening the rain slackened, the torrent quickly subsided, and the following morning beheld only a small stream flowing where the day before the waters of a mighty river had swept along. A bright sun lit up the scene of yesterday's destruction and displayed so complete a change in the appearance of the valley that we could not recognize it for the same.

On returning to Din-yuan-ing[1] we equipped our caravan, bartered away our bad camels, bought new ones, and on the morning of the 26th July started on our journey. Thanks to our Peking passport, and still more to the presents we bestowed on the *tosalakchi* who acted as regent during the prince's absence, we were able to hire two guides to escort us to the border of Ala-shan where we were to obtain others, and for this purpose the *yamen* (or magistracy) of Ala-shan issued an official document; in this way we continued to obtain guides from one *banner*[2] to another; a matter of great importance, for our road lay through the wildest part of the Gobi, in a meridional direction from Ala-shan to Urga,[3] and we could not possibly have found our way without them.

Another long series of hardships now awaited us. We suffered most from the July heat, which at midday rose to 113° Fahr. in the shade and at night was never less than 73°. No sooner did the sun appear above the horizon than it scorched us mercilessly. In the daytime the heat enveloped us on all sides, above from the sun, below from the burning ground; the wind, instead of cooling the atmosphere, stirred the lower strata and made it even more intolerable.

The air, too, was terribly dry; no dew fell, and rain-clouds dispersed without sending more than a few drops to earth. We observed this interesting phenomenon several times, particularly in southern Ala-shan near the Kan-su mountains where the rain as it fell met the lower heated atmosphere and passed off in steam before reaching the earth. Thunderstorms rarely occurred, but the wind was incessant night and day, and sometimes blew with great violence chiefly from the south-east and south-west. On calm days tornadoes were frequent about the middle of the day or a little later. To avoid the heat as much as possible we rose before daybreak; tea-drinking

[1] Tzehu, forty miles north-west of Ninghsia.
[2] Section of a tribe.
[3] Ulan Bator, Outer Mongolia.

and loading the camels, however, took up so much time that we never got away before four or even five o'clock in the morning. We might have lightened the fatigue considerably by night-marching, but in that case we should have had to forego the survey which formed so important a part of our labours. The line on the map marking our route from Din-yuan-ing to Urga is barely over a foot long, yet it was obtained at the cost of forty-four marches, mostly accomplished in the burning midday heat of the desert.

The commencement of our journey was unpropitious, for on the sixth day after we left Din-yuan-ing we lost our faithful friend 'Faust', and we ourselves nearly perished in the sands.

It was on the 31st July; we had left Djarataidabas and had taken the direction of the Khan-ula mountains; our guide having informed us that a march of eighteen miles lay before us that day, but that we should pass two wells about five miles apart.

Having accomplished that distance, we arrived at the first, and after watering our animals proceeded in the full expectation of finding the second, where we intended to halt; for though it was only seven in the morning, the heat was overpowering. So confident were we that the Cossacks proposed to throw away the supply of water that we had taken in the casks in order not to burden our camels needlessly, but fortunately I forbade their doing this. After nearly seven miles more, no well was to be seen, and the guide announced that we had gone out of our road. So he proceeded to the top of a hillock in the immediate neighbourhood to obtain a view over the surrounding country, and soon afterwards beckoned to us to follow. On rejoining him, he assured us where he purposed passing the night was scarcely four miles farther. We took the direction indicated. In the meanwhile it was near midday and the heat intolerable. A strong wind stirred the hot lower atmosphere, enveloping us in sand and saline dust. Our animals suffered frightfully, especially the dogs, obliged to walk over the burning sand. We stopped several times to give them drink and to moisten their heads as well as our own. But the supply of water now failed! Less than a gallon remained, and this we reserved for the last extremity. 'How much farther is it?' was the question we constantly put to our guide who invariably answered that it was near, that we should see it from the next sand-hill or the one after; and so we passed on upwards of seven miles without having seen a sign of the promised well. In the meanwhile the unfortunate 'Faust' lay down and moaned, giving us to understand that he was quite unable to walk. I then told my companion and guide to ride on, charging the latter to take 'Faust' on his camel as he was completely exhausted. After they had ridden a mile in advance of the caravan the guide pointed out the spot where he said the well should be, apparently about three miles off. Poor 'Faust's' doom was sealed; he was seized with fits, and Mr. Pyltseff, finding it was impossible to hurry on, and too far to ride back to the caravan for a glass of water, waited till we came up, laying 'Faust' under a clump of saxaul and covering him with saddle-felt. The poor dog became less conscious every minute, gasped two or three times, and expired. Placing his body on one of the packs, we moved on again, sorely doubting whether there were really any well in the place pointed out to us by the guide, for he had already deceived us more than once. Our situation at this moment was desperate. Only a few glasses of water were left, of which we took into our mouths just enough to moisten our parched tongues; our bodies seemed on fire, our heads swam, and we were close upon fainting. In this last extremity I desired a Cossack to take a small vessel and to ride as hard as he could to the well, accompanied by the guide, ordering him to fire at the latter if he attempted to run away. They were soon hidden in a cloud of dust which filled the air, and we toiled onwards in their tracks in the most anxious suspense. At length, after half an hour, the Cossack appeared. What news does he bring? and spurring our jaded horses which could hardly move their legs to meet him we learned with the joy of a man who has been snatched from the jaws of death that the well had been found! After a draught of fresh water from the vessel-ful that he brought, and having wet our heads, we rode in the direction pointed out, and soon reached the well of Boro-Sondji. It was now two-o'clock in the afternoon; we had, therefore, been exposed for nine consecutive hours to frightful heat, and had ridden upwards of twenty miles.

After unloading the camels, I sent a Cossack back with the Mongol for the pack which had been left on the road, by the side of which our other (Mongol) dog who had been with us nearly two years was laid. The poor brute had lain down underneath the pack but was still alive, and after getting a draught of water he was able to follow the men back to camp. Notwithstanding the complete prostration of our physical and moral energies, we felt the loss of 'Faust' so keenly that we could eat nothing, and slept but little all night. The following morning we dug a small grave and buried in it the remains of our faithful friend.

*Mongolia, the Tangut Country and Northern Tibet.* By N. M. Prejevalski, 1876.

# Charles Montagu Doughty
## 1843-1926

ARABIA has exerted a powerful attraction upon British travellers, and some of the finest books of travel describe that gaunt, sterile peninsula and its uncalculable, intriguing peoples. Indisputably the greatest Arabian traveller and writer was Charles Doughty. Sympathetic and comprehending, his coolness and intrepidity brought him through many critical moments. As a scholar he did much to establish the archaeology of Arabia on sound lines, while the minuteness and accuracy of his observations have made *Arabia Deserta* the standard source book on that country. It was to become indeed the 'Bible' of T. E. Lawrence during the 1914-18 war. It is the excellence of his highly individual literary style which particularly commends him to English readers; precise and strong, yet full of imagery, capturing in a few vivid strokes the heart of an incident or a landscape, it has had many imitators but no peers. The extract below describes a critical moment on his journey through Najd from Buraida to Taif in 1878.

★     ★     ★

The mad sherif had the knife again in his hand! and his old gall rising, 'Show me all that thou hast,' cries he, 'and leave nothing; or now will I kill thee.' Where was Maabub whom I had not seen since yester-evening? In him was the faintness and ineptitude of Arab friends. 'Remember the bread and salt which we have eaten together, Salem!' 'Show it all to me, or now by Ullah I will slay thee with this knife.' More bystanders gathered from the shadowing places; some of them cried out, 'Let us hack him in morsels, the cursed one! What hinders, fellows, let us hack him in morsels!' 'Have patience a moment, and send these away.' Salem, lifting his knife, cried, 'Except thou show me all at the instant, I will slay thee!' But rising and a little retiring from them I said, 'Let none think to take away my pistol!' which I drew from my bosom.

What should I do now? The world was before me; I thought, shall I fire if the miscreants come upon me, and no shot amiss? I might in the first horror reload—my thelul[1] was at hand; and if I could break away from more than a score of persons, what then?—repass the Ri'a, and seek Sh'aara again where 'Ateyban often come in to water? Which failing I might ride at adventure; and though I met with no man in the wilderness, in two or three days, it were easier to end thus than to be presently rent in pieces. I stood between my jaded thelul, that could not have saved her rider, and the sordid crew of camel-men advancing to close me in. They had no fire-arms. Fheyd approached and I gave back pace for pace; he opened his arms to embrace me! There was but a moment, I must slay him, or render the weapon, my only defence; and my life would be at the discretion of these wretches. I bade him come forward boldly. There was not time to shake out the shot, the pistol was yet suspended from my neck by a strong lace. I offered the butt to his hands. Fheyd seized the weapon! They were now in assurance of their lives and the booty; he snatched the cord and burst it. Then came his companion Salem; and they spoiled me of all that I had; and first my aneroid came into their brutish hands, then my purse that the black-hearted Siruan had long worn in his Turkish bosom at Kheybar. Salem feeling no reals[2] therein gave it over to his confederate Fheyd to whom fell also my pocket thermometer which, when they found to be but a toy of wood and glass, he restored it to me again, protesting with nefarious solemnity that other than this he had nothing of mine! Then these robbers sat down to divide the prey in their hands. The lookers-on showed a cruel countenance still, and reviling and threatening me, seemed to await Salem's rising, to begin 'hewing in pieces the Nasrany.'[3]

Salem and his confederate Fheyd were the most dangerous Arabs that I have met with; for the natural humanity of the Arabians was corrupted in them by the strong contagion of the government towns. I saw how impudently the robber sherif attributed all the best of the stealth to himself! Salem turned over the pistol-machine in his hand; such Turk's tools he had seen before at Mecca. But as he numbered the ends of the bullets in the chambers, the miscreant was dismayed;

[1] Riding camel.
[2] Spanish coin, used as currency.
[3] The Christian.

and thanked his God which had delivered him from these six deaths! He considered the perilous instrument and gazed on me, and seemed to balance in his heart whether he should not prove its shooting against the Nasrany. 'Akhs—akhs!' cried some hard hostile voices, 'Look how he carried this pistol to kill the Moslemin! Come now and we will hew him piecemeal. How those accursed Nasranies are full of wicked wiles! O thou! How many Moslems hast thou killed with that pistol?' 'My friends, I have not fired it in the lands of the Arabs. Salem, remember 'Ayn ez-Zeyma! Thou camest with a knife to kill me, but did I turn it against thee? Render therefore thanks to Ullah! and remember the bread and the salt, Salem.'

He bade his drudge Fheyd shoot off the pistol, and I dreaded he might make me his mark. Fheyd fired the first shots in the air; the chambers had been loaded nearly two years, but one after another they were shot off—and that was with a wonderful resonance in this silent place of rocks. Salem said, rising, 'Leave one of them!' This last shot he reserved for me; and I felt miserable to die here by their barbarous hands without defence. 'Fheyd,' he said again, 'is all sure?—and one remains?'

Salem glared upon me, and perhaps had indignation that I did not say 'dakhilak'; the tranquility of the kafir troubled him. When he was weary, he went to sit down and called me, 'Sit,' quoth he, 'beside me.' 'You hear the savage words of these persons; remember, Salem, you must answer for me to the sherif.' 'The sherif will hang thee, Nasrany! Ullah curse the Yahud and Nasara.' Some of the camel-men said, 'Thou wast safe in thine own country, thou mightest have continued there; but since thou art come into the land of the Moslemin, God has delivered thee into our hands to die:—so perish all the Nasara and be burned in hell with your father, Sheytan.' 'Look!' I said to them, 'Good fellows—for the most fault is your ignorance, ye think I shall be hanged tomorrow; but what if the sherif esteem me more than you all, who revile me today! If you deal cruelly with me you will be called to an account. Believe my words! Hasseyn will receive me as one of the ullema; but with you men of the people, his subjects, he will deal without regard.' 'Thou shalt be hanged,' they cried again, 'O thou cursed one!' And after this they dispersed to their several halting places.

Soon afterward there came over to us the Mecca burgess, who now had alighted under some trees at little distance. From this smooth personage, a flower of merchants in the holy city—though I appealed to his better mind, that he should speak to Salem, I could not draw a human word; and he abstained from evil. He gazed his fill, and forsook me to go again to his hareem. I watched him depart, and the robber sherif was upbraiding me that I had 'hidden' the things and my pistol! In this I received a shock and became numbed to the world. I sat in a swoon and felt that my body rocked and shivered; and thought now they had mortally wounded me with a knife or shot, for I could not hear, I saw light thick and confusedly. But coming slowly to myself, so soon as I might see ground I saw there no blood. I felt a numbness and deadness at the nape of the neck. Afterward I knew that Fheyd had inhumanly struck me there with his driving-stick—and again, with all his force.

I looked up and found them sitting by me. I said faintly, 'Why have you done this?' *Fheyd*: 'Because thou didst withhold the pistol.' 'Is the pistol mine or thine? I might have shot thee dead, but I remembered the mercy of Ullah.' A caravaner sat by us eating—one that ceased not to rail against me; he was the man who assailed me in the night, and had brought so much mischief upon me. I suddenly caught his hand with the bread, and putting some in my mouth, I said to him, 'Enough, man! there is bread and salt between us.' The wretch allowed it, and said not another word. I have never found any but Salem a truce-breaker of the bread and salt—but he was of the spirituality.

There came one riding to us on an ass! It was Abd-el-Aziz! He and Maabub had heard the shots as they sat resting at some distance yonder. For they, who were journeying together to et-Tayif, had arrived here in the night-time and I was not aware of it. Maabub now sent this young man (unworthy of the name of Bessam) to know what the shots meant, and what were become of the Nasrany— whether he yet lived? Abd-el-Aziz, seeing the pistol in Salem's hands and his prisoner alive, asked, 'Wherefore had he taken away the man's pistol?' I said to him, 'You see how these ignorant men threaten me; speak some word to them for thine uncle Abdullah's sake.' But he, with sour fanatical looks; 'Am I a Frenjy?'—and mounting again, he rode out of sight.

After these haps Salem, having now the spoil in his hands and fearing to lose it again at et-Tayif,[1] had a mind to send me down to Jidda[2] on the Bessam's thelul. 'Ha! Khalil, we are become brothers; Khalil, are we not now good friends? There is nothing more betwixt us. What sayest thou? Wilt thou then that we send thee to Jidda, and I myself ride with thee on the thelul?' But I answered, 'I go to visit the sherif at Tayif, and you to accuse me there and clear yourselves before him; at Jidda you would be put in prison.' Some bystanders cried, 'Let him go to et-Tayif.'

A messenger returned from Maabub bidding Salem, Khalil and Fheyd come to him. As we went I looked back, and saw Fheyd busy to rifle my camel-bags!—after that he followed us. The young Bessam was sitting under the shadow of some rocks with Maabub. 'Are you men?' quoth Maabub. 'Are you men who have so dealt with this stranger?' I told him how they robbed me, and what I had suffered at their hands. I was yet (and long afterward) stunned by the blows on the neck. *Maabub*: 'Sherif Salem, thou art to bring this stranger to our lord Hasseyn at et-Tayif, and do him no wrong by the way. How canst thou rob and wound one who is committed to thy trust, like the worst Beduin thieves? But I think verily that none of the Beduw would do the like.' *Salem*: 'Is not this a Nasrany? He might kill us all by the way; we did but take his pistol because we were afraid.' *Maabub*: 'Have you taken his silver from him and his other things because ye were afraid? I know thee, Salem! but thou wilt have to give account to our lord the Sherif.' So he dismissed us; and we returned to our place.

It came into my mind, bye and bye, to go again to Maabub; the sand was as burning coals under my bare feet, so that after every few steps I must fall on my knees to taste a moment's relief. Maabub was Umbrella-bearer of the Sherif, and an old faithful servitor of his brother, the late sherif. 'Wherefore, I asked, had he so strangely forsaken me hitherto? Or how could he commit me to that murderous Salem whom he himself called a mad sherif? Did he look to

[1] Some fifty miles south-east of Mecca.
[2] The Red Sea port for Mecca.

see me alive at Tayif?—I am now without defence; at the next turn he may stab me; do thou therefore ride with me on the thelul!'— 'Khalil, because of an infirmity (sarcocele) I cannot mount in a saddle.' When I said I would requite his pains, the worthy Negro answered, 'That be far from me, for it is my duty which I owe to our lord, the sherif, but if thou have a remedy for my disease, I pray thee, remember me at et-Tayif.' The young Bessam had fever, with a daily crisis. It came on him at noon; and then he who lately would not speak a word to shelter the Frenjy's life, with a puling voice (as they are craven and unmanly), besought me to succour him. I answered, 'At et-Tayif!' Had he aided me at the first, for his good uncle's sake, I had not now been too faint to seek for remedies. I promised, if he would ride with me tonight, to give him a medicine to cut the fever, tomorrow; but Arabs put no trust in distant promises.

It drew to the mid-afternoon, when I heard we should remove; and then the foolish young Bessam bade me rise and help to load the carpets on his camel. I did not deny him; but had not much strength; and Maabub, blaming the rashness of the young man, would have me sit still in the shadow—Maabub rode seated on the load of carpets, and when the camel arose under him, the heavy old Negro was nigh falling. Once more I asked him not to forsake me, and to remember how many were the dark hours before us on the road.

*Travels in Arabia Deserta*. By C. M. Doughty. Jonathan Cape, 1936. Permission to quote given by the Misses Doughty.

# Marc Aurel Stein
## 1862-1943

MANY European explorers and archaeologists travelled in Central Asia in the decades before World War I. But none outrivalled the Anglo-Hungarian archaeologist and geographer, Aurel Stein. Supported by the Indian Government he made three great central Asian journeys from 1900 to 1915. That of 1906–8 was perhaps the most striking. Crossing the Hindu Kush he travelled round the great Takla Makan desert to examine the intriguing lake, Lop Nor, and continued across the Southern Gobi in the tracks of medieval explorers. Here he picked up and traced the half-buried remains of the ancient wall and defence system. An astonishing discovery was made in the Tunhuang oasis at the western end of the wall. Here he found the cave-temples of the 'Thousand Buddhas' and an incredibly rich collection of early Buddhist MSS sealed up, probably for eight hundred years, in a small cell. These were closely related to the MSS collected by Hsuan-tsang (see above, p. 3). To obtain access to them Stein made successful play on his devotion to that pilgrim, as he relates below. These MSS revolutionized knowledge of early Chinese art and of the history of Buddhism. Single-minded in his devotion to Asian archaeology, regardless of comfort, immensely learned, with a prodigious memory, Stein is the type representative of the scholar-explorer.

\*    \*    \*

More than once before, my well-known attachment to the memory of Hsuan-tsang, the greatest of those pilgrims, had been helpful in securing me a sympathetic hearing both among the learned and the simple. Wang Tao-shih, too, had probably heard about it. So surrounded by these tokens of lingering Buddhist worship, genuine though distorted, I thought it appropriate to tell Wang Tao-shih,[1] as well as my poor Chinese would permit, of my devotion to the saintly traveller; how I had followed his footsteps from India for over ten thousand li across inhospitable mountains and deserts [to

[1] The priest in charge of the MSS.

Tunhuang]; how in the course of this pilgrimage I had traced to its present ruins, however inaccessible, many a sanctuary he had piously visited and described; and so on.

I confess it never cost me any effort to grow eloquent on the subject of my 'Chinese patron saint', whose guidance had so often proved fruitful for my own work. But now it was made doubly easy by the gleam of lively interest which I caught in the Tao-shih's eyes, otherwise so shy and fitful. As Chiang,[1] in reply to interjected questions, elaborated details and made the most of my familiarity with Hsuan-tsang's authentic records and the distant scenes of his travels, I could read the impression made in the Taoist priest's generally puzzling countenance. Very soon I felt sure that the Tao-shih, though poorly versed in and indifferent to things Buddhist, was quite as ardent an admirer in his own way of 'T'ang-seng',[2] the great 'monk of the T'ang period', as I am in another.

I had ocular proof of this when he took us outside into the spacious newly built loggia in front of the temple, and showed us with pride how he had caused all its walls to be decorated by a local Tun-huang artist with a series of quaint but spirited frescoes representing characteristic scenes from the great pilgrim's adventures. They were those fantastic legends which have transformed Hsuan-tsang in popular belief throughout China into a sort of saintly Munchausen. It is true they are not to be found in the genuine memoirs and biography. But what did that little difference in our respective conceptions of the hero matter? Gladly I let my delightfully credulous cicerone expound in voluble talk the wonderful stories of travel which each fresco panel depicted. Here the holy pilgrim was seen snatched up to the clouds by a wicked demon and then restored again to his pious companions through the force of his prayer or magic. Two queer-looking figures—one horse, one bull-headed—were represented as his constant attendants. Elsewhere he was shown forcing a ferocious dragon which had swallowed his horse to restore it again, and so on.

But the picture in which I displayed particular interest showed a

[1] Stein's interpreter.
[2] i.e., Hsuan-tsang.

theme curiously adapted to our own case, though it was not till later that I appealed again and again to the moral it pointed. There was 'T'ang-seng' standing on the bank of a violent torrent, and beside him his faithful steed laden with big bundles of manuscripts. To help in ferrying across such a precious burden a large turtle was seen swimming towards the pilgrim. Here was clearly a reference to the twenty pony-loads of sacred books and relics which the historical traveller managed to carry away safely from India. But would the pious guardian read this obvious lesson aright, and be willing to acquire spiritual merit by letting me take back to the old home of Buddhism some of the ancient manuscripts which chance had placed in his keeping? For the time being it seemed safer not to tackle that question. Yet when I took my leave of the Tao-shih I instinctively felt that a new and more reliable link was being established between us.

I left the Ssu-yeh behind to make the most of the favourable impression produced, and to urge an early loan of the promised manuscript specimens. But the priest had again become nervous and postponed their delivery in a vague way 'until later'. There was nothing for me but to wait.

All doubt, however, disappeared in the end. Late at night Chiang groped his way to my tent in silent elation with a bundle of Chinese rolls which Wang Tao-shih had just brought him in secret, carefully hidden under his flowing black robe, as the first of the promised 'specimens'. The rolls looked unmistakably old as regards writing and paper, and probably contained Buddhist canonical texts; but Chiang needed time to make sure of their character. Next morning he turned up by day-break and with a face expressing both triumph and amazement reported that these fine rolls of paper contained Chinese versions of certain 'Sutras' from the Buddhist canon which the colophons declared to have been brought from India and translated by Hsuan-tsang himself. The strange chance which thus caused us to be met at the very outset by the name of my Chinese patron saint, and by what undoubtedly were early copies of his labours as a sacred translator, struck both of us as a most auspicious omen. Was it not 'T'ang-seng' himself, so Chiang declared, who at the opportune moment had revealed the hiding-place of that manuscript hoard to an ignorant priest in order to prepare for me, his admirer and disciple from distant India, a fitting antiquarian reward on the westernmost confines of China proper?

Of Hsuan-tsang's authorship, Wang Tao-shih in his ignorance could not possibly have had any inkling when he picked up that packet of 'specimens'. Chiang-ssu-yeh realized at once that this discovery was bound to impress the credulous priest as a special interposition on my behalf of the great traveller of sacred memory. So he hastened away to carry the news to the Tao-shih, and, backed up by this visible evidence of support from the latter's own cherished saint, to renew his pleading for free access to the hidden manuscript store. The effect was most striking. Before long Chiang returned to report that the portent could be trusted to work its spell. Some hours later he found the wall blocking the entrance to the recess of the temple removed, and on its door being opened by the priest, caught a glimpse of a room crammed full to the roof with manuscript bundles. I had purposely kept away from the Tao-shih's temple all the forenoon, but on getting this news I could no longer restrain my impatience to see the great hoard myself. The day was cloudless and hot, and the 'soldiers' who had followed me about during the morning with my cameras, were now taking their siesta in sound sleep soothed by a good smoke of opium. So accompanied only by Chiang I went to the temple.

I found the priest there evidently still combating his scruples and nervous apprehensions. But under the influence of that quasi-divine hint he now summoned up courage to open before me the rough door closing the narrow entrance which led from the side of the broad front passage into the rock-carved recess, on a level of about four feet above the floor of the former. The sight of the small room disclosed was one to make my eyes open wide. Heaped up in layers, but without any order, there appeared in the dim light of the priest's little lamp a solid mass of manuscript bundles rising to a height of nearly ten feet, and filling, as subsequent measurement showed, close on five hundred cubic feet. The area left clear within the room was just sufficient for two people to stand in. It was manifest that in this 'black hole' no examination of the manuscripts would be possible, and also that the digging out of all its contents would cost a good deal of physical labour.

A suggestion to clear out all the bundles into the large cellar of the cave-temple, where they might have been examined at ease, would have been premature; so much oppressed at the time was Wang Tao-shih by fears of losing his position—and patrons—by the rumours which any casual observers might spread against him in the oasis. So for the present I had to rest content with his offer to take out a bundle or two at a time, and to let us look rapidly through their contents in a less cramped part of the precincts. Fortunately the restorations carried out by him, besides the fine loggia already mentioned, included a kind of large ante-chapel, having on either side a small room provided with a door and paper-covered windows. So here a convenient 'reading-room' was at hand for this strange old library, where we were screened from any inquisitive eyes, even if an occasional worshipper dropped in to 'kotow' before the huge and ugly Buddha statue now set up in the temple.

While the Tao-shih was engaged in digging out a few bundles, I closely examined the passage wall behind which this great deposit of manuscripts had been hidden. The priest had told us that, when he first settled at the 'Thousand Buddhas' some eight years before, he found the entrance to this cave-temple almost completely blocked by drift sand. Judging from the condition of the other caves near by and the relatively low level of this particular temple, it is probable that this accumulation of drift sand rose to ten feet or more at the entrance. Keeping only a few labourers at work from the proceeds of pious donations, at first coming driblet-like with lamentable slowness, our Tao-shih had taken two or three years to lay bare the whole of the broad passage, some forty feet deep. When this task had been accomplished, and while engaged in setting up new statues in place of the decayed old stucco images occupying the dais of the cellar, he had noticed a small crack in the frescoed wall to the right of the passage. There appeared to be a recess behind the plastered surface instead of the solid conglomerate from which the cells and its approach are hewn; and on widening the opening he discovered the small room with its deposit such as I now saw it.

Walled into the west face of the room had been found a large slab of black marble covered with a long and neatly engraved Chinese inscription. It had subsequently been removed and set up in a more accessible place on the left-hand wall of the passage. This inscription records imperial eulogies of a Chinese pilgrim named Hung-pien, who had visited India, and after returning with relics and sacred texts had apparently settled at these shrines to devote his remaining years to translating and other pious labours. As it is dated in the year corresponding to A.D. 851, it was clear to me from the first that the deposit of the manuscripts must have taken place some time after the middle of the ninth century.

*Ruins of Desert Cathay.* By M. Aurel Stein. Macmillan, 1912. Vol. 2.

# Wilfred Thesiger
## 1910–

WILFRED THESIGER was born in Addis Abbaba, the eldest son of
the British Minister in Ethiopia, and was early influenced by the
strange sights and romantic ceremonies of this ancient African
kingdom. A conventional education at Eton and Oxford only confirmed in him a preference for out-of-the-way places and savage
peoples; in 1933–4 he explored the Danakil country of Abyssinia
and the Aussa Sultanate, and from 1935 to 1940 he served in the
Sudan Political Service. During the Second World War he saw fighting in the Ethiopian, Syrian and Western Desert campaigns and won
the D.S.O., but it was not until after the end of hostilities that he
found his true bent. His two crossings of the Rub' al Khali, the
'Empty Quarter' of Southern Arabia, in 1945–49, were undertaken
on behalf of the Anti-Locust Research Centre, and the account of
the journeys in *Arabian Sands* stands comparison with the finest
travel books of the past. The extract describes his traverse of the
Uruq al Shaiba, the area of the highest sand-dunes, bordering on
southern Oman. Thesiger has also lived and travelled in the wild
marsh country of southern Iraq, in the Hindu Kush, the Karakoram
and Morocco.

&starf;      &starf;      &starf;

We rested for a while on the sand, not troubling to talk, until al Auf
rose to his feet and said 'Come on'. Some small dunes built up by
cross-winds ran in curves parallel with the main face across the back
of these downs. Their steep faces were to the north and the camels
slithered down them without difficulty. These downs were brick-
red, splashed with deeper shades of colour; the underlying sand,
exposed where it had been churned up by our feet, showing red of a
paler shade. But the most curious feature was a number of deep
craters resembling giant hoof-prints. These were unlike normal
crescent-dunes, since they did not rise above their surroundings,
but formed hollows in the floor of hard undulating sand. The salt
flats far below us looked very white.

We mounted our camels. My companions had muffled their faces in their head-cloths and rode in silence, swaying to the camels' stride. The shadows on the sand were very blue, of the same tone as the sky; two ravens flew northward, croaking as they passed. I struggled to keep awake. The only sound was made by the slap of the camels' feet, like wavelets lapping on a beach.

To rest the camels we stopped for four hours in the late afternoon on a long gentle slope which stretched down to another salt-flat. There was no vegetation on it and no salt-bushes bordered the plain below us. Al Auf announced that we would go on again at sunset. While we were feeding I said to him cheerfully, 'Anyway, the worst should be over now that we are across the Uruq al Shaiba.' He looked at me for a moment and then answered, 'If we go well tonight we should reach them tomorrow.' I said, 'Reach what?' and he replied, 'The Uruq al Shaiba,' adding, 'Did you think what we crossed today was the Uruq al Shaiba? That was only a dune. You will see them tomorrow.' For a moment I thought he was joking, and then I realized that he was serious, that the worst of the journey which I had thought was behind us was still ahead.

It was midnight when at last al Auf said, 'Let's stop here. We will get some sleep and give the camels a rest. The Uruq al Shaiba are not far away now.' In my dreams that night they towered above us higher than the Himalayas.

Al Auf woke us again while it was still dark. As usual bin Kabina made coffee, and the sharp-tasting drops which he poured out stimulated but did not warm. The morning star had risen above the dunes. Formless things regained their shape in the first dim light of dawn. The grunting camels heaved themselves erect. We lingered for a moment more beside the fire; then al Auf said 'Come,' and we moved forward. Beneath my feet the gritty sand was cold as frozen snow.

We were faced by a range as high as, perhaps even higher than, the range we had crossed the day before, but here the peaks were steeper and more pronounced, rising in many cases to great pinnacles, down which the flowing ridges swept like draperies. These sands, paler coloured than most we had crossed, were very soft, cascading round our feet as the camels struggled up the slopes.

Remembering how little warning of imminent collapse the dying camels had given me twelve years before in the Danakil country, I wondered how much more these camels would stand, for they were trembling violently whenever they halted. When one refused to go on we heaved on her head-rope, pushed her from behind, and lifted the loads on either side as we manhandled the roaring animal upward. Sometimes one of them lay down and refused to rise, and then we had to unload her, and carry the water-skins and the saddle-bags ourselves. Not that the loads were heavy. We had only a few gallons of water left, and some handfuls of flour.

We led the trembling, hesitating animals upward along great sweeping ridges where the knife-edged crests crumbled beneath our feet. Although it was killing work, my companions were always gentle and infinitely patient. The sun was scorching hot and I felt empty, sick, and dizzy. As I struggled up the slope, knee-deep in shifting sand, my heart thumped wildly and my thirst grew worse. I found it difficult to swallow; even my ears felt blocked, and yet I knew that it would be many intolerable hours before I could drink. I would stop to rest, dropping down on the scorching sand, and immediately it seemed I would hear the others shouting, 'Umbarak, Umbarak'; their voices sounded strained and hoarse.

It took us three hours to cross this range.

On the summit were no gently undulating downs such as we had met the day before. Instead, three smaller dune-chains rode upon its back, and beyond them the sand fell away to a salt-flat in another great empty trough between the mountains. The range on the far side seemed even higher than the one on which we stood, and behind it were others. I looked round, seeking instinctively for some escape. There was no limit to my vision. Somewhere in the ultimate distance the sands merged into the sky, but in that infinity of space I could see no living thing, not even a withered plant to give me hope. There is nowhere to go, I thought. We cannot go back and our camels will never get up another of these awful dunes. We really are finished. The silence flowed over me, drowning the voices of my companions and the fidgeting of their camels.

We went down into the valley, and somehow—and I shall never know how the camels did it—we got up the other side. There, utterly exhausted, we collapsed. Al Auf gave us each a little water, enough to wet our mouths. He said, 'We need this if we are to go on.' The midday sun had drained the colour from the sands. Scattered banks of cumulus cloud threw shadows across the dunes and salt-flats, and added an illusion that we were high among Alpine peaks, with frozen lakes of blue and green in the valley, far below. Half asleep, I turned over, but the sand burnt through my shirt and woke me from my dreams.

Two hours later al Auf roused us. As he helped me load my camel, he said, 'Cheer up, Umbarak. This time we really are across the Uruq al Shaiba,' and when I pointed to the ranges ahead of us, he answered, 'I can find a way through those; we need not cross them.' We went on till sunset, but we were going with the grain of the country, following the valleys and no longer trying to climb the dunes. We should not have been able to cross another. There was a little fresh *qassis* on the slope where we halted. I hoped that this lucky find would give us an excuse to stop here for the night, but, after we had fed, al Auf went to fetch the camels, saying, 'We must go on again while it is cool if we are ever to reach Dhafara.'

We stopped long after midnight and started again at dawn, still exhausted from the strain and long hours of yesterday, but al Auf encouraged us by saying that the worst was over. The dunes were certainly lower than they had been, more uniform in height and more rounded, with fewer peaks. Four hours after we had started we came to rolling uplands of gold and silver sand, but still there was nothing for the camels to eat.

A hare jumped out from under a bush, and al Auf knocked it over with his stick. The others shouted 'God has given us meat.' For days we had talked of food; every conversation seemed to lead back to it. Since we had left Ghanim I had been always conscious of the dull ache of hunger, yet in the evenings my throat was dry even after my drink, so that I found it difficult to swallow the dry bread Musallim set before us. All day we thought and talked about that hare, and by three o'clock in the afternoon could no longer resist stopping to cook it. Mabkhaut suggested, 'Let's roast it in its skin in the embers of a fire. That will save our water—we haven't got much left.' Bin Kabina led the chorus of protest. 'No, by God!

Don't even suggest such a thing'; and turning to me he said, 'We don't want Mabkhaut's charred meat. Soup. We want soup and extra bread. We will feed well today even if we go hungry and thirsty later. By God, I am hungry!' We agreed to make soup. We were across the Uruq al Shaiba and intended to celebrate our achievement with this gift from God. Unless our camels foundered we were safe; even if our water ran out we should live to reach a well.

Musallim made nearly double our usual quantity of bread while bin Kabina cooked the hare. He looked across at me and said, 'The smell of this meat makes me faint.' When it was ready he divided it into five portions. They were very small, for an Arabian hare is no larger than an English rabbit, and this one was not even fully grown. Al Auf named the lots and Mabkhaut drew them. Each of us took the small pile of meat which had fallen to him. Then bin Kabina said, 'God! I have forgotten to divide the liver,' and the others said, 'Give it to Umbarak.' I protested, saying that they should divide it, but they swore by God that they would not eat it and that I was to have it. Eventually I took it, knowing that I ought not, but too greedy for this extra scrap of meat to care.

# Edmund Hillary
## 1919–

MOUNTAINEERS in the Himalaya, besides grappling with the highest and some of the most difficult peaks in the world, also explored considerable areas of the earth's surface. Between the wars, when entry into Nepal was prohibited, many British expeditions assaulted Mount Everest from the north. After 1945 political conditions in Nepal changed and permission to attempt the summit from the south was granted. Following Eric Shipton's reconnaissance from the expedition of 1951 and the unsuccessful Swiss attempts the next year, the British expedition of 1953 led by Sir John Hunt conquered the summit, the news of their success happily reaching the outside world on H.M. Queen Elizabeth II's Coronation Day. Hunt's expedition was notable for thoroughness of organization, careful and meticulous planning and quality of leadership. But in the final event success depended on the skill and endurance of the team of mountaineers. The South Peak of Everest was climbed by Charles Evans and Tom Bourdillon on May 26th, and three days later Edmund Hillary and Tenzing achieved the summit. In this extract Sir Edmund describes their final climb from South Peak to the summit (29,141 feet).

*　　*　　*

It was with some relief that we finally reached some firmer snow higher up and then chipped steps up the last steep slopes and cramponed on to the South Peak. It was now 9 a.m. We looked with some interest at the virgin ridge ahead. Both Bourdillon and Evans had been depressingly definite about its problems and difficulties and we realized that it could form an almost insuperable barrier. At first glance it was certainly impressive and even rather frightening. On the right, great contorted cornices, overhanging masses of snow and ice, stuck out like twisted fingers over the ten thousand foot drop of the Kangshung Face. Any move on to these cornices could only bring disaster. From the cornices the ridge dropped steeply to the left until the snow merged with the great rock face sweeping up

70

from the Western Cwm.[1] Only one encouraging feature was apparent. The steep snow slope between the cornices and the rock precipices seemed to be composed of firm, hard snow. If the snow proved soft and unstable, our chances of getting along the ridge were few indeed. If we could cut a trail of steps along this slope, we could make some progress at least.

We cut a seat for ourselves just below the southern summit and removed our oxygen. Once again I worked out the mental arithmetic that was one of my main preoccupations on the way up and down the mountain. As our first partly full bottle of oxygen was now exhausted, we had only one full bottle left. Eight hundred litres of oxygen at three litres per minute? How long could we last? I estimated that this should give us four and a half hours of going. Our apparatus was now much lighter, weighing just over twenty lb, and as I cut steps down off the southern summit I felt a distinct sense of freedom and well-being quite contrary to what I had expected at this great altitude.

As my ice-axe bit into the first steep slope of the ridge, my highest hopes were realized. The snow was crystalline and firm. Two or three rhythmical blows of the ice-axe produced a step large enough even for our oversized high altitude boots and, the most encouraging feature of all, a firm thrust of the ice-axe would sink it half-way up the shaft, giving a solid and comfortable belay. We moved one at a time. I realized that our margin of safety at this altitude was not great and that we must take every care and precaution. I would cut a forty-foot line of steps, Tenzing belaying me while I worked. Then in turn I would sink my shaft and put a few loops of the rope around it and Tenzing, protected against a breaking step, would move up to me. Then once again as he belayed me I would go on cutting. In a number of places the overhanging ice cornices were very large indeed and in order to escape them I cut a line of steps down to where the snow met the rocks on the west. It was a great thrill to look straight down this enormous rock face and to see, eight thousand feet below us, the tiny tents of the Camp IV in the Western Cwm. Scrambling on the rocks and cutting handholds in the snow, we were able to shuffle past these difficult portions.

[1] The valley of the great glacier up which the route of the Expedition lay.

On one of these occasions I noted that Tenzing, who had been going quite well, had suddenly slowed up considerably and seemed to be breathing with difficulty. The Sherpas had little idea of the workings of an oxygen set and from past experience I immediately suspected his oxygen supply. I noticed that hanging from the exhaust tube of his oxygen mask were icicles, and on closer examination found that this tube, some two inches in diameter, was completely blocked with ice. I was able to clear it out and gave him much-needed relief. On checking my own set I found that the same thing was occurring, though it had not reached the stage to have caused me any discomfort. From then on I kept a much closer check on this problem.

The weather for Everest seemed practically perfect. Insulated as we were in all our down clothing and windproofs, we suffered no discomfort from cold or wind. However, on one occasion I removed my sunglasses to examine more closely a difficult section of the ridge, but was very soon blinded by the fine snow driven by the bitter wind and hastily replaced them. I went on cutting steps. To my surprise I was enjoying the climb as much as I had ever enjoyed a fine ridge in my own New Zealand Alps.

After an hour's steady going we reached the foot of the most formidable-looking problem on the ridge—a rock step some forty feet high. We had known of the existence of this step from aerial photographs and had also seen it through our binoculars from Thyangboche. We realized that at this altitude it might well spell the difference between success and failure. The rock itself, smooth and almost holdless, might have been an interesting Sunday afternoon problem to a group of expert rock climbers in the Lake District, but here it was a barrier beyond our feeble strength to overcome. I could see no way of turning it on the steep rock bluff on the west, but fortunately another possibility of tackling it still remained. On its east side was another great cornice, and running up the full forty feet of the step was a narrow crack between the cornice and the rock. Leaving Tenzing to belay me as best he could, I jammed my way into this crack, then kicking backwards with my crampons I sank their spikes deep into the frozen snow behind me and levered myself off the ground. Taking advantage of every little rock-hold and all the force of knee, shoulder and arms I could muster, I literally cramponed backwards up the crack, with a fervent prayer that the cornice would remain attached to the rock. Despite the considerable effort involved, my progress although slow was steady, and as Tenzing paid out the rope I inched my way upwards until I could finally reach over the top of the rock and drag myself out of the crack on to a wide ledge. For a few moments I lay regaining my breath and for the first time really felt the fierce determination that nothing now could stop us reaching the top. I took a firm stance on the ledge and signalled to Tenzing to come on up. As I heaved hard on the rope Tenzing wriggled his way up the crack and finally collapsed exhausted at the top like a giant fish when it has just been hauled from the sea after a terrible struggle.

I checked both our oxygen sets and roughly calculated our flow rates. Everything seemed to be going well. Probably owing to the strain imposed on him by the trouble with his oxygen set, Tenzing had been moving rather slowly but he was climbing safely, and this was the major consideration. His only comment on my inquiring of his condition was to smile and wave along the ridge. We were going so well at three litres per minute that I was determined now if necessary to cut down our flow rate to two litres per minute if the extra endurance was required.

The ridge continued as before. Giant cornices on the right, steep rock slopes on the left. I went on cutting steps on the narrow strip of snow. The ridge curved away to the right and we had no idea where the top was. As I cut around the back of one hump, another higher one would swing into view. Time was passing and the ridge seemed never-ending. In one place, where the angle of the ridge had eased off, I tried cramponing without cutting steps, hoping this would save time, but I quickly realized that our margin of safety on these steep slopes at this altitude was too small, so I went on step-cutting. I was beginning to tire a little now. I had been cutting steps continuously for two hours, and Tenzing, too, was moving very slowly. As I chipped steps around still another corner, I wondered rather dully just how long we could keep it up. Our original zest had now quite gone and it was turning more into a grim struggle. I then realized that the ridge ahead, instead of still monotonously

73

rising, now dropped sharply away, and far below I could see the North Col and the Rongbuk glacier. I looked upwards to see a narrow snow ridge running up to a snowy summit. A few more whacks of the ice-axe in the firm snow and we stood on top.

From the book *The Conquest of Everest*. By Sir John Hunt. Copyright 1954 by Sir John Hunt. Reprinted by permission of E. P. Dutton & Co., Inc.

# AFRICA

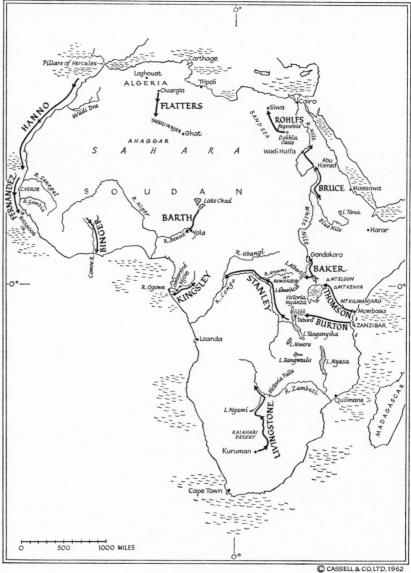

AFRICA

# Hanno
## fl. 500 B.C.

THE Carthaginian commercial empire was based upon extensive settlement and trade relations in the regions around the western Mediterranean. Partly owing to the character of Carthaginian history, the evidence for these activities is fragmentary and difficult to interpret. A Greek version, however, of a trading and exploratory expedition along the north-west African coast under the leadership of a certain Hanno has survived. There appear to be three themes mixed in this account; a colonizing expedition along the coast immediately west of the Straits of Gibraltar; a short voyage from the Wadi Dra to the Senegal river, and a longer voyage to the south. The latter has excited much controversy. Conservative commentators accept the 'Mountaine full of great trees' as Cape Verde, 'the loftie Mountaine called the Chariot of the Gods' as a summit in Guinea, perhaps Mt. Kakoulima; the 'fierie rivers' as grass fires, and the people with 'bodies all over hairie' as some primitive tribe. Bolder critics make the voyage continue much further south; they see the fiery mountain as an active volcano (Mount Camerun being an obvious candidate) and the hairy people as gorillas. The latter identification is certainly unacceptable. Hanno's inclusion in the Elizabethan Richard Hakluyt's collection of voyages is interesting.

★    ★    ★

The Carthaginians determined that Hanno should saile without Hercules Pillars,[1] and there build Cities of the Liby-phinicians. He set saile with threescore Ships of fiftie Oares a peece, conducting with him a great multitude of men and women, to the number of thirty thousand, with victuals and all other necessaries. We arrived at the Pillars, and passed them, and having sailed without them two daies, we built the first Citie, calling it Thymiaterium. It had round about it very large Champaignes. After turning toward the West,

---

[1] i.e. beyond the Strait of Gibraltar.

77

we came to a promontorie of Africa, called Soloente, covered all over with woods. And having here built a Temple to Neptune, we sailed halfe a day towards the East, till we arrived at a Fen, which is situated not farre from the Sea, very full of great and long Canes[1]; and there were in it feeding Elephants and many other creatures. Then having gone about a daies saile beyond that Fenne we built Cities on the Sea Coast, calling them by their proper names Murus, Caricus, Gitta, Acra, Melitta and Arambis. Departing from thence we came to the great River Lixus[2] which descends from Africa. By it there were certaine men called Lixitae, feeders of Cattell, tending their flockes; with whom wee continued so long that they became verie familiar. Moreover up in the Countrie above them the Negros inhabited, who will not traffique with any, and their Countrie is verie barbarous and full of wilde Beasts, and environed with high Mountaines from which, as they say, issues the River Lixus, and round about the Mountains inhabit men of divers shapes which have their abiding in Canes; they runne swifter then horses, as the Lixians report; from thence taking some Interpreters we sailed by a desart Countrie towards the South two daies. And then wee vered one day towards the East, where in the bottome of a Gulfe we found a like Iland,[3] that was five furlongs in compasse, which we inhabited, naming it Cerne, and by the way that we had sailed we judged that that Iland was opposite to Carthage, for the Navigation from Carthage to the Pillars, and from thence to Cerne seemed equall. Parting from thence, and sailing by a great River called Crete, we arrived at a Lake which had in it three Ilands greater then Cerne. From whence sailing the space of a day, we came to the further part of the Lake; there we saw very high Mountaines which overlooked all the Lake where were savage people cloathed in beasts skins, who chased us away with stones, not suffering us to land; sailing from thence we came to another great and large streame[4] full of Croco-diles and River-horses. From thence turning backe againe, wee returned to Cerne. Sailing then twelve daies Southerly, not going farre from the coast, which was peopled with Negros, who upon

[1] These could mean caves.  
[2] The Wadi Dra.  
[3] Hern island, Rio Ouro.  
[4] Probably the Senegal river.

sight of us fled away, and spake so, as the Lixitae that were with us understood them not. The last day we arrived at a Mountaine full of great trees, the wood whereof was odoriferous and of various colours.[1] Having now coasted two daies by this Mountaine, wee found a deepe and troublesome race of Sea; on the side whereof towards the land was a plaine, where by night we saw fires kindled on every side, distant one from the other some more some lesse. Having watered here, we sailed by the land five daies so that we arrived in a great Bay, which our Interpreters said was called Hesperus his horne. In this there was a great Iland and in the Iland a Lake which seemed a Sea, and in this there was another Iland;[2] where having landed, by day we saw nothing but woods, but in the night many fires were kindled, and we heard Phifes (fifes) and the noise and sound of Cimbals and Drummes, and besides infinite shouts; so that wee were exceedingly afraid, and our Diviners commanded us to abandon the Iland; then swiftly sailing from thence, we passed a Countrie smelling of Spices from which some fierie Rivers fall into the Sea, and the land is so hot that men are not able to goe in it; therefore being somewhat affrighted we suddenly hoised out our sailes, and running along in the maine the space of foure daies, we saw by night the Country full of flames, and in the middest an exceeding high fire, greater then all the rest, which seemed to reach unto the Starres; but wee saw this after in the day time, which was a very loftie Mountaine, called $\theta\epsilon\hat{\omega}\nu$ $o\chi\eta\mu\alpha$ that is, the Chariot of the Gods.[3] But having sailed three daies by fierie Rivers, we arrived in a Gulfe called Notuceras, that is, the South horne; in the inner part thereof there was a little Iland like unto the first which had a Lake in it, and in that there was another Iland full of Savage men, but the women were more; they had their bodies all over hairie, and of our Interpreters they were called Gorgones; we pursued the men but could take none, for they fled into precipices and defended themselves with stones; but we tooke three of the women, which did nothing but bite and scratch those that led them, and would not follow them. Therefore they killed them and fled

[1] Cape Verde.
[2] The Bissagos Islands.
[3] Perhaps Mt. Kakoulima, but see introductory note.

them, and brought their skins to Carthage; and because victuals failed us, we sailed no further.

'The Navigation of Hanno, a Carthaginian Captaine on the coasts of Africa . . . ' From *Purchas His Pilgrimes*, 1903–5. Maclehose, ed., vol I.

# Alvaro Fernandes
## fl. 1446

THE first stage in the opening up of the sea route to India was the long and toilsome exploration of the coasts of Western Africa by Portuguese navigators. The principal inspirer of these voyages was Prince Henry, known as 'The Navigator', grandson of John of Gaunt.

It was a squire of his court, Gil Eannes, who opened this period by rounding Cape Bojador in 1434. Others followed in his wake, somewhat intermittently as political and other considerations dictated, and with varying success. Alvaro Fernandes, nephew of João Gonzalves Zarco, Captain of Madeira, in 1445 sailed beyond Cape Verde and, as described in this extract, undertook a second voyage in 1446, when he reached a more southerly point than earlier voyagers on this coast. Alvaro had been instructed by his uncle not to indulge in slave-raiding, but to press on southwards. Though he did not avoid some strife with the natives, it was this advice which was no doubt responsible for his success in passing beyond the estuary of the Gambia.

*     *     *

One of the signs by which a noble heart is recognized is that it hath no contentment in small matters, but ever seeketh some betterment, that its honour may be increased among the deeds of the noble both in its own land and outside it. And this may we justly say of João Gonzalvez (Zarco), captain of the island (of Madeira), for he, not satisfied by the other voyage that his ship had made in the previous year to the land of the Negroes, made ready once more to dispatch there that same Alvaro Fernandez with his caravel well armed, and charged him to make his way still further onward to the utmost of his power, and to toil for some booty which by its novelty and greatness might give testimony of the good will he had to serve that lord who had brought him up. Now Alvaro Fernandez undertook this matter as an honourable burden, like one who had no less desire to carry through the mandate which his uncle had laid upon him.

And when the ship had been provisioned, they made their voyage straight to Cape Verde, whereat in the past year they had captured the two Guineas of whom we have spoken in another place, and thence they passed on to the Cape of Masts,[1] and made a stay there to put some men on shore. And for the sole purpose of seeing the land, seven of them joined together, and these, when they had been landed upon the beach, discovered the footprints of men leading along a certain path. And they followed them up and reached a well where they found goats which it seemeth the Guineas had left there, and this would be, I think, because they perceived that they were being followed. The Christians went so far and no further, for they dared not pursue their course, and returning to their caravel, they voyaged on, and putting out their boat, found on land some elephant's dung of the bigness of a man, according to the judgement of those that saw it; and because it seemed not a place wherein to make booty they returned again to their caravel.

And so journeying along the sea coast, in a few days they went on shore again, and came upon a village, and its inhabitants issued forth like men who showed they had a will to defend their houses, and among them came one armed with a good buckler and an assegai in his hand. And Alvaro Fernandez seeing him, and judging him to be the leader of the band, went stoutly at him, and gave him such a great wound with his lance that he fell dead, and then he took from him his shield and assegai; and these he brought home to the Infant along with some other things, as will be related further on. Now the Guineas, perceiving that man to be dead, paused from their fighting, and it appeared to our men to be neither the time nor the place to withdraw them from that fear.

But rather they returned to their ship and on the next day landed a little way distant from there, where they espied some of the wives of those Guineas walking. And it seemeth that they were going nigh to a creek collecting shell-fish, and they captured one of them who would be as much as thirty years of age with a son of hers who would be of about two, and also a young girl of fourteen years who had well-formed limbs and also a favourable presence for a Guinea; but the strength of the woman was much to be marvelled at, for not one of
[1] Red Cape, just beyond Cape Verde.

the three men who came upon her but would have had a great labour in attempting to get her to the boat. And so one of our men, seeing the delay they were making, during which it might be that some of the dwellers of the land would come upon them, conceived it well to take her son from her and to carry him to the boat; and love of the child compelled the mother to follow after it, without great pressure on the part of the two who were bringing her.

From this place they went on further for a certain distance until they lighted upon a river[1] into the which they entered with the boat, and in some houses that they found they captured a woman and after they had brought her to the caravel, they returned once more to the river, intending to journey higher up in order to try and make some good booty.

And as they were pursuing their voyage thus, there came upon them four or five boats of Guineas prepared like men who would defend their land, and our men in the boat were not desirous to try a combat with them, seeing the great advantage their enemies had, and especially because they feared the great peril that lay in the poison with which they shot. And so they began to retreat to their ship as well as they could, but seeing how one of those boats was much in front of the others, they turned round upon it, but it returned towards its companions, and as our men were trying to reach it before it escaped (for it seemeth that it was already distant a good way from the company) their boat came so near that one of those Guineas made a shot at it and happened to hit Alvaro Fernandez with an arrow in the leg. But since he had already been warned of its poison, he drew out that arrow very quickly and had the wound washed with urine and olive oil, and then annointed it very well with theriack, and it pleased God that it availed him, although his health was in very troublous case, for during certain days he was in the very act of passing away from life.

The others on the caravel, although they saw their captain thus wounded, desisted not from voyaging forward along that coast until they arrived at a narrow strip of sand stretching in front of a great bay and here they put out their boat and went inside to see what kind of land they would find; and when they were in sight of

[1] Probably the Gambia.

83

the beach they saw coming towards them full a hundred and twenty Guineas, some with shields and assegais, others with bows. And as soon as they came near the water these began to play and dance like men far removed from any sorrow; but our men in the boat, wishful to escape from the invitation to that festival, returned to their ship. And this took place a hundred and ten leagues beyond Cape Verde, and all that coast trendeth commonly to the south.[1]

And this caravel went further this year than all the others, wherefore with right good will a guerdon of two hundred doubloons was granted unto it, that is to say a hundred which the Infant Don Pedro, who was then Regent, ordered to be given, and another one hundred which it obtained from the Infant Don Henry. And had it not been for the illness of Alvaro Fernandez, by which he was much disabled, the caravel would have gone further still, but it was obliged to return from that last place I have mentioned.

It came straight to the Isle of Arguim and thence to the Cape of the Ransom where they found that Ahude Meymam of whom we have already spoken at times in this history. And although they did not carry an interpreter, yet by making signs they obtained a negress whom the Moors gave them in exchange for some cloths they brought with them, and had they not brought so little they could have obtained much more, judging by the desire that the Moors showed. And thence they made their voyage towards the Kingdom, where they received the doubloons as I have already said, together with many other guerdons from the Infant their lord who was very joyful at their coming on account of the advance they had made in their expedition.

[1] 110 leagues south of Cape Verde would place them in the neighbourhood of Conakry.

Azurara, Gomes Eannes de: *The Chronicle of the discovery and Conquest of Guinea.* Trsl. ed. by C. R. Beazley and E. Prestage. *Hakluyt Soc.*, ser. I, v. 100. Of how Alvaro Fernandez returned again to the land of the Negroes, and of the things he accomplished there.

# James Bruce
## 1730–1794

Bruce came of an old Scottish family, the Bruces of Kinnaird in Stirlingshire, married a Miss Allan in 1754, and joined her brother in the wine trade. He acquired a taste for travel and an interest in Arabic while in Spain and Portugal on business, and in 1763 was appointed British Consul in Algiers with a commission to study the ancient ruins of the region. In 1768 he set forth to seek the source of the Nile, and arrived at Gondar, then the capital of Abyssinia, early in 1770.

He spent three years at the court of the young king, making himself useful as a doctor and popular as a sportsman, but hampered, by the civil war then raging, from pursuing his quest. He managed to reach the source of the Blue Nile at Geesh, south of Lake Tana (previously visited by Portuguese Fathers in the sixteenth century), on 14th November, 1770. He returned to Cairo by way of Sennar, Nubia and the White Nile early in 1773; the extract below is from his account of this part of his journey. His *Travels*, published in 1790, was received with some incredulity, despite the fact that it was a sober and carefully observed account of all he had seen. He died in retirement at Kinnaird in 1794.

★    ★    ★

On the 14th [November, 1772], at seven in the morning we left Assa Nagga,[1] our course being due north. At one o'clock we alighted among some acacia-trees at Waadi el Halboub, having gone twenty-one miles. We were here at once surprised and terrified by a sight surely one of the most magnificent in the world. In that vast expanse of desert, from W. and to N.W. of us, we saw a number of prodigious pillars of sand at different distances, at times moving with great celerity, at others stalking on with a majestic slowness; at intervals we thought they were coming in a very few minutes to overwhelm us and small quantities of sand did actually more than

[1] The places named by Bruce are halts on the caravan route across the great bend of the Nile from Abou Hamed to Wadi Halfa.

once reach us. Again they would retreat so as to be almost out of sight, their tops reaching to the very clouds. There the tops often separated from the bodies, and these, once disjoined, dispersed in the air and did not appear more. Sometimes they were broken near the middle as if struck with a large cannon shot. About noon they began to advance with considerable swiftness upon us, the wind being very strong at north. Eleven of them ranged alongside of us about the distance of three miles. The greatest diameter of the largest appeared to me at that distance as if it would measure ten feet. They retired from us with a wind at S.E. leaving an impression upon my mind to which I can give no name, though surely one ingredient in it was fear, with a considerable deal of wonder and astonishment. It was in vain to think of flying; the swiftest horse or fastest sailing ship could be of no use to carry us out of this danger, and the full persuasion of this riveted me as if to the spot where I stood, and let the camels gain on me so much in my state of lameness that it was with some difficulty I could overtake them.

The effect this stupendous sight had upon Idris was to set him to his prayers, indeed rather to his charms, for, besides the name of God and Mahomet, all the rest of the words were mere gibberish and nonsense. This created a violent altercation between him and Ismael the Turk, who abused him for not praying in the words of the Koran, maintaining, with apparent great wisdom at the same time, that nobody had charms to stop these moving sands but the inhabitants of Arabia Deserta.

The Arabs to whom this inhospitable spot belongs are the Adelaia. They too are Jaheleen or Arabs of Benu Koreish. They are said to be a harmless race, and to do no hurt to the caravans they meet; yet I very much doubt, had we fallen in with them they would not have deserved the good name that was given them. We went very slowly today, our feet being sore and greatly swelled. The whole of our company were much disheartened (except Idris), and imagined that they were advancing into whirlwinds of moving sand, from which they should never be able to extricate themselves; but before four o'clock in the afternoon these phantoms of the plain had all of them fallen to the ground and disappeared. In the evening we came to Waadi Dimokea where we passed the night, much disheartened, and our fear more increased when we found, upon wakening in the morning, that one side was perfectly buried in the sand that the wind had blown above us in the night.

From this day, subordination, though not entirely ceased, was fast on the decline; all was discontent, murmuring, and fear. Our water was greatly diminished, and that terrible death by thirst began to stare us in the face, and this was owing in a great measure to our own imprudence. Ismael, who had been left sentinel over the skins of water, had slept so soundly that this had given an opportunity to a Tucorory to open one of the skins that had not been touched, and serve himself out of it at his own discretion. I suppose that, hearing somebody stir, and fearing detection he had withdrawn himself as speedily as possible without taking time to tie the mouth of the girba, which we found in the morning with scarce a quart of water in it.

On the 15th, at a quarter past seven in the morning we left Waadi Dimokea, keeping a little to the westward of north, as far as I could judge, just upon the line of Syene. The same ridge of hills being on our right and left as yesterday, in the centre of these appeared Del Aned. At twenty minutes past two o'clock in the afternoon we came to an opening in the ridge of rocks; the passage is about a mile broad, through which we continued till we alighted at the foot of the mountain Del Aned. The place is called Waadi Del Aned.

The same appearance of moving pillars of sand presented themselves to us this day in form and disposition like those we had seen at Waadi Halboub, only they seemed to be more in number and less in size. They came several times in a direction close upon us; that is, I believe, within less than two miles. They began immediately after sunrise like a thick wood, and almost darkened the sun. His rays shining through them for near an hour gave them an appearance of pillars of fire. Our people now became desperate. The Greeks shrieked out, and said it was the day of judgement. Ismael pronounced it to be hell, and the Tucorories that the world was on fire. I asked Idris if ever he had before seen such a sight? He said he had often seen them as terrible, though never worse; but what he feared most was that extreme redness in the air which was a sure presage of the coming of the simoom. I begged and entreated Idris that he would not say one word of that in the hearing of the people, for they had already felt it at Imphanzara in their way from Ras el Feel to Teawa, and again at the Acaba of Gerri before we came to Chendi, and they were already nearly distracted at the apprehension of finding it here.

At half past four o'clock in the afternoon we left Waadi Del Aned, our course a little more to the westward than the direction of Syene. The sands which had disappeared yesterday scarcely shewed themselves at all this day, and at a great distance from the horizon. This was, however, a comfort but of short duration. I observed Idris took no part in it, but only warned me and the servants that upon the coming of the simoom we should fall upon our faces with our mouths upon the earth, so as not to partake of the outward air as long as we could hold our breath. We alighted at six o'clock at a small rock in the sandy ground without trees or herbage, so that our camels fasted all that night. This place is called Ras el Seah or, by the Bishareen, El Mout, which signifies death, a name of bad omen.

On the 16th, at half past ten in the forenoon we left El Mout, standing in the direction close upon Syene. Our men, if not gay, were however in better spirits than I had seen them since we left Gooz. One of our Barbarins had even attempted a song; but Hagi Ismael very gravely reproved him by telling him that singing in such a situation was a tempting of Providence. There is, indeed, nothing more different than active and passive courage. Hagi Ismael would fight but he had not strength of mind to suffer. At eleven o'clock, while we contemplated with great pleasure the rugged top of Chiggre to which we were fast approaching and where we were to solace ourselves with plenty of good water, Idris cried out with a loud voice, 'Fall upon your faces for here is the simoom.' I saw from the S.E. a haze come, in colour like the purple part of the rainbow, but not so compressed or thick. It did not occupy twenty yards in breadth and was about twelve feet high from the ground. It was a kind of blush upon the air and it moved very rapidly, for I scarce could turn to fall upon the ground with my head to the northward, when I felt the heat of its current plainly upon my face. We all lay flat on the ground as if dead, till Idris told us it was blown over. The meteor or purple haze which I saw was indeed passed, but the light air that still blew was of heat to threaten suffocation. For my part I found distinctly in my breast that I had imbibed a part of it, nor was I free of an asthmatic sensation till I had been some months in Italy at the baths of Poretta near two years afterwards.

*Travels to Discover the Source of the Nile,* 1768–73. By James Bruce. Edinburgh, 1790. Vol. IV.

# David Livingstone
## 1813-1873

THE powers of endurance, the sturdy independence and the high-minded enthusiasm which make Livingstone the greatest of African explorers were learnt young. He was born at Blantyre, one of a pious and devoted family, and at the age of ten went to work in the local cotton mill where he mastered Latin while machine-minding. He worked his way through Glasgow University and, having qualified as a doctor, was sent by the London Missionary Society to Kuruman in Bechuanaland where he worked under the veteran missionary and traveller, Robert Moffatt, whose daughter he married. His journeys into the interior in search of sites for new mission stations took him across the Kalahari and in 1851 he reached the Zambezi. From Linyanti on the Chobe, Livingstone travelled west across the Zambezi–Congo watershed to Loanda in Portuguese West Africa and thence back to the east coast at Quilimane, discovering the Victoria Falls and perfecting in his mind a great design for opening up the interior of Africa to the 'commerce and Christianity' which would defeat the slave trade. This great journey lasted from 1853 to 1856, and in 1858 he was appointed to lead an expedition sponsored by the British Government up the Zambezi to establish centres for trade and for missions. Though results were disappointing at the time, the six years he spent on the Zambezi and in Nyasaland paved the way for later development in Central Africa. From 1866 to 1873 Livingstone travelled alone throughout Central Africa, in failing health and obsessed by a preoccupation with the Nile sources. He died in the swamps of Lake Bangweulu near the head-waters of the Congo, and such was the devotion of the Africans who were with him that they carried his body back to Quilimane whence it was sent home to be buried in Westminster Abbey.

In the following extract he describes an early stage in his trans-continental journey of 1853–6. He was crossing Northern Bechu-analand to the swamps of the Chobe river which falls into the

Zambezi about fifty miles up-stream from the Victoria Falls. The Sanshureh is a southern arm of the Chobe.

*  *  *

I may mention that the valley on its northern side, named Kandehai, is as picturesque a spot as is to be seen in this part of Africa. The open glade, surrounded by forest trees of various hues, had a little stream meandering in the centre. A herd of reddish-coloured antelopes (pallahs) stood on one side near a large baobab, looking at us, and ready to run up the hill; while gnus, tsessebes and zebras gazed in astonishment at the intruders. Some fed carelessly, and others put on the peculiar air of displeasure which these animals sometimes assume before they resolve on flight. A large white rhinoceros came along the bottom of the valley with his slow sauntering gait without noticing us; he looked as if he meant to indulge in a mud bath. Several buffaloes with their dark visages stood under the trees on the side opposite to the pallahs. It being Sunday, all was peace, and from the circumstances in which our party was placed we could not but reflect on that second stage of our existence which we hope will lead us into scenes of perfect beauty. If pardoned in that free way the Bible promises, death will be a glorious thing; but to be consigned to wait for the Judgement-day, with nothing else to ponder on but sins we would rather forget, is a cheerless prospect.

Our Bushmen wished to leave us and, as there was no use in trying to thwart these independent gentlemen, I paid them and allowed them to go. The payment, however, acted as a charm on some strangers who happened to be present, and induced them to volunteer their aid.

The game hereabouts is very tame. Koodoos and giraffes stood gazing at me as a strange apparition when I went out with the Bushmen. On one occasion a lion came at daybreak, and went round and round the oxen. I could only get a glimpse of him occasionally from the waggon-box but, though barely thirty yards off, I could not get a shot. He then began to roar at the top of his voice, but the oxen continuing to stand still, he was so disgusted that he went off, and continued to use his voice for a long time in the distance. I could not see that he had a mane; if he had not, then even the maneless variety can use their tongues. We heard others also roar, and when they found they could not frighten the oxen they became equally angry. This we could observe in their tones.

As we went north the country became very lovely; many new trees appeared, the grass was green, and often higher than the waggons; the vines festooned the trees among which appeared the real banian (*Ficus indica*) with its drop-shoots, and the wild date and palmyra, and several other trees which were new to me; the hollows contained large patches of water. Next came watercourses, now resembling small rivers, twenty yards broad and four feet deep. The further we went the broader and deeper these became; their bottoms contained great numbers of deep holes made by elephants wading in them; in these the oxen floundered desperately, so that our waggon-pole broke compelling us to work up to the breast in water for three hours and a half; yet I suffered no harm.

We at last came to the Sanshureh which presented an impassable barrier, so we drew up under a magnificent baobab-tree (lat. 18° 4′ 27″ S., long. 24° 6′ 20″ E.), and resolved to explore the river for a ford. The great quantity of water we had passed through was part of the annual inundation of the Chobe; and this, which appeared a large deep river, filled in many parts with reeds and having hippopotami in it, is only one of the branches by which it sends its superabundant water to the south-east. From the hill N'gwa a ridge of higher land runs to the north-east, and bounds its course in that direction. We, being ignorant of this, were in the valley, and the only gap in the whole country destitute of tsetse. In company with the Bushmen I explored all the banks of the Sanshureh to the west till we came into tsetse on that side. We waded a long way among the reeds in water breast deep, but always found a broad deep space free from vegetation, and unfordable. A peculiar kind of lichen which grows on the surface of the soil becomes detached and floats on the water, giving out a very disagreeable odour, like sulphuretted hydrogen, in some of these stagnant waters.

We made so many attempts to get over the Sanshureh, both to the west and east of the waggon, in the hope of reaching some of the Makololo on the Chobe, that my Bushmen friends became quite tired of the work. By means of presents I got them to remain some days, but at last they slipped away by night, and I was fain to take one of the strongest of my still weak companions and cross the river in a pontoon, the gift of Captains Codrington and Webb. We each carried some provisions and a blanket, and penetrated about twenty miles to the westward in the hope of striking the Chobe. It was much nearer to us in a northerly direction, but this we did not then know. The plain over which we splashed the whole of the first day was covered with water ankle deep and thick grass which reached above the knees. In the evening we came to an immense wall of reeds, six or eight feet high, without any opening admitting of a passage. When we tried to enter, the water always became so deep that we were fain to desist. We concluded that we had come to the banks of the river we were in search of, so we directed our course to some trees which appeared in the south in order to get a bed and a view of the adjacent locality. Having shot a leche and made a glorious fire, we got a good cup of tea and had a comfortable night. While collecting wood that evening, I found a bird's nest consisting of live leaves sewn together with threads of the spider's web. Nothing could exceed the airiness of this pretty contrivance; the threads had been pushed through small punctures and thickened to resemble a knot. I unfortunately lost it. This was the second nest I have seen resembling that of the tailor-bird of India.

Next morning, by climbing the highest trees, we could see a fine large sheet of water, but surrounded on all sides by the same impenetrable belt of reeds. This is the broad part of the river Chobe, and is called Zabesa. Two tree-covered islands seemed to be much nearer to the water than the shore on which we were, so we made an attempt to get to them first. It was not the reeds alone we had to pass through; a peculiar serrated grass which at certain angles cut the hands like a razor was mingled with the reed, and the climbing convolvulus with stalks which felt as strong as whipcord bound the mass together. We felt like pigmies in it, and often the only way we could get on was by both of us leaning against a part and bending it down till we could stand upon it. The perspiration streamed off our bodies, and as the sun rose high, there being no ventilation among the reeds, the heat was stifling, and the water, which was up to the knees, felt agreeably refreshing. After some hours' toil we reached one of the islands. Here we met an old friend, the bramble-bush. My strong moleskins were quite worn through at the knees, and the leather trousers of my companion were torn and his legs bleeding. Tearing my handkerchief in two, I tied the pieces round my knees, and then encountered another difficulty. We were still forty or fifty yards from the clear water, but now we were opposed by great masses of papyrus which are like palms in miniature, eight or ten feet high and an inch and a half in diameter. These were laced together by twining convolvulus so strongly that the weight of both of us could not make way into the clear water. At last we fortunately found a passage prepared by a hippopotamus. Eager as soon as we reached the island to look along the vista to clear water, I stepped in and found it took me at once up to my neck.

Returning nearly worn out, we proceeded up the bank of the Chobe till we came to the point of departure of the branch Sans-hureh; we then went in the opposite direction, or down the Chobe, though from the highest trees we could see nothing but one vast expanse of reed, with here and there a tree on the islands. This was a hard day's work, and when we came to a deserted Bayeiye hut on an anthill, not a bit of wood or anything else could be got for a fire, except the grass and sticks of the dwelling itself. I dreaded the 'tampans', so common in all old huts, but outside of it we had thousands of mosquitoes, and cold dew began to be deposited, so we were fain to crawl beneath its shelter.

We were close to the reeds and could listen to the strange sounds which are often heard there. By day I had seen water-snakes putting up their heads and swimming about. There were great numbers of otters (*Lutra inunguis*, F. *Cuvier*), which have made little spoors all over the plains in search of the fishes, among the tall grass of these flooded prairies; curious birds, too, jerked and wriggled among these reedy masses, and we heard human-like voices and unearthly sounds, with splash, guggle, jupp, as if rare fun were going on in their uncouth haunts. At one time something came near us, making a splashing like that of a canoe or hippopotamus; thinking it to be the Makololo, we got up, listened, and shouted; then discharged a gun several times, but the noise continued without intermission for an hour. After a damp cold night we set to, early in the morning, at our work of exploring again, but left the pontoon in order to lighten our labour. The ant-hills are here very high, some thirty feet, and of a base so broad that trees grow on them, while the lands, annually flooded, bear nothing but grass. From one of these ant-hills we discovered an inlet to the Chobe and, having gone back for the pontoon, we launched ourselves on a deep river, here from eighty to one hundred yards wide. I gave my companion strict injunctions to stick by the pontoon in case a hippopotamus should look at us; nor was this caution unnecessary, for one came up at our side and made a desperate plunge off. We had passed over him. The wave he made caused the pontoon to glide quickly away from him.

We paddled on from midday till sunset. There was nothing but a wall of reed on each bank and we saw every prospect of spending a supperless night in our float, but just as the short twilight of these parts was commencing, we perceived on the north bank the village of Moremi, one of the Makololo, whose acquaintance I had made in our former visit and who was not located on the island Mahonta (lat. 17° 58′ S., long. 24° 6′ E.). The villagers looked as we may suppose people do who see a ghost, and in their figurative way of speaking said, 'He has dropped among us from the clouds, yet came riding on the back of a hippopotamus! We Makololo thought no one could cross the Chobe without our knowledge, but here he drops among us like a bird.'

Next day we returned in canoes across the flooded lands and found that in our absence the men had allowed the cattle to wander into a very small patch of wood to the west containing the tsetse; this carelessness cost me ten fine large oxen. After remaining a few days, some of the head men of the Makololo came down from Linyanti with a large party of Barotse, to take us across the river. This they did in fine style, swimming and diving among the oxen more like alligators than men, and taking the waggons to pieces and carrying them across on a number of canoes lashed together. We were now among friends; so going about thirty miles to the north, in order to avoid the still flooded lands on the north of the Chobe, we turned westwards towards Linyanti (lat. 18°/17′ 20″ S., long. 23° 50′ 9″ E.), where we arrived on the 23rd of May, 1853.

This is the capital town of the Makololo, and only a short distance from our waggon-stand of 1851 (lat. 18° 20′ S., long. 23° 50′ E.).

*Missionary Travels and Researches in South Africa.* By David Livingstone. 1857.

# Heinrich Barth
## 1821-1865

HEINRICH BARTH, a native of Hamburg, probably did more than anyone, by persevering travel and painstaking observation, to discover to the world that part of Africa north of the Niger-Benue confluence which today largely constitutes Northern Nigeria. His reputation rests on the six years (from 1849 to 1855) which he spent, on an expedition backed by the British Foreign Office, travelling between Lake Chad on the east and Timbuktu on the west, the story of which is contained in his five volume *Travels*. His most important achievement was to locate the upper reaches of the Benue river, in a sally south from Lake Chad in 1851; this discovery is described in the extract below. His later journeys between Sokoto and Timbuktu were also noteworthy. Barth's minute and pertinent account of the Kingdom of Bornu and the Fulani Empire as he knew them merited the award of the Royal Geographical Society's Patron's Medal in 1865. He was made Professor of Geography at Berlin University in 1863, and continued to travel in the Middle East until his death at the early age of forty-four.

★     ★     ★

Wednesday, June 18th [1851]. At an early hour we left the inhospitable place of Sulléri. It was a beautiful fresh morning, all nature being revived and enlivened by the last night's storm. My companions, sullen and irritated, quarrelled among themselves on account of the selfish behaviour of Ibrahima. As for me, I was cheerful in the extreme and borne away by an enthusiastic and triumphant feeling, for today I was to see the river [the Benue].

The neighbourhood of the water was first indicated by numbers of high ant-hills which, as I shall have occasion to observe more fully in the course of my narrative, abound chiefly in the neighbourhood of rivers; they were here ranged in almost parallel lines and afforded a very curious spectacle. We had just passed a small village or rúmde, where not a living soul was to be seen, the people having all gone forth to the labours of the field, when the lively Mohammedu came

97

running up to me and exclaimed, 'Gashí, gashí, dútsi-n-Alantíka ké nan' ('Look! look! that is Mount Alantíka').[1] I strained my eyes and saw at a great distance to the S.W. a large but insulated mountain mass rising abruptly on the east side and forming a more gradual slope towards the west, while it exhibited a rather smooth and broad top, which certainly must be spacious as it contains the estates of seven independent pagan chiefs. Judging from the distance, which was pretty well known to me, I estimated the height of the mountain at about eight thousand feet above the plain or about nine thousand feet of absolute elevation; but it may be somewhat less.

Here there was still cultivated ground, exhibiting at present the finest crop of masr, called, 'bútalí' by the Fúlbe of A'damáwa; but a little further on we entered upon a swampy plain (the savannas of A'damáwa), overgrown with tall rank grass, and broken by many large hollows full of water, so that we were obliged to proceed with great caution. This whole plain is annually (two months later) entirely under water. However, in the middle of it, on a little rising ground which looks as if it were an artificial mound, lies a small village, the abode of the ferrymen of the Bénuwé, from whence the boys came running after us—slender well-built lads, accustomed to fatigue and strengthened by daily bathing; the younger ones quite naked, the elder having a leathern apron girt round their loins. A quarter of an hour afterwards we stood on the bank of the Bénuwé.

It happens but rarely that a traveller does not feel disappointed when he first actually beholds the principal features of a new country, of which his imagination has composed a picture from the description of the natives; but although I must admit that the shape and size of the Alantíka as it rose in rounded lines from the flat level did not exactly correspond with the idea which I had formed of it, the appearance of the river far exceeded my most lively expectations. None of my informants had promised me that I should just come upon it at that most interesting locality—the Tépe—where the mightier river is joined by another of very considerable size, and that in this place I was to cross it. My arrival at this point, as I have stated

[1] The Alantika Mountains lie south of Yola, along the west bank of the R. Faro.

before, was a most fortunate circumstance. As I looked from the bank over the scene before me I was quite enchanted, although the whole country bore the character of a desolate wilderness; but there could scarcely be any great traces of human industry near the river as, during its floods, it inundates the whole country on both sides. This is the general character of all the great rivers in these regions, except they are encompassed by very steep banks.

The principal river, the Bénuwé, flowed here from east to west in a broad and majestic course, through an entirely open country, from which only here and there detached mountains started forth. The banks on our side rose to twenty-five, and in some places to thirty feet, while just opposite to my station behind a pointed headland of sand, the Fáro[1] rushed forth, appearing from this point not much inferior to the principal river, and coming in a fine sweep from the south-east where it disappeared in the plain but was traced by me, in thought, upwards to the steep eastern foot of the Alantíka. The river, below the junction, keeping the direction of the principal branch but making a slight bend to the north, ran along the northern foot of Mount Bágelé, and was there lost to the eye, but was followed in thought through the mountainous region of the Báchama and Zína to Hamárruwa, and thence along the industrious country of Korórofa, till it joined the great western river the Kwára or Niger and, conjointly with it, ran towards the great ocean.

On the northern side of the river another detached mountain, Mount Taife, rose, and behind it the Bengo, with which Mount Fúro seemed connected, stretching out in a long line towards the north-west. The bank upon which we stood was entirely bare of trees with the exception of a solitary and poor acacia, about one hundred paces further up the river, while on the opposite shore, along the Fáro and below the junction, some fine clusters of trees were faintly seen.

I looked long and silently upon the stream; it was one of the happiest moments in my life. Born on the bank of a large navigable river, I had from my childhood a great predilection for river-scenery; and although plunged for many years in the too exclusive study of antiquity, I never lost this native instinct. As soon as I left

[1] The Faro river, a south bank tributary of the Benue, west of Yola.

home and became the independent master of my actions, I began to combine travel with study, and to study while travelling, it being my greatest delight to trace running waters from their sources, and to see them grow into brooks, to follow the brooks, and see them become rivers, till they at last disappeared in the all-devouring ocean. I had wandered all around the Mediterranean with its many gulfs, its beautiful peninsulas, its fertile islands—not hurried along by steam, but slowly wandering from place to place, following the traces of the settlements of the Greeks and Romans around this beautiful basin once their terra incognita. And thus, when entering upon the adventurous career in which I subsequently engaged, it had been the object of my most lively desire to throw light upon the natural arteries and hydrographical network of the unknown regions of Central Africa. The great eastern branch of the Niger was the foremost to occupy my attention, and, although for some time uncertain as to the identity of the river of A'damáwa with that laid down in its lower course by Messrs. W. Allen, Laird and Oldfield, I had long made up my mind on this point, thanks to the clear information received from my friend Ahmed bel Mejúb. I had now with my own eyes clearly established the direction and nature of this mighty river; and to an unprejudiced mind there could no longer be any doubt that this river joins the majestic watercourse explored by the gentlemen just mentioned. Hence I cherish the well-founded conviction that along this natural highroad European influence and commerce will penetrate into the very heart of the continent, and abolish slavery, or rather those infamous slave-hunts and religious wars, destroying the natural germs of human happiness which are spontaneously developed in the simple life of the pagans, and spreading devastation and desolation all around. . . .

At length a canoe arrived, the largest of the two that were actually employed, and a long bargaining commenced with the eldest of the canoemen, a rather short and well-set lad. Of course as the chief of the caravan I had to pay for all, and there being three camels and five horses to be carried over, it was certainly a difficult business. It cannot, therefore, be regarded as a proof of exorbitant demands that I had to pay five 'dóras', a sum which in Kúkawa would buy two oxen loads of Indian corn. I allowed all the people to go before me, in order to prevent the canoemen from exacting something more from them.

There was considerable difficulty with my large camel-bags which were far too large for the canoes, and which several times were in danger of being upset; for they were so unsteady that the people were obliged to kneel down on the bottom, and keep their equilibrium by holding with both hands on the sides of the boat. Fortunately I had laid my tent-poles at the bottom of the canoe, so that the water did not reach the luggage; but owing to the carelessness of the Hajji's companions all his books were wetted, to his utmost distress; but I saw him afterwards shedding tears, while he was drying his deteriorated treasures on the sandy beach of the headland. The horses as they crossed, swimming by the sides of the canoe, had to undergo great fatigue, but desperate was the struggle of the camels, which were too obstinate to be guided by the frail vessels and had to be pushed through alone, and could only be moved by the most severe beating; the camel of the Hajji was for a while given up in despair by the whole party. At length they were induced to cross the channel, the current carrying them down to a great distance, and our whole party arrived safe on the sandy beach of the headland, where there was not a bit of shade. This whole headland for two or three months every year is covered with water, although its chief part which was overgrown with tall reed-grass was at present about fifteen feet above the surface.

*Travels and Discoveries in North and Central Africa, 1849–55.* By Heinrich Barth. 1857. Vol 2.

# Richard Francis Burton
## 1821-1900

FAMOUS as an Arabic scholar, as an anthropologist and as a traveller in both Asia and Africa, Burton's name is particularly linked with the search for the Nile sources. In 1854, while still an officer in the Indian Army, he visited the forbidden city of Harar in Abyssinia, and in 1858 he and John Hanning Speke penetrated the interior of Africa, starting from Zanzibar and reaching the eastern shore of Lake Tanganyika; their arrival there is described below. Burton maintained that the Victoria N'yanza, which Speke visited alone on the way back, was not the true source of the Nile (as Speke rightly insisted), and the controversy lasted for many years. Speke, who died in a shooting accident in 1864 at the height of his quarrel with Burton, was finally justified by the discoveries of Stanley in 1874-77 and in 1887-90. Burton was a man of great ability but his quarrelsome temperament and unconventional attitudes prevented his ever achieving the public recognition he felt was his due. He held consular appointments in West Africa, in South America, the Middle East, and in Trieste and was knighted in 1887. His devoted wife, Isabella Arundell, destroyed his papers on his death, making it even more difficult for posterity to assess this brilliant but cross-grained man.

★    ★    ★

The 7th of February [1858] led us over broken ground, encumbered by forest and cut by swamps, with higher levels on the right hand, till we again fell into the marshes and fields of the river valley. The district on the other side of the river,[1] called Jambeho, is one of the most flourishing in Uvinza; its villages of small bird-nest huts, and its carefully hoed fields of grain and sweet potato affected the eye, after the dreary monotony of a jungle-march, like the glimmer of a light at the end of a night-march, or the discovery of land at the conclusion of a long sea voyage. The village ferry was instantly put

[1] This is the Malagarazi which falls into Lake Tanganyika south of Ujiji.

into requisition and the chief, Ruwere, after receiving as his 'dash'
eight cloths, allowed us to purchase provisions. At that season,
however, the harvest of grain and sweet potatoes had not been
got in, and for their single old hen the people demanded an exorbitant price. We hastened, despite all difficulties, to escape from the
place of pestilence, which clouds of mosquitoes rendered as uncomfortable as it was dangerous.

The next day ushered in our departure with drizzling rain which
drenched the slippery paths of red clay; the asses, wild with wind
and weather, exposed us to accident in a country of deep ravines
and rugged boulders. Presently diverging from the Malagarazi, we
passed over the brow of a low tree-clad hill above the junction of
the Rusugi River, and followed the left bank of this tributary as far
as its nearer ford. The Rusugi, which drains the northern highlands
into the Malagarazi, was then about a hundred yards in width·
the bottom is a red ocherish soil, the strong stream, divided in the
centre by a long low strip of sand and gravel, flowed at that time
breast-deep, and its banks—as usual with rivers in these lands—
deeply cut by narrow watercourses, rendered travelling unusually
toilsome. At the Rusugi Ford the road separates into a northern and
a southern branch, a hill-spur forming the line of demarcation.
The northern strikes off to the district of Parugerero on the left
bank, where a shallower ford is found; the place in question is a
settlement of Wavinza containing from forty to fifty bee-hive huts
tenanted by salt diggers. . . .

We followed the southern line which crosses the Rusugi River at
the branch islet. Fords are always picturesque. The men seemed to
enjoy the washing; their numbers protected them from the croco-
diles which fled from their shouting and splashing; and they even
ventured into deep water where swimming was necessary. We
crossed as usual on a 'unicorn' of negroids, the upper part of the
body supported by two men, and the feet resting upon the shoulders
of a third—a posture somewhat similar to that affected by gentlemen
who find themselves unable to pull off their own boots. Then,
remounting, we ascended the grassy rise on the right of the stream,
struggled, slipped, and slided over a muddy swamp, climbed up a
rocky and bushy ridge, and found ourselves ensconced in a ragged

and comfortless kraal upon the western slopes within sight of some deserted salt-pans below.

On the 9th February, we descended from the ridge upon which the kraal was placed, and traversed a deep swamp of black mud, dotted in the more elevated parts with old salt-pans and pits, where broken pottery and blackened lumps of clay still showed traces of human handiwork. Beyond this lowland, the track, striking off from the river-valley and turning to the right, entered toilsome ground. We crossed deep and rocky ravines with luxuriant vegetation above, and with rivulets at the bottom trickling towards the Malagarazi, by scrambling down and swarming up the roughest steps of rock, boulder, and knotted tree-root. Beyond these difficulties lay woody and stony hills, whose steep and slippery inclines were divided by half a dozen waters, all more or less troublesome to cross. The porters, who were in a place of famine, insisted upon pushing on to the utmost of their strength; after six hours' march, I persuaded them to halt in the bush upon a rocky hill where the neighbouring descent supplied water. The Fundi visited the valley of the Rusugi River and, finding a herd of the Mbogo or Bos Caffer, brought home a welcome addition to our well-nigh exhausted rations.

The 10th February saw us crossing the normal sequence of jungly and stony 'neat's-tongues', divided by deep and grassy swamps which, stagnant in the dry weather, drain after rains the northern country to the Malagarazi River. We passed over by a felled tree trunk an unfordable rivulet, hemmed in by a dense and fetid thicket; and the asses summarily pitched down the muddy bank into the water, swam across and wriggled up the slimy off-side like cats. Thence a foul swamp of black mire led to the Ruguvu or Luguvu River, the western boundary of Uvinza and the eastern frontier of Ukaranga. This stream, which can be forded during the dry season, had spread out after the rains over its borders of grassy plain; we were delayed till the next morning in a miserable camping ground, a mud-bank thinly veiled with vegetation, in order to bridge it with branching trees. An unusual downfall during the night might have caused serious consequences; provisions had now disappeared, moreover the porters considered the place dangerous.

The 10th February began with the passage of the Ruguvu River where again our goods and chattels were fated to be thoroughly sopped. I obtained a few corn-cobs from a passing caravan of Wanyamwezi and charged them with meat and messages for the party left behind. A desert march similar to the stage last travelled led us to the Unguwwe or Uvungwe River, a shallow, muddy stream, girt in as usual by dense vegetation; and we found a fine large kraal on its left bank. After a cold and rainy night we resumed our march by fording the Unguwwe. Then came the weary toil of fighting through tiger and spear-grass with reeds, rushes, a variety of ferns, before unseen, and other lush and lusty growths clothing a succession of rolling hills, monotonous swellings, where the descent was ever a reflection of the ascent. The paths were broken, slippery, and pitted with deep holes; along their sides where the ground lay exposed to view a conglomerate of ferruginous red clay—suggesting a resemblance to the superficies of Londa, as described by Dr. Livingstone—took the place of the granites and sandstones of the eastern countries, and the sinking of the land towards the Lake became palpable. In the jungle were extensive clumps of bamboo and rattan, the former small, the latter of poor quality; the bauhinia or black-wood, and the salsaparilla vine abounded; wild grapes of diminutive size and of the austerest flavour appeared for the first time upon the sunny hill-sides which Bacchus ever loves, and in the lower swamps plantains grew almost wild. In parts the surface was broken into small deep hollows from which sprang pyramidal masses of the hugest trees. Though no sign of man here met the eye, scattered fields and plantations showed that villages must be somewhere near. Sweet water was found in narrow courses of black mud which sorely tried the sinews of laden man and beast. Long after noon we saw the caravan halted by fatigue upon a slope beyond a weary swamp; a violent storm was brewing and whilst half the sky was purple black with nimbus, the sun shone stingingly through the clear portion of the empyrean. But these small troubles were lightly borne; already in the far distance appeared walls of sky-blue cliff with gilded summits, which were as a beacon to the distressed mariner.

On the 13th February we resumed our travel through screens of lofty grass which thinned out into a straggling forest. After about an hour's march, as we entered a small savannah, I saw the Fundi alluded to running forward and changing the direction of the caravan. Without supposing that he had taken upon himself this responsibility, I followed him. Presently he breasted a steep and stony hill, sparsely clad with thorny trees; it was the death of my companion's riding-ass. Arrived with toil—for our fagged beasts now refused to proceed—we halted for a few minutes upon the summit. 'What is that streak of light which lies below?' I inquired of Seedy Bombay. 'I am of the opinion,' quoth Bombay, 'that that is the water.' I gazed in dismay; the remains of my blindness, the veil of trees, and a broad ray of sunshine illuminating but one reach of the Lake had shrunk its fair proportions. Somewhat prematurely I began to lament my folly in having risked life and lost health for so poor a prize, to curse Arab exaggeration, and to propose an immediate return, with the view of exploring the Nyanza or Northern Lake. Advancing, however, a few yards, the whole scene suddenly burst upon my view, filling me with admiration, wonder and delight. It gave local habitation to the poet's fancy. . . .

Nothing, in sooth, could be more picturesque than this first view of the Tanganyika Lake, as it lay in the lap of the mountains, basking in the gorgeous tropical sunshine. Below and beyond a short foreground of rugged and precipitous hill-fold, down which the footpath zigzags painfully, a narrow strip of emerald green, never sere and marvellously fertile, shelves towards a ribbon of glistening yellow sand, here bordered by sedgy rushes, there cleanly and clearly cut by the breaking wavelets. Further in front stretch the waters, an expanse of the lightest and softest blue, in breadth varying from thirty to thirty-five miles and sprinkled by the crisp east wind with tiny crescents of snowy foam. The background in front is a high and broken wall of steel-coloured mountain, here flecked and capped with pearly mist, there standing sharply pencilled against the azure air; its yawning chasms, marked by a deeper plum colour, fall towards dwarf hills of mound-like proportions which apparently dip their feet in the wave. To the south, and opposite the long low point behind which the Malagarazi River discharges the red loam suspended in its violent stream, lie the bluff headlands and capes of Uguhha and, as the eye dilates, it falls upon a cluster of outlying islets, speckling a sea-horizon. Villages, cultivated lands, the frequent canoes of the fishermen on the waters, and on a nearer approach the murmurs of the waves breaking upon the shore give a something of variety, of movement, of life to the landscape which, like all the fairest prospects in these regions, wants but a little of the neatness and finish of Art—mosques and kiosks, palaces and villas, gardens and orchards—contrasting with the profuse lavishness and magnificence of nature, and diversifying the unbroken *coup d'œil* of excessive vegetation, to rival, if not to excel, the most admired scenery of the classic regions. The riant shores of this vast crevasse appeared doubly beautiful to me after the silent and spectral mangrove-creeks on the East-African seaboard, and the melancholy, monotonous experience of desert and jungle scenery, tawny rock and sun-parched plain or rank herbage and flats of black mire. Truly it was a revel for soul and sight! Forgetting toils, dangers, and the doubtfulness of return, I felt willing to endure double what I had endured; and all the party seemed to join me in joy. My purblind companion[1] found nothing to grumble at except the 'mist and glare before his eyes.' Said bin Salim looked exulting—he had procured for me this pleasure—the monoculous Kemadar grinned his congratulations and even the surly Baloch made civil salaams.

[1] Captain John Hanning Speke.

*The Lake Regions of Central Africa.* By Richard F. Burton. 1860. Vol. 2.

# Samuel White Baker
## 1821-1893

BAKER came of a well-to-do family, originally of Bristol, with interests in West Indian sugar. He early decided on the life of a pioneer and traveller, founded an agricultural settlement in Ceylon and for some years indulged to the full his passion for big game hunting and his expertise in firearms. In 1861, in tune with the fashion of the times, he decided to go exploring in Africa. He had in mind to join J. H. Speke and Augustus Grant who were known to be on their way from the south on an expedition to discover for certain whether the Victoria N'yanza, visited for the first time by Speke on his expedition with Burton in 1858, was the source of the Nile. With his wife Florence, Baker travelled up the Nile from Khartoum and met Speke and Grant at Gondokoro and learnt that at any rate the main source of the Nile had been discovered. Was there no leaf of the laurel for him to pluck? asked Baker, and Speke suggested his seeking the second great lake south of Gondo-koro and establishing its place as part of the Nile system. The Bakers reached this second lake, which they named the Albert N'yanza, on 14th March, 1864; the extract below is from his description of the approaches to the lake.

\*      \*      \*

Having at length started, we arrived in the afternoon at the Kafoor[1] river, at a bend from the south where it was necessary to cross over in our westerly course. The stream was in the centre of a marsh, and although deep, it was so covered with thickly matted water-grass and other aquatic plants that a natural floating bridge was established by a carpet of weeds about two feet thick; upon this waving and unsteady surface the men ran quickly across, sinking merely to the ankles, although beneath the tough vegetation there was deep water. It was equally impossible to ride or to be carried over this treacherous surface; thus I led the way, and begged Mrs. Baker to follow me on foot as quickly as possible, precisely in my tracks. The river was

[1] The Kafu river which flows into the Victoria Nile just above Masindi Port.

about eighty yards wide, and I had scarcely completed a fourth of the distance and looked back to see if my wife followed close to me, when I was horrified to see her standing in one spot, and sinking gradually through the weeds, while her face was distorted and perfectly purple. Almost as soon as I perceived her, she fell, as though shot dead. In one instant I was by her side; and with the assistance of eight or ten of my men, who were fortunately close to me, I dragged her like a corpse through the yielding vegetation, and up to our waists we scrambled across to the other side, just keeping her head above the water; to have carried her would have been impossible as we should all have sunk together through the weeds. I laid her under a tree and bathed her head and face with water, as for the moment I thought she had fainted; but she lay perfectly insensible, as though dead, with teeth and hands firmly clenched and her eyes open but fixed. It was a *coup de soleil*. . . .

I laid her carefully in a miserable hut, and watched beside her. I opened her clenched teeth with a small wooden wedge and inserted a wet rag, upon which I dropped water to moisten her tongue which was dry as fur. The unfeeling brutes that composed the native escort were yelling and dancing as though all were well; and I ordered their chief at once to return with them to Kamrasi, as I would travel with them no longer. At first they refused to return until at length I vowed that I would fire into them should they accompany us on the following morning. Day broke, and it was a relief to have got rid of the brutal escort. They had departed and I had now my own men and the guides supplied by Kamrasi.

There was nothing to eat in this spot. My wife had never stirred since she fell by the *coup de soleil*, and merely respired about five times in a minute. It was impossible to remain; the people would have starved. She was laid gently upon her litter and we started forward on our funeral course. I was ill and broken-hearted and I followed by her side through the long day's march over wild park-lands and streams with thick forest and deep marshy bottoms; over undulating hills and through valleys of tall papyrus rushes which, as we brushed through them on our melancholy way, waved over the litter like the black plumes of a hearse. We halted at a village and again the night was passed in watching. I was wet and coated with mud from the swampy marsh, and shivered with ague; but the cold within was greater than all. No change had taken place; she had never moved. I had plenty of fat, and I made four balls of about half a pound, each of which would burn for three hours. A piece of a broken water-jar formed a lamp, several pieces of rag serving for wicks. So in solitude the still calm night passed away as I sat by her side and watched. In the drawn and distorted features that lay before me I could hardly trace the same face that for years had been my comfort through all the difficulties and dangers of my path. Was she to die? Was so terrible a sacrifice to be the result of my selfish exile?

Again the night passed away. Once more the march. Though weak and ill, and for two nights without a moment's sleep, I felt no fatigue, but mechanically followed by the side of the litter as though in a dream. The same wild country diversified with marsh and forest. Again we halted. The night came, and I sat by her side in a miserable hut with the feeble lamp flickering while she lay as in death. She had never moved a muscle since she fell. . . .

The morning broke; my lamp had just burnt out and, cramped with the night's watching, I rose from my low seat, and seeing that she lay in the same unaltered state I went to the door of the hut to breathe one gasp of the fresh morning air. I was watching the first red streak that heralded the rising sun, when I was startled by the words, 'Thank God,' faintly uttered behind me. Suddenly she had awoke from her torpor, and with a heart overflowing I went to her bedside. Her eyes were full of madness! She spoke; but the brain was gone!

I will not inflict a description of the terrible trial of seven days of brain fever with its attendant horrors. The rain poured in torrents, and day after day we were forced to travel for want of provisions, not being able to remain in one position. Every now and then we shot a few guinea-fowl, but rarely; there was no game although the country was most favourable. In the forests we procured wild honey, but the deserted villages contained no supplies, as we were on the frontier of Uganda and M'tese's people had plundered the district. For seven nights I had not slept, and although as weak as a reed, I had marched by the side of her litter. Nature could resist no longer. We reached a village one evening; she had been in violent convulsions successively—it was all but over. I laid her down on her litter within a hut, covered her with a Scotch plaid, and I fell upon my mat insensible, worn out with sorrow and fatigue. My men put a new handle to the pickaxe that evening, and sought for a dry spot to dig her grave!

*Mrs. Baker, however, made a spectacular recovery and the journey continued. . . .*

. . . Fortunately there were many fowls in this village; we found several nests of fresh eggs in the straw which littered the hut; these were most acceptable after our hard fare, and produced a good supply of soup.

Having rested for two days we again moved forward, Mrs. Baker being carried on a litter. We now continued on elevated ground, on the north side of a valley running from west to east, about sixteen miles broad and exceedingly swampy. The rocks composing the ridge upon which we travelled due west were all gneiss and quartz, with occasional breaks, forming narrow valleys, all of which were swamps choked with immense papyrus rushes that made the march very fatiguing. In one of these muddy bottoms one of my riding oxen that was ill stuck fast and we were obliged to abandon it, intending to send a number of natives to drag it out with ropes. On arrival at a village, our guide started about fifty men for this purpose, while we continued our journey.

That evening we reached a village belonging to a head-man, and very superior to most that we had passed on the route from M'rooli; large sugar-canes of the blue variety were growing in the fields and I had seen coffee growing wild in the forest in the vicinity. . . .

The name of this village was Parkāni. For several days past our guides had told us that we were very near to the lake, and we were now assured that we should reach it on the morrow. I had noticed a lofty range of mountains at an immense distance west, and I had imagined that those mountains formed the western frontier of the M'-wootan N'zige, and that the lake was actually within a march of

Parkāni. I could not believe it possible that we were so near the object of our search. The guide Rabonga now appeared and declared that if we started early on the following morning we should be able to wash in the lake by noon!

That night I hardly slept. For years I had striven to reach the 'sources of the Nile'.[1] In my nightly dreams during that arduous voyage I had always failed, but after so much hard work and perseverance the cup was at my very lips, and I was to drink at the mysterious fountain before another sun should set—at that great reservoir of Nature that ever since creation had baffled all discovery.

I had hoped and prayed and striven through all kinds of difficulties, in sickness, starvation, and fatigue, to reach that hidden source; and when it had appeared impossible, we had both determined to die upon the road rather than return defeated. Was it possible that it was so near and that tomorrow we could say, 'the work is accomplished'?

The 14th March—the sun had not risen when I was spurring my ox after the guide who, having been promised a double handful of beads on arrival at the lake, had caught the enthusiasm of the moment. The day broke beautifully clear, and having crossed a deep valley between the hills, we toiled up the opposite slope. I hurried to the summit. The glory of our prize burst suddenly upon me! There, like a sea of quicksilver, lay far beneath the grand expanse of water—a boundless sea horizon on the south and south-west, glittering in the noon-day sun; and on the west, at fifty or sixty miles' distance, blue mountains rose from the bosom of the lake to a height of about seven thousand feet above its level.

It is impossible to describe the triumph of that moment; here was the reward for all our labour—for the years of tenacity with which we had toiled through Africa. England had won the sources of the Nile! Long before I reached this spot, I had arranged to give three cheers with all our men in English style in honour of the discovery, but now that I looked down upon the great inland sea lying nestled in the very heart of Africa, and thought how vainly mankind had sought these sources throughout so many ages, and reflected that I had been the humble instrument permitted to

[1] See introductory note.

unravel this portion of the great mystery when so many greater than I had failed, I felt too serious to vent my feelings in vain cheers for victory, and I sincerely thanked God for having guided and supported us through all dangers to the good end.

*Albert N'yanza: Great Basin of the Nile.* By Samuel W. Baker. 1872.

# Gerhard Rohlfs
## 1832-1896

ROHLFS, who was born at Vegesack near Bremen, first became aware of Africa when he enlisted in 1855 in the Foreign Legion in Algeria and took part, as an apothecary's assistant, in the conquest of Great Kabylia. In July 1862 he started from Tangier disguised as a Muhammadan physician; then followed a series of expeditions into the interior of North Africa, including a traverse from Tripoli across the desert, down the Benue to its confluence with the Niger, and finally to Lagos. In 1873 he commanded an expedition which marched for thirty-six days across the Libyan desert to Siwa Oasis, and some of his experiences are described below. In 1878-9 he penetrated as far as the Oasis of Kufra. He received the Patron's Medal of the R.G.S. for 1868 for 'his extensive and important travels in the interior of Northern Africa.'

$$\star \quad \star \quad \star$$

So, by the 5th February [1874], everything was ready, and next morning we began our march across the Sand Sea.[1] We had water and provisions for twenty days, having left much superfluous food including several hundredweights of dates and biscuit at Regenfeld.[2] We had to maintain a north-north-west course, or 340°, since this direction from Regenfeld should lead us to the Oasis of Jupiter Ammon (Siwa) should we fail to find a way to the west through the Sand Sea. Without doubt, a difficult undertaking, but one which I favoured for other reasons—among them the fact that I had previously visited Siwa and was therefore familiar with the topography not only of the small oasis, but also of its environs and particularly of the significant extensive escarpment. On this journey from Dachel[3] via Regenfeld to Siwa, as throughout the whole expedition, Jordan maintained a route survey as though at sea by astronomical determination of latitude each evening, longitude

[1] The eastern Libyan desert.
[2] The name Rohlfs had given to his first camp, where rain had fallen.
[3] The oasis of Dakhla.

determination on rest days, and continous compass observations on the march. . . .

If we had had, with the rain, to endure a hard fight, so we were chilled on our first march by a cutting cold wind from a storm blowing up from the north—truly no laughing matter—for we were as close as could be to the rain of sand, and had to struggle continuously against a dense cloud of sand. Climbing over several high dunes, we nevertheless marched for nine hours that day.

We were still on Nubian limestone, and on the second day also there was not the slightest trace of vegetation. It was as though we were on a completely lifeless planet. If one hung back momentarily, the caravan was lost to sight, and one was sensible in the limitless expanse of a loneliness which affected the firmest minds alarmingly. The deeper we penetrated into the Sand Sea, the stronger this feeling grew. If wind or storm is a sign of life, their absence, troublesome though they were to us, made an almost crushing impression. Nothing but sand and sky! At sea, the face of the waters is never still, save in a profound calm; here, in the Sand Sea, nothing but the numbing little gusts of the last Simoom recall the great common life of the earth; otherwise, everything is dead.

On the second day we marched for eight hours only, yet we were by no means in such comfortless monotony as surrounded us some days later, for on 8th February at about 2 p.m. we struck a depression bounded on the north by a steeply ascending scarp with foothills. But to the east and west sand-dunes confronted us, destroying the hope that here in the midst of the Sand Sea we had come upon a firm surface of continuous rock. Near a self-standing rock pillar which from a distance stood out like a gigantic signpost or a factory chimney, I found, by a crack in the rock, a snake several feet in length (*coelo-peltis insignita*, a species widely distributed through North Africa and Syria.) As I approached this object, which I at first thought to be artificial, to examine it more closely, the snake basked for a moment but as soon as it saw me it disappeared into the crack. To capture it a whole rock slab had to be raised. This was done with the help of a servant, summoned by a revolver shot, and the snake was killed by blows on the head and was later preserved in spirit. How did this animal exist? Perhaps on birds which, strewn in numbers on the ground, had, exhausted by their wanderings, soon found their graves in the Libyan desert. Perhaps also, small insects, lizards, mice and jerboas are to be found, for here, where the topography displayed a different formation and there was some vegetation, in particular Aristida grass, dissection threw no light on the food of the snake. Zittel found only some sand grains in its stomach. Yet the animal had a rich layer of fat which could well nourish it during hibernation. Isolated outliers displayed singular rock formations and rounded boulders, perched on pillars and two to four feet in diameter, bedecked their slopes.

Above all this region was rich in oyster shells and ammonites, and on account of these latter fossils which we struck here for the first time, Zittel named this scarp the 'Ammonite Mountains'. Clearly we had left the region of Nubian sandstone behind us and were now on limestone. An indescribably rich life must have pulsated here in an earlier epoch; enormous banks of oysters and various other mussels of prehistoric age were to be found here. So rich a life flourishes today only in tropical seas, and the contrast strikes one all the more strongly here, for now all is dead—only the traces of the former life which ruled here so many thousands of years ago. We camped in the evening on a stony Hammada, but at the foot of a giant dune.

The next day we continued along this hundred metre-high dune on easy ground where Aristida grass sprouted here and there. We also saw a Fennek and numerous traces of animals disclosed that some four-footed beasts have withdrawn from the oases. Indeed, the fragments of ostrich eggs scattered everywhere prove that this shy bird, probably in order to hatch her brood in safety, seeks the loneliness of the Sand Sea to nest. We found new and old egg shells, polished by the drifting sand, over the whole Sand Sea. No area safer from pursuit than this desert could the ostrich have chosen and, in search of food, what are distances of fifty, even one hundred miles, to the fast-moving bird?

But conditions became progressively worse, the desert more alarming. On 10th February I wrote in my journal: 'I have nothing to record, except that we march steadily downwards and are in a sand sea.'

As one would imagine, our order of march was always pretty much the same, as also the rest of our life. The camel which marched best led the way, attended by one of the servants, the others tied in single file behind it. Our riding camels all had names both with us and the servants; Zittel's camel was known as the Baron, Jordan's as the Little Dog, and my own as the Giant. All the others were distinguished by a characteristic, and named after it.

Most of the time we went on foot, to maintain direction—our meal-times were approximately the same as on the march from Sint to Dachel. As we had saved all our cases for this trip, our table was well furnished, and even wine was not lacking. On arrival, a glass of Hennessy's brandy and biscuits much enjoyed! Water was plentiful and good; only our fuel began to run out, and our hen-coop and some cases had been condemned to be burnt. Then on 11th February, in the middle of the Sand Sea we discerned plants of Tulch (*Acacia tayal*) some with stems as thick as an arm, and only the tops sticking out of the sand. These were quickly collected. Fulgerites and, as usual, fragments of ostrich eggs were often seen during that day.

It was absolutely necessary to give the animals a rest day, so on 12th February we remained at the spot which we had reached the day before. We named it 'Sandheim', and Jordan fixed its position as lat. 26° 52' N., long. 26° 32' E. The magnetic declination was 7° 5' west, the altitude approximately 720 feet above sea level. From Regenfeld we had been descending appreciably.

Here we were able to water the camels—if not freely at least with a ration of water from the iron tanks, as a reward for their troublesome march! This was the first time that camels in the Sahara had been watered in this way. We always left the empty tanks behind as useless rubbish; so, in hundreds of years' time, empty bottles, water tanks and cases will mark our route through the Libyan Sand Sea.

February 13th and 14th were spent in the harsh Sand Sea; during nine-hour marches on each day we never struck solid rock. Although still among great accumulations of sand, we finally came for the first time on clean swept rock again, which was also encountered on the following days and which, according to Zittel, was a freshwater limestone formation. In the evening of the same day sparse vegetation appeared, the dunes lost their chain-like appearance, and the roads or sand paths formed by them disappeared. On 17th February the character of the region completely changed, and the next day we had descended so low that often aneroid readings showed that we were below sea-level. The dunes were markedly lower and had lost their north-south direction; they were now much more chaotic for no apparent reason. Above all we were on solid rock, which Zittel identified as undoubtedly a freshwater limestone. The camels had had no water for seventeen days. Vegetation was richer, principally Belbel (*Anabasis articulata*) and Aristida, and we noticed the tracks of jackals, jerboas, and lizards. The true Libyan sand sea was now behind us, but we had yet to reach the safe haven of the oasis of Jupiter Ammon.

On February 19th we finally emerged from the dunes. Thinking it better to proceed to the east of Siwa, where we must inevitably strike the southerly road from Beharieh, I altered course on this day from 340° to a more northerly direction. At 11 a.m. I at last sighted the first *allem*—without doubt a signpost set up by men.

There was great jubilation when after fourteen days we struck the first traces of human activity.

[The following afternoon the caravan entered Siwa.]

*Drei Monate in der libyschen Wüste*. Von Gerhard Rohlfs. Kassel, 1875. Trsl. by G.R.C.

# Henry Morton Stanley
## 1841-1904

STANLEY's first appearance on the African scene was as the leader of the expedition financed by the *New York Herald* which brought relief to Livingstone in 1871. Born John Rowlands, illegitimate and unwanted, Stanley was brought up in the workhouse of St. Asaph in North Wales. He went to sea in 1858 and, landing at New Orleans, sought his fortune for some years in America where he was befriended by a kindly merchant, Henry Morton Stanley, who gave him his name. Stanley led a roving life as a soldier, a sailor and, with increasing success, as a journalist, reporting the British Abyssinian campaign of 1867 and the Ashanti campaign of 1873 for the *New York Herald*, in addition to his scoop in 'finding Livingstone'. He regarded himself as Livingstone's natural heir and, on the latter's death, determined on the great trans-continental journey of 1874-7 when he visited Uganda, circumnavigated Lakes Victoria and Tanganyika and established the course of the Congo by sailing down it to the sea. In 1878 he took service with King Leopold of the Belgians with whom he was joint founder of the Congo Free State. His second trans-continental journey, from west to east as leader of the expedition for the relief of Emin Pasha in 1887-9, finally determined the main outlines of Central African geography. Ruthless in the field and unpopular at home, Stanley was nevertheless a redoubtable explorer of immense fortitude and ability. The fight described in the extract below took place during the long journey down the Congo to the sea, at the junction of the Congo (called by Stanley 'the Livingstone') with the Aruwimi river.

★   ★   ★

February 1 [1877]—The sun came out above the forest, round and large and bright, shooting broad gleams of light into the island shades, and lighting up their gloom until they seemed most envied retreats. Not for us, however. Destiny urged us on. There were no retreats for us. Man refused us, and the forest rejected us, for it had nothing to support us.

119

Almost straight the river [i.e. the Congo] flows—north-west half west. The right bank to which we again cling is steep and high, and crowned with solemn woods. At the water line is yellow clay; above it, alluvium and vegetable mould on which a hundred varieties of tropical plants flourish. Presently we are made aware that we are approaching settlements, by a number of ditches excavated in the lower banks, at an obtuse angle to the course of the river which, during the flooding season, will become filled by the full river and the resort of numerous fish. We had observed this before. The larger islands and banks ever since leaving the Stanley Falls, exhibited proofs of that love of the natives for fish which has stimulated them to undertake these laborious excavations, often over a hundred yards in length, to plait basket-traps and reedy fences at the mouths of creeks, to manufacture coils of stout rope out of plantain and palm (Hyphene) fibre, large cord nets, to plant great poles in the middle of cataracts, and undeterred by its dangers, to risk their lives daily in fish-catching.

About 8 p.m. we came in view of a market-place near which there were scores of small canoes. The men at once rushed into them and advanced all round us. We refrained a long time, but finally, as they began to get brave by our quiescence and to launch their wooden spears, which they proceeded to do unanimously as soon as somebody cried out 'Mutti'—sticks—we were obliged to reply to them with a few shots which compelled them to scamper away ahead of us. Drums then awakened the whole country and horns blew deafening blasts. Some canoes pertinaciously followed us. We came about 10 a.m. to another market-green. Here, too, warriors were ready and the little canoes, like wasps, hovered round us, and again we had recourse to our weapons. The little canoes with loud threats disappeared quickly down river; the land warriors rushed away into the woods. We did not wish to hurry, because the faster we proceeded the quicker we found we were involved in trouble. We therefore loitered languidly; rest was so rare that it became precious when we obtained it.

At noon I observed the sun, and found we were in north latitude 0° 50′ 17″. We resumed our journey, rowing at a steady though not a fast pace. We had descended the river for about an hour when we came again in sight of those waspish little canoes, and from the left bank, three thousand yards off, canoes were seen heading across the river at a terrific pace, while horns blew and drums beat. We heard shouts of defiance or threats, we knew not which—we had become indifferent to the incessant noise and continued fury.

In these wild regions our mere presence excited the most furious passions of hate and murder, just as in shallow waters a deep vessel stirs up muddy sediments. It appeared to be a necessity, then why should we regret it? Could a man contend with the inevitable?

At 2 p.m., heralded by savage shouts from the wasp swarm, which from some cause or other are unusually exultant, we emerge out of the shelter of the deeply wooded banks in presence of a vast affluent, nearly two thousand yards across at the mouth. As soon as we have fairly entered its waters, we see a great concourse of canoes hovering about some islets which stud the middle of the stream. The canoe-men, standing up, give a loud shout as they discern us, and blow their horns louder than ever. We pull briskly on to gain the right bank, and come in view of the right branch of the affluent when, looking up-stream, we see a sight that sends the blood tingling through every nerve and fibre of the body, arouses not only our most lively interest, but also our most lively apprehensions—a flotilla of gigantic canoes bearing down upon us, which both in size and numbers utterly eclipse anything encountered hitherto! Instead of aiming for the right bank, we form in line, and keep straight down river, the boat taking position behind. Yet after a moment's reflection, as I note the numbers of the savages, and the daring manner of the pursuit, and the desire of our canoes to abandon the steady compact line, I give the order to drop anchor. Four of our canoes affect not to listen until I chase them and threaten them with my guns. This compelled them to return to the line, which is formed of eleven double canoes anchored ten yards apart. The boat moves up to the front and takes position fifty yards above them. The shields are next lifted by the non-combatants, men, women and children, in the bows and along the outer lines as well as astern, and from behind these, the muskets and rifles are aimed.

We have sufficient time to take a view of the mighty force bearing down on us, and to count the number of the war-vessels which have been collected from the Livingstone and its great affluent. There are fifty-four of them! A monster canoe leads the way with two rows of upstanding paddles, forty men on a side, their bodies bending and swaying in unison as with a swelling barbarous chorus they drive her down towards us. In the bow, standing on what appears to be a platform, are ten prime young warriors, their heads gay with feathers of the parrot, crimson and grey; at the stern, eight men, with long paddles whose tops are decorated with ivory balls, guide the monster vessel; and dancing up and down from stem to stern are ten men who appear to be chiefs. All the paddles are headed with ivory balls, every head bears a feather crown, every arm shows gleaming white ivory armlets. From the bow of the canoe streams a thick fringe of the long fibre of the Hyphene palm. The crashing sound of large drums, a hundred blasts from ivory horns, and a thrilling chant from two thousand human throats do not tend to soothe our nerves or to increase our confidence. However, it is 'neck or nothing'. We have no time to pray, or to take sentimental looks at the savage world, or even to breathe a sad farewell to it. So many other things have to be done speedily and well.

As the foremost canoe comes rushing down, and its consorts on either side beating the water into foam, and raising their jets of water with their sharp prows, I turn to take a last look at our people, and say to them:

'Boys, be firm as iron; wait until you see the first spear and then take good aim. Don't fire all at once. Keep aiming until you are sure of your man. Don't think of running away, for only your guns can save you.'

Frank is with the *Ocean* on the right flank, and has a choice crew and a good bulwark of black wooden shields. Manwa Sera has the *London Town*—which he has taken in charge instead of the *Glasgow*— on the left flank, the sides of the canoe bristling with guns, in the hands of tolerably steady men.

The monster canoe aims straight for my boat as though it would run us down; but, when within fifty yards off, swerves aside and, when nearly opposite, the warriors above the manned prow let fly their spears, and on either side there is a noise of rushing bodies. But every sound is soon lost in the ripping, crackling musketry. For five minutes we are so absorbed in firing that we take no note of anything else; but at the end of that time we are made aware that the enemy is re-forming about two hundred yards above us.

Our blood is up now. It is a murderous world, and we feel for the first time that we hate the filthy, vulturous ghouls who inhabit it. We therefore lift our anchors and pursue them up-stream along the right bank, until rounding a point we see their villages. We make straight for the banks and continue the fight in the village streets with those who have landed, hunt them out into the woods, and there only sound the retreat, having returned the daring cannibals the compliment of a visit.

While mustering my people for re-embarkation, one of the men came forward and said that in the principal village there was a 'Meskiti', a 'pembe'—a church, or temple, of ivory—and that ivory was 'as abundant as fuel'. In a few moments I stood before the ivory temple which was merely a large circular roof supported by thirty-three tusks of ivory, erected over an idol four feet high, painted with camwood dye, a bright vermilion, with black eyes and beard and hair. The figure was very rude, still it was an unmistakable likeness of a man. The tusks being wanted by the Wangwana, they received permission to convey them into the canoes. One hundred other pieces of ivory were collected in the shape of log wedges, long ivory war-horns, ivory pestles to pound cassava into meal and herbs for spinach, ivory armlets and balls, and ivory mallets to beat the fig-bark into cloth.

The stores of beautifully carved paddles, ten feet in length, some of which were iron-pointed, the enormous six-feet-long spears, which were designed more for ornament than use, the splendid long knives, like Persian kummars, and bright iron-mounted sheaths with broad belts of red buffalo and antelope-hide, barbed spears, from the light assegai to the heavy double-handed sword-spear, the tweezers, hammers, prickers, hole-burners, hairpins, fish-hooks, hammers, arm and leg-rings of iron and copper, iron beads and wrist-bands, iron bells, axes, war-hatchets, adzes, hoes, dibbers, etc., proved the people on the banks of this river to be clever, intelligent, and more advanced in the arts than any hitherto observed since we commenced our descent of the Livingstone. The architecture of their huts, however, was the same, except the conical structure they had erected over their idol. Their canoes were much larger than those of the Mwana Ntaba above the Stanley Falls, which had crocodiles and lizards carved on them. Their skull-caps of basket-work, leopard, civet, and monkey skins, were similar to those that we had observed in Uregga. Their shields were like those of the Wariwa. There were various specimens of African wood-carving in great and small idols, stools of ingenious pattern, double benches, walking-staffs, spear-staffs, flutes, grain-mortars, mallets, drums, clubs, troughs, scoops and canoe-balers, paddles, porridge spoons, etc. Gourds also exhibited taste in ornamentation. Their earthenware was very superior, their pipes of an unusual pattern—in short, everything that is of use to a well-found African village exhibited remarkable intelligence and prosperity.

Evidences of cannibalism were numerous in the human and 'soko' skulls that grinned on many poles and the bones that were freely scattered in the neighbourhood near the village garbage heaps and the river banks, where one might suppose hungry canoe-men to have enjoyed a cold collation on an ancient matron's arm. As the most positive and downright evidence, in my opinion, of this hideous practice was the thin forearms of a person that was picked up near a fire with certain scorched ribs which might have been tossed into the fire after being gnawed. It is true that it is but circumstantial evidence, yet we accepted them as indubitable proofs. Besides, we had been taunted with remarks that we would furnish them with meat supplies—for the words meat and today have but slight dialectic difference in many languages.

We embarked in our canoes at 5 p.m., and descending the affluent came to the confluence again and then, hugging the right bank, appeared before other villages; but after our successful resistance to such a confederation of chiefs and the combined strength of three or four different tribes, it was not likely that one small settlement would risk an encounter.

*Through the Dark Continent. By H. M. Stanley, 1860.*

# Louis-Gustave Binger
## 1856–1937

DESCRIBED in an official obituary as 'one of the creators of French West Africa . . . the hardy pioneer of the Ivory Coast,' Louis-Gustave Binger did more than any traveller of his time to open up the country in the great bend of the Niger. In the era of the 'Scramble for Africa' Binger's travels had a political object in view, but he was more than a simple pioneer in the interests of his country. Coming to West Africa first on military duty, he showed himself a great natural explorer and in 1887 he embarked on the three-year journey on which his fame chiefly rests and for which, in 1899, he received the Founder's Medal of the R.G.S. In 1892 Binger undertook the delimitation of the boundary between the British Gold Coast and the French Ivory Coast, of which latter territory he became Governor in 1893. The extract which follows describes a stage of his journey down the Comoé river, Ivory Coast, approaching Attakrou, a town about a hundred and thirty miles from the sea. Suffering from a painful hernia, he is glad of the occasional delay while porters are collected.

★     ★     ★

Saturday, March 2nd [1889]—I don't altogether mind [the delay] because the enforced rest is really a necessity; I am still very far from well, and my good Treich is up to the eyes with everything to see to; the start in the morning, the organization of the supplies, the convoy, etc. All I have strength for is to keep the journal up to date.

It is about four o'clock: I am on tenterhooks, and the inertia, or rather the total lack of any sense of urgency, or of desire for activity on the part of these people fidgets me to death. I think of tomorrow, of the departure which we have so looked forward to, of the hours which we must lose while we gather our eight wretched canoe-men; what is more, it is no good even thinking that the whole of our party will be able to go by canoe. Benié puts forward excellent arguments for making them go on foot, and only half our baggage and men will be able to leave with us.

Sunday, March 3rd—We were up by half past three this morning, and an hour later enjoying a monkey stew, warmed up from last night, and some grilled bananas. All was said to be ready, but at half past six the crew were still running around looking for the paddles, and we did not embark until a quarter past seven.

What a relief at last to wave good-bye with my ragged felt hat, and what bliss it was for me to be able, even for a short time, to have a change from that exhausting travel in a litter! My servant Boukary had arranged my bedding in the canoe in such a way that I was able to lie back against the baggage arranged to serve as a pillow. The swelling in my groin is less painful, but I feel the fever coming on again. I have my notebook, my two compasses and my umbrella, which has been extremely useful during the day-time.

On leaving Attakrou the river flows almost in a circle, but the general direction is to the south, and there is bottom throughout. At the end of about an hour we leave to our right a wide beach of white sand, then, about a quarter of an hour afterwards, we arrive at a pretty wooded islet opposite which, on the left bank, is the little village of Akhiékrou or Akhiékourou. Two women doing their washing go to call the village chief, and he brings us two gin bottles of palm wine. There is no need for skilled manœuvres to bring the canoe to its moorings; the channel is so shallow (hardly ten centi-metres of water) that the boat grounds of its own accord, and we can enjoy the good palm wine at our ease.

A few moments after passing the islet and the village, we reach the mouth of a little river in the right bank, about four metres wide, which flows through an absolute cradle of greenery. Just as I am marvelling at the smoothness of our progress, the river turns at a sharp angle, makes a twist, and we are faced with three pretty difficult falls, one after another. The first goes fairly easily, the channel being just in midstream; but for the two others we have to manœuvre carefully to find the way, which is right over on the left bank. Hardly are we away from these obstructions than we reach a point called Ebohoré situated about half-way between Attakrou and Satticran, a real chaos of rocks and of little oyster-beds. It takes a whole hour to overcome this awkward passage; not that there are rapids or dangerous places, only the constant risk of being stranded and the need to manœuvre from one bank to the other so as to get the canoes through with the least possible damage. Half an hour later, we have negotiated successively two minor falls: the first by a channel in midstream, the second, which embraces an islet, can only be got through by hugging the right bank. Here we come to a fine, swift current, very deep, where one can really get along. On our left we sweep past the village of Mangokourou opposite which is the landing stage used by the Morénou people. This splendid current is checked up-stream of Satticran by an easy fall in midstream, then by a big island facing the mouth of a rivulet on the right bank, five metres wide. Several strong rhythmic paddle-strokes bring us along-side the sand-bank on the left and, a few moments later, we arrive at Satticran where our men have been waiting some two hours; it is half past four in the afternoon. It is impossible to imagine how tiring a ten-hour canoe voyage can be; what is more, instead of taking a stroll round the village, I now have to sit down and trans-cribe our first day of navigation, so as to be able to lie down with a clear conscience and ease my discomfort.

Thanks to the good offices of the chief at Attakrou we are very well received at Satticran. The villagers offer us sugar-cane, pineapple, bananas and yams which, with a good quarter of dried monkey-meat, makes us a delicious dinner! My men make themselves a gigantic stew with the smoked venison from Attakrou. During the evening the people at Angoikhé, a little village a kilometre down-stream, come to see us. Though quite exhausted, I collect informa-tion on tomorrow's route for our porters, who must do a double journey on foot through the forest to Aniasué; they will follow the river from Anghoikhé to Assémanone and only ford one river, five or six metres wide and flowing between Ammoaconkrou, the residence of the chief of Indenié, and the village of Zébédou—Treich crossed it in 1887. Tomorrow, eight of our men must come back to Kabrankrou to carry me in my litter from here to Aniasué.

Tomorrow's details settled, we try to sleep. Alas! the pain from which I suffer brings on a fever which makes me delirious, in spite of quinine. Tossing through the night, not only can I get no rest but my good Treich does not close an eye, forestalling my least wish and asking me, each time I turn over in my bed, whether there is anything I need.

Monday, March 4th. At first light our porters are off. Treich and I embark in our frail boat, taking with us some bananas grilled over the fire to serve for breakfast. The swift current is checked by a shallow rapid at Zébédou, and the fall at Assémaone allows us to navigate rapidly enough; unfortunately, from this last village to Darou—situated in a right-angled bend of the river—the bed is obstructed by a series of rapids through which the stream runs sometimes to the right, sometimes to the left, causing us to lose much precious time. Before Darou, the river is nearly dry, and the local people cross as and when they like to get to Morénou, to which the path takes off on the right bank opposite the village.

At Kabrankrou the river flows towards Aniasué by a series of loops which take a long time to navigate, but progress is quite straightforward despite a number of rapids. At Kabrankrou itself there is one quite difficult one, two metres above the level of the water, through which we find a narrow passage on the right.

During the stretch through the meanders of Kabrankou to Aniasué there is only one village on the left bank at about the half-way mark called Bourouattakrou. According to our crew the chief of the village had a fine canoe to sell for which he would probably want two to three gold ounces (between 90 and 120 francs). Naturally our first care when we disembarked was to find out whether this canoe had yet found a purchaser. We had our answer that evening: it had been sold two days before to the people at Arikokrou, so there was no point in considering it further. . . .

Thursday, March 7th. We left this morning at daybreak, a quarter to six. The sufferings of a sick man carried in a litter can hardly be told; although the porters show the best will in the world one is for ever being bumped against trees and creepers throughout the winding length of the road. In order to clear the path, the natives have cut down the young trees to about eighty centimetres to one metre from the ground, and this leaves a forest of stakes on which one might be impaled at any moment. As in the course of one's passage one brushes against the trees and creepers, they let fall bits of dead wood, ants' nests stuck in the branches, dry leaves and rotten boughs, all in a blinding shower. One can count oneself lucky not to be injured or maimed by some great lump of old wood suspended twenty metres or more above one's head, which could be dislodged at a touch. Of sunshine, not a gleam; throughout this thirty-day journey a half-darkness broods over the forest which exhausts the spirit. One craves for the daylight, to see the grass—because here the ground is carpeted only with the young shoots of trees and the litter of pineapples. No ferns, no flowers, nothing to uplift the heart or speak to the soul—the monotony of these regions is terrible.

And yet, is there not something truly grand and mysterious about the forest? How gladly could one wander here were it not for the thought of tomorrow! How the silence impresses one! Neither wind nor sun penetrate this vastness! Only a hundred metres from a village one might be alone in the world. One hardly notices the birds: they live in the treetops enjoying at once the sun and the shade and we cannot hear their twittering as we wend our way, for it is lost in the hacking sound of the knives with which the natives clear the path, cutting away at creepers and trees sometimes twenty centimetres thick. From time to time, however, one hears the game scampering away in the undergrowth with a crash of branches as it breaks through to safety; probably, for all the noise, only a little gazelle, the size of a goat. During the halts, seated by the way to enjoy some cold boiled yams or a few bananas, a joyous band of monkeys passes overhead at twenty to fifty metres, their cries drowned by the cracking of the dead twigs which pour down on your head and drive you under cover.

These forests are so awe-inspiring that the sight of even the roughest path crossing your own gives you infinite joy; you say to yourself: 'Then there are others in these solitudes!' When these paths become more frequent and, above all, when they lead in another direction to one's own, courage wells up. 'A garden path!' We are near a village but, alas, sometimes it lies two mortal hours ahead.

Oh joy! How one's heart leaps up! One feels alive again when, a few minutes later, a half dug-out tree trunk, a canoe in the making, lies across the way; little by little, plantations of oil palms, a wider path, a banana grove, and then the tops of dun-coloured roofs covered with dead leaves or tawny palms, the sound of cockcrow, or the rhythmic clack and rattle betraying the presence of a weaver.

Oh, that cockcrow! How the fancy has deluded me! Dropping with fatigue, struggling on with difficulty, not knowing whether we should come soon to the village, the ear on the qui vive, we keep thinking we hear it. 'What welcome shall we get?' we ask each other. Alas, our longing for the end of the road deceives us into mistaking for the reality the hallucination of a tired mind, and when, after two more hours on the march, we reach the longed-for village, the cock is as sound asleep as the villagers.

*Du Niger au Golfe de Guinée par le Pays de Kong et de Mossi*. By L.-G. Binger. Librairie Hachette, Paris, 1889. Vol. 2. Trsl. by D.M.

# Joseph Thomson
## 1858-1895

JOSEPH THOMSON was both an explorer in the heroic tradition of Livingstone, and a pioneer of the new commercial development of Africa. He studied geology at Edinburgh University and was only twenty-one when he was appointed geologist and naturalist to the Royal Geographical Society's expedition to East Central Africa. When the leader, Keith Johnston, died at an early stage of the journey, Thomson unhesitatingly took command and led the expedition successfully to Lakes Nyasa and Tanganyika and back to the coast. In 1882 the R.G.S. sent him to pioneer a route from the east coast to the Nile headwaters through the country of the warlike Masai, from Mombasa by way of Mt. Kilimanjaro and Mt. Kenya to the north-east corner of Lake Victoria. This journey is described in the extract below. He received the Patron's Medal in 1885 for this feat of exploration during which he made important geological observations, being the first traveller to understand and describe the formation of the Great African Rift Valley. In 1885 he headed a trade mission to the Sultans of Sokoto and Gando in Nigeria, and in 1890 entered the service of Cecil Rhodes in Northern Rhodesia. His incessant journeys, and a riding accident when in Morocco in 1888, undermined his health and he died at the early age of thirty-seven.

★    ★    ★

On the 3rd of May [1883] we proceeded to take the important step of crossing the threshold of the dangerous region [of the Masai tribe], carrying with us about eight days' food. Leaving the forest country round the base of Kibonoto and traversing a rich and varied scene, we suddenly emerged at a height of six thousand feet, on a great treeless plain covered with a close and succulent coating of grass quite undistinguishable from the pasture of more temperate climates. In the immediate foreground the country spread out before us in gently waving plains diversified by low, rounded ridges, small humpy hills or volcanic cones, well described in the lines of Bryant, extending as they do—

131

'In airy undulations far away,
As if the ocean in his gentlest swell
Stood still, with all his rounded billows fix'd,
And motionless for ever.'

Such is the country: but see its inhabitants! There, towards the base of Kilimánjaro, are three great herds of buffalo slowly and leisurely moving up from the lower grazing-grounds to the shelter of the forest for their daily snooze and rumination in its gloomy depths. Farther out on the plains enormous numbers of the harmless but fierce-looking wildebeest continue their grazing, some erratic members of the herd gambolling and galloping about with waving tail and strange, uncouth movements. Mixed with these are to be seen companies of that loveliest of all large game, the zebra, conspicuous in their beautiful striped skin, here marching with stately step, with heads down bent, there enjoying themselves by kicking their heels in mid-air or running open-mouthed in mimic fight, anon standing as if transfixed, with heads erect and projecting ears, watching the caravan pass. But these are not all. Look! Down in that grassy bottom there are several specimens of the great, unwieldy rhinoceros, with horns stuck on their noses in a most offensive and pugnacious manner. Over that ridge a troop of ostriches are scudding away out of reach of danger, defying pursuit, and too wary for the stalker. See how numerous are the herds of hartebeest, and notice the graceful pallah springing into mid-air with great bounds as if in pure enjoyment of existence. There also among the tall reeds near the marsh you perceive the dignified waterbuck, in twos and threes, leisurely cropping the dewy grass. The wart-hog, disturbed at his morning's feast, clears off in a bee-line with tail erect, and with a steady military trot truly comical. These do not exhaust the list, for there are many other species of game. Turn in whatever direction you please, they are to be seen in astonishing numbers, and so rarely hunted, that unconcernedly they stand and stare at us, within gun-shot.

Look, now, farther ahead. Near a dark line of trees which conspicuously mark out the course of the Ngare N'Erobi (cold stream) in the treeless expanse around, you observe in the clear morning air columns of curling smoke, and from the vicinity strange long dark lines are seen to emerge like the dark columns of an advancing army. The smoke marks the kraals of the Masai and the advancing lines are their cattle moving towards the pasture-ground. If you will now imagine a long line of men moving in single file across this prairie region, carrying boxes, bales, packages of iron wire, etc., headed by myself, and brought up in the rear by Martin,[1] while a cold, piercing wind blows with the freezing effect suggestive of an early spring in Scotland, you will be able to form a picture of the scene which presented itself on that memorable morning in April. In order to find a frame for the picture, just glance round at the circle of mountains. There to the right rises Mount Meru, now seen in all its simple but grand proportions, forming a fitting pillar to the 'door' of the Masai. On your left stands the second great pillar, Kibo. From these circles an apparently almost unbroken range of mountains, rising into the picturesque masses of Donyo Erok and Ndapduk in the north, and finally sweeping round in the less conspicuous ranges of the Guaso N'Ebor (white water) in the direction of Nguru-ma-ni and the cold heights of Gelei, behind which lies unseen the still active volcano of Donyo Engai.

Let us now hurry forward, for the day is big with fate! As we stride on, continually tempted to try our 'shooting-irons', the Masai begin to appear. First a woman, well-dressed in bullock's-hide and loaded with wire, beads, and chains, appears driving a donkey before her as she wends her way fearlessly towards Kibonoto to buy the vegetable food eaten by the married people and children. It is war to the death between the male Masai and Wa-chaga, but a treaty allows the women to go unhurt and without protection. Next, two or three poor men are descried engaged in the menial task of herding and tending the cattle. As we near the kraals the El-Moran (warriors or unmarried men) begin to turn out in parties to see the 'latest thing' in men. They do not hurry themselves, however. They survey you leisurely, and by neither word nor sign betray any feelings of astonishment. As we pass them in succession we pluck some grass and gravely shake hands. Addressing them as

[1] James Martin was a Maltese sailor who accompanied Thomson throughout the Masailand expedition.

El-Moran, we wait till an inarticulate sound intimates they have ears. Then we say 'Subai,' to which they reply 'Ebai,' and our introduction is over. Greatly struck by the unnusual manners of these savages, so different from the notion we have formed of them, we move on, not a bit inconvenienced by crowding or annoyed by rude remarks.

Before noon we had all reached the ice-cold waters of the snow-fed Ngare N'Erobi, which rises in its full volume at the base of the mountain. We camped in a sharp bend of the stream where it almost surrounds a bit of level sward. Our first care, of course, was to make the *bomba*[1], and thoroughly fortify ourselves. So far everything had gone on swimmingly, though I was quite bewildered by my unexpected reception, and felt as if there was something portentous in the whole affair.

The news of our arrival soon spread. The Masai men and women began to crowd into camp, and we mutually surveyed each other with equal interest. The women had all the style of the men. With slender, well-shaped figures, they had brilliant dark eyes, Mongolian in type, narrow, and with an upward slant. Their expression was distinctly lady-like (for natives), and betrayed their ideas in more ways than one. Obviously they felt that they were a superior race, and that all others were but as slaves before them.

[1] A defensive work built of branches, boulders, etc.

*Through Masai Land.* By Joseph Thomson. 3rd edition, 1885.

# Paul François Xavier Flatters
## 1832 — 1881

IN the 'seventies of the last century the French were much pre-
occupied with the project of a Trans-Saharan railway. In 1879
Colonel Flatters was ordered to pioneer a route from Algeria to
some point between the Niger and Lake Chad. This now seems a
bad choice, since this route would traverse the rocky Ahaggar
massif in the central Sahara, which rises in places to ten thousand
feet. But the great obstacle was the hostile attitude of the Tuareg
tribesmen (the 'veiled warriors'), independent, fanatic and warlike,
who were readier to listen to the Turks than to the French. The
government, however, decided that the Mission should not be a
military one. Flatters was to rely on negotiating a passage. The
extract relates the outcome of this policy. On his first attempt
Flatters had to extricate his party from a perilous position in northern
Ahaggar, some four hundred miles south of Ouargla. On the
second he was less fortunate. Emboldened by their earlier success the
Tuareg ambushed Flatters' party, and he and many others were
killed, only a handful surviving the terrible return journey. Lieut.
Henri Brosselard, who wrote the following account, was the
surveyor of the first expedition.

★    ★    ★

Why did Haji Ikhenoukhen[1] not reply? Why was he hesitating?
What was causing the delay? He was clearly influenced by other
preoccupations than those of the lesser chiefs with whom we had
dealt so far. He had doubtless considered it his duty to forward the
communications from the Chief of the Mission to the Turkish
government agents at Tripoli. They were referring them to their
sovereign, who had himself perhaps to take the advice of a friendly
nation. This might go on indefinitely and end with a simple refusal
to allow us to proceed.

Would it not pay to be bold, and without waiting for a reply,
which should not have been so long delayed if it was to prove favour-

[1] The aged chief of the Azdjer Tuareg.

135

able, to continue our journey? If we had been organized on a military footing; if in place of our Chambaa followers[1] we had had soldiers on camels to direct the caravan such as the Smala of Laghouat; if, in a word, we had been in a position to call in case of need on two hundred men trained in the use of arms, disciplined and reliable; if, on the other hand, the government instructions had authorized Colonel Flatters to take whatever steps the circumstances might require and to renounce if necessary the accomplishment of his enterprise by peaceful means, then perhaps this would have indeed been at once the wisest, the most prudent and most useful course. But in the position in which we were, we could not adopt this solution. Each day witnessed the arrival in the vicinity of the camp of fresh tribesmen who installed themselves some distance away, less to honour us than to keep watch and to extract presents from us. Their language was full of the most admirable sentiments; to listen to them, the country was open to us and we would receive the warmest welcome wherever we might choose to go. But to these friendly feelings there were always reservations regarding Ikhenoukhen's decision—he was now being represented to us as the sole sovereign and master of the country—and unceasing demands for presents.

We began to see clearly the real intentions of the Azdjer in inducing us to enter their territory and in leading us in the direction of Rhat (Ghat). For them it was a matter of seizing for their own profit and to the detriment of the Hoggar, their neighbours and rivals, a prey which they believed to be rich and hoped to be easy. The tales of the Chambaa and various incidents which had impressed them during their stay with us had apparently caused them to abandon the idea of pillaging us by main force—but they had not abandoned their intention of depriving us of all we had brought with us. What they did not dare to seize at one swoop they hoped to force us to surrender piecemeal. Since assembling in strength near the lake and virtually beleaguering our camp, they felt themselves masters of the situation. This showed itself at every turn in their speech and attitude, however careful they were to reiterate constantly their protestations of friendship.

Their demands became such that we were obliged to keep our

[1] Tribesmen, notoriously unreliable, from the vicinity of Ouargla.

baggage almost continually locked up, and to hide every object of value we wished to retain. How many times have I seen one ot these bandits, lance in hand, enter my tent in search of booty? . . .

To enter into *pourparlers* with Ahitaghen[1] in an attempt to negotiate a passage through his territory, after having failed in our first plans, was now almost impossible, and could have no other effect than to require from us new sacrifices which our resources would not allow us to meet. Having seen us enter his domain through the Azdjer country, Ahitaghen would easily realize the motives which had forced us to turn to him, he would unscrupulously abuse the necessity which had driven us hither, and we should have definitely broken with the Azdjer Tuareg uselessly and without result.

Ten of the Ifoghas, who had accompanied us to lake Menghough[2] and who had been engaged as guides, went off on the pretext of seeking the provisions required for the journey. They never returned and gave no sign of life. Great anxiety was displayed by our Chambaa who were proclaiming loudly that all was lost and that we were to become the prey of the Tuareg. In anticipation of a catastrophe they began skilfully but unscrupulously to ally themselves with our future conquerors. I cannot say that they had started to plan treachery and to bargain for the price of their defection, but they certainly took precautions to be in at the sharing of the spoils. Groups gradually formed among them, they spoke in low tones and seemed to be preparing for an approaching event. Each day the Chambaa on one pretext or another withdrew a little further from our tents, while the few Beni-Tour who had followed us drew nearer, as though to keep watch on us.

All these symptoms were too serious to pass unnoticed and they demanded rapid and energetic action. Colonel Flatters realized this and suddenly gave the order to reload the camels and resume the march. We took the track to the south, circling the lake to descend the other side to the plain. But we had scarcely advanced five hundred yards before we came face to face with one hundred

---

[1] Chief of the Hoggar Tuareg.
[2] A small lake in a rock basin, surrounded by dunes, near which the expedition was encamped.

Tuareg drawn up for battle with lances at the ready and seemingly resolved to dispute our advance. The Tuareg had organized themselves, having elected leaders, and seemed disposed to accept battle.

We were obliged to halt and to pitch camp again. M. le Chatelier, sent to parley with the Azdjer, returned with the elected leaders. The latter declared to the colonel in the most formal manner that as Haji Ikhenoukhen had not authorized us to proceed they would oppose our departure.

It was all clear, precise and formal. The position had developed quite simply; the Tuareg considered us to be their prisoners. . . .

The moment was decisive; they must allow us to pass or fight.

In every possible way we had to be positive about the true intentions of the Tuareg and the fate planned for us. This was Colonel Flatters' purpose in making as though to resume his march. This move had succeeded; we now knew what faced us. He at once began to parley with the enemy, and embarked on a series of conferences lasting forty-eight hours during which time he had no rest. Finally he held a council of war with the officers of the Mission and with the greatest simplicity explained the position. . . .

When he was finished, each of us in turn gave his opinion, and it was unanimously decided that the next day before dawn the caravan would march in the direction of Laghouat via Ouargla to replenish supplies. The colonel also wrote to Ahitaghen, the Hoggar chief, to ask whether, if it were necessary, he would agree to our passage through his territory when the Mission resumed its work. In sum, we must retreat and for the moment at least abandon our enterprise. As we left the council we wept with rage.

We occupied ourselves preparing to leave; our servants overhauled the camel saddles and filled our water casks.

Tuesday, April 20th passed in this fashion. During the night while I was in charge of the camp guard, I saw the colonel approaching.

'Can you,' he asked me, 'count upon your men of the Bataillon d'Afrique?'

'Yes,' I replied, 'they will do as they are ordered.'

'Good. Tomorrow, before daybreak, you will load the camels and the caravan will set out silently to get out of the dunes and reach the plain. All must be done as quietly as possible. You, with Captain Masson, and your men will form the rear guard. If the Tuareg should pursue us, you will halt at the entrance to the defile which you will hold at all cost until the caravan is safe. If necessary, fight to the last man so long as the caravan escapes.'

Towards four in the morning I roused Captain Masson, and in a short time the camels were loaded and had begun the descent. We remained at our post until the last camel was in position on the plain. When day broke we had the satisfaction of watching the caravan disappear over the grassy plain of the Wadi Tijoujelt.

The Tuareg, when they awoke and could no longer see the camp, fell into agitated disorder as though completely taken by surprise. They ran hither and thither questioning and seeming to await orders which they were astonished not to receive, since no one came forward to take command. It was to this confusion which reigned at first that we owed our freedom from attack and the opportunity to rejoin the caravan without a shot being fired.

During the negotiations of the previous evening with the Azdjer chiefs, the colonel, realizing that an attack was inevitable and imminent, and despairing of obtaining help, had decided to purchase their neutrality. That was why on the following morning the Tuareg, seeing the caravan leave, were astonished not to receive orders to bar our way. They sought everywhere for those who should have given the signal for attack, but they were nowhere to be found. They had taken advantage of the dark to decamp, carrying into the desert the price of their treason.

*Voyage de la Mission Flatters au pays des Touareg Azdjers.* By Henri Brosselard. Paris, 1883. Trsl. by G.R.C.

# Mary Kingsley
## 1862-1900

MARY KINGSLEY was the daughter of George Henry Kingsley, and niece of Charles Kingsley. Her interests were primarily scientific and after the death of her parents, to whom she was a devoted daughter, she decided to visit West Africa for zoological research. She was chiefly interested in fish, but hardly less so in the customs of the people, and came to hold strong and controversial views on the administration of colonial territories. She travelled as a trader and frequently upheld the rights of her fraternity as opposed to those of the missionaries. Her visits among the savage and unpredictable Fan tribe are as noteworthy as was her prowess as a navigator in the tangled creeks of the Niger and Cross river mouths. Wearing long skirts, and armed only with an umbrella and her packet of trade goods, she comes brilliantly to life in the long, breathless passages of the two books she wrote about her years on 'The Coast'.

The extract below describes part of her journey through what was then the French Congo, up the Ogowe river and into the interior from Njole which lies up-stream from Lambaréné now celebrated as the site of Albert Schweitzer's settlement. It took place in 1893.

★     ★     ★

The Ogowe is broad at Njole and its banks not mountainous as at Talagouga; but as we go on it soon narrows, the current runs more rapidly than ever, and we are soon again surrounded by the mountain range. Great masses of black rock show among the trees on the hillsides, and under the fringe of fallen trees that hang from the steep banks. Two hours after leaving Njole we are facing our first rapid. Great grey-black masses of smoothed rock rise up out of the whirling water in all directions. These rocks have a peculiar appearance which puzzled me at the time, but in subsequently getting used to it accepted it quietly and admired. When the sun shines on them they have a soft light blue haze round them like a halo. The effect produced by this, with the forested hill-sides and the little beaches of glistening white sand was one of the most perfect things I have ever seen.

We kept along close to the right-hand bank, dodging out of the way of the swiftest current as much as possible. Ever and again we were unable to force our way round projecting parts of the bank, so we then got up just as far as we could to the point in question, yelling and shouting at the tops of our voices. M'bo said, 'Jump for bank, sar,' and I 'up and jumped,' followed by half the crew. Such banks! sheets, and walls, and rubbish heaps of rock, mixed up with trees fallen and standing. One appalling corner I shall not forget, for I had to jump at a rock wall and hang on to it in a manner more befitting an insect than an insect-hunter, and then scramble up it into a close-set forest, heavily burdened with boulders of all sizes. I wonder whether the rocks or the trees were there first? There is evidence both ways, for in one place you will see a rock on the top of a tree, the tree creeping out from underneath it, and in another place you will see a tree on the top of a rock, clasping it with a network of roots and getting its nourishment, goodness knows how, for these are by no means tender, digestible sandstones, but uncommon hard gneiss and quartz which has no idea of breaking up into friable small stuff, and which only takes on a high polish when it is vigorously sanded and canvassed by the Ogowe. While I was engaged in climbing across these promontories, the crew would be busy shouting and hauling the canoe round the point by means of the strong chain provided for such emergencies fixed on to the bow. When this was done, in we got again and paddled away until we met our next affliction.

M'bo had advised that we should spend our first night at the same village that M. Alegret did; but when we reached it, a large village on the north bank, we seemed to have a lot of daylight still in hand, and thought it would be better to stay at one a little higher up, so as to make a shorter day's work for tomorrow, when we wanted to reach Kondo Kondo; so we went against the bank just to ask about the situation and character of the up-river villages. The row of low, bark huts was long, and extended its main frontage close to the edge of the river bank. The inhabitants had been watching us as we came, and when they saw we intended calling that afternoon they charged down to the river-edge hopeful of excitement. They had a great deal to say, and so had we. After compliments, as they say, in excerpts of diplomatic communications, three of their men took charge of the conversation on their side, and M'bo did ours. To M'bo's questions they gave a dramatic entertainment as answer, after the manner of these brisk, excitable Fans. One chief, however, soon settled down to definite details, prefacing his remarks with the silence-commanding 'Azuna! Azuna!' and his companions grunted approbation of his observations. He took a piece of plantain leaf and tore it up into five different-sized bits. These he laid along the edge of our canoe at difference intervals of space, while he told M'bo things, mainly scandalous, about the characters of the villages these bits of leaf represented, save of course about bit A, which represented his own. The interval between the bits was proportional to the interval between the villages, and the size of the bits was proportional to the size of the village. Village number four was the only one he should recommend our going to. When all was said, I gave our kindly informants some heads of tobacco and many thanks. Then M'bo sang them a hymn with the assistance of Pierre half a line behind him in a different key, but every bit as flat. The Fans seemed impressed, but any crowd would be by the hymn-singing of my crew, unless they were inmates of deaf and dumb asylums. Then we took our farewell, and thanked the village elaborately for its kind invitation to spend the night there on our way home, shoved off and paddled away in great style just to show those Fans what Igalwas could do.

We hadn't gone two hundred yards before we met a current coming round the end of a rock reef that was too strong for us to hold our own in, let alone progress. On to the bank I was ordered and went; it was a low slip of rugged confused boulders and fragments of rocks, carelessly arranged, and evidently under water in the wet season. I scrambled along, the men yelled and shouted and hauled the canoe, and the inhabitants of the village, seeing we were becoming amusing again, came, legging it like lamp-lighters, after us, young and old, male and female, to say nothing of the dogs. Some good souls helped the men haul, while I did my best to amuse the others by diving headlong from a large rock on to which I had elaborately climbed, into a thick clump of willow-leaved shrubs. They applauded my performance vociferously, and then assisted my efforts to extricate myself, and during the rest of my scramble they kept close to me, with keen competition for the front row, in hopes that I would do something like it again. But I refused the encore, because, bashful as I am, I could not but feel that my last perform- ance was carried out with all the superb reckless abandon of a Sarah Bernhardt, and a display of art of this order should satisfy any African village for a year at least. At last I got across the rocks on to a lovely little beach of white sand, and stood there talking, surrounded by my audience, until the canoe got over its difficulties and arrived almost as scratched as I; and then we again said farewell and paddled away, to the great grief of the natives, for they don't get a circus up above Njole every week, poor dears.

Now there is no doubt that that chief's plantain-leaf chart was an ingenious idea and a credit to him. There is also no doubt that the Fan mile is a bit Irish, a matter of nine or so of those of ordinary mortals, but I am bound to say I don't think, even allowing for this, that he put those pieces far enough apart. On we paddled a long way before we picked up village number one, mentioned in that chart. On again, still longer, till we came to village number two. Village number three hove in sight high up on a mountain-side soon after, but it was getting dark and the water worse, and the hill-sides growing higher and higher into nobly shaped mountains, forming with their forest-graced steep sides, a ravine that, in the gathering gloom, looked like an alley-way made of iron, for the foaming Ogowe. Village number four we anxiously looked for; village num- ber four we never saw; for round us came the dark, seeming to come out on to the river from the forests and the side ravines, where for some hours we had seen it sleeping, like a sailor with his clothes on in bad weather. On we paddled, looking for signs of village fires and seeing them not. The Erdgeist knew we wanted something, and seeing how we personally lacked it, thought it was beauty; and being in a kindly mood, gave it us, sending the lovely lingering flushes of his afterglow across the sky which, dying, left it that divine deep purple velvet which no one has dared to paint. Out in it came the great stars blazing high above us, and the dark round us was be- gemmed with fire-flies; but we were not as satisfied with these things as we should have been; what we wanted were fires to cook by and dry ourselves by, and all that sort of thing. The Erdgeist did not understand, and so left us when the afterglow had died away, with only enough starlight to see the flying foam of the rapids ahead and around us, and not enough to see the great trees that had fallen from the bank into the water. These, when the rapids were not too noisy, we could listen for because the black current rushes through their branches with an impatient 'lish, swish'; but when there was a rapid roaring close alongside we ran into those trees, and got ourselves mauled, and had ticklish times getting on our course again. Now and again we ran up against great rocks noisily fighting in the arena of the white water. Still on we poled and paddled. About 8 p.m. we came to a corner, a bad one; but we were unable to leap on to the bank and haul round, not being able to see either the details or the exact position of the said bank, and we felt, I think naturally, disinclined to spring in the direction of such bits of country as we had had experience of during the afternoon with nothing but the aid we might have got from a compass hastily viewed by the transitory light of a lucifer match, and even this would not have informed us how many tens of feet of tree fringe lay between us and the land, so we did not attempt it. One must be careful at times, or nasty accidents may follow. We fought our way round that corner, yelling defiance at the water, and dealt with succeeding corners on the *vi et armis* plan, breaking, ever and anon, a pole. About 9.30 we got into a savage rapid. We fought it inch by inch. The canoe jammed herself on some barely sunken rocks in it. We shoved her off over them. She tilted over and chucked us out. The rocks round being just awash, we survived and got her straight again, and got into her and drove her unmercifully; she struck again and bucked like a bronco, and we fell in heaps upon each other, but stayed inside that time—the men by the aid of their intelligent feet, I by clinching my hands into the bush rope lacing which ran round the rim of the canoe and the meaning of which I did not understand when I left Talagouga. We sorted ourselves out hastily and sent her at it again. Smash went a sorely tried pole and a paddle. Round and round we went in an exultant whirlpool which, in a light-hearted, maliciously joking way, hurled us tail first out of it into the current. Now the grand point in these canoes of having both ends alike declared itself; for at this juncture all we had to do was to revolve on our own axis and commence life anew with what had been the bow for the stern. Of course we were defeated, we could not go up any further without the aid of our lost poles and paddles, so we had to go down for shelter somewhere, anywhere, and down at a terrific pace in the white water we went. While hitched among the rocks the arrangement of our crew had been altered, Pierre joining M'bo in the bows; this piece of precaution was frustrated by our getting turned round, so our position was what you might call precarious, until we got into another whirlpool, when we persuaded nature to start us right end on. This was only a matter of minutes, whirlpools being plentiful, and then M'bo and Pierre, provided with our surviving poles, stood in the bows to fend us off rocks, as we shot towards them; while we midship paddles sat, helping to steer, and when occasion arose, which did with lightning rapidity, to whack the whirlpools with the flat of our paddles to break their force. Cook crouched in the stern concentrating his mind on steering only. A most excellent arrangement in theory and the safest practical one no doubt, but it did not work out what you might call brilliantly well; though each department did its best. We dashed full tilt towards high rocks, things twenty to fifty feet above water. Midship backed and flapped like fury; M'bo and Pierre received the shock on their poles; sometimes we glanced successfully aside and flew on; sometimes we didn't. The shock being too much for M'bo and Pierre they were driven back on me, who got flattened on to the cargo of bundles which, being now firmly tied in, couldn't spread the confusion further aft; but the shock of the canoe's nose against the rock did so in style, and the rest of the crew fell forward on to the bundles, me, and themselves. So shaken up together were we several times that night, that it's a wonder to me, considering the hurry, that we sorted ourselves out correctly with our own particular legs and arms. And although we in the middle of the canoe did some very spirited flapping, our whirlpool-breaking was no more successful than M'bo and Pierre's fending off, and many a wild waltz we danced that night with the waters of the River Ogowe.

*Travels in West Africa.* By Mary H. Kingsley. 1897. Pp. 168–74.

# NORTH AMERICA

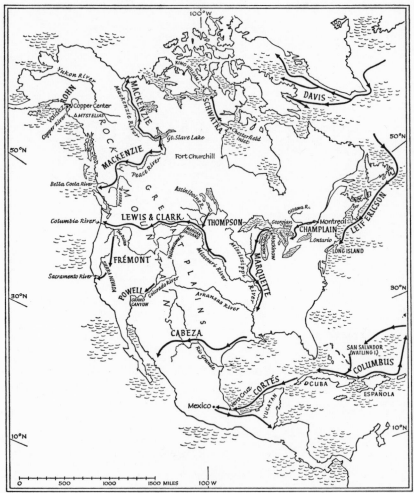

100°W

DAVIS

KING WILLIAM I.

SCHWATKA

Yukon River

Copper Center

VALDEZ

ST JOHN

Copper River

MT ST ELIAS

Mackenzie River

MACKENZIE

50°N

R O C K Y

M O U N T A I N S

MACKENZIE

Gt. Slave Lake

Fort Churchill

Chesterfield Inlet

Peace River

50°N

Bella Coola River

Assiniboine R.

Columbia River

LEWIS & CLARK

THOMPSON

Georgian Bay

Ottawa R.

CHAMPLAIN

Montreal

LEIF ERICSON

FRÉMONT

The Dalles

Yellowstone R.

MANDAN INDIANS

Missouri River

Mississippi River

MARQUETTE

Muskingum

L. Ontario

LONG ISLAND

Sacramento River

SIERRA NEVADA

POWELL

GRAND CANYON

Colorado River

G R E A T

P L A I N S

Arkansas River

30°N

30°N

CABEZA

Rio Grande

SAN SALVADOR (WATLING I.)

COLUMBUS

CORTÉS

Vera Cruz

CUBA

ESPAÑOLA

Mexico

YUCATAN

10°N

10°N

0    500    1000    1500 MILES    100 W

© CASSELL & CO. LTD. 1962

# N·AMERICA

# Leif Ericson

## c. 1002

THOUGH attempts have been made to establish that America was first reached by the Irish or Welsh—to go no further back into history—it is now generally accepted that the Norsemen were the first Europeans to reach that continent. This discovery was part of the general outward movement from Scandinavia which in the early Middle Ages brought the Norsemen to the British Isles, Normandy, Sicily, Southern Italy and as far as Constantinople. Iceland was colonized by Norse settlers in the ninth century A.D. As a result of internal strife, one Eric the Red was exiled, and sailing westwards discovered and later colonized Southern Greenland about A.D. 985. His explorations were extended by his son, Leif Ericson, who in A.D. 1002 sighted and sailed along the northeastern coasts of America. The story of his exploits was later written down and incorporated in the Norse Sagas. The exact extent of his voyage has been the subject of much controversy but it seems clear from the details given that he visited parts of Labrador, Newfoundland, and Nova Scotia; from the story about the grapes it has been argued that the most southerly point reached was in the neighbourhood of New York.

$\star$     $\star$     $\star$

Now the next event to be recorded (after the death of Olaf Tryggvason, September 1000) is that Bjarni Herjulfson came over from Greenland to Earl Eric (who became the ruler of a large part of Norway after Olaf's death), and the earl gave him a good reception. Bjarni told the story of his voyage when he saw the strange lands, but people thought that he had been lacking in curiosity, since he had nothing to report about those countries, and some fault was found with him on this account.[1] Bjarni was made an officer of the earl's court, but the following summer he went out to Greenland.

There was now much talk of exploration. Leif, Eric the Red's

---

[1] Driven off his course by a storm during a voyage to Greenland, Olaf had probably sighted the coast of North America.

son from Brattahlid, went to Bjarni Herjulfson and bought a ship of him, and engaged a crew of thirty-five men. Leif asked his father Eric still to be leader of the expedition. Eric excused himself, saying that he was now an old man, and less fitted to bear all the hardships than formerly. Leif said that he was still the member of the family who would bring the best luck; Eric thereupon gave way to Leif, and as soon as they were ready for it he rode from home, and came to within a short distance of the ship. The horse which Eric was riding stumbled, and he fell off and hurt his foot. Then Eric said, 'I am not fated to discover more countries than this in which we are now settled, and we ought not to bear one another company any longer.' So Eric went home to Brattahlid, but Leif went on board with his companions, thirty-five men. There was a southerner (a German) on the expedition called Tyrker.

Now they prepared their ship, and when they were ready they put to sea, and they found first the country which Bjarni found last. There they sailed up to the land, and having cast anchor and lowered a boat, went ashore and saw no grass there. The background was all great glaciers, and all the intermediate land from the sea to the glaciers was like one flat rock, and the country seemed to them destitute of value. Then Leif said, 'We have not failed to land, like Bjarni; now I will give this country a name, and call it Helluland (the land of flat stone).[1] Thereupon they returned on board, after which they sailed to sea and discovered the second land. Again they sailed up to the land and cast anchor, then lowered the boat and went ashore. This land was low-lying and wooded, and wherever they went there were wide stretches of white sand, and the slope from the sea was not abrupt. Then Leif said, 'This land shall be given a name from its resources, and shall be called Markland (woodland),[2] after which they returned to the ship as quickly as possible. And they sailed after that in the open sea with a north-east wind, and were out two days before they saw land, towards which they sailed, and having come to an island which lay to the north of the mainland they landed on it, the weather being fine, and looked round; and they perceived that there was a dew on the grass, and it

[1] Generally identified with Newfoundland.
[2] Nova Scotia.

came about that they put their hands in the dew, and carried it to their mouths, and thought that they had never known anything so sweet as that was. Then they went back to the ship and sailing into the sound which lay between the island and the cape which ran north from the mainland they steered a westerly course past the cape. It was very shallow there at low tide, so that their ship ran aground, and soon it was a long way from the ship to the sea. But they were so very eager to get to land that they would not wait for the tide to rise under their ship, but hurried ashore where a river came out of a lake; but when the sea had risen under their ship they took the boat and rowed to the ship, and took her up the river and afterwards into the lake, where they cast anchor, and carrying their leather kitbags ashore they put up shelters, but later, on deciding to pass the winter there, they made large houses.

There was no want of salmon, either in the river or the lake, and bigger salmon than they had seen before; the amenities of the country were such, as it seemed to them, that no cattle would need fodder there in the winter; there came no frost in the winter, and the grass did not wither there much. Day and night were more equally divided there than in Greenland or Iceland; on the shortest day the sun was up over the (Icelandic) marks for both nones and breakfast time.

Now when they had finished building their houses, Leif said to his men, 'Now I will divide our party into two, and have the country explored, and one half shall stay at home in camp while the other explores the country, going no further than they can return by the evening, and not separating.' And so for a time they did this, Leif sometimes going with the explorers and at others staying at home in camp. Leif was a big, strong man, the handsomest of men in appearance, and clever; in fact he was in all respects an excellent commander.

It happened one evening that a man of their party was missing, and this was Tyrker the southerner. Leif was much distressed at this, for Tyrker had been long with his father and him, and had been very fond of Leif as a child; so now Leif, after finding great fault with his men, prepared to look for him, taking a dozen men with him. But when they had got a little way from camp Tyrker came towards them, and was received with joy. Leif saw at once that his foster-father was in good spirits.

Tyrker had a projecting forehead and a very small face with roving eyes; he was a small and insignificant man, but handy at every kind of odd job.

Then Leif said to him, 'Why are you so late, my foster-father, and why did you separate from your companions?' Tyrker at this spoke for a long time in German, rolling his eyes and grimacing, but the others did not distinguish what he was saying. But a little later he said in Norse, 'I did not go much further than you, (but) I have found something fresh to report. I found vines and grapes.' 'Is that true, foster-father?' said Leif. 'Certainly it is true,' he replied, 'for I was born where there was no lack of vines or grapes.'

Now they slept that night, but in the morning Leif said to his crew, 'We will now do two things, keeping separate days for each; we will gather grapes and cut down vines, and fell wood, to make a cargo for my ship,' and this suggestion was adopted. The story goes that their pinnance was full of grapes. So a cargo was cut for the ship, and in spring they made ready and sailed away, and Leif gave the country a name according to its resources, and called it Wineland[1].

So after this they put to sea, and the breeze was fair till they sighted Greenland, and the mountains under its glaciers. Then a man spoke up and said to Leif, 'Why are you steering the ship so much into the wind?' 'I am paying attention to my steering,' replied Leif, 'but to something else as well. What do you see that is strange?' They said they could see nothing remarkable. 'I do not know,' said Leif, 'whether it is a ship or a reef that I see.' Then they saw it, and said that it was a reef. But Leif was longer sighted than they, so that he saw men on the reef. 'Now,' said Leif, 'I wish that we should beat up wind, so as to reach them if they need our help and it is necessary to assist them, and if they are not peaceably disposed we are masters of the situation and they are not.' So they came up to the reef, and lowered their sail and cast anchor: and they launched a second dinghy that they had with them. Then Tyrker asked who was the captain (of the shipwrecked party). 'His name is

[1] A portion of the eastern coast of the United States; its exact location is hotly disputed.

Thori,' was the reply, 'and he is a Norseman, but what is your name?' Leif told his name. 'Are you a son of Eric the Red of Brattahlid?' said Thori. Leif assented. "Now," said Leif, 'I will take you all on board my ship, and as much of your stuff as the ship can hold.' They agreed to these terms, and afterwards they sailed to Ericsfjord with this freight, until they came to Brattahlid where they unloaded the ship. After that Leif invited Thori and Gudrid his wife, and three other men to stay with him, and procured lodgings for the rest of the crews, both Thori's men and his own. Leif took fifteen men from the reef; he was subsequently called Leif the lucky. So Leif gained both wealth and honour. That winter Thori's folk were much attacked by sickness, and Thori and a great part of his crew died.

*The Norse Discoverers of America; The Wineland Sagas*. Trsl. by G. M. Gathorne-Hardy. Clarendon Press, 1921.

# Christopher Columbus
## 1451-1506

THERE are many theories concerning the birthplace of Christopher Columbus (known to the Spaniards as Cristoval Colon and to the Italians as Cristoforo Colombo). The best authenticated and most widely held opinion is that he was born in poor circumstances in Genoa about A.D. 1451. After offering his services in vain to the King of Portugal, he went to Spain and secured the patronage of Queen Isabella. It is just possible that he had heard of the Norse voyages to Greenland and North America, but undoubtedly his imagination was fired by the stories of the riches of Cathay (China) and Zipangu (Japan) brought back to Western Europe by Marco Polo nearly two centuries earlier. His plan, probably inspired by the Italian geographer, Paolo Toscanelli (1397-1482) was to reach the reputedly rich and populous islands of eastern Asia by sailing westwards. Owing to miscalculating the size of the earth, he was convinced, on reaching the West Indies, that he had achieved his aim. Columbus's personality was complex and baffling, the extent and standard of his knowledge and capabilities difficult to assess, and his motives doubtless mixed; but, whether or to what extent he had been forestalled by others, the date of his arrival in the New World—September 1492—is a landmark in world history.

The following account—in the nature of an 'official despatch'—is the earliest at all complete account of his achievement by the Admiral of the 'Ocean Sea' himself. Traces of his acquaintance with legends of the East are evidenced by his remarks on the sweetness of the birds' song, the gold and spices, and the Great Khan.

★ ★ ★

Sir, As I know that you will be pleased at the great victory with which Our Lord has crowned my voyage, I write this to you, from which you will learn how in thirty-three days I passed from the Canary Islands to the Indies with the fleet which the most illustrious king and queen, our sovereigns, gave to me. And there I found very many islands filled with people innumerable, and of them all I have

154

taken possession for their highnesses, by proclamation made and with the royal standard unfurled, and no opposition was offered to me. To the first island which I found I gave the name San Salvador (Watlings Island), in remembrance of the Divine Majesty who has marvellously bestowed all this; the Indians call it 'Guanahani'. To the second, I gave the name Isla de Santa Maria de Concepcion (Rum Cay); to the third, Fernandina (Long Island); to the fourth, Isabella (Crooked Island); to the fifth, Isla Juana (Cuba), and so to each I gave a new name.

When I reached Juana I followed its coast to the westward, and I found it to be so extensive that I thought that it must be the mainland, the province of Catayo (Cathay). And since there were neither towns nor villages on the seashore but only small hamlets, with the people of which I could not have speech because they all fled immediately, I went forward on the same course, thinking that I should not fail to find great cities and towns. And at the end of many leagues, seeing that there was no change and that the coast was bearing me northwards, which I wished to avoid, since winter was already beginning and I proposed to make from it to the south, and as moreover the wind was carrying me forward, I determined not to wait for a change in the weather and retraced my path as far as a certain harbour known to me. And from that point I sent two men inland to learn if there were a king or great cities. They travelled three days' journey and found an infinity of small hamlets and people without number, but nothing of importance. For this reason they returned.

I understood sufficiently from other Indians whom I had already taken that this land was nothing but an island. And therefore I followed its coast eastwards for one hundred and seven leagues to the point where it ended. And from that cape, I saw another island, distant eighteen leagues from the former, to the east, to which I at once gave the name 'Española'. And I went there and followed its northern coast, as I had in the case of Juana, to the eastward for one hundred and eighty-eight great leagues in a straight line. This island and all the others are very fertile to a limitless degree, and this island is extremely so. In it there are many harbours on the coast of the sea, beyond comparison with others which I know in Christendom, and many rivers, good and large, which is marvellous. Its lands are high, and there are in it very many sierras and very lofty mountains beyond comparison with the island of Teneriffe. All are most beautiful, of a thousand shapes, and all are accessible and filled with trees of a thousand kinds and tall, and they seem to touch the sky. And I am told that they never lose their foliage, as I can understand, for I saw them as green and as lovely as they are in Spain in May, and some of them were flowering, some bearing fruit, and some in another stage according to their nature. And the nightingale was singing and other birds of a thousand kinds in the month of November there where I went. There are six or eight kinds of palm which are a wonder to behold on account of their beautiful variety, but so are the other trees and fruits and plants. In it are marvellous pine groves, and there are very large tracts of cultivatable lands, and there is honey, and there are birds of many kinds and fruits in great diversity. In the interior are mines of metals, and the population is without number. Española is a marvel.

The sierras and mountains, the plains and arable lands and pastures, are so lovely and rich for planting and sowing, for breeding cattle of every kind, for building towns and villages. The harbours of the sea here are such as cannot be believed to exist unless they have been seen, and so with the rivers, many and great, and good waters, the majority of which contain gold. In the trees and fruits and plants there is a great difference from Juana. In this island, there are many spices and great mines of gold and of other metals.

The people of this island, and of all the other islands which I have found and of which I have information, all go naked, men and women, as their mothers bore them, although some women cover a single place with the leaf of a plant or with a net of cotton which they make for the purpose. They have no iron or steel or weapons, nor are they fitted to use them, not because they are not well built men and of handsome stature but because they are very marvellously timorous. They have no other arms than weapons made of canes cut in seeding time, to the ends of which they fix a small sharpened stick. And they do not dare to make use of these, for many times it has happened that I have sent ashore two or three men to some town to have speech, and countless people have come out to them, and as soon as they have seen my men approaching they have fled, even a father not waiting for his son. And this, not because ill has been done to anyone; on the contrary, at every point where I have been and have been able to have speech, I have given to them of all that I had, such as cloth and many other things, without receiving anything for it; but so they are incurably timid. . . .

And I gave a thousand handsome good things which I had brought in order that they might conceive affection, and more than that, might become Christians and be inclined to the love and service of their highnesses and of the whole Castilian nation, and strive to aid us and to give us of the things which they have in abundance and which are necessary to us. And they do not know any creed and are not idolators; only they all believe that power and good are in the heavens, and they are very firmly convinced that I, with these ships and men, came from the heavens, and in this belief they everywhere received me, after they had overcome their fear. And this does not come because they are ignorant; on the contrary, they are of a very acute intelligence and are men who navigate all those seas, so that it is amazing how good an account they give of everything, but it is because they have never seen people clothed or ships of such a kind.

And as soon as I arrived in the Indies, in the first island which I found, I took by force some of them in order that they might learn and give me information of that which there is in those parts, and so it was that they soon understood us, and we them, either by speech or signs, and they have been very serviceable. I still take them with me, and they are always assured that I come from Heaven, for all the intercourse which they have had with me; and they were the first to announce this wherever I went, and the others went running from house to house and to the neighbouring towns with loud cries of, 'Come! Come to see the people from Heaven!' So all, men and women alike, when their minds were set at rest concerning us, came, so that not one, great or small, remained behind, and all brought something to eat and drink which they gave with extraordinary affection. In all the island they have very many canoes, like rowing *fustas*, some larger, some smaller, and some are larger than a *fusta* of eighteen benches. They are not so broad because they are made of a single log of wood, but a *fusta* would not keep up with them in rowing, since their speed is a thing incredible. And in these they navigate among all those islands, which are innumerable, and carry their goods. One of these canoes I have seen with seventy and eighty men in her and each one with his oar.

In all these islands I saw no great diversity in the appearance of the people or in their manners and language. On the contrary, they all understand one another, which is a very curious thing, on account of which I hope that their highnesses will determine upon their conversion to our holy faith, towards which they are very inclined.

I have already said how I went one hundred and seven leagues in a straight line from west to east along the seashore of the island Juana, and as a result of that voyage I can say that this island is larger than England and Scotland together[1] for, beyond these one hundred and seven leagues, there remain to the westward two provinces to which I have not gone. One of these provinces they call 'Avan',[2] and there the people are born with tails; and these provinces cannot have a length of less than fifty or sixty leagues, as I could understand from those Indians whom I have and who know all the islands.

The other, Española, has a circumference greater than all Spain, from Colibre (Collioure) by the sea coast to Fuenterabia in Vizcaya[3], since I voyaged along one side one hundred and eighty-eight great leagues in a straight line from west to east. It is a land to be desired and, seen, it is never to be left. And in it, although of all I have taken possession for their highnesses and all are more richly endowed than I know how, or am able to say, and I hold them all for their highnesses so that they may dispose of them as, and as absolutely as, of the Kingdom of Castile, in this Española, in the situation most convenient and in the best position for the mines of gold; and for all intercourse as well with the mainland here as with that there, belonging to the Grand Khan, where will be great trade and gain, I have taken possession of a large town, to which I gave the name *Villa de Navidad*, and in it I have made fortifications and a fort, which

[1] A considerable over-estimate.
[2] Perhaps Havana.
[3] Another over-estimate.

now will by this time be entirely finished; and I have left in it sufficient men for such a purpose with arms and artillery and provisions for more than a year, and a *fusta*, and one, a master of all seacraft, to build others, and great friendship with the king of that land, so much so, that he was proud to call me and to treat me as a brother.[1]

Done in the caravel, off the Canary Islands,[2] on the fifteenth of February, in the year one thousand four hundred and ninety-three.

At your orders.                                                    El Almirante.

---

[1] When Columbus returned, however, the fort had been destroyed and the garrison slaughtered.
[2] Columbus was in fact off Santa Maria, in the Azores.

Letter of Columbus on his first voyage. Probably addressed to Louis de Santangel and printed at Barcelona in 1493. Jane, C.: Voyages of Columbus, vol. I (Hakluyt Soc. ser. ii. vol. 65, 1930.)

# Hernando Cortés
## 1485-1547

THE second and decisive leap forward of Spanish power in the New World was the work of Hernando Cortés, the outstanding character among the 'second generation' of Spanish *conquistadores*. After making a reputation and acquiring some wealth in Cuba, he was sent by the Governor, Diego Velazquez, in 1518 on what was planned as a relatively modest expedition to recently discovered Yucatan. Cortés, however, staked all on one throw, and boldly embarked upon the conquest of the Aztec empire of Mexico with an army of five hundred men, fifteen horses and six cannon. Having seized the capital, Tenochtitlan (Mexico City), he was forced to retreat but, reorganizing his forces and aided by dissensions among his opponents, he finally subjugated it in 1521. Cortés displayed all the qualities of a Renaissance despot with a zest for life and power; he combined courage, ruthlessness, enterprise and diplomacy with a lively interest in the world around him, as is evidenced by his understanding of native life, and in the account below of the volcano Popocatepetl. The second extract illustrates his pertinacity and ingenuity on his hazardous march overland to Honduras in the years 1524-26 to consolidate Spanish rule in that province.

★    ★    ★

Eight leagues from this city of Cholula[1] there are two marvellously high mountains[2] whose summits still at the end of August are covered with snow so that nothing else can be seen of them. From the higher of the two both by day and night a great volume of smoke often comes forth and rises up into the clouds as straight as a staff, with such force that although a very violent wind continuously blows over the mountain range yet it cannot change the direction of the column. Since I have ever been desirous of sending your Majesty a very particular account of everything that I met with in this land, I was eager to know the secret of this which seemed to

[1] The scene of a bloody contest on Cortés's first march to Mexico City.
[2] Popocatepetl (17,887 feet) and Ixtoccihuatl.

me not a little marvellous, and accordingly sent ten men such
as were well fitted for the expedition with certain natives to guide
them to find out the secret of the smoke where and how it arose.
These men set out and made every effort to climb to the summit
but without success on account of the thickness of the snow, the
repeated wind storms in which ashes from the volcano were blown
in their faces and also the great severity of the temperature, but
they reached very near the top, so near in fact that being there when
the smoke began to rush out, they reported that it did so with such
noise and violence that the whole mountain seemed like to fall
down; thereupon they descended, bringing a quantity of snow and
icicles for us to see, which seemed a novelty indeed, it being so hot
everywhere in these parts according to the opinion of explorers up
to now; especially since this land is said to be in the twentieth degree
of altitude where great heat is always found. . . .

I was more cast down at the sight of this arm or inlet of the sea[1]
than I could possibly describe. To pass it was impossible on account
of its width and the lack of canoes, but even had we them for the
men and baggage the horses would have been unable to get across,
for lining either bank were great marshes and large tree roots
surrounding them, so that for this and other reasons any idea of
getting them across was quite impossible. Yet to attempt to retrace
our steps would, it was obvious, mean the death of us all, on account
of the wretched roads we had followed and the heavy falls of rain
that had since taken place. For we were aware that the river in its
rise must have swept away all the bridges we had made, and to
build them again would be a matter of tremendous difficulty since
the men were now all wearied out. In addition we bethought us
that we had now eaten all the stores to be had on the road and
should we return would find nothing more to eat; for I had many
men and horses with me, including in addition to the Spaniards
more than three thousand native Mexicans. Yet the obstacle to our
further progress remained as I have described to your Majesty,
and so formidable a one that the wit of man was powerless to
remedy it, had not God, Who is the true remedy and succour of

[1] This was the Rio Tabasco, in the state of that name.

those in affliction or want, put it into my mind. I took the little canoe which the Spaniards whom I had sent on ahead had used and had the river sounded from one bank to the other, when it was found that there was an average depth of four arms' length. I ordered lances to be tied together to examine the bottom and another two arms' length of mud was discovered, so that the total depth amounted to six arms' length.

Accordingly as a desperate remedy I determined to make a bridge over it. I immediately ordered wood to be got to those measurements, of some nine to ten arms' length, allowing for what would rise above the surface of the water. I ordered the Indian chieftains who had accompanied me to cut and bring wood of this length, each one according to the number of his followers. Meanwhile the Spaniards and I began to drive in the stakes, using rafts and the small canoe with two others which were found later, but to all the task seemed impossible to accomplish. Some even whispered behind my back that it would be better to turn back before all the men should be worn out and unable through weakness and hunger to do so. Indeed the murmur grew so loud among my men that they almost dared to say it to my face. Upon this, seeing them so discontented (and in truth they had reason to be since the task was truly overpowering and they had now nothing to eat but roots and herbs) I ordered them to abandon work on the bridge, saying that I would complete it with the help of the Indians. Forthwith I called all the native chieftains together and bade them consider in what plight we were, that we must either pass over or perish. I therefore begged them very earnestly to urge on their people that the bridge might be finished, and once crossed we should enter upon a great province called Acalan where there was great abundance of provisions and where we could encamp; moreover I reminded them that in addition to the stores to be found in that land I had ordered stores to be brought up to us in canoes from the ships and that therefore in that province we should have abundance of everything; in addition to all this I promised them that when we returned to Mexico they should be very fully rewarded by me in your Majesty's name. They promised me they would undertake the work, and began forthwith to divide it out among themselves, working at it with such skill and speed that in four days they had finished it and all the horses and men were able to pass over. Moreover it will take more than ten years to destroy it, provided it is not interfered with by the hand of man; and even so almost the only method would be to burn it, for it contains more than a thousand stakes the smallest of which is about the thickness of a man's body, to say nothing of smaller logs which are beyond number. And I can assure your Majesty that I think there is no man who could rightly declare after what plan or fashion the natives built this bridge; all that one can say is that it is the most extraordinary thing one has ever seen.

No sooner had the men and horses reached the other side than we came upon a great marsh fully two bow-shots broad and the most frightful thing that ever my men set eyes on. All the horses, riderless as they were, sank up to the saddle-cloths, nothing else appearing above the slime. To attempt to urge them on was but to make them sink the deeper, in such wise that we lost all hope of being able to get a single horse across, and thought that they must all perish. Nevertheless we set to and placed bundles of grass and large branches underneath them on which they were borne up, and no longer sank, matters being thus somewhat relieved. Then as we were busy going thither and thither in our task a lane of water and slime opened up in the middle so that the horses could swim a little, by which help it pleased God that they should all escape without injury, although so fatigued and utterly worn out that they could hardly remain on their feet.

*Hernando Cortés: Five Letters, 1519-1526.* Trsl. by J. B. Morris. Archer House, Inc., 1929.

# Alvar Nuñez Cabeza da Vaca
## 1507-1559

In June 1527 an expedition of six hundred soldiers and colonists, under Pamfilo de Narvaez, sailed from Cuba to open up the country north of the Gulf of Mexico. After an amazing series of shipwrecks and disasters along the coast west of Florida and Louisiana, Alvar Nuñez Cabeza da Vaca, one of the survivors, passed five years as a trader among the Indians of the Texas coastlands. Finally, with three other survivors of the expedition, he succeeded in escaping and making his way to Mexico. His route appears to have lain from the lower Rio Colorado (Texas) to the Rio Grande and thence approximately due westwards to the Rio Sonora near the present town of Ures, where he met a band of Spanish slave-hunters. The extract printed here describes his experiences while traversing western Texas between the Rio Pecos and the Rio Grande.

★ ★ ★

We left there and travelled through so many sorts of people of such diverse languages, the memory fails to recall them. They ever plundered each other, and those that lost, like those that gained, were fully content. We drew so many followers that we had not use for their services. While on our way through these vales, every Indian carried a club three palms in length, and kept on the alert. On raising a hare, which animals are abundant, they surround it directly and throw numerous clubs at it with astonishing precision. Thus they cause it to run from one to another; so that, according to my thinking, it is the most pleasing sport which can be imagined, as oftentimes the animal runs into the hand. So many did they give us that night when we stopped we had eight or ten back-loads apiece. Those having bows were not with us; they dispersed about the ridge in pursuit of deer; and at dark came bringing five or six for each of us, besides quail, and other game. Indeed, whatever they either killed or found, was put before us, without themselves daring to take anything until we had blessed it, though they should be

164

expiring of hunger, they having so established the rule, since marching with us.

The women carried many mats, of which the men made us houses, each of us having a separate one, with all his attendants. After these were put up, we ordered the deer and hares to be roasted, with the rest that had been taken. This was done by means of certain ovens made for the purpose. Of each we took a little and the remainder we gave to the principal personage of the people coming with us, directing him to divide it among the rest. Every one brought his portion to us, that we might breathe upon and give it our benediction, for not until then did they dare eat any of it. Frequently we were accompanied by three or four thousand persons, and as we had to breathe upon and sanctify the food and drink for each, and grant permission to do the many things they would come to ask, it may be seen how great was the annoyance. The women first brought us prickly pears, spiders, worms, and whatever else they could gather; for even were they famishing, they would eat nothing unless we gave it them.

In company with these, we crossed a great river[1] coming from the north, and passing over some plains thirty leagues in extent, we found many persons coming a long distance to receive us, who met us on the road over which we were to travel, and welcomed us in the manner of those we had left.

From this place was another method of receiving us, as respects the pillage. Those who came out in the ways to bring us presents were not plundered; but on our coming into their houses, themselves offered us all they had as well as the houses. We gave the things to the chief personages who accompanied us, that they should divide them; those who were despoiled always followed us until coming to a populous country, where they might repair their loss. They would tell those among whom we came, to retain everything and make no concealment, as nothing could be done without our knowledge, and we might cause them to die, as the sun revealed everything to us. So great was their fear that during the first days they were with us, they continually trembled, without daring even

[1] Rio Grande.

to speak or raise their eyes to the heavens. They guided us through more than fifty leagues of desert, over rough mountains, which being dry were without game, and in consequence we suffered much from hunger.

At the termination we forded a very large river,[1] the water coming up to our breasts. From this place, many of the people began to sicken from the great privation and labour they had undergone in the passage of those ridges, which are sterile and difficult in the extreme. They conducted us to certain plains at the base of the mountains, where people came to meet us from a great distance, and received us as the last had done, and gave so many goods to those who came with us that the half were left because they could not be carried. I told those who gave, to resume the goods that they might not lie there and be lost; but they answered they could in no wise do so, as it was not their custom after they had bestowed a thing to take it back; so considering the articles no longer of value, they were left to perish.

We told these people that we desired to go where the sun sets, and they said inhabitants in that direction were remote. We commanded them to send and make known our coming; but they strove to excuse themselves the best they could, the people being their enemies, and they did not wish to go to them. Not daring to disobey, however, they sent two women, one of their own, the other a captive from that people; for the women can negotiate even though there be war. We followed them, and stopped at a place where we agreed to wait. They tarried five days; and the Indians said they could not have found anybody.

We told them to conduct us towards the north; and they answered, as before, that except afar off there were no people in that direction, and nothing to eat, nor could water be found. Notwithstanding all this, we persisted, and said we desired to go in that course. They still tried to excuse themselves in the best manner possible. At this we became offended, and one night I went out to sleep in the woods apart from them; but directly they came to where I was, and remained all night without sleep, talking to me in great fear, telling me how terrified they were, beseeching us to be no longer

[1] They were probably recrossing the Rio Grande.

angry, and said that they would lead us in the direction it was our wish to go, though they knew they should die on the way.

Whilst we still feigned to be displeased lest their fright should leave them, a remarkable circumstance happened, which was that on the same day many of the Indians became ill, and the next day eight men died. Abroad in the country, wheresoever this became known, there was such dread that it seemed as if the inhabitants would die of fear at sight of us. They besought us not to remain angered, nor require that more of them should die. They believed we caused their death by only willing it, when in truth it gave us so much pain that it could not be greater; for, beyond their loss, we feared they might all die, or abandon us of fright, and that other people thenceforward would do the same, seeing what had come to these. We prayed to God, our Lord, to relieve them; and from that time the sick began to get better. . . .

The sick having recovered, and three days having passed since we came to the place, the women whom we sent away returned and said they had found very few people; nearly all had gone for cattle, being then in the season. We ordered the convalescent to remain and the well to go with us, and that at the end of two days' journey those women should go with two of our number to fetch up the people, and bring them on the road to receive us. Consequently, the next morning the most robust started with us. At the end of three days' travel we stopped, and the next day Alonzo del Castillo set out with Estevanico the negro, taking the two women as guides. She that was the captive led them to the river which ran between some ridges, where was a town at which her father lived; and these habitations were the first seen, having the appearance and structure of houses.

Here Castillo and Estevanico arrived and, after talking with the Indians, Castillo returned at the end of three days to the spot where he had left us, and brought five or six of the people. He told us he had found fixed dwellings of civilization, that the inhabitants lived on beans and pumpkins, and that he had seen maize. This news the most of anything delighted us, and for it we gave infinite thanks to our Lord. Castillo told us the negro was coming with all the population to wait for us in the road not far off. Accordingly we left and, having travelled a league and a half, we met the negro and the people coming to receive us. They gave us beans, many pumpkins, calabashes, blankets of cowhide and other things. As this people and those who came with us were enemies and spoke not each other's language, we discharged the latter, giving them what we received, and we departed with the others. Six leagues from there, as the night set in we arrived at the houses where great festivities were made over us. We remained one day, and the next set out with these Indians. They took us to the settled habitations of others, who lived upon the same food. . . .

Two days being spent while we tarried, we resolved to go in search of the maize. We did not wish to follow the path leading to where the cattle are, because it is towards the north, and for us very circuitous, since we ever held it certain that going towards the sunset we must find what we desired.

Thus we took our way, and traversed all the country until coming out at the South Sea. Nor was the dread we had of the sharp hunger through which we should have to pass (as in verity we did, throughout the seventeen days' journey of which the natives spoke) sufficient to hinder us. During all that time in ascending by the river they gave us many coverings of cowhide; but we did not eat of the fruit. Our sustenance each day was about a handful of deer-suet which we had a long time been used to saving for such trials. Thus we passed the entire journey of seventeen days, and at the close we crossed the river and travelled other seventeen days.

As the sun went down upon some plains that lie between chains of very great mountains, we found a people who for the third part of the year eat nothing but the powder of straw and, that being the season when we passed, we also had to eat of it, until reaching permanent habitations, where was abundance of maize brought together. They gave us a large quantity in grain and flour, pumpkins, beans, and shawls of cotton. With all these we loaded our guides, who went back the happiest creatures on earth. We gave thanks to God, our Lord, for having brought us where we had found so much food.

Some houses are of earth, the rest all of cane mats. From this point we marched through more than a hundred leagues of country, and continually found settled domiciles, with plenty of maize and beans. The people gave us many deer and cotton shawls better than those of New Spain, many beads and certain corals found on the South Sea, and fine turquoises that come from the north. Indeed they gave us everything they had. To me they gave five emeralds made into arrow-heads, which they use at their singing and dancing. They appeared to be very precious. I asked whence they got these; and they said the stones were brought from some lofty mountains that stand towards the north, where were populous towns and very large houses, and that they were purchased with plumes and the feathers of parrots.

Among this people the women are treated with more decorum than in any part of the Indias we had visited. They wear a shirt of cotton that falls as low as the knee, and over it half-sleeves with skirts reaching to the ground, made of dressed deer-skin. It opens in front and is brought close with straps of leather. They soap this with a certain root that cleanses well, by which they are enabled to keep it becomingly. Shoes are worn. The people all came to us that we should touch and bless them, they being very urgent, which we could accomplish only with great labour, for sick and well all wished to go with a benediction. Many times it occurred that some of the women who accompanied us gave birth; and so soon as the children were born the mothers would bring them to us that we should touch and bless them.

These Indians ever accompanied us until they delivered us to others; and all held full faith in our coming from heaven. While travelling, we went without food all day until night, and we ate so little as to astonish them. We never felt exhaustion, neither were we in fact at all weary, so inured were we to hardship. We possessed great influence and authority; to preserve both, we seldom talked with them. The negro was in constant conversation; he informed himself about the ways we wished to take, of the towns there were, and the matters we desired to know.

We passed through many and dissimilar tongues. Our Lord granted us favour with the people who spoke them, for they always understood us, and we them. We questioned them and received their answers by signs, just as if they spoke our language and we theirs; for, although we knew six languages, we could not everywhere avail ourselves of them, there being a thousand differences.

*Spanish Explorers in the Southern United States, 1528–43*. Edited by F. W. Hodge and T. H. Lewis. New York, Barnes and Noble, 1925.

# Samuel de Champlain
## 1567-1635

THE exploration and settlement of Canada was inaugurated by the Frenchman Jacques Cartier who in 1535 ascended the St. Lawrence River as far as the Lachine rapids and established a settlement at Montreal. The next decisive step, the move into the Great Lakes region, was inspired and initiated by Samuel de Champlain, the founder of Quebec. In 1613 he discovered the Ottawa river and two years later ascended it and thence passed to the shores of Lake Huron—the first European to do so—as narrated in this extract. After the events described therein, he joined a Huron party to raid the Iroquois to the south of Lake Ontario. The raid failed and Champlain was wounded, but he was carried on the return journey by his allies. Champlain's importance in Canadian history lies not in his own explorations but in the dynamic influence he exerted on his fellow countrymen.

★     ★     ★

On the ninth of the said month [July 1615] I embarked[1] with two others, namely one of our interpreters and my own man, accompanied by ten savages, in the said two canoes, which is all they could carry, inasmuch as they were heavily loaded and encumbered with clothing, which hindered me from taking more men.

We continued our voyage up the river St. Lawrence some six leagues, and into the Rivière des Prairies, which empties into the said river, leaving the St. Louis rapid five or six leagues farther upstream on our left hand. We passed several little rapids in this stream and then entered a lake, crossing which we again entered the river where I had been before, which leads to the Algonquins, a distance of eighty-nine leagues from the St. Louis rapid; and of that river I have given ample description and an account of my discoveries in my preceding book, printed in the year 1614. For that reason I shall not speak of it in this work but shall pursue my journey as far as the lake of the Algonquins, at which point we entered a

[1] Champlain had come up the St. Lawrence from Quebec.

river[1] which flows into the said lake, up which we went some thirty-five leagues past a great number of rapids, either by portage or by tracking, through an ill-favoured region full of pines, birches and a few oaks, very rocky, and in many places rather hilly. Moreover it is quite a wilderness, being barren and uninhabited except for a few Algonquin savages, called Otaguottouemins, who dwell in that country and live by hunting and by the fish they catch in the rivers, ponds and lakes with which the country is well provided. It is true that God appears to have been pleased to give this frightful and abandoned region some things in their season for the refreshment of man and of the inhabitants of these parts; for I can assure you that along the streams there are such a great quantity of blue-berries, which is a small fruit very good to eat, and many raspberries and other small fruits, and in such plenty that it is marvellous. These people who live there dry these fruits for their winter supply, just as we do plums in France for Lent. We left that river which comes from the north and is the one by which the savages go to the Saguenay, and for the purpose of bartering furs for tobacco. This place is in latitude 46°,[2] being very pleasant to look at, although unproductive.

Continuing our way by land, after leaving the river of the Algonquins, we passed through several lakes, where the savages carry their canoes, until, on the twenty-sixth day of the said month, after having made, either by land or by the lakes, twenty-five leagues or thereabouts, we entered the Lake of the Nipissings,[3] in the latitude of 46° 15'. This done, we reached the lodges of the savages, where we stayed two days. They gave us a very kind reception and were in goodly number; they are a race who cultivate the soil very little. . . .

During the time I was with them, the chief of these people and other of their head men feasted us on several occasions, according to their custom, and took the trouble to go fishing and hunting in order to entertain us as daintily as they could. These tribes were in number quite seven or eight hundred souls, who live usually on the lake

[1] The Ottawa River.
[2] Mattawa, in lat. 46° 18' N.
[3] Lake Nipissing.

where are a great number of very pretty islands, and among others one more than six leagues long, on which are three or four fine ponds and a number of beautiful meadows. It is bordered by very fine woods containing plenty of game that haunts these little ponds where the savages catch fish. The north side of the lake is very pleasant; there are fair meadows for pasturing cattle and many little streams discharging into the lake.

At that time they were fishing in a lake[1] very abundant in many kinds of fish; among others a very good one, which is a foot in length and also other varieties which the savages catch in order to dry and to lay up in store. This lake is some eight leagues wide and twenty-five long, and into it flows a river which comes from the north-west,[2] up which they go to trade the goods which we give them in barter and exchange for their furs, with those who dwell there, who live by the chase and by fishing. It is a country stocked with great numbers both of animals, birds and fish.

Having rested two days with the chief of the said Nipissings, we re-embarked in our canoes and entered a river[3] flowing out of this lake, and made some thirty-five leagues along it, and passed several little rapids, some by portaging, others by running them, as far as Lake Attigouautan.[4] This whole region is even more unprepossessing than the former, for I did not see in the whole length of it ten acres of arable land, but only rocks and a country somewhat hilly. It is quite true that near Lake Attigouautan we found some Indian corn, but in small quantity; and here our savages went and gathered squashes, which seemed to us good, for our provisions were beginning to fail, through the bad management of the said savages, who ate so heartily at the start that towards the end very little remained, although we made but one meal a day. It is true, as I have stated above, that there was no lack of blue-berries and raspberries; for otherwise we should have been in danger of starvation.

We met with three hundred men of a tribe named by us the *Cheveux relevés*, or 'High Hairs', because they had them elevated and

[1] Lake Nipissing.
[2] Sturgeon river.
[3] French river.
[4] Lake Huron, at Georgian Bay.

arranged very high and better combed than our courtiers, and there is no comparison, in spite of the irons and methods these have at their disposal. This seems to give them a fine appearance. They wear no breech cloths, and are much carved about the body in divisions of various patterns. They paint their faces with different colours and have their nostrils pierced and their ears fringed with beads. When they leave their homes they carry a club. I visited them and gained some slight acquaintance and made friends with them. I gave a hatchet to their chief who was as happy and pleased with it as if I had made him some rich gift and, entering into conversation with him, I asked him about his country, which he drew for me with charcoal on a piece of tree-bark. He gave me to understand that they had come to this place to dry the fruit called blue-berries, to serve them as manna in the winter when they can no longer find anything. . . .

The next day we parted, and continued our journey along the shore of this Lake of the Attigouautans, in which there are a great number of islands; and we made about forty-five leagues, keeping along the shore of this lake. It is very large, being nearly four hundred leagues in length,[1] from east to west, and fifty leagues wide, and in view of its great size I named it the Freshwater Sea. It abounds in many kinds of excellent fish, both those we have and those we have not, and principally in trout, which are of enormous size; I have seen some that were as much as four and a half feet long, and the smallest one sees are two and a half feet in length. Also pike of like size, and a certain kind of sturgeon, a very large fish and marvellously good to eat. The country bordering upon this lake along the north shore is partly rugged and partly flat, uninhabited by savages and slightly covered with trees including oaks. Then afterwards we crossed a bay[2] which forms one of the extremities of the lake, and made some seven leagues until we reached the country of the Attigouautan, and came on the first of August to a village called Otoüacha. Here we found a great change in the country, this part being very fine, mostly cleared, with many hills and several streams

[1] An exaggerated estimate.
[2] Georgian Bay.

which make it an agreeable district. I went to look at their Indian corn which at that time was far advanced for the season.

This district seemed to me very pleasant in contrast to such a bad country as that through which we had just come. On the morrow I went to another village called Carmaron, distant a league from this one, where they received us very kindly, making a feast for us with their bread, squash and fish; as to meat it is very scarce there. The chief of this village begged me hard to stay there, which I could not grant him, but returned to our own village. Here on the second night, having gone outside the lodge to escape the fleas, which were very numerous and a great pest to us, a shameless girl came boldly up to me, offering to keep me company, which I declined with thanks, sending her away with gentle remonstrances, and I passed the night with some of the savages.

On the morrow I left that village to go to another, called Toua-guainchain, and to another called Tequenonquiaye, in both of which the inhabitants received us very kindly, giving us the best cheer they could with their Indian corn served in various ways. This country is so very fine and fertile that it is a pleasure to travel about in it.

Thence I had them conduct me to Carhagouha,[1] which is enclosed for defence and protection by a triple wooden palisade, thirty-five feet high. In this village lived Father Joseph, whom we found there and were very glad to see him in good health, he on his side being no less delighted; for he expected nothing less than to see me in that country. And on the twelfth day of August the reverend Father celebrated the holy mass, and a cross was set up near a little cabin apart from the village, which the savages built while I was staying there and waiting for our Indians to get ready and prepare to go on the war-path, which took them a very long time.

And seeing how long a time they took to make up their full strength and that I should have time to visit their country, I decided to go by small stages from village to village as far as Cahiagué,[2] where the whole army was to rendezvous, distant fourteen leagues from Carhagouha; and we set out from this village on the fourteenth of August with ten of my companions. I visited five of the principal

[1] Two miles from Thunder Bay.
[2] Near Hawkestone on Lake Simcoe.

villages, enclosed by wooden palisades, as far as Cahiagué, the chief village of the country, which contains two hundred fairly large lodges and where all the warriors were to assemble. Now in all these villages they received us very courteously with some modest welcome. This whole region which I visited on foot extends for some twenty to thirty leagues, and is very fine, being in latitude 44° 30′, and a well cleared country where they plant much Indian corn, which comes up very well, as do also squashes and sunflowers from the seeds of which they make oil wherewith they annoint their heads. The region is crossed by many streams which empty into the lake. . . .

On the seventeenth of August I arrived at Cahiagué, where I was received with great joy and gratitude by all the savages of the country who had abandoned their project, thinking they would see me no more and that the Iroquois had captured me, as I have mentioned above.

*The Works of Samuel de Champlain.* Vol. II, trsl. and ed. by H. P. Biggar. Champlain Soc., Toronto, 1929.

# Jacques Marquette
## 1637-1675

AFTER Champlain had carried French influence into the Great Lakes region, the French intensified their search for the 'Great River of the West', which it was hoped, would lead to the Pacific Ocean. Information on the headwaters of a large river having been received from travellers, Frontenac, the Governor of French Canada, sent the Jesuit, Father Marquette, to descend the river. In 1673, accompanied by an official, the Sieur Jolliet, he left Mackinaw, a missionary post on Lake Michigan, travelled down the Wisconsin river to the Mississippi ('Great Water') which they descended to its junction with the Arkansas. Before they turned back, it was clear from the general direction of the river that it must flow into the Gulf of Mexico, and not into the Pacific Ocean. Marquette died two years later in the course of his missionary work. His remarkable forecast in the concluding paragraph of the extract, that the Pacific Ocean could be reached by the Missouri River (Pekitanoui) was justified by the expedition of Lewis and Clark. (See below.)

\*     \*     \*

We knew that there was, three leagues from Maskoutens, a river[1] emptying into the Mississippi; we knew too, that the point of the compass we were to hold to reach it, was the west-south-west; but the way is so cut up by marshes and little lakes that it is easy to go astray, especially as the river leading to it is so covered with wild oats, that you can hardly discover the channel. Hence, we had good need of our two guides, who led us safely to a portage of twenty-seven hundred paces, and helped us to transport our canoes to enter this river, after which they returned, leaving us alone in an unknown country, in the hands of Providence.

Our route was southwest, and after sailing about thirty leagues, we perceived a place which had all the appearances of an iron mine, and in fact, one of our party who had seen some before, averred that

[1] The Wisconsin river.

the one we had found was very good and very rich. It is covered with three feet of good earth, very near a chain of rock, whose base is covered with fine timber. After forty leagues on this same route, we reached the mouth of our river,[1] and finding ourselves at $42\frac{1}{2}°$ N., we safely entered the Mississippi on the 17th of June with a joy that I cannot express.

Here then we are on this renowned river, of which I have endeavoured to remark attentively all the peculiarities.

Having descended as far as $41° 28'$, following the same direction, we find that turkeys have taken the place of game, and the *pisikous*, or wild cattle,[2] that of other beasts. We call them wild cattle, because they are like our domestic cattle; they are not longer, but almost as big again, and more corpulent; our men having killed one, three of us had considerable trouble in moving it.

We advanced constantly, but as we did not know where we were going, having already made more than a hundred leagues without having discovered anything but beasts and birds, we kept well on our guard. Accordingly we make only a little fire on the shore at night to prepare our meal, and after supper keep as far off from it as possible, passing the night in our canoes, which we anchor in the river pretty far from the bank. Even this did not prevent one of us being always as a sentinel for fear of a surprise.

Proceeding south and south-southwest, we find ourselves at $41°$ north; then at $40°$ and some minutes, partly by southeast and partly by southwest, after having advanced more than sixty leagues since entering the river, without discovering anything.

At last, on the 25th June, we perceived footprints of men by the waterside, and a beaten path entering a beautiful prairie. We stopped to examine it, and concluding that it was a path leading to some Indian village, we resolved to go and reconnoitre; we accordingly left our two canoes in charge of our people, cautioning them strictly to beware of a surprise; then M. Jollyet and I undertook this rather hazardous discovery for two single men, who thus put them-

[1] To the south of Prairie du Chien, Wisconsin, in $43° 3'$ N.
[2] i.e., bison.

selves at the discretion of an unknown and barbarous people. We followed the little path in silence, and having advanced about two leagues, we discovered a village on the banks of the river,[1] and two others on a hill, half a league from the former. Then, indeed, we recommended ourselves to God, with all our hearts; and having implored His help, we passed on undiscovered, and came so near that we even heard the Indians talking. We then deemed it time to announce ourselves, as we did by a cry, which we raised with all our strength, and then halted without advancing any further. At this cry the Indians rushed out of their cabins, and having probably recognized us as French especially seeing a black gown, or at least having no reason to distrust us, seeing we were but two, and had made known our coming, they deputed four old men to come and speak with us. Two carried tobacco-pipes well-adorned, and trimmed with many kinds of feathers. They marched slowly, lifting their pipes towards the sun, as if offering them to him to smoke, but yet without uttering a single word. They were a long time coming the little way from the village to us. Having reached us at last, they stopped to consider us attentively. I now took courage, seeing these ceremonies, which are used by them only with friends, and still more on seeing them covered with stuffs, which made me judge them to be allies. I therefore spoke to them first, and asked them who they were; they answered that they were Ilinois and, in token of peace, they presented their pipes to smoke. They then invited us to their village where all the tribe awaited us with impatience. These pipes for smoking are called in the country calumets, a word that is so much in use that I shall be obliged to employ it in order to be understood, as I shall have to speak of it frequently.

At the door of the cabin in which we were to be received, was an old man awaiting us in a very remarkable posture; which is their usual ceremony in receiving strangers. This man was standing, perfectly naked, with his hands stretched out and raised towards the sun, as if he wished to screen himself from its rays, which nevertheless passed through his fingers to his face. When we came near him, he paid us this compliment: 'How beautiful is the sun, O Frenchmen,

[1] Perhaps the Desmoines River.

when thou comest to visit us! All our town awaits thee, and thou shalt enter all our cabins in peace.' He then took us into his, where there was a crowd of people who devoured us with their eyes, but kept a profound silence. We heard, however, these words occasionally addressed to us: 'Well done, brothers, to visit us!'

As soon as we had taken our places, they showed us the usual civility of the country, which is to present the calumet. You must not refuse it, unless you would pass for an enemy, or at least for being impolite. It is, however, enough to pretend to smoke. While all the old men smoked after us to honour us, some came to invite us on behalf of the great sachem of all the Ilinois to proceed to his town, where he wished to hold a council with us. We went with a good retinue, for all the people who had never seen a Frenchman among them could not tire looking at us; they threw themselves on the grass by the wayside, they ran ahead, then turned and walked back to see us again. All this was done without noise, and with marks of a great respect entertained for us. . . .

The council was followed by a great feast which consisted of four courses, which we had to take with all their ways; the first course was a great wooden dish full of sagamity, that is to say, of Indian meal boiled in water and seasoned with grease. The master of ceremonies, with a spoonful of sagamity, presented it three or four times to my mouth as we would do with a little child; he did the same to M. Jollyet. For the second course, he brought in a second dish containing three fish; he took some pains to remove the bones, and having blown upon it to cool it, put it in my mouth, as we would food to a bird; for the third course, they produced a large dog, which they had just killed, but learning that we did not eat it, it was withdrawn. Finally, the fourth course was a piece of wild ox, the fattest portions of which were put into our mouths.

After this feast we had to visit the whole village, which consists of full three hundred cabins. While we marched through the streets an orator was constantly haranguing to oblige all to see us without being troublesome; we were everywhere presented with belts, garters, and other articles made of the hair of the bear and wild cattle, dyed red, yellow, and grey. These are their rarities, but not being of consequence we did not burthen ourselves with them.

We slept in the sachem's cabin, and the next day took leave of him, promising to pass back through his town in four moons. He escorted us to our canoes with nearly six hundred persons, who saw us embark, evincing in every possible way the pleasure our visit had given them. On taking leave, I personally promised that I would return the next year to stay with them, and instruct them. . . .

We take leave of our Ilinois about the end of June at three o'clock in the afternoon, and embark in sight of all the tribe, who admire our little canoes, having never seen the like.

We descend, following the course of the river, towards another called Pekitanoui,[1] which empties into the Mississippi, coming from the northwest, of which I have something considerable to say after I have related what I have remarked of this river. . . .

As we coasted along rocks frightful for their height and length, we saw two monsters painted on one of these rocks, which startled us at first, and on which the boldest Indian dare not gaze long. They are as large as a calf, with horns on the head like a deer, a fearful look, red eyes, bearded like a tiger, the face somewhat like a man's, the body covered with scales, and the tail so long that it twice makes the turn of the body, passing over the head and down between the legs, and ending at last in a fish's tail. Green, red, and a kind of black are the colours employed. On the whole, these two monsters are so well painted that we could not believe any Indian to have been the designer, as good painters in France would find it hard to do as well; besides this, they are so high upon the rock that it is hard to get conveniently at them to paint them. This is pretty nearly the figure of these monsters, as I drew it off. [Drawing omitted.]

As we were discoursing of them, sailing gently down a beautiful, still, clear water, we heard the noise of a rapid into which we were about to fall. I have seen nothing more frightful; a mass of large trees, entire, with branches, real floating islands, came rushing from the mouth of the river Pekitanoui, so impetuously, that we could

[1] The Missouri river.

not, without great danger, expose ourselves to pass across. The agitation was so great that the water was all muddy and could not get clear.

Pekitanoui is a considerable river which, coming from very far in the northwest, empties into the Mississippi. Many Indian towns are ranged along this river and I hope by its means to make the discovery of the Red or California sea. We judged by the direction the Mississippi takes that if it keeps on the same course it has its mouth in the Gulf of Mexico.

(*Shortly after, without further incident, Marquette reached his turning point, the junction with the Arkansas.*)

'Father Marquette on the Mississippi', from J. G. Shea's *Discovery and Exploration of the Mississippi Valley*, 1852.

# Alexander Mackenzie
## 1755-1820

THE search for the Western sea (Pacific Ocean) was taken over from the French by British fur-traders, who pioneered the routes westwards from the Great Lakes. The first to reach the long-sought-for sea was Alexander Mackenzie, a servant of the Hudson's Bay Company. On his first journey, he travelled by canoe down the Slave River and along the northern shores of the Great Slave Lake. Finding a river which flowed out from its north-west corner, he continued down it and eventually reached the estuary of the river which now bears his name, as related in the first extract. The Mackenzie, however, entered not the Pacific, but the Arctic Ocean, which had been sighted earlier by Samuel Hearne. The problem of a route to the west, therefore, remained to be solved. Four years later, he pushed westwards and southwards from the Slave River to the source of the Peace River on the Rocky Mountains' watershed. For a short time he continued his river voyage down the Fraser River, but for reasons given in the second extract, decided to return up-stream and then follow the Indian trails due westwards to the Ocean. He finally reached the Pacific on 22nd July, 1793 at the mouth of the Bella Coola River, the first European to have crossed the American continent north of Mexico.

I

[1789, July 14]. It blew very hard from the north-west since the preceding evening. Having sat up till three in the morning, I slept longer than usual, but about eight one of my men saw a great many animals in the water which he first supposed to be pieces of ice.[1] About nine, however, I was awakened to resolve the doubts which had taken place respecting this extraordinary appearance. I immediately perceived that they were whales, and having ordered the canoe to be prepared we embarked in pursuit of them. It was, indeed,

[1] The party was now in the estuary of the Mackenzie river.

a very wild and unreflecting enterprise, and it was a very fortunate circumstance that we failed in our attempt to overtake them, as a stroke from the tail of one of these enormous fish would have dashed the canoe to pieces. We may, perhaps, have been indebted to the foggy weather for our safety, as it prevented us from continuing our pursuit. Our guide informed us that they are the same kind of fish which are the principal food of the Esquimoes, and they were frequently seen as large as our canoe. The part of them which appeared above the water was altogether white, and they were much larger than the largest porpoise.

About twelve the fog dispersed, and being curious to take a view of the ice I gave orders for the canoe to be got in readiness. We accordingly embarked, and the Indians followed us. We had not, however, been an hour on the water, when the wind rose on a sudden from the north-east and obliged us to tack about, and the return of the fog prevented us from ascertaining our distance from the ice; indeed, from this circumstance, the island which we had so lately left was but dimly seen. Though the wind was close we ventured to hoist the sail, and from the violence of the swell it was by great exertions that two men could bale out the water from our canoe. We were in a state of actual danger, and felt every corresponding emotion of pleasure when we reached the land. The Indians had fortunately got more to windward so that the swell in some measure drove them on shore, though their canoes were nearly filled with water; and had they been laden, we should have seen them no more. As I did not propose to satisfy my curiosity at the risk of similar dangers, we continued our course along the islands which screened us from the wind. I was now determined to take a more particular examination of the islands in the hope of meeting with parties of the natives from whom I might be able to obtain some interesting intelligence, though our conductor discouraged my expectations by representing them as very shy and inaccessible people. At the same time he informed me that we should probably find some of them if we navigated the channel which he had originally recommended us to enter.

At eight we encamped on the eastern end of the island which I had named the Whale Island. It is about seven leagues in length, east and west by compass, but not more than half a mile in breadth. We saw several red foxes, one of which was killed. There was also five or six very old huts on the point where we had taken our station. The nets were now set, and one of them in five fathom water, the current setting north-east by compass. This morning I ordered a post to be erected close to our tents, on which I engraved the latitude of the place, my own name, the number of persons which I had with me, and the time we remained there.

## II

[1793, June 22]. My people had listened with great attention to the relation which had been given me, and it seemed to be their opinion that it would be absolute madness to attempt a passage through so many savage and barbarous nations. My situation may, indeed, be more easily conceived than expressed: I had no more than thirty days provision remaining, exclusive of such supplies as I might obtain from the natives, and the toil of our hunters, which, however, was so precarious as to be matter of little dependence: besides, our ammunition would soon be exhausted, particularly our ball, of which we had not more than an hundred and fifty, and about thirty pounds weight of shot, which, indeed, might be converted into bullets, though with great waste.

The more I heard of the river,[1] the more I was convinced it could not empty itself into the ocean to the north of what is called the River of the West, so that with its windings, the distance must be very great. Such being the discouraging circumstances of my situation, which were now heightened by the discontents of my people, I could not but be alarmed at the idea of attempting to get to the discharge of such a rapid river, especially when I reflected on the tardy progress of my return up it even if I should meet with no obstruction from the natives; a circumstance not very probable, from the numbers of them which would then be on the river; and whom I could have no opportunity of conciliating in my passage down, for the reasons which have been already mentioned.

[1] The Fraser river, down which he had been travelling. Mackenzie later struck westwards overland.

At all events, I must give up every expectation of returning this season to Athabasca. Such were my reflections at this period; but instead of continuing to indulge them, I determined to proceed with resolution and set future events at defiance. At the same time I suffered myself to nourish the hopes that I might be able to penetrate with more safety, and in a shorter period, to the ocean by the inland, western communication.

To carry this project into execution I must have returned a considerable distance up the river, which would necessarily be attended with a very serious inconvenience, if I passed over every other; as in a voyage of this kind, a retrograde motion could not fail to cool the ardour, slacken the zeal and weaken the confidence of those who have no greater inducement in the undertaking than to follow the conductor of it. Such was the state of my mind at this period, and such the circumstances by which it was distressed and distracted. . . .

[1789, June 23]. It was now, however, absolutely necessary that I should come to a final determination which route to take; and no long interval of reflection was employed before I preferred to go over land; the comparative shortness and security of such a journey were alone sufficient to determine me. I accordingly proposed to two of the Indians to accompany me, and one of them readily assented to my proposition.

I now called those of my people about me who had not been present at my consultation with the natives, and after passing a warm eulogium on their fortitude, patience, and perseverance, I stated the difficulties that threatened our continuing to navigate the river, the length of time it would require, and the scanty provision we had for such a voyage. I then proceeded for the foregoing reasons to propose a shorter route, by trying the overland road to the sea. At the same time, as I knew from experience, the difficulty of retaining guides, and as many circumstances might occur to prevent our progress in that direction, I declared my resolution not to attempt it unless they would engage, if we could not after all proceed overland, to return with me and continue our voyage to the discharge of the waters whatever the distance might be. At all events, I declared, in the most solemn manner, that I would not abandon my design of reaching the sea, if I made the attempt alone, and that I did not despair of returning in safety to my friends.

This proposition met with the most zealous return, and they unanimously assured me that they were as willing now as they had ever been, to abide by my resolutions, whatever they might be, and to follow me wherever I should go. I therefore requested them to prepare for an immediate departure, and at the same time gave notice to the man who had engaged to be our guide to be in readiness to accompany us. When our determination to return up the river was made known, several of the natives took a very abrupt departure; but to those who remained I gave a few useful articles, explaining to them at the same time the advantages that would result to them if their relations conducted me to the sea, along such a road as they had described. I had already given a moose skin to some of the women for the purpose of making shoes which were now brought us; they were well sewed but ill shaped, and a few beads were considered as a sufficient remuneration for the skill employed on them. Mr. Mackay, by my desire, engraved my name, and the date of the year on a tree.

*Voyages . . . through the Continent of North America to the Frozen and Pacific Oceans, 1789-93.* By Alexander Mackenzie, 1801.

# David Thompson
## 1770-1857

DAVID THOMPSON, an official of the Hudson's Bay Company, landed at Fort Churchill in 1785; and in the following years acquired, as trader and surveyor, an unrivalled knowledge of the country between the Great Lakes and the Pacific, continuing and greatly extending the work of Alexander Mackenzie. The extract gives a good picture of the man and the conditions in which he was accustomed to work. Thompson's worth was not appreciated by the H.B.C., and in 1797 he joined their rivals, the North-West Company, who recognized his value as a surveyor. His map, drawn in 1814, was for long the only reliable authority for north-western America. He describes a winter journey from the junction of the Assiniboine and Souris rivers southwards through unsurveyed territory to the Mandan Indian villages on the Missouri River, North Dakota, with the object of inducing them to trade.

★     ★     ★

[28th November, 1797]. I was readily supplied with everything I required which was chiefly ammunition, tobacco and a few trinkets for expenses. For my service I had two horses. M. Jussomme[1] had one, and the men thirty dogs, their own property; each two hauled a flat sled upon which their venture was lashed; these dogs had all been traded from the Stone Indians, who make great use of them in their encampments. They were all like half dog, half wolf, and always on the watch to devour everything they could get their teeth on; they did not do willing work, and most of them had never hauled a flat sled, but the Canadians soon break them in by constant flogging in which they seem to take great delight; when on the march the noise was intolerable, and made me keep two or three miles ahead.

As my journey to the Missisourie[2] is over part of the Great Plains I shall give it in the form of a journal; this form, however dull, is

---

[1] The guide and interpreter, conversant with the Mandan language.
[2] i.e. Missouri River.

the only method in my opinion that can give the reader a clear idea of them. With our three horses and thirty dogs with their sleds, we crossed the Stone River on the ice; the snow on the ground was three inches in depth. We went about six miles and put up in the woods of the Mouse River,[1] which joins the Stone Indian River about two miles below the house. The dogs, unused to hauling, going anywhere and everywhere from the men, who employed themselves all the way in swearing at, and flogging them until we put up, when the dogs were unharnessed, a piece of line tied round the neck of each, and one or both fore feet were brought through it to keep them quiet and from straying away. At 8 pm the thermometer twenty degrees below zero. . . .

December 3rd. At 8 am three (degrees above freezing point) at 8 pm three (degrees above freezing point) the weather was now mild but a WNW gale came on with snow and high drift (so) that we could not see a fourth a mile from us. And our journey is over open plains from one patch of wood to another patch, for the Mouse River on which we are camped has woods only in places, and many miles distant from each other. And these patches of wood must be kept in sight to guide over the plains and none of the men knew the use of the compass, and did not like to trust it. We could not proceed and the tent was disagreeable with smoke.

December 4th. 7 am four above zero WSW gale of wind. At 9 am we set off, and went eleven miles to a grove of oaks, ash, elm, nut trees, and other hard woods; which are always the woods of this river. At this place we came to five tents of Stone Indians, who as usual received us with kindness; they did not approve of our journey to the Missisourie and informed us that some skirmishes had taken place between the Mandane and Sieux Indians in which the latter lost several men, which they attributed to the ammunition furnished to the former by the trading parties from the Stone Indian River, such as ours were; and that they had determined to waylay us, and plunder us of all we had, and also take all our scalps, and they warned us to be on our guard; I did not like this news, but the men paid no attention to it, thinking it proceeded from hatred

[1] Now the Souris river.

to the Mandanes. We then followed the river banks for seven miles, and camped at 4 pm. The river is about twenty yards wide, at present the water very low.

December 5th. 7 am Ther. thirteen below zero, became mild, in the afternoon a WSW gale came on and increased to a storm by 6 pm. M. Jussomme, our guide, informed us that he would now take the great traverse to the Turtle Hill; we were early up, and by 7.30 am set off. He led us about south four miles to a small grove of aspins on the banks of a brook thence about six miles to the Turtle Brook from the hill; thence S by W seven miles; we now came on a rising ground at 1 pm but the Turtle Hill was not in sight; and all before and around us a boundless plain; and M. Jussomme could not say where we were; the weather appeared threatening and preparing for a storm; our situation was alarming; and anxiety (was) in the face of every man, for we did not know to which hand to turn ourselves for shelter. I mounted my horse and went to the highest ground near us, and with my telescope viewed the horizon all around, but not the least vestige of woods appeared; but at due north-west from us, where there appeared the tops of a few trees like oaks. They anxiously inquired if I saw woods. I told them what I had seen and that with my old soldier I should guide myself by the compass, and directly proceed as the woods were far off; McCrachan and a Canadian joined us; the other six conferred among themselves what to do, they had no faith in the compass on land, and thought best to march in some direction until they could see woods with their own eyes; but had not proceeded half a mile before all followed us, thinking there would be a better chance of safety by being all together. The gale of wind came on and kept increasing. The snow was four to six inches in depth with a slight crust on it. We held on almost in despair of reaching the woods; fortunately the dogs were well broken in and gave us no trouble. Night came upon us and we had carefully to keep in file, at times calling to each other to learn that none were missing. At length at 7 pm, thank good Providence, we arrived at the woods, very much fatigued; walking against the storm was as laborious as walking knee-deep in water. We got up our tent and placed ourselves under shelter. Although we had taken six hours on this last course, yet I found by my observations we had come only thirteen miles.

December 6th. A heavy westerly gale of wind with mild weather. The horses and dogs as well as ourselves were too much fatigued to proceed. Two bison bulls were killed, though very tough, kept away hunger and fed the dogs.

December 7th. At 7 am Ther. twenty-five, only five degrees below the freezing-point, a fine mild day. We proceeded five miles up the Mouse River to an old trading house called 'Ash House' from the plenty of those fine trees; it had to be given up, from its being too open to the incursions of the Sieux Indians. Two Stone Indians came to us. They said their camp was not far off. M. Jussomme's mare and my yellow horse had both become lame of each one foot, and could proceed no further through the plains, each of these horses had one white foot and three black feet; the white foot of each was lame in the same manner, the hair of the white foot was worn away by the hard snow, and a small hole in the flesh also above the hoof. The three black feet had not a hair off them. My other horse was dark brown with four black feet. As the horses of this country have no shoes the colour of the hoof is much regarded; the yellow hoof with white hair is a brittle hoof and soon wears away; for this reason, as much as possible, the natives take only black hoofed horses on their war expeditions. As the camp of Stone Indians were going to the house of Mr. John McDonell to trade we delivered the horses to the care of an old Indian to be taken to the house. M. Jussomme was now without a horse and had to purchase dogs.

December 8th. 7 am Ther. eighteen below zero. A cold day which was employed in hunting, without success. I observed for latitude and longitude.

December 9th. 7 am Ther. twenty-six below zero. We went up the river SW seven and a half miles to eight tents of Stone Indians who treated us with hospitality, and each of us got a good meal. Learning that we were going to the Missisourie, they warned us to beware of the Sieux Indians whom they thought would lie in wait for us at the Dog Tent Hills, and (to) keep on our guard against a surprise. We offered a high reward to a young man to guide us to the Mandane Villages, but however tempting the offer, neither himself nor any other would accept the offer. They plainly told us that we might expect to find Sieux Indians on our road, and they were not on good terms with the Mandanes. We went about three miles and put up in view of the Turtle Hill. We are near the place, where in 1794, fifteen tents of Stone Indians were destroyed by a large war party of Sieux Indians, although of the same nation. From their own accounts, some forty or fifty years ago a feud broke out and several were killed and wounded on both sides; about five hundred tents separated from the main body, and took up their hunting grounds on the Red River and the plains stretching north-westward along the right bank of the Saskatchewan River to within three hundred miles of the mountains; and being in alliance and strict confederacy with the Nahathaways, who accompanied them to war, they were powerful, and with their allies made their brethren, the Sieux Nation, feel the weight of their resentment for several years until the small-pox of 1782 came, which involved them all in one common calamity, and very much reduced the numbers of all parties. The Sieux had lost several of their men, who went to hunt but did not return, and suspicion fell on the Stone Indians and their allies. They determined on revenge, and the destruction of these fifteen tents was the result. The Sieux afterwards found the loss of their men was by the Chippaways, their never-ceasing enemies, and deeply regretted what they had done; the old men made an apology and proffered peace, which was accepted in 1812, and a reunion took place; and in this peace their allies and confederates were included; and which continues to this day.

December 10th. 7 am Ther. twenty below zero. The hummock of woods on the Turtle Hill, which was our mark, gave our course by the compass S. 30° E. As we had to cross a plain of twenty-two miles, and having felt the severe changes of weather, I desired the men to follow close in file, for they now had faith in the compass. At 7.30 am our bit of a caravan set off; as the dogs were fresh we walked at a good pace for some time, a gentle south wind arose and kept increasing; by 10 am it was a heavy gale, with high drift and dark weather, so much so that I had to keep the compass in my hand, for I could not trust to the wind. By noon it was a perfect storm; we had no alternative but to proceed, which we did slowly and with great labour, for the storm was ahead, and the snow drift in our faces. Night came on, I could no longer see the compass, and had to trust to the wind; the weather became mild with small rain, but the storm continued with darkness; some of the foremost called to lie down where we were, but as it was evident we were ascending a gentle rising ground we continued and soon, thank good Providence, my face struck against some oak saplings, and I passed the word that we were in the woods, a fire was quickly made, and as it was on an elevated place it was seen afar off. As yet the only one with me was my servant who led the horse, and we anxiously awaited the others; they came hardly able to move, one, and then another, and in something more than half an hour, nine had arrived; each with dogs and sleds, but one man, and a sled with the dogs were missing; to search for the latter was useless; but how to find the former we were at a loss, and remained so for another half an hour, when we thought we heard his voice; the storm was still raging, we extended ourselves within call of each other; the most distant man heard him plainly, went to him, raised him up, and with assistance brought him to the fire, and we all thanked the Almighty for our preservation. He told us he became weak, fell several times, and at length he could not get up, and resigned himself to perish in the storm, when by chance lifting up his head he saw the fire, this gave him courage; stand he could not but shuffled away on hands and knees through the snow, bawling with all his might until we fortunately heard him. We threw the tent over some oak saplings and got under shelter from showers of rain, hail and sleet. At 7.30 pm Ther. thirty-six, being four degrees above the freezing-point; by a south wind making in little more than twelve hours a difference of temperature of fifty-six degrees. I had weathered many a hard gale, but this was the most distressing day I had yet seen.

*David Thompson's narrative of his explorations in Western America, 1784–1812.* Ed. by J. B. Tyrrell. Champlain Soc., Toronto, 1916.

# Meriwether Lewis and William Clark
## 1774-1809          1770-1838

THE first American expedition to the Pacific Ocean followed immediately on the Louisana Purchase, 1803, with which it formed part of American expansion to the West. Attention had been drawn to the Pacific coast by the activities of fur traders, including Russian, in the north-west and of whalers, also of several nationalities. It was plain that a political vacuum existed in that region, and Thomas Jefferson was determined that the Power to fill it should be the United States. The first step was to examine and report on the country, the routes across it and the condition of its inhabitants with a view to establishing effective occupation, though the expedition was ostensibly 'for the purpose of extending the external commerce of the United States'. The expedition, a military one, was placed under the charge of Captain Lewis of the First Infantry, a man with much experience of the frontier. The first stage of the journey lay up the Missouri by water as far as possible, thence by land to its source and across the divide to the western coast in the vicinity of the Columbia River. The success of the expedition depended upon the party obtaining horses from the Indian tribes for transport from the divide to a westerly flowing and navigable river. The extract illustrates the astuteness and tact by which the pertinacious Lewis secured this vital assistance. The expedition finally struck the Columbia River and descended it to its mouth, reached in November 1805.

★     ★     ★

Tuesday, August 13th 1805. At the distance of five miles the road, after leading us down a long descending valley[1] for two miles, brought us to a large creek about ten yards wide; this we passed and on rising the hill beyond it had a view of a handsome little valley to our left of about a mile in width through which from the appearance of the timber I conjectured that a river passed. We had proceeded about four miles through a wavy plain parallel to the

[1] Lewis had just crossed the continental divide by the Lembi Pass.

194

valley or river bottom when at the distance of about a mile we saw two women, a man and some dogs on an eminence immediately before us. They appeared to view us with attention and two of them after a few minutes sat down as if to wait our arrival. We continued our usual pace towards them. When we had arrived within half a mile of them I directed the party to halt and leaving my pack and rifle I took the flag which I unfurled and advanced singly towards them. The women soon disappeared behind the hill, the man continued until I arrived within a hundred yards of him and then likewise absconded. Though I frequently repeated the word *tab-ba-bone* sufficiently loud for him to have heard it.

I now hastened to the top of the hill where they had stood but could see nothing of them. The dogs were less shy than their masters. They came about me pretty close. I therefore thought of tying a handkerchief about one of their necks with some beads and other trinkets and then let them loose to search their fugitive owners thinking by this means to convince them of our pacific disposition towards them, but the dogs would not suffer me to take hold of them; they also soon disappeared. I now made a signal for the men to come on, they joined me and we pursued the back track of these Indians which lead us along the same road which we had been travelling. The road was dusty and appeared to have been much travelled lately both by men and horses.

We had not continued our route more than a mile when we were so fortunate as to meet with three female savages. The short and steep ravines which we passed concealed us from each other until we arrived within thirty paces. A young woman immediately took to flight, an elderly woman and a girl about twelve years old remained. I instantly laid by my gun and advanced towards them. They appeared much alarmed but saw that we were too near for them to escape by flight. They therefore seated themselves on the ground, holding down their heads as if reconciled to die which they expected no doubt would be their fate; I took the elderly woman by the hand and raised her up repeated the word *tab-ba-bone* and stripped up my shirt sleeve to show her my skin; to prove to her the truth of the assertion that I was a white man, for my face and hands, which have been constantly exposed to the sun, were quite as dark as their own. They appeared instantly reconciled, and the men coming up, I gave these women some beads a few moccasin awls some pewter looking-glasses and a little paint.

I directed Drewyer to request the old woman to recall the young woman who had run off to some distance by this time, fearing she might alarm the camp before we approached and might so exasperate the natives that they would perhaps attack us without inquiring who we were. The old woman did as she was requested and the fugitive soon returned almost out of breath. I bestowed an equivalent portion of trinkets on her with the others. I now painted their tawny cheeks with some vermilion which with this nation is emblematic of peace. After they had become composed I informed them by signs that I wished them to conduct us to their camp that we were anxious to become acquainted with the chiefs and warriors of their nation. They readily obeyed and we set out, still pursuing the road down the river. We had marched about two miles when we met a party of about sixty warriors mounted on excellent horses who came in nearly full speed. When they arrived I advanced towards them with the flag leaving my gun with the party about fifty paces behind me. The chief and two others who were a little in advance of the main body spoke to the women, and they informed them who we were and exultingly showed the presents which had been given them. These men then advanced and embraced me very affectionately in their way which is by putting their left arm over your right shoulder clasping your back, while they apply their left cheek to yours and frequently vociferate the word *ah-hi-e, ah-hi-e* that is, I am much pleased, I am much rejoiced. Both parties now advanced and we were all caressed and besmeared with their grease and paint till I was heartily tired of the national hug. I now had the pipe lit and gave them smoke; they seated themselves in a circle around us, and pulled off their moccasins before they would receive or smoke the pipe. This is a custom among them as I afterwards learned indicative of a sacred obligation of sincerity in their profession of friendship given by the act of receiving and smoking the pipe of a stranger. Or which is as much as to say that they wish they may always go barefoot if they are not sincere; a pretty heavy penalty if they are to march through the plains of their country.

After smoking a few pipes with them I distributed some trifles among them, with which they seemed much pleased particularly with the blue beads and vermilion. I now informed the chief that the object of our visit was a friendly one, that after we should reach his camp I would undertake to explain to him fully those objects, who we were, from whence we had come and whither we were going; that in the meantime I did not care how soon we were in motion, as the sun was very warm and no water at hand. They now put on their moccasins, and the principal chief Ca-me-ah-wait made a short speech to the warriors. I gave him the flag which I informed him was an emblem of peace among white men and now that it had been received by him it was to be respected as the bond of union between us. I desired him to march on, which he did and we followed him; the dragoons moved on in squadron in our rear. After we had marched about a mile in this order he halted them and gave a second harangue; after which six or eight of the young men rode forward to their encampment and no further regularity was observed in the order of march. I afterwards understood that the Indians we had first seen this morning had returned and alarmed the camp; these men had come out armed cap-à-pie for action, expecting to meet with their enemies the Minnetares of Fort de Prairie whom they call Pah-kees. They are armed with bows, arrows and shields except three whom I observed with small pieces such as the N.W. Company furnish the natives with which they had obtained from the Rocky Mountain Indians on the Yellow Stone river with whom they are at peace. On our arrival at their encampment on the river in a handsome level and fertile bottom at the distance of four miles from where we had first met them, they introduced us to a lodge made of willow brush and an old leather lodge which had been prepared for our reception by the young men which the chief had dispatched for that purpose.

Here we were seated on green boughs and the skins of antelopes. One of the warriors then pulled up the grass in the centre of the lodge forming a small circle of about two feet in diameter. The chief next produced his pipe and native tobacco and began a long ceremony of the pipe.

I now explained to them the objects of our journey, etc. All the women and children of the camp were shortly collected about the lodge to indulge themselves with looking at us, we being the first white persons they had ever seen. After the ceremony of the pipe was over I distributed the remainder of the small articles I had brought with me among the women and children. By this time it was late in the evening and we had not tasted any food since the evening before. The chief informed us that they had nothing but berries to eat and gave us some cakes of serviceberries and choke berries which had been dried in the sun; of these I made a hearty meal, and then walked to the river, which I found about forty yards wide, very rapid, clear and about three feet deep.[1] Cameahwait informed me that this stream discharged itself into another doubly as large at the distance of half a day's march which came from the S.W. But he added on further inquiry that there was but little more timber below the junction of those rivers than I saw here, and that the river was confined between inaccessible mountains, was very rapid and rocky insomuch that it was impossible for us to pass either by land or water down this river to the great lake where the white men lived as he had been informed. This was unwelcome information but I still hoped that this account had been exaggerated with a view to detain us among them. As to timber I could discover not any that would answer the purpose of construction canoes or in short more than was barely necessary for fuel.

These people had been attacked by the Minnetares of Fort de Prairie this spring and about twenty of them killed and taken prisoners. On this occasion they lost a great part of their horses and all their lodges except that which they had erected for our accommodation; they were now living in lodges of a conic figure made of willow brush. I still observe a great number of horses feeding in every direction around their camp and therefore entertain but little doubt but we shall be enabled to furnish ourselves with an

[1] The Lemi River, a tributary of Salmon River. The 'great lake' was the Pacific Ocean.

adequate number to transport our stores even if we are compelled to travel by land over these mountains. On my return to my lodge an Indian called me in to his bower and gave me a small morsel of the flesh of an antelope boiled and a piece of a fresh salmon roasted; both which I ate with a very good relish. This was the first salmon I had seen and perfectly convinced me that we were on the waters of the Pacific Ocean.

This evening the Indians entertained us with their dancing nearly all night. At 12 o'clock I grew sleepy and retired to rest, leaving the men to amuse themselves with the Indians. I observe no essential difference between the music and manner of dancing among this nation and those of the Missouri. I was several times awoke in the course of the night by their yells but was too much fatigued to be deprived of a tolerable sound night's repose.

*The Journals of Lewis and Clark.* Edited by Bernard De Voto. Houghton Mifflin Company, 1953. (Spelling modernized.)

# John Charles Frémont
## 1813-1890

AFTER Lewis and Clark had accomplished the first overland crossing of what was to become United States territory to the Pacific, numerous government explorers were at work in the West seeking practical routes and trying to sort out the complicated structure of the Rocky Mountains, the great basins and the western Sierra. The greatest of these men, and the last before the finding of gold in California brought a host of miners, hunters and migrants into the area, was Colonel J. C. Frémont, a tough and at times ruthless explorer with a good eye for country and high qualifications as a surveyor. On an early journey he examined the Great Salt Lake of Utah, first sighted in 1824. In 1843 he embarked upon an expedition to explore the unknown country south of the Columbia River towards California. With a party of twenty-five he pushed southwards from Fall River, and after a very difficult passage of the Sierra Nevada, as described in the extract, reached the fringe of white settlement near the Sacramento River, northern California. Frémont's topographical work was of great importance, but it was soon to be absorbed in the surveys which preceded the construction of the great transcontinental railways.

★     ★     ★

February 10. Taplin was sent back with a few men to assist Mr. Fitzpatrick; and continuing on with three sleighs carrying a part of the baggage, we had the satisfaction to encamp within two and a half miles of the head of the hollow, and at the foot of the last mountain ridge.[1] Here two large trees had been set on fire, and in the holes, where the snow had been melted away, we found a comfortable camp. . . .

The elevation of the camp, by the boiling point, is 8,050 feet. We are now a thousand feet above the level of the South Pass in the

[1] Frémont was crossing the Sierra Nevada, some seventy miles north of the present Yosemite National Park.

Rocky Mountains; and still we are not done ascending. The top of a flat ridge near was bare of snow, and very well sprinkled with bunch grass, sufficient to pasture the animals two or three days; and this was to be their main point of support. This ridge is composed of a compact trap, or basalt, of a columnar structure; over the surface are scattered large boulders of porous trap. The hills are in many places entirely covered with small fragments of volcanic rock.

Putting on our snow-shoes, we spent the afternoon in exploring a road ahead. The glare of the snow, combined with great fatigue, had rendered many of the people nearly blind; but we were fortunate in having some black silk handkerchiefs, which, worn as veils, very much relieved the eye.

February 11. High wind continued, and our trail this morning was nearly invisible—here and there indicated by a little ridge of snow. Our situation became tiresome and dreary, requiring a strong exercise of patience and resolution.

In the evening I received a message from Mr. Fitzpatrick, acquainting me with the utter failure of his attempt to get our mules and horses over the snow—the half-hidden trail had proved entirely too slight to support them, and they had broken through, and were plunging about or lying half-buried in snow. He was occupied in endeavouring to get them back to his camp; and in the meantime sent to me for further instructions. I wrote to him to send the animals immediately back to their old pastures; and, after having made mauls and shovels, turn in all the strength of his party to open and beat a road through the snow, strengthening it with branches and boughs of the pines.

February 12. We made mauls, and worked hard at our end of the road all the day. The wind was high, but the sun bright, and the snow thawing. We worked down the face of the hill, to meet the people at the other end. Towards sundown it began to grow cold, and we shouldered our mauls, and trudged back to camp.

February 13. We continued to labour on the road; and in the course of the day had the satisfaction to see the people working down the face of the opposite hill, about three miles distant. During the morning we had the pleasure of a visit from Mr. Fitzpatrick, with the information that all was going on well. A party of Indians had passed on snow-shoes, who said they were going to the western side of the mountain after fish. This was an indication that the salmon were coming up the streams; and we could hardly restrain our impatience as we thought of them, and worked with increased vigour.

The meat train did not arrive this evening, and I gave Godey leave to kill our little dog (Tlamath), which he prepared in Indian fashion; scorching off the hair, and washing the skin with soap and snow, and then cutting it up into pieces,which were laid on the snow. Shortly afterwards, the sleigh arrived with a supply of horse meat; and we had tonight an extraordinary dinner—pea soup, mule, and dog. . . .

February 16. We had succeeded in getting our animals safely to the first grassy hill; and this morning I started with Jacob on a reconnoitring expedition beyond the mountain. We travelled along the crests of narrow ridges, extending down from the mountain in the direction of the valley from which the snow was fast melting away. On the open spots was tolerably good grass, and I judged we should succeed in getting the camp down by way of these. Towards sundown we discovered some icy spots in a deep hollow; and, descending the mountain, we encamped on the head water of a little creek, where at last the water found its way to the Pacific.

The night was clear and very long. We heard the cries of some wild animals which had been attracted by our fire, and a flock of geese passed over during the night. Even these strange sounds had something pleasant to our senses in this region of silence and desolation.

We started again early in the morning. The creek acquired a regular breadth of about twenty feet, and we soon began to hear the rushing of the water below the ice surface over which we travelled to avoid the snow; a few miles below we broke through, where the water was several feet deep, and halted to make a fire and dry our clothes. We continued a few miles farther, walking being very laborious without snow-shoes.

I was now perfectly satisfied that we had struck the stream on which Mr. Sutter lived; and, turning about, made a hard push, and reached the camp at dark. Here we had the pleasure to find all the remaining animals, fifty-seven in number, safely arrived at the grassy hill near the camp; and here, also, we were agreeably surprised with the sight of an abundance of salt. Some of the horse-guard had gone to a neighbouring hut for pine-nuts, and discovered unexpectedly a large cake of very white fine-grained salt, which the Indians told them they had brought from the other side of the mountain; they used it to eat with their pine-nuts, and readily sold it for goods.

On the 19th, the people were occupied in making a road and bringing up the baggage; and, on the afternoon of the next day, February 20, 1844, we encamped with the animals and all the *matériel* of the camp, on the summit of the Pass in the dividing ridge, a thousand miles by our travelled road from the Dalles of the Columbia.

The people, who had not yet been to this point, climbed the neighbouring peak to enjoy a look at the valley.

The temperature of boiling water gave for the elevation of the encampment 9,338 feet above the sea.

This was two thousand feet higher than the South Pass in the Rocky mountains, and several peaks in view rose several thousand feet still higher. Thus, at the extremity of the continent, and near the coast, the phenomenon was seen of a range of mountains still higher than the great Rocky mountains themselves. This extraordinary fact accounts for the Great Basin, and shows that there must be a system of small lakes and rivers here scattered over a flat country, and which the extended and lofty range of the Sierra Nevada prevents from escaping to the Pacific ocean. Latitude 38° 44'; longitude 120° 28'. [The South Fork, American River.]

Thus this pass in the Sierra Nevada, which so well deserves its name of snowy mountain, is eleven degrees west and about four degrees south of the South Pass.

February 21. We now considered ourselves victorious over the mountain; having only the descent before us, and the valley under our eyes, we felt strong hope that we should force our way down. But this was a case in which the descent was not facile. Still deep fields of snow lay between, and there was a large intervening space of rough-looking mountains, through which we had yet to wind our way. Carson[1] roused me this morning with an early fire, and we were all up long before day, in order to pass the snow-fields before the sun should render the crust soft. We enjoyed this morning a scene, at sunrise, which even here was unusually glorious and beautiful. Immediately above the eastern mountains was repeated a cloud-formed mass of purple ranges, bordered with bright yellow gold; the peaks shot up into a narrow line of crimson cloud, above which the air was filled with a greenish orange; and over all was the singular beauty of the blue sky. Passing along a ridge which commanded the lake on our right, of which we began to discover an outlet through a chasm on the west, we passed over alternating open ground and hard-crusted snow-fields which supported the animals, and encamped on the ridge after a journey of six miles. The grass was better than we had yet seen, and we were encamped in a clump of trees twenty or thirty feet high, resembling white pine. With the exception of these small clumps the ridges were bare; and, where the snow found the support of the trees, the wind had blown it up into banks ten or fifteen feet high. It required much care to hunt out a practicable way, as the most open places frequently led to impassable banks.

We had hard and doubtful labour yet before us, as the snow appeared to be heavier where the timber began further down, with few open spots. Ascending a height, we traced out the best line we could discover for the next day's march, and had at least the consolation to see that the mountain descended rapidly. The day had been one of April; gusty, with a few occasional flakes of snow; which in the afternoon enveloped the upper mountain in clouds. We watched them anxiously, as now we dreaded a snow-storm. Shortly afterwards we heard the roll of thunder and, looking towards the valley, found it all enveloped in a thunderstorm. For us, as connected with the idea of summer, it had a singular charm; and we watched its progress with excited feelings until nearly sunset, when the sky cleared off brightly, and we saw a shining line of water directing its course towards another, a broader and larger sheet. We knew that these could be no other than the Sacramento and the

[1] Kit Carson, the famous frontier man.

bay of San Francisco; but, after our long wandering in rugged mountains, where so frequently we had met with disappointments, and where the crossing of every ridge displayed some unknown lake or river, we were yet almost afraid to believe that we were at last to escape into the genial country of which we had heard so many glowing descriptions, and dreaded again to find some vast interior lake, whose bitter waters would bring us disappointment. On the southern shore of what appeared to be the bay could be traced the gleaming line where entered another large stream; and again the Buenaventura rose up in our minds.

February 23. This was our most difficult day: we were forced off the ridges by the quantity of snow among the timber, and obliged to take to the mountain-sides, where, occasionally, rocks and a southern exposure afforded us a chance to scramble along. But these were steep, and slippery with snow and ice; and the tough evergreens of the mountain impeded our way, tore our skins, and exhausted our patience. Some of us had the misfortune to wear moccasins with parfleche soles, so slippery that we could not keep our feet, and generally crawled across the snow-beds. Axes and mauls were necessary today, to make a road through the snow. Going ahead with Carson to reconnoitre the road, we reached in the afternoon the river which made the outlet of the lake. Carson sprang over, clear across a place where the stream was compressed among rocks, but the parfleche sole of my moccasin glanced from the icy rock, and precipitated me into the river. It was some few seconds before I could recover myself in the current, and Carson, thinking me hurt, jumped in after me, and we both had an icy bath. We tried to search a while for my gun, which had been lost in the fall, but the cold drove us out; and making a large fire on the bank, after we had partially dried ourselves we went back to meet the camp. We afterwards found that the gun had been slung under the ice which lined the banks of the creek.

Using our old plan of breaking the road with alternate horses, we reached the creek in the evening, and encamped on a dry open place in the ravine.

Another branch which we had followed here comes in on the

left; and from this point the mountain wall, on which we had travelled today, faces to the south along the right bank of the river, where the sun appears to have melted the snow; but the opposite ridge is entirely covered. Here among the pines the hill-side produces but little grass—barely sufficient to keep life in the animals. We had the pleasure to be rained upon this afternoon; and grass was now our greatest solicitude. Many of the men looked badly; and some this evening were giving out.

[But the worst of the journey was over, and on March 6th they reached the outskirts of white settlement near the Sacramento.]

*Report of the Exploring Expedition to the Rocky Mountains, 1842, and to Oregon and North California, 1843-4.* By J. C. Frémont. Washington, 1845.

# John Wesley Powell
## 1834-1902

THE final phase in the exploration of the West was the individual examination of the geographical features, and particularly of the great rivers. Perhaps the most outstanding and dangerous task was the navigation of the Colorado River, in its course through the Grand Canyon, the walls of which rise seven thousand feet above water-level. Major J. W. Powell, with a party of nine, in four specially built boats left Green River City on 24th May 1869 to descend the Green and Colorado Rivers. On reaching the entrance to the Grand Canyon, three men decided to abandon the party. Powell persisted in the attempt, and after some exciting experiences successfully passed through the Canyon, as described below. Powell, as a result of his observations in the West gained great distinction as a geologist, and was one of the founders of the science of geomor- phology—the study of land forms.

★   ★   ★

August 28—At last daylight comes, and we have breakfast without a word being said about the future. The meal is as solemn as a funeral. After breakfast I ask the three men if they still think it best to leave us. The elder Howland thinks it is, and Dunn agrees with him. The younger Howland tries to persuade them to go on with the party, failing in which, he decides to go with his brother.

Then we cross the river. The small boat is very much disabled, and unseaworthy. With the loss of hands consequent on the depar- ture of the three men, we shall not be able to run all of the boats, so I decide to leave my *Emma Dean*.

Two rifles and a shot-gun are given to the men who are going out. I ask them to help themselves to the rations and take what they think to be a fair share. This they refuse to do, saying they have no fear but that they can get something to eat; but Billy, the cook, has a pan of biscuits prepared for dinner, and these he leaves on a rock.

Before starting, we take our barometers, fossils, the minerals and some ammunition from the boat, and leave them on the rocks. We are going over this place as light as possible. The three men help us lift our boats over a rock twenty-five or thirty feet high, and let them down again over the first fall, and now we are all ready to start. The last thing before leaving, I write a letter to my wife, and give it to Howland. Sumner gives him his watch, directing that it be sent to his sister, should he not be heard from again. The records of the expediton have been kept in duplicate. One set of these is given to Howland, and now we are ready. For the last time, they entreat us not to go on, and tell us that it is madness to set out in this place; that we can never get safely through it; and, further, that the river turns again to the south into the granite, and a few miles of such rapids and falls will exhaust our entire stock of rations, and then it will be too late to climb out. Some tears are shed; it is rather a solemn parting; each party thinks the other is taking the dangerous course.

My old boat left, I go on board of the *Maid of the Cañon*. The three men climb a crag that overhangs the river to watch us off. The *Maid of the Cañon* pushes out. We glide rapidly along the foot of the wall, just grazing one great rock then pull out a little into the chute of the second fall, and plunge over it. The open compartment is filled when we strike the first wave below, but we cut through it, and then the men pull with all their power towards the left wall, and swing clear of the dangerous rock below all right. We are scarcely a minute in running it, and find that, although it looked bad from above, we have passed many places that were worse.

The other boat follows without more difficulty. We land at the first practicable point below and fire our guns, as a signal to the men above that we have come over in safety. Here we remain a couple of hours, hoping that they will take the smaller boat and follow us. We are behind a curve in the cañon, and cannot see up to where we left them, and so we wait until their coming seems hopeless, and push on.

And now we have a succession of rapids and falls until noon, all of which we run in safety. Just after dinner we come to another bad place. A little stream comes in from the left, and below there is a fall, and still below another fall. Above, the river tumbles down, over and among the rocks, in whirlpools and great waves, and the waters are lashed into mad, white foam. We run along the left, above this, and soon see that we cannot get down on this side, but it seems possible to let down on the other. We pull up-stream again for two or three hundred yards and cross. Now there is a bed of basalt on this northern side of the cañon, with a bold escarpment that seems to be a hundred feet high. We can climb it, and walk along its summit to a point where we are just at the head of the fall. Here the basalt is broken down again, so it seems to us, and I direct the men to take a line to the top of the cliff and let the boats down along the wall. One man remains in the boat, to keep her clear of the rocks, and prevent her line from being caught on the projecting angles. I climb the cliff, and pass along to a point just over the fall, and descend by broken rocks, and find that the break of the fall is above the break of the wall, so that we cannot land; and that still below the river is very bad, and that there is no possibility of a portage. Without waiting further to examine and determine what shall be done, I hasten back to the top of the cliff, to stop the boats from coming down. When I arrive, I find the men have let one of them down to the head of the fall. She is in swift water, and they are not able to pull her back; nor are they able to go on with the line, as it is not long enough to reach the higher part of the cliff, which is just before them; so they take a bight around a crag. I send two men back for the other line. The boat is in very swift water, and Bradley is standing in the open compartment, holding out his oar to prevent her from striking against the foot of the cliff. Now she shoots out into the stream, and up as far as the line will permit, and then, wheeling, drives headlong against the rock, then out and back again, now straining on the line, now striking against the rock. As soon as the second line is brought we pass it down to him; but his attention is all taken up with his own situation, and he does not see that we are passing the line to him. I stand on a projecting rock, waving my hat to gain his attention, for my voice is drowned by the roaring of the falls. Just at this moment, I see him take his knife from its sheath, and step forward to cut the line. He has evidently decided that it is better to go over with the boat as it is, than to wait for her to be broken to pieces. As he leans over, the boat sheers again into the stream, the stem-post breaks away, and she is loose. With perfect composure Bradley seizes the great scull oar, places it in the stern rowlock, and pulls with all his power (and he is an athlete) to turn the bow of the boat down stream, for he wishes to go bow down rather than to drift broadside on. One, two strokes he makes, and a third just as she goes over, and the boat is fairly turned, and she goes down almost beyond our sight, though we are more than a hundred feet above the river. Then she comes up again on a great wave, and down and up, then around behind some great rocks, and is lost in the mad, white foam below. We stand frozen with fear, for we see no boat. Bradley is gone, so it seems. But now, away below, we see something coming out of the waves. It is evidently a boat. A moment more, and we see Bradley standing on deck, swinging his hat to show that he is all right. But he is in a whirlpool. We have the stem-post of his boat attached to the line. How badly she may be disabled we know not. I direct Sumner and Powell to pass along the cliff, and see if they can reach him from below. Rhodes, Hall, and myself run to the other boat, jump aboard, push out, and away we go over the falls. A wave rolls over us, and our boat is unmanageable. Another great wave strikes us, the boat rolls over, and tumbles and tosses, I know not how. All I know is that Bradley is picking us up. We soon have all right again, and row to the cliff, and wait until Sumner and Powell can come. After a difficult climb they reach us. We run two or three miles farther, and turn again to the northwest, continuing until night, when we have run out of the granite once more.

August 29—We start very early this morning. The river still continues swift, but we have no serious difficulty, and at twelve o'clock emerge from the Grand Cañon of the Colorado.

*Exploration of the Colorado River of the West 1869–72.* By J. W. Powell. Washington, 1875.

# Oscar Rohn
## 1870-1923

ALASKA was the last great area of the continental United States to be explored, the work only being completed in this century, though its coasts had been frequented by the Russians for two hundred years. Serious examination of the interior followed the purchase of the territory by the United States in 1867. But the great impetus followed the discovery of gold twenty years later. To establish routes of supply to the mining settlements, the government put a number of expeditions in the field. That, of which Oscar Rohn was a member, had as its object the pioneering of a route through the Wrangel Mountains to the Copper River and Copper Centre. The extract from the official Report describes his experiences in seeking a route over the Nezeria glacier, north of Valdez, to the Copper River valley. Some one hundred fifty miles to the north-west of the area in which Rohn was working rises Mt. McKinley (20,300 feet), the highest summit in North America.

*　　　*　　　*

When morning broke September 1 the storm was still raging and we were obliged to remain in camp. It was with great difficulty that we kept our tent from blowing away. We had no way of making a fire, so had to spend our time in our blankets to keep warm. On the morning of the 2nd the weather, though still cold, had cleared and we started out very early. At ten o'clock we had reached the foot of the summit bench where our goods were cached. From here the best, and in fact the only, course seemed to be right up the middle of the glacier. On either side were tremendous cataracts, which seemed to preclude all possibility of crossing them. We had not gone a quarter of a mile from the cache, however, before the crevasses became so numerous and so large that we decided, before going farther with our loads, to explore ahead. Ordinarily crevasses are not continuous for long distances. Splinters, one end of which join one side and the other the opposite side, cut diagonally across them. This offers an opportunity to make headway even over badly crevassed areas.

On this glacier, however, we found two sets of heavy crevasses at nearly right angles to each other, cutting into isolated rectangular blocks, over which it was all but impossible to make headway. This condition was aggravated by the loose snow of the previous day, which had everywhere built snow bridges across the crevasses, often completely masking them, so that to avoid walking deliberately into a crevasse it was impossible to take a step in any direction without first carefully feeling the way with a stick. Fastened together with a life-line about our waists, one felt his way carefully ahead, while the other followed in his steps at the end of the line in order to check his fall should he break through. In this way we worked back and forth, and often, when about ready to give up and return, we would manage to find a wedge or snow-bridge strong enough to bear our weight, and thus enable us to get to the next block ahead.

At 2 p.m. that afternoon, after four hours of most trying work, we had made but a quarter of a mile. We had, however, crossed the worst part, and had now reached an elevation at which the crust of the snow was beginning to be sufficiently strong to bear our weight over the crevasses. From here on the grade was slight, and we reached the summit, a distance of about three miles, without difficulty. From the summit we could see nothing but a broad, smooth plain of snow which seemed to break down abruptly some eight or ten miles ahead.

I felt that life was too short to permit of taking the chances involved in attempting to bring our outfit over the route we had travelled that morning, and we decided to turn back, unless in some way we could manage to make our way over the great bench or cataract on the easterly side. This we undertook on our way back, and after many fruitless attempts we finally succeeded in making our way down. While exceedingly difficult, this route was free from the treacherous snow and we decided to attempt to get our goods over. Our outfit weighed somewhat over four hundred pounds, which was more than we could possibly handle on one trip. We concluded, therefore, to take one half of it and on the first clear day attempt to cross the summit and reach a point on the opposite side at which we would camp, and from here return for the rest.

The next morning broke clear, and at nine o'clock we were at the top of the bench with our loads. From here on the surface was bare and smooth, with a covering of six or eight inches of snow, over which we made good time. In view of the difficulty we had experienced in reaching the summit, we were much concerned regarding the possibility of getting down on the opposite side. . . . The most favourable condition we could hope for was that the zone would occur on the bench and that it would be possible to get around both over a moraine bordering on the glacier at this point. Indications from the summit favoured this supposition, and as we approached the top of the bench we came in sight of a moraine along its western edge. However, when within two miles of this the crust of the snow began giving away, and soon after we began stepping through it into cracks. As yet these were narrow, but conditions along the edge of the glacier and the conformation of the valley before us indicated larger ones. The surface was perfectly smooth and gave no evidence of its treacherous nature.

We were standing at this point discussing the situation and considering what next to do, when suddenly the surface of the glacier began swaying up and down in a most amazing manner. At the time I took this to be an earthquake, due to a fracture at some point in the glacier, but later I learned that it was the great earthquake which shook the entire country around. A careful survey of the situation showed us that there was only one possible way of reaching the moraine, and that was squarely down the middle of the valley before us. We accordingly fastened ourselves together with a line about our waists, tied our sleds together and, each carrying a stick with which to span a crack and support himself in case he went through, we started out, trusting we might not meet a crevasse too wide for these means to save us if one fell through. Slipping into unexpected openings up to our knees or our waist every few paces, and not knowing at what moment a large opening would take us in bodily, travelling was uncomfortable, to say the least; but there being only one course to pursue, we pushed ahead as best we could, and at the end of two seemingly long hours we reached the moraine.

Here we camped and prepared supper, after which we explored ahead and, to our great satisfaction, found that the moraine on which we were camped continued along the glacier for several miles, leaving little doubt but that over it we should be able to reach the plain below. At this time of the year days on the summit free from storm and blizzards are rare, and with the question of getting down disposed of, the next matter of importance was to get the remainder of our loads over the summit before bad weather again set in.

The next morning found us ready to leave camp at the first sign of day. The sky was overcast but the summit was clear when we started out, and we hoped it would remain so. The necessity of picking our way carefully had obliged us on the previous day to expose our eyes frequently to the intense glare of the snow, and before night we had experienced symptoms of snow-blindness which this morning grew rapidly worse in the cold wind which blew from the summit. While going over the divide where the travelling was good we were able to keep our eyes covered most of the time, but on working on the bench it was necessary to use both eyes and to have them uncovered. Before we reached the top of this bench with our loads on the return journey both of my eyes were all but useless and one of McNeer's was totally blind. Whether his other eye would hold out and enable us to get back to the camp was a serious question. With the prospect of wandering about on the top of the glacier in a blizzard, without food or blankets and unable to see staring us in the face, crossing crevasses caused us little concern that afternoon. In fact, by the time we got to the crevasses the pain in our eyes was such that neither of us cared seriously how soon we fell into one. McNeer's eye, although most painful, retained its sight and enabled us to reach camp, where we took to our blankets and did not again leave them until the morning of the second day. We were in an exposed position and, the blizzard now raging threatening to blow down our tent, we managed to pack up and move the tent about a quarter of a mile into the ravine. The next day McNeer's eye was so much improved that he decided to explore ahead. He returned shortly and reported a bunch of sheep a mile or two away on the mountain side. This was welcome news, and I urged him to make every effort possible to secure one, a fact which I regretted when night came on and he had not returned to camp. When he finally did come, about an hour after dark, he reported having cached a dressed carcass about three miles ahead on the trail. He had become so engrossed in his sheep hunt that he had failed to notice that night was coming on, and in consequence had to take reckless chances in making his way back to camp over the glacier and moraine.

My eyes being considerably improved, the following morning we began packing our goods down the moraine, and on the afternoon of the second day after, had them once more loaded on our sleds on smooth ice at the foot of the great bench. Now that the question of getting over the glacier was practically disposed of, the subject of absorbing interest was which river drainage we had reached, the Copper or Tanana. From the summit we had seen a large open valley, seemingly at the foot of the glacier and leading off towards the north-west. Now we found this valley was cut off by a range of low, moraine-like hills, which caused the glacier to turn slightly to the east, and as we travelled on down we saw more and more of a wide, open valley leading to the east. The glacier headed directly for this valley, and we were about satisfied that this was the Tanana River, when we saw that the drainage was towards and not away from it, and that the river from the foot of the glacier turned abruptly around a prominent mountain opposite the foot of the glacier on the left-hand side. We were now satisfied that the river entered the valley to the north-west and that it was, without a question, Copper River.

We spent one more night on the ice, and the following day, shortly after noon, we came to the foot of the glacier, which, being free from a terminal moraine, enabled us to go down easily and to make camp with our goods on solid ground that night. We had been on the glacier just fifteen days, and during this time we had nothing to eat but frozen bread, bacon, and mutton, except oatmeal or corn-meal mush and a little tea. We had cut up the wood we carried into shavings, and by burning these in a furnace-like enclosure and constant fanning, about a hat full would suffice to heat a skillet of water to boiling. In this way we managed to have some warm tea and mush twice a day during the time we were on the glacier with not more than twenty pounds of wood.

'Exploration in Wrangle Mountain District (Alaska).' By Oscar Rohn, in *Copper River Exploring Expedition, Capt. W. R. Abercrombie, U.S. Infantry, commanding, 1899.* Washington, 1900.

# SOUTH AMERICA

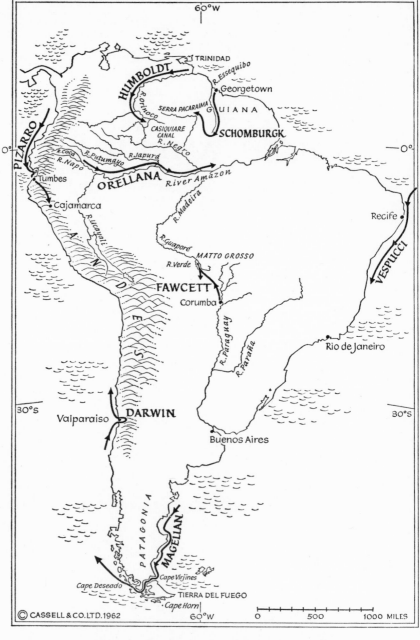

S·AMERICA

Labels on the map:

60°W

TRINIDAD
R. Essequibo
HUMBOLDT
Georgetown
R. Orinoco
SERRA PACARAIMA
GUIANA
CASIQUIARE CANAL
R. Negro
SCHOMBURGK

PIZARRO

0°
R. Coca
R. Putumayo
R. Japurá
R. Napo
Tumbes
ORELLANA
River Amazon
0°

Cajamarca
R. Ucayati
R. Madeira
Recife

A
N
D
E
S
R. Guaporé
MATTO GROSSO
R. Verde
FAWCETT
Corumba
VESPUCCI

Rio de Janeiro
R. Paraguay
R. Paraña

30°S
Valparaiso
DARWIN
30°S

Buenos Aires

PATAGONIA
MAGELLAN

Cape Deseado
Cape Virjines
TIERRA DEL FUEGO
Cape Horn
© CASSELL & CO. LTD. 1962
60°W
0        500        1000 MILES

# Amerigo Vespucci
## 1451-1512

THE discovery by Columbus was followed by numerous Spanish and Portuguese voyages, the details and results of which are by no means clear. The most enigmatical of these explorers was Amerigo Vespucci—another Italian, for he was a native of Florence —after whom the new continent was named. He served both Portugal and Spain, and is credited by some with having made four voyages in all. He eventually rose to be Chief Pilot of Spain, so that it is difficult for his denigrators to challenge his professional competence, though this has been exaggerated by his advocates. The following extract from the narrative of his 'third' voyage, 1501-2, describes his experiences on the coast of north-eastern Brazil. The expedition continued south-westwards, Vespucci claiming to have reached 50° S. latitude, that is to within about four hundred miles of the entrance to the Straits of Magellan. Whatever the truth about Vespucci's claims as an explorer may be, he was undoubtedly the first great popularizer of the wonders of the New World.

★　　★　　★

4 Sept., 1504. We left this port of Ethiopia,[1] and sailed south-west a quarter south, so that in sixty-seven days we came to a land which was distant seven hundred leagues to the south-west of this said port. In those sixty-seven days we had the most contrary weather ever encountered at sea by man—rains, storms and tempests. These beset us because we were in a very unpropitious season, for the greater part of our voyage was ever near the equator, where in the month of June it is winter. And we found the days and nights to be equal, and shadows always fell towards the south. It pleased God to reveal to us a new land on the 17th day of August. Anchoring half a league off-shore, we put out our boats to see whether the land was inhabited by human beings, and what it was like. We found people who were worse than brutes. Your Magnificence will understand that at the outset we saw no one, but we perceived clearly

[1] In the neighbourhood of the modern Dakar, West Africa.

that it was peopled from the many indications around. We took possession of it for the most serene King.[1] We found it a very pleasant green land, of fair appearance lying five degrees south of the equator. On this day we returned to the ships and, as we had much need of water and wood, agreed to return the following day to procure these necessities. Having landed, we saw some people on a hilltop, gazing at us and not daring to approach. They were naked, and of the same colour and form as those we had seen before. Though we endeavoured to induce them to draw near and to speak with us, we failed to win their confidence. In view of their obstinacy, and as it was already late in the day, we returned to the ships, leaving many bells, mirrors, and other trifles on the beach, where they could be seen. When we had put out to sea, they came down from the hill, and approaching the articles which we had left, marvelled greatly at them. On this day we obtained nothing except water. The next morning we saw from the ships that the people on the shore were making much smoke; and, thinking that they were signalling to us, we went ashore, where we found a multitude assembled. They remained at a distance from us, motioning us to accompany them inland. Whereupon two of our Christians asked permission from our captain to take the risk of venturing inland with them to ascertain what manner of people they were, and whether they had any riches, spices or drugs. They pleaded so strongly that the captain consented. Equipped with many articles of barter, they left us with orders to return within the five days we would wait for them. They took their way inland and we awaited their return in the ships. Almost every day people came to the beach, but would not speak with us. On the seventh day we went ashore, and found that they had brought their women with them. When we leaped ashore, the men of that land sent many of their women to talk with us. Seeing that they lacked confidence, we agreed to send one of our men to them, a very active youth, while we, to reassure them, returned to the boats. When he approached them, they made a great circle round him, touching him in amazement. While this was going on, we saw a woman coming down the hill, carrying a great club in her hand. When she reached the place where our Christian stood, she

[1] King Manuel of Portugal.

came up behind him, and raising her club, dealt him so severe a blow that he fell dead to the ground. On the instant the other women seized him by the feet, and dragged him towards the hill, while the men rushed to the beach, shooting off their bows and arrows. This put such fear into our people, who were in the boats made fast to the shore, that, under the shower of arrows which were shot into our boats, no one thought of taking up his weapons. Nevertheless, we discharged four mortar shots at them, without hitting anyone; but, on hearing the reports, they all fled towards the hill where the women were already cutting the Christian to pieces. Over a great fire which they had built they roasted him before our eyes, showing us many pieces before eating them. And the men conveyed by signs how they had killed and eaten the other two Christians, the which grieved us exceedingly. To see with our own eyes the cruelty with which they had treated the dead man was an intolerable injury to us all. More than forty of us wished to jump ashore to avenge so cruel a death, and an act so bestial and inhuman, but the captain-major would not give his consent; and thus they remained unpunished for this great affront. We left them with much ill-will, and shamed at our captain's behaviour.

Departing this place, we continued our voyage to the east-south-east, for so the land trended. We hove to many times, but never found people willing to treat with us. And we sailed so far that we found the land turning towards the south-west. When we had rounded a cape, to which we gave the name of Cape St. Augustine, we began to sail to the south-west. And this cape is one hundred and fifty leagues east of the first land seen, where they murdered our Christians, in eight degrees south of latitude.[1] Sailing on we sighted one day many people assembled on the beach to see the marvel of our ships and our manner of sailing. We approached them, anchored in a good place, and putting ashore in the boats, found the people better natured than the others. Although it was hard work to gain their confidence, nevertheless we made friends and traded with them. We stayed in this place five days and here we found canafistula very large, green and dry, and higher than the tree-tops. We decided to carry off two men from this place that they

[1] They were then in the neighbourhood of the modern port of Recife.

might teach us the language, and three came of their own free will, to make the journey to Portugal.

Letter from Amerigo Vespucci to Piero Sodarini, 1504. Trsl. by G.R.C. from the text in E. Levillier's *Amerigo Vespucci*. Buenos Aires, 1951.

# Francisco Pizarro
## 1476-1541

THE Central American peninsula was crossed and the Pacific Ocean first sighted by Vasco Nuñez de Balboa in 1513. Twenty years later, after a reconnaissance, Pizarro, lured on by reports of great wealth, landed near Tumbes on the Pacific coast of South America with a small company of adherents and began his assault on the Inca kingdom of Peru. This extract written by his secretary describes the first traverse of the Andes by Europeans. On the day following their arrival at Cajamarca (the point at which this extract ends) Pizarro and his men fell, without warning, upon the Indians, seized the Inca, Atahualpa, and put his army to flight. Atahualapa was subsequently murdered, and Peru with all its riches passed under Spanish control with little further opposition.

Having arrived at the foot of the mountains they rested for a day to arrange the order for the ascent. The Governor,[1] after taking counsel with experienced officers, resolved to leave the rear guard and baggage, taking with him forty horse and sixty foot. He entrusted the remainder to the care of a captain, and ordered him to follow with much circumspection, telling him that he would receive instructions as to what he was to do.

Having made these arrangements, the Governor commenced the ascent. The horsemen led their horses up until, at noon, they reached a pallisaded fort on the top of a hill, in a narrow part of the road where, with few Christians, the way might be made good against a great army. It was so steep that, in places, they had to ascend by steps, and there was no other place but the road by which the ascent could be effected. This pass was ascended without its being defended by anyone. The fortress was surrounded by stone walls, and was built on a hill with steep rocks on all sides. Here the Governor stopped to rest and have some food. The cold is so great

1 Francisco Pizarro.

on these mountains that some of the horses, accustomed to the warmth of the valleys, were frost-bitten.

Thence the Governor went to sleep at a village, and sent a messenger to the forces in his rear, with the news that they might safely advance through the pass, and with orders that they were to push on so as to pass the night at the fortress. The Governor lodged that night at a village, in a strong house surrounded by a masonry wall, as extensive as a fort of Spain, with its doorways. If the people had had the artists and tools of Spain, this surrounding wall could not have been better built. The people of this village had taken up arms, except some women and a few Indians. The Governor ordered a captain to take two from amongst the Indians, and to examine each separately touching the affairs of that land, asking them where Atabaliba[1] was, and if he intended peace or war. The captain learnt from them that Atabaliba had reached Caxamalca[2] three days before with a large force; but they knew nothing of his intentions. They said, however, that they had always heard that Atabaliba wished to have peace with the Christians. The people of the village were on his side.

Towards sunset one of the Indians who had gone with the messenger arrived and said that he had been sent back by his master when he was near Caxamalca, because he had encountered two messengers of Atabaliba who were coming behind him and would arrive next day. He reported that Atabaliba was at Caxamalca, and that there were no armed men on the road. The Governor sent back this intelligence to the captain in charge of the baggage, by a letter, in which he was told that the Governor would make but a short march next day in order that the Captain might join him and that the whole force would then advance together. The next morning the Governor marched with his troops, still ascending the mountains, and stopped on a plain on the summit, near some springs of water, to wait for those who were still behind. The Spaniards rested in the cotton tents they brought with them, making fires to protect themselves from the cold of the mountains. For on the plains of

[1] Atahualpa, the son of the Inca, Huayna Capac.
[2] Cajamarca, a town in the Andes about a hundred miles from the sea, where Atahualpa had his headquarters.

Castile it is not colder than on these heights, which are clear of trees, but covered with a grass, like short esparto. There are a few stunted trees and the water is so cold that it cannot be drunk without being first warmed.

After the Governor had rested here for a short time the rear guard arrived, and also the messengers sent by Atabaliba, who brought ten sheep. Being brought before the Governor, and having made their obeisances, they said, 'Atabaliba has sent these sheep for the Christians, and he would know the day on which they will arrive at Caxamalca that he may send out provisions on the road.' The Governor received them well, and said that he rejoiced at their arrival with a message from his brother Atabaliba, and that he would come as quickly as possible. After they had eaten food, and had some rest, the Governor questioned the messengers touching the affairs of their land, and respecting the wars waged by Atabaliba. . . .

The Governor, believing that all that this Indian had told him, on the part of Atabaliba, was intended to astonish the Christians, and make them understand his power and skill, also said to the messenger, 'I well believe that what you have told me is true because Atabaliba is a great lord, and I am informed that he is a good soldier. Yet I would have you to know that my Lord the Emperor, who is King of Spain and of all the Indies and of Tierra Firme, and Lord over all the World, has many servants who are greater lords than Atabaliba, and his captains have fought and taken much greater lords than either Atabaliba, his brother, or his father. The Emperor has sent me to these lands to bring the inhabitants to a knowledge of God and, in his service, I have defeated greater lords than Atabaliba, with these few Christians that are with me now. If he should wish for my friendship and to receive me peacefully, as other lords have done, I shall be his good friend, and I will assist him in his conquest, leaving him in his present state; for I go through these lands to discover the other sea. But if he should wish for war, I will make war, as I have done against the chief of the island of Santiago, and against the chief of Tumbes, and against all others who have wished to have war with me. I make war upon no one, nor do I molest any one, unless war is made upon me.'

When the messengers heard these things, they were at first so astounded that they could not speak, to think that so few Spaniards could have performed such wonderful things. After a time they expressed a wish to go with this reply to their lord, and to tell him that the Christians would come quickly, in order that he might send out provisions on the road. The Governor dismissed them. The next morning he continued the march, still over the mountains, and that night he slept at some villages he came to in a valley. As soon as the Governor arrived there came the chief messenger whom Atabaliba had first sent with the present of the fountains like fortresses and who came to Caran[1] by way of Caxas. The Governor was very glad to see him and inquired after Atabaliba. The messenger answered that he was well and that he had sent ten sheep for the Christians. He spoke very freely and from his conversation he seemed to be an intelligent man.

When he had completed his speech the Governor asked the interpreters what he had said. They answered that he had repeated the same as had been said by the other messengers the day before; but that he had added many arguments, praising the greatness of his lord and the vast power of his army and assuring the Governor that Atabaliba would receive him in peace and that he desired to have him as a friend and a brother. The Governor answered with fair words such as the other had used. This ambassador was served as a lord, and had five or six cups of fine gold from which he drank, and he gave the Spaniards *chica*[2] to drink out of them, which he brought with him. He said that he desired to go to Caxamalca with the Governor.

Next morning the Governor started, his way leading over the mountains as before, and he reached a village of Atabaliba, where he rested for one day. . . .

Next day the Governor departed and slept on a plain, intending to reach Caxamalca at noon the day after, as they told him it was near. Here messengers arrived from Atabaliba, with food for the Christians. Early next morning the Governor started, with his

[1] Zaran, a town through which Pizarro had already passed.
[2] A fermented liqueur made from maize.

troops in order of battle, and marched to within a league of Caxa-malca. Here he waited for his rear guard to join him. All the troops got their arms ready, and the Governor formed the Spaniards, horse and foot, three deep, to enter the town. In this order the Governor advanced, sending messengers to Atabaliba, that he might come and meet him at the town of Caxamalca. On reaching the entrance to Caxamalca they saw the camp of Atabaliba at a distance of a league in the skirts of the mountains. The Governor arrived at this town of Caxamalca on Friday, the 15th of November, 1532, at the hour of vespers. In the middle of the town there is a great open space surrounded by walls and houses. The Governor occupied this position, and sent a messenger to Atabaliba, to announce his arrival, to arrange a meeting, and that he might show him where to lodge. Meanwhile he ordered the town to be examined, with a view to discovering a stronger position where he might pitch the camp. He ordered all the troops to be stationed in the open space, and the cavalry to remain mounted, until it was seen whether Atabaliba would come.

*Narrative of the Conquest of Peru, 1547.* By Francisco Xeres. Trsl. by C. R. Markham. Hakluyt Soc., ser. 1, v. 47.

# Francisco Orellana
## 1500-1550

AFTER his conquest of Peru, Francisco Pizarro sent his youngest brother Gonzalo in 1539 to explore the 'Cinamon Land', east of Quito and on the Amazonian flanks of the Andes. Pizarro's party of four thousand men spent several months making their way through equatorial forest and down the Rio Coca. With his force greatly reduced in numbers, by the assaults of Indians and the hostile environment, Pizarro finally decided to send a party down the Coca, which he was told joined a large river at no great distance. The party was then to return with fresh supplies. Francisco Orellana, the commander, however, continued downstream, on the grounds that the reported supplies were non-existent and that it was impossible to return against the strong current. But his enemies said that his motive was to obtain the lordship of the newly discovered country from the King of Spain. Whatever the truth may be, Orellana thus discovered the great river Amazon, which he descended to the sea (26th August, 1541), and then sailed to Trinidad. The extract below describes his adventures down the upper Amazon between the mouths of the Putumayo and the Japura. The narrative is by Friar Gaspar de Carvajal, who took part in the expedition.

★     ★     ★

Up to this point they had made two hundred leagues in nine days, having lost seven companions, who had died of hunger during their former sufferings. They now determined (in order not to exhaust the Indians) to depart on the feast of Candlemas. Twenty leagues further on, a stream flowed into the river on the right hand, which was so swollen that at the point of junction with the larger stream, the water struggled with such violence that the Spaniards expected to have been lost. Escaped from this danger, for the next two hundred leagues that they traversed, they met with no habitations and suffered much from toil and dangers, until they arrived at some villages where the Indians seemed to be quite off their guard. In order not to disturb them the captain ordered twenty soldiers to land and ask them for food. The Indians were delighted to see the Spaniards and gave them plenty of provisions, turtles and parrots. Orellana then went to a village at another part of the river where he met with no resistance. The natives gave him provisions; and, continuing the voyage in sight of villages, on another day some Indians in four canoes came to the vessel, and offered the captain some turtles, good partridges and fish; they were much pleased and invited Orellana to come and see their chief who was named Aparia and who now approached with more canoes. The Indians and Christians landed, and the chief Aparia came and was well received by captain Orellana, who treated him to a discourse on the law of God and the grandeur of the King of Castile, all which the Indians listened to with much attention. Aparia inquired if he had seen the Amazons whom in his language they call Coniapuyara, meaning Great Lord. He added that his people were few, while the Amazons were numerous. Continuing the conversation, the captain begged the chief to name all the lords in the country. Having enumerated twenty, he ended saying that all were children of the sun, and that as such he ought to hold them as friends. They were rejoiced, and supplied plenty of provisions of good quality; and the captain took possession of the land, placing a cross on a high place, at which the Indians expressed wonder and satisfaction.

When Captain Orellana found that he met with a cordial reception, he determined to build the brigantine at this place; and it pleased God that there should be an engraver in his company who, though ship-building was not his business, proved of great use. The timber having been cut and prepared with great labour, which the men endured with much willingness, in thirty-five days she was launched, caulked with cotton, and the seams payed with pitch which was given them by the Indians.

At this time four tall Indians came to the captain, dressed and adorned with ornaments, and with hair reaching from the head to the waist. With much humility they placed food before the captain, and said that a great chief had sent them to inquire who these strangers were and whence they came. Orellana gave them some articles of barter which they valued very much, and he spoke to them in the same way as he had done to the others, and so they departed. The Spaniards passed all Lent at this place, and all the Christians confessed to the two priests who were in the company, and the priests preached to them, and urged them to endure the hardships they would have to encounter with constancy, until there should be an end of them.

The new brigantine being completed, and fit to navigate the sea, they set sail on the fourth of April from the residence of Aparia, and voyaged for eighty leagues without encountering a single warlike Indian. The river passed through an uninhabited country, flowing from forest to forest, and they found no place where they could either sleep or fish. Thus with herbs and a little toasted maize for food, they went on until the 6th of May, when they reached an elevated place which appeared to have been inhabited. Here they stopped to fish, and it happened that the engraver, who had been so useful in building the vessel, killed a guana with his cross-bow. The creature was in a tree near the river, and fell into the water. A soldier named Contreras also caught a large fish with a hook and, as the hook was small and the fish was large, it was necessary to take hold of it with his hand; and when it was opened, the nut of the cross-bow was found in its stomach. . . .

On the twelfth of May they arrived at the province of Machiparo, which is thickly peopled and ruled by another chief named Aomagua. One morning they discovered a number of canoes full of warlike Indians with large shields made of the skins of lizards and dantas, beating drums, and shouting with threats that they would eat the Christians. The latter collected their vessels together but met with a great misfortune in finding that their powder had become damp and that they were thus unable to load their arquebusses. The Indians approached with their bows, and the cross-bows did them some damage; and thus, while reinforcements continued to arrive, a gallant conflict was maintained. In this way they descended the river, engaged in a running fight until they reached a place where there was a great crowd in the ravines. Half the Spaniards then landed and followed the Indians to their village; and as it appeared large and the people were numerous, the ensign returned to make his report to

Orellana, who was defending the vessels against the Indians, who were attacking him from their canoes.

Understanding that there was a quantity of provisions in the village, the captain ordered a soldier, named Cristoval de Segovia, to take it. He started with twelve companions, who loaded themselves with supplies, but were attacked by more than two thousand Indians, whom they resisted with such vigour that they forced them to retreat, and retained the food, with only two Spaniards wounded. But the Indians returned with reinforcements, and pressing on the Spaniards wounded four. Cristoval de Segovia, though he wished to retire to the ships, said that he would not leave the Indians with the victory, nor place his retreat in such peril and, making a gallant resistance, he succeeded in retiring in safety. In the meanwhile another body of Indians attacked the vessels from two sides and, having fought for more than two hours, it pleased the Lord to assist the Spaniards and some, of whom little was expected, performed wonderful deeds of valour. Such were the acts of Cristoval de Aguilar, Blas de Medina, and Pedro de Ampudia.

The Indians having retired, the wounded, who amounted to eighteen, were ordered to be attended to. All recovered except Ampudia, a native of Ciudad Roderigo, who died of his wounds in eight days. In this encounter the value of the commander's example was shown; for Orellana did not, because he commanded, cease to fight like any common soldier; while his good disposition, his form, his promptitude, and forethought animated the soldiers.

'Voyage of Francisco Orellana down the River of the Amazons, 1540.' From Antonio de Herrera's *General History of the Western Indies*. Trsl. by C. R. Markham, Hakluyt Society, ser. i, vol. 24, 1859.

# Alexander von Humboldt
## 1769-1859

ALEXANDER VON HUMBOLDT, 'the father of modern geography', mentioned earlier in connection with Asian exploration, based his life-work largely on his observations and experiences during several years' travel in Central and South America (1799–1804). His main purpose was to determine a large number of astronomical positions—to improve the maps of the country—and, in co-operation with Aimé Bonpland, to collect botanical specimens. But he also amassed a great amount of scientific, political and economic information on the countries through which he passed. He penetrated to the headwaters of the Orinoco, and solved the problem of the 'Casiquiari Canal', the waterway linking the Orinoco and the Amazon river systems, by traversing it by canoe as related in this extract. Later he published the results of his travels in many volumes, wrote his *Kosmos*, an attempt to describe the universe on scientific lines, and encouraged and supported much subsequent research. Humboldt's contribution to the evolution of geography was his insistence upon observation in the field, on the interrelation of natural phenomena, and on the virtue of clear, vivid writing.

★    ★    ★

May 6th. We embarked at sunrise, after having carefully examined the bottom of our canoe. It had become thinner, but had received no crack in the portage. We reckoned that the same boat would still bear the voyage of three hundred leagues, which remained for us to make, in going down the Rio Negro, ascending the Cassiquiare, and redescending the Orinoco as far as Angostura. The Pimichin, which is called a rivulet (*caño*), is as broad as the Seine opposite the gallery of the Tuileries; but small trees that love the water, corossals and achras, narrow the bed so much that there remains open a channel of only fifteen or twenty toises (100–130 feet). Next to the Rio Chagre this river is one of the most celebrated in America for the number of its windings; eighty-five are reckoned, which greatly lengthen it. They often form a right angle, and occur every two or three leagues (5 to $7\frac{1}{2}$ miles). To determine the difference of longitude between the landing-place[1] and the point where we were to enter the Rio Negro, I took by the compass the course of the Caño Pimichin, and noted the time during which we followed the same direction. The velocity of the current was only 2·4 feet in a second; but our canoe made by rowing 4·6 feet. The *embarcadero* of the Pimichin appeared to me to be eleven thousand toises (40 miles) west of its mouth, and 0° 2' west of the mission of Javita. This *caño* is navigable during the whole year, and has but one *raudal*,[2] which is somewhat difficult to go up; its banks are low, but rocky. After having followed for four hours and a half the windings of this narrow channel, we at length entered the Rio Negro.

The morning was cool and beautiful. We had been confined thirty-six days in a narrow boat, so unstable that it would have been overset by any person rising imprudently from his seat, without warning the rowers to preserve her trim, by leaning on the opposite side. We had suffered severely from the sting of insects, but we had withstood the insalubrity of the climate; we had passed without accident the great number of falls of water and bars that impede the navigation of the rivers and often render it more dangerous than long voyages by sea. After all we had endured, I may be permitted, perhaps, to speak of the satisfaction we felt in having reached the tributary streams of the Amazon, having passed the isthmus that separates two great systems of rivers, and in being sure of having fulfilled the most important object of our voyage, the astronomical determination of the course of that arm of the Orinoco, which falls into the Rio Negro, and of which the existence has been alternately proved and denied for half a century.[3] In proportion as we draw near to an object we have long had in view, its interest seems to augment. The uninhabited banks of the Cassiquiare, covered with forests, without memorials of times past, then occupied my imagination, as do now the banks of the Euphrates or the Oxus, celebrated in the annals of civilized nations. In that interior part of the New Continent we almost accustomed ourselves to regard men as not being

[1] On a tributary of the Rio Negro.
[2] Rapids.
[3] The so-called 'Casiquiare Canal'.

essential to the order of nature. The earth is loaded with plants, and nothing impedes their free development. An immense layer of mould manifests the uninterrupted action of organic powers. The crocodiles and the boas are masters of the river; the jaguar, the pecari, the dante, and the monkeys traverse the forest without fear and without danger; there they dwell as in an ancient inheritance. This aspect of animate nature in which man is nothing has something in it strange and sad. To this we reconcile ourselves with difficulty on the ocean and amid the sands of Africa; though in these scenes, where nothing recalls to mind our fields, our woods and our streams, we are less astonished at the vast solitude through which we pass. Here, in a fertile country adorned with eternal verdure, we seek in vain the traces of the power of man; we seem to be transported into a world different from that which gave us birth. These impressions are so much the more powerful in proportion as they are of longer duration. A soldier, who had spent his whole life in the missions of the Upper Orinoco, slept with us on the bank of the river. He was an intelligent man who, during a calm and serene night, pressed me with questions on the magnitude of the stars, on the inhabitants of the Moon, on a thousand subjects of which I was as ignorant as himself. Being unable by my answers to satisfy his curiosity, he said to me in a firm tone, 'With respect to men, I believe there are no more above than you would have found if you had gone by land from Javita to Cassiquiare. I think I see in the stars, as here, a plain covered with grass, and a forest (*mucho monte*) traversed by a river.' In citing these words, I paint the impression produced by the monotonous aspect of those solitary regions. May this monotony not be found to extend itself to the journal of our navigation, and tire the reader accustomed to the description of the scenes and historical memorials of the ancient continent! . . .

[May 23rd.] Our canoe was not ready to receive us till near three o'clock in the afternoon.[1] It had been filled with an innumerable quantity of ants during the navigation of the Cassiquiare; and the *toldo*, or roof of palm-leaves, beneath which we had again to remain

[1] Humboldt had passed from the Rio Negro via the Casiquiare to the Orinoco, which river he was about to descend.

stretched out during twenty-two days, was freed with difficulty from these insects. We employed part of the morning in repeating to the inhabitants of Esmeralda the questions which we had already put to them on the existence of a lake towards the east. We showed copies of the maps of Surville and Le Cruz to old soldiers who had been posted in that mission ever since its first establishment. They laughed at the pretended communication of the Orinoco with the Rio Idapa, and at the *White Sea*, which the former river was supposed to cross. What we politely call geographical fictions appeared to them lies of the other world (*mentiras de por alla*). These good people could not comprehend how men, in making the map of a country, which they had never visited, could pretend to know things in minute detail of which persons who lived on the spot were ignorant. The lake Parima, the Sierra Mey, the springs that separate at the point where they issue from the earth, were entirely unknown at Esmeralda. We were repeatedly assured, that no one had ever been to the east of the Raudal of the Guahariboes and that beyond this point, according to the opinion of some of the natives, the Orinoco descends like a small torrent from a group of mountains inhabited by the Coroto Indians. I urge these circumstances because, if at the time of the royal expedition of the boundaries, or after that memorable occasion, any white man had actually reached the sources of the Orinoco and the pretended lake Parima, the tradition would have been preserved in the nearest mission, which must have been passed in order to make so important a discovery. Now the three persons who had knowledge of the labours of the expedition of the boundaries, Father Caulin, La Cruz, and Surville have published notions on the origin of the Orinoco that are diametrically opposite to each other. How could these contradictions have existed if, instead of having founded their maps on calculations and hypotheses framed at Madrid, those learned men had had before their eyes the narrative of one real journey. . . .

*Personal Narrative of Travels to the Equatorial Regions of the New Continent, 1799-1804.* By Alexander von Humboldt. Trsl. by H. M. Williams, 2nd ed. 1827. Vol. 5.

# Robert Hermann Schomburgk
## 1804-1865

ROBERT SCHOMBURGK, a German by birth who became a naturalized British subject, was one of the generation of travellers inspired by the example of Alexander von Humboldt. A geologist and naturalist by training, with experience of the West Indies, he secured the support of the Royal Horticultural Society and the Royal Geographical Society for his project to explore the interior of British Guiana, 1833. He proved himself also to be a good traveller and surveyor, and succeeded in linking the surveys of the colony to those of Humboldt. As a botanist he is perhaps best known for his discovery of the giant water lily, *Victoria regia*. The extract from the narrative by his brother, Richard, describes the ascent of a summit in the Humirida range, the eastern portion of the Serra Pacaraima, south of Roraima (8,620 feet). Through these rugged sandstone highlands— of the type which have given rise to legends of 'lost worlds'—runs the divide between the rivers of Guiana and the northern tributaries of the Amazon. For his work in Guiana he received the Gold Medal of the Royal Geological Society in 1840. He subsequently entered the Colonial Service and was knighted.

★     ★     ★

(24th Oct. 1842.) We set out upon the dangerous enterprise. Between and over colossal sandstone rocks, up went the trail. At the end of an hour we had not reached half-way although our strength was exhausted: the panting breast, the trembling knee that every few minutes required a moment's rest, and the scorching sun, from which we were quite unprotected, exhausted the remainder of our strength. We were really in a bad way and yet we Europeans held nothing but a stick in our hands, while the Indians, steeped in perspiration and carrying their load by means of a broad band over the forehead, clambered over the masses of stone with as much ease and agility as if these were level ground and the glowing orb a cooling shade. Our long procession glided like a snake up the mountain side and the outlook, front and back, was of so strange a nature that it was even able to captivate us, exhausted as we were, on the repeated occasions that we were forced to rest.

After many an hour's climb we reached the five hundred foot high sandstone wall. For us to commence its ascent at once along the dangerous trail that the Indians had been forced to use was impossible, our lost strength had at least to be partly recuperated. A quantity of moss and lichens put a little life into the gloomy fabric; its cracks and crevices were filled with several orchids, e.g. *Epidendrum*, and a small shrub belonging to the *Piperaceae*, the roots of which had entangled the rocks in a regular network; it was by its help that we would have to climb the ravines hewn out of the main massif. The possibility of the climb was indeed dependent upon this same network, but this again required above everything else intrepid courage, the complete and free use of the hands, and the close investigation of the stability of the roots and projecting stones in the weathered and decayed sandstone wall, before one could trust the weight of one's body to them. A slip of the foot before the hand could steady itself at the halt that this growth or that chink offered, the loss of one's balance, or the breaking of a root, not only meant a most horrible smash for the unfortunate fellow himself, but the probable death of a large number of his followers.

A start was made on the daring enterprise. We Europeans followed immediately next to the guides. The procession clambered zig-zag, one following the other at a fixed distance and swinging from step to landing up the wall. I shuddered the first time I looked below; the brown figures were climbing up the rocks like ants, and the thought that with the bursting of a forehead band, the load might lose its sole and only support, and in falling knock over one of the men following, made me shut my eyes, and not dare look behind again. No noise interrupted the dead silence which was only now and then broken by the plunge of a stone that had crumbled its way loose.

With the arrival at the top of the men ahead of me, I also threw myself quite out of breath on the more secure flat and took another peep down the steep wall, but had to close my eyes and hasten away, because every moment I imagined I should be hearing the death-cry of someone who had fallen over. As each of the climbers reached the ridge he uttered a loud shout of triumph like those before him. In the course of three hours the last of the party finally reached the top, and now for the first time the anxious breast could breathe with freedom and one could appreciate in dumb delight the beautiful panorama which stretched beneath and near him in its absolutely infinite wealth of charm. Upon our entrance to the valley of the Muyang we had rejoiced from the very bottom of our hearts over the wonderful landscape—the same thing here, and yet again another one opposite. Shall I describe it as more beautiful? I don't know. The magic of the moment excluded comparisons. In the solemn stillness of virgin nature, the valley of the Muyang, strewn over with many a luxuriant oasis, stretched itself before us at our feet, but the eye sought in vain the roof of the house that we had left a few hours before; the work of man had been buried in the wantonness of Nature. Not a sign of active life, no noise of busy human hands disturbed the deep solemn calm in which Nature looked proudly up towards us, and held us spell-bound. Towards the S.E. and W. innumerable mountain chains melted away into the surface of a green wavy sea; only in the S.E. and in the far W. did the gloomy bleak rock masses of Mairari and in the S.W. the peculiar steeple-like Mareppa-Emba—the latter with a height of 3,500 feet—rise above this sea of vegetation, over which somewhat further to the W. the Erimitipu, and in W. by S. the Ucaraima soared to a height of 3,690 feet. The rocky wall was by no means the summit of Humirida, which we had still to climb before we could sweep our gaze freely towards the north.

It seemed as if the pure current of air blowing cool around us brought new strength with it, so wonderfully quickly did we feel refreshed for the continuation of the journey. Between the fissures of the sandstone layers there sprouted several orchids, namely the former species of *Epidendrum* and a beautiful *Odontoglossum*, with which a little orchid set with sedge-like leaves was associated, but unfortunately no longer in bloom. Besides these orchids, the *Marcetia taxifolia DeC.*, decked with rose blossoms, had chosen the crevices and clefts for its place of stay; this plant, that was seen here for the first time, I had taken for an Erica in the distance. As we reached the real mountain top, a broad and glorious highland interrupted by insignificant hills and refreshing green clumps of woodland and bush, lay before us in the N.W., N., and N.E., until the high mountain ranges again limited the far horizon. We followed a course now straight for the north, until a thick cluster of arboreal growths attracted my attention from the mountains. It was composed of extraordinary ferns. Their bare stems, several feet in circumference, soon branched dichotomously, these branches tapering off at their extremities into long grass-like broad leaves.

We partook of our meagre breakfast close by an abandoned house, refreshed ourselves in the cool waters of the Zuappi, and after packing up my botanical treasures proceeded on our way through the magic garden when a forest, with its edges bordered with gigantic twenty to thirty-foot high cactus columns, soon received us. Innumerable palms raised their proud crowns of fronds above the mighty foliage trees, the extensive boughs of which were almost completely covered with the dependent cercus as well as with a motley intricacy of immense tillandsiae, orchids and ferns, while countless creepers and rope-vines, from the thickness of an arm to that of a human body, running up their trunks like ropes in odd sorts of twists and tangles, wound themselves from branch to branch whence they either ran straight down or hung in rings and loops and changed the forest into a fairy grove. The further we went, the richer and more varied became the vegetation.

Humeseta consisted of five houses, two of which however were still under construction, and fifty red-painted residents who, inquisitive and surprised, were gazing at us pale-faced strangers with our extraordinary baggage. Even before actual arrival, our two Indians had come out to meet us with the hardly encouraging information that here also we should only find just enough provisions as would prevent us starving. The luckless war which, like the Trojan, a woman had kindled, had likewise brought scarcity and want into this dale.

Through being repeated so often during the past few days disappointment had almost become habitual, but alas, our pinched and discontented stomachs would not accustom themselves to hunger. Chaffing and smiling in sympathy our followers looked first at their emaciated figures and loosely hanging folds of skin and then at the piece of cassava bread hardly the size of their hand, and the two half-ripe plantains that fell to each one's lot when the provisions were divided. However much the stomach might want, the mouth was silent; with stoical equanimity our men had withstood the enforced strain of several days' fast with more than usual endurance; they knew it was not our fault, and quietly and willingly fulfilled the duties, now doubly heavy, that they had undertaken. Though their mouths were silent their very appearance made open complaint. Had anyone in Germany told me that within three or four days hunger could turn an otherwise healthy man into a skeleton, I should immediately have come out with an emphatic 'no'! With the South American Indians this is, however, not only possible, but is actually the case. Even at the end of the second day, after the curtailing of the accustomed rations, the ribs and remaining bones became more and more prominent over the hitherto fleshy figures, the fat body fell in, and like someone else's clothes the otherwise well-stuffed skin of the belly, hung down in folds. However incredible the following may appear, it is nevertheless true that after they had consumed their share of the rations all at one go, one would think them unable to get another morsel past their lips for the next twenty-four hours—yet they puckered up this wobbly skin in their hands to show us how much more they still wanted before its previous well-to-do condition could be restored. This fulness of body is resumed just as quickly as it is lost.

*Travels in British Guiana, 1840–4.* By Richard Schomburgk. Trsl. by W. E. Roth. 2 vols. Georgetown, 1923.

# Charles Darwin
## 1809-1882

CHARLES DARWIN, a young naturalist fresh from Cambridge, sailed in H.M.S. *Beagle* under the command of Captain Fitzroy, in December 1831. On this voyage of circumnavigation, he was observing and pondering on many facts which he later employed in formulating his epoch-making work, *The Origin of Species*. Though he visited few if any entirely unknown places, he was in any sense of the word 'an explorer'. His 'Journal of researches into the natural history and geology of the countries visited during the voyage of H.M.S. *Beagle*', deals mainly with South America, with the exception of Brazil, and forms part of the remarkable contribution of British naturalists to our knowledge of that continent. (Others of note are A. R. Wallace, who formulated the theory of natural selection simultaneously with Darwin, and H. W. Bates.) The extract illustrates Darwin's ability to deduce a general theory from his field observations—in this case the geological history of the Andean valleys and river terraces in the Pleistocene. Darwin, through his theories of evolution which stimulated the correlation and orderly arrangement of observed facts, had a profound influence on geographical thinking, an influence which is not always fully appreciated. Darwin left the *Beagle* at Valparaiso and crossed the Andes via Santiago and the Portillo pass, to Mendoza, returning by the Uspallata pass.

★     ★     ★

March 19th [1835[. We rode during this day to the last, and therefore most elevated house in the valley. The number of inhabitants became scanty; but wherever water could be brought on the land, it was very fertile. All the main valleys in the Cordillera are characterized by having, on both sides, a fringe or terrace of shingle and sand, rudely stratified, and generally of considerable thickness. These fringes evidently once extended across the valleys, and were united; and the bottoms of the valleys in northern Chile, where there are no streams, are thus smoothly filled up. On these fringes the roads are generally carried, for their surfaces are even, and they rise with a very gentle slope up the valleys; hence, also, they are easily cultivated by irrigation. They may be traced up to a height of between seven and nine thousand feet, where they become hidden by the irregular piles of debris. At the lower end or mouths of the valleys, they are continuously united to those land-locked plains (also formed of shingle) at the foot of the main Cordillera, which I have described in a former chapter as characteristic of the scenery of Chile, and which were undoubtedly deposited when the sea penetrated Chile, as it now does the more southern coasts. No one fact in the geology of South America interested me more than these terraces of rudely stratified shingle. They precisely resemble in composition, the matter which the torrents in each valley would deposit if they were checked in their course by any cause, such as entering a lake or arm of the sea; but the torrents, instead of depositing matter, are now steadily at work wearing away both the solid rock and these alluvial deposits, along the whole line of every main valley and side valley. It is impossible here to give the reasons, but I am convinced that the shingle terraces were accumulated, during the gradual elevation of the Cordillera, by the torrents delivering, at successive levels, their detritus on the beach-heads of long narrow arms of the sea, first high up the valleys, then lower and lower down as the land slowly rose. If this be so, and I cannot doubt it, the grand and broken chain of the Cordillera, instead of having been suddenly thrown up, as was till lately the universal, and still is the common opinion of the geologists, has been slowly upheaved in mass, in the same gradual manner as the coasts of the Atlantic and Pacific have risen within the recent period.

A multitude of facts in the structure of the Cordillera, on this view receive a simple explanation.

The rivers which flow in these valleys ought rather to be called mountain-torrents. Their inclination is very great, and their water the colour of mud. The roar which the Maypu made as it rushed over the great rounded fragments was like that of the sea. Amidst the din of rushing waters, the noise from the stones, as they rattled one over another, was most distinctly audible even from a distance. This rattling noise, night and day, may be heard along the whole course of the torrent. The sound spoke eloquently to the geologist; the thousands and thousands of stones, which, striking against each other, made the one dull uniform sound, were all hurrying in one direction. It was like thinking of time, where the minute that now glides past is irrecoverable. So was it with these stones; the ocean is their eternity, and each note of that wild music told of one more step towards their destiny.

It is not possible for the mind to comprehend, except by a slow process, any effect which is produced by a cause repeated so often, that the multiplier itself conveys an idea, not more definite than the savage implies when he points to the hairs of his head. As often as I have seen beds of mud, sand and shingle, accumulated to the thickness of many thousand feet, I have felt inclined to exclaim that causes, such as the present rivers and the present beaches, could never have ground down and produced such masses. But, on the other hand, when listening to the rattling noise of these torrents, and calling to mind that whole races of animals have passed away from the face of the earth, and that during this whole period, night and day, these stones have gone rattling onwards in their course, I have thought to myself, can any mountains, any continent, withstand such waste?

In this part of the valley, the mountains on each side were from three to eight thousand feet high, with rounded outlines and steep bare flanks. The general colour of the rock was dullish purple and the stratification very distinct. If the scenery was not beautiful it was remarkable and grand. We met during the day several herds of cattle, which men were driving down from the higher valleys in the Cordillera. This sign of the approaching winter hurried our steps, more than was convenient for geologizing. The house where we slept was situated at the foot of a mountain, on the summit of which are the mines of S. Pedro de Nolasko. Sir F. Head marvels how mines have been discovered in such extraordinary situations, as the bleak summit of the mountain of S. Pedro de Nolasko. In the first place, metallic veins in this country are generally harder than the surrounding strata; hence, during the gradual wear of the hills, they project above the surface of the ground. Secondly, almost every labourer, especially in the northern parts of Chile, understands something about the appearance of ores. In the great mining provinces of Coquimbo and Copiapo, firewood is very scarce, and men search for it over every hill and dale; and by this means nearly all the richest mines have there been discovered. Chanuncillo, from which silver to the value of many hundred thousand pounds has been raised in the course of a few years, was discovered by a man who threw a stone at his loaded donkey, and thinking that it was very heavy he picked it up and found it full of pure silver; the vein occurred at no great distance, standing up like a wedge of metal. The miners, also, taking a crowbar with them, often wander on Sundays over the mountains. In this south part of Chile, the men who drive cattle into the Cordillera, and who frequent every ravine where there is a little pasture, are the usual discoverers.

20th. As we ascended the valley the vegetation, with the exception of a few pretty alpine flowers, became exceedingly scanty; and of quadrupeds, birds, or insects, scarcely one could be seen. The lofty mountains, their summits marked with a few patches of snow, stood well separated from each other; the valleys being filled up with an immense thickness of stratified alluvium. The features in the scenery of the Andes which struck me most, as contrasted with the other mountain chains with which I am acquainted, were—the flat fringes sometimes expanding into narrow plains on each side of the valleys—the bright colours, chiefly red and purple, of the utterly bare and precipitous hills of porphyry—the grand and continuous wall-like dykes—the plainly-divided strata which, where nearly vertical, formed the picturesque and wild central pinnacles, but where less inclined, composed the great massive mountains on the outskirts of the range—and lastly, the smooth conical piles of fine and brightly coloured detritus, which sloped up at a high angle from the base of the mountains, sometimes to a height of more than two thousand feet.

I frequently observed, both in Tierra del Fuego and within the Andes, that where the rock was covered during the greater part of the year with snow, it was shivered in a very extraordinary manner into small angular fragments. Scoresby has observed the same fact in Spitzbergen. The case appears to me rather obscure, for that part of the mountain which is protected by a mantle of snow, must be less subject to repeated and great changes of temperature than any other part. I have sometimes thought that the earth and fragments of stone on the surface, were perhaps less effectually removed by slowly percolating snow water than by rain, and therefore that the appearance of a quicker disintegration of the solid rock under the snow, was deceptive. Whatever the cause may be, the quantity of crumbling stone on the Cordillera is very great. Occasionally in the spring, great masses of this detritus slide down the mountains and cover the snow-drifts in the valleys, thus forming natural ice-houses. We rode over one, the height of which was far below the limit of perpetual snow.

*The Voyage of the Beagle*. By Charles Darwin. Everyman edition. 1906.

# Percy Harrison Fawcett
## 1867-1925

COLONEL P. H. FAWCETT, a regular Artillery officer, was the last British, if not the last great, explorer of South America in the classical tradition. A man of powerful physique, courageous and determined, he was ideally fitted to combat the obstacles to the exploration of tropical South America. Added to these qualities, he was technically qualified as a surveyor and cartographer, but above all. he was a born pathfinder, undeterred by natural or human opposition. Allied to these practical faculties was an imaginative streak, amounting almost to mysticism, which grew stronger with the years. He was convinced from legends he encountered and his own experiences that a legendary city was to be found in the interior of Brazil, and it was in search of this that he disappeared in 1925. The following incident occurred when Fawcett was leading a Bolivian frontier demarcation party in 1908. The Rio Verde is in eastern Bolivia; its source locates a point on the boundary with Brazil.

★　　★　　★

We started on foot on September 15th (1908); six days later the peons ran out of food; we others shared out what there was of our supplies but by the 23rd this had gone too. We found some palmettos and ate the 'cabbages', but they made an unsatisfying meal and even weakened us. On September 25th we saw a turkey—but it saw us first! On the 30th there was the heart-breaking labour of hacking a way through a *tacuara* forest—a kind of bamboo which sends out a tangle of branches armed with wait-a-bit thorns. Next day we found a bees' nest and, very hungry indeed, pounced on it. The honey had fermented and it doubled us up with violent stomach-ache. On October 2nd one of the dogs found a bird's nest with four large sky-blue eggs in it. The dog received one as a reward, and the other three did very little except make us more conscious of hunger. On the following day we reached the source of the river, finding there a few Chonta palms, with nuts about the size of marbles, and almost as hard.

'Well, we've got here all right,' said Fisher; 'but how are we going to get back?'

Certainly not by the way we came, I thought. 'We'll find a way all right. We don't have to follow the river any more. I expect we can get out over the hills.'

'I hope to God we can!' muttered Urquhart.

Fisher said something about, 'Leave our bones here, most likely!'

Possibly we should, but we were going to make a fight for it, anyhow.

'That's enough!' I said. 'We're going to get out. Pull yourselves together and look cheerful. If the peons think we're giving up they'll never have the guts to stick it out. If we've got to die, we'll die walking—see!'

We were starving now—really starving. The tendency to trip and fall showed a growing weakness, yet we still found no difficulty in carrying our packs, weighing now about thirty pounds. The voices of the others and the sounds of the forest seemed to come from a vast distance, as though through a long tube, for the deafness of famine was upon us. Our position seemed absolutely hopeless. Tremendous effort was needed to take observations and make a triangulation connecting the source of the river with Villa Bella, but the work had to be done or our sufferings would be to no purpose—that is, if we ever escaped from this hell! Remembering the game-infested forests of the Guaporé, the peons were inclined to be mutinous, and who could blame them? Even had we wished to, it was out of the question to return the way we had come, for observations would not be possible, and we should be held up for certain amongst the lagoons.

Above us towered the Ricardo Franco Hills, flat-topped and mysterious, their flanks scarred by deep *quebradas*. Time and the foot of man had not touched those summits. They stood like a lost world, forested to their tops, and the imagination could picture the last vestiges there of an age long vanished. Isolated from the battle with changing conditions, monsters from the dawn of man's existence might still roam those heights unchallenged, imprisoned and protected by unscalable cliffs. So thought Conan Doyle when later in London I spoke of these hills and showed photographs of them.

He mentioned an idea for a novel on Central South America and asked for information which I told him I should be glad to supply. The fruit of it was his *Lost World* in 1912, appearing as a serial in the *Strand Magazine*, and subsequently in the form of a book that achieved widespread popularity.

In an effort to find a way out in that direction we struck up into the hills, but to our despair found those deep canyons in the mountain-sides impossible to cross. Time and time again we were brought to a standstill at the edge of some ghastly precipice, returning dejected to the starting-point, each time with diminished strength. How long could we carry on was the vital question. Unless food was obtained soon we should be too feeble to make our way out by any route, and one more expedition would never be heard of again!

The *capataz* of the peons was missing, and I suspected that he had laid himself down to die, as Indians will when there appears to be no hope. I searched for him, found his tracks, and eventually ran him to earth in the *monte*, or scrub forest, sitting, his back to a tree, weeping like a heart-broken girl.

'Come on,' I said, taking his shoulder. 'Up on your feet, man! What's the matter with you?'

'Leave me alone!' he wailed, shaking my hand away. 'Let me die. I want to die—I can't stand it any longer!'

Kindness is no good in these cases, however sympathetic you may feel. I took out my hunting-knife and jabbed it into his ribs till he cried out and sprang up.

'Oh no you don't!' I said. 'You're not going to lie down and die just like that. If you die, you die on your feet—unless you prefer the knife.'

He said nothing, but caught his breath with a last sob and staggered off towards the camp, regarding me, no doubt, as a fiend.

I called the party together and told them of my intentions.

'Our only hope is to follow the watershed. I believe it will bring us out. We can't escape by way of the hills, nor by the way we came, so it's our one chance.'

There was a groan of dismay, for it meant staking our lives on a mere hope. I called Fisher and Urquhart.

'Better take the peons' guns away from them at the first

opportunity. To their way of thinking it's going in the wrong direction to follow the watershed, and they may desert. Without guns they won't dare to, for fear of Indians!'

Indians were not far away now. At night we saw their fires here and there, but never a savage showed himself. It was bitterly disappointing that they avoided us so obstinately, for we should have welcomed them in the hope of obtaining something to eat.

Again on the move, we encountered another difficulty. The ground was covered with hard, slippery bunch grass on the top of loose pebbles. At every step or two we slipped, and in our weakened condition often fell grovelling. It was then that an almost superhuman effort was required to get up again, for our packs seemed to pin us down. How good it would have been to lie there—just lie and rest! The peons had to be driven on with threats and blows, and the effort to keep them on the move stimulated our own flagging energies. I have never struck these people in anger, and the apparent brutality of my treatment now went sorely against the grain, but it was with the sole object of forcing them to make a fight for their lives.

Voracious looks were frequently cast at the dogs, though they were nothing but skin and bones—like ourselves. I had firmly quashed all suggestions that they be killed and eaten. For one thing, I'm too much of a dog-lover and for another, they might have helped us to find food. Somehow they had managed to keep alive by hunting, though what they found we were unable to discover. They did not appear to be exhausted, yet now they just curled up in the grass, went to sleep, and never wakened. A more peaceful and even beautiful demise could not be imagined. The Indian peons wanted to follow their example—to lie down and sleep themselves out of life. Instead they were goaded on.

It was a miracle that saved us—at least, for me it was then, and always will be, the nearest thing to what we like to call a miracle. On October 13th, feeling that we had come to our last gasp, I did what I had never known to fail when the need was sufficiently pronounced, and that is to pray audibly for food. Not kneeling, but turning east and west, I called for assistance—forcing myself to know that assistance would be forthcoming. In this way did I pray, and within fifteen minutes a deer showed itself in a clearing three hundred yards away.

The others saw it at the same time, and a breathless silence fell as I unslung my rifle. It was almost hopeless range for a violently kicking Winchester carbine; and at the end of one's tether from hunger or thirst the sight is not reliable, nor is it easy to hold the rifle steady.

'For God's sake don't miss, Fawcett!' The hoarse whisper came from close behind me. Miss! As I sighted along the shaking barrel I knew the bullet would find its mark. The power that answered my prayer would see that it did. Never have I made a cleaner kill—the animal dropped with severed spine where it stood!

The peons wolfed their portions, skin, fur and all. What a pity the dogs had not survived a few days longer! Our troubles were over. Next day we found a bees' nest full of excellent honey; on the 15th we at last found a way down the cliffs to the forests of the Guaporé, and on the 18th we came to a small negro settlement where coarse sugar made from boiled cane juice was to be had.

Strangely enough, sugar was the thing we had hungered for more than anything else. In our dreams we had gorged ourselves on sugar-coated delicacies, and in the agony of our waking hours discussed repeatedly what sweet things we would most enjoy eating. As you may imagine, we ate far too much head-sugar that day at the settle-ment—we gorged ourselves on it—we ate till we could eat no more.

Nightfall saw us doubled up with agony in our hammocks, groaning with the pain, until relieved by vomiting.

On October 19th we arrived back at Villa Bella, whose sad streets and empty houses cheered us after the utter loneliness of the forest. We had left stores here, and condensed milk and Quaker oats made a considerably healthier diet for us than sugar. As strength came back, it was with a growing realization that we had escaped only by a miracle.

A jubilant telegram from General Pando was awaiting me here. Anticipating our safe return he sent his congratulations, and asked for an address to which he could send the money owing to us. Little did he guess how close the Verde had come to putting a premature end to our work. The river was explored at last, and its course found to differ entirely from the guesswork in 1873. Its source was in springs, not in a lake as had been thought. Our complete set of observations would enable every mile of it to be accurately mapped, thus saving about 1,200 square miles of valuable country for Bolivia. Our hardships and sufferings were fully justified.

We followed the telegraph line to the Jauru, not too bad a tramp over a fairly good trail, and dropped down from the hills of Aguape into Porto Esperidiao, an *estancia* on the river. Here we procured a large canoe which took us to Caxocira. A hospitable Brazilian fed us well and supplied us with a boat to Descalvados, where we arrived on November 18th.

Our reception was chilly. Someone had spread a malicious rumour to the effect that we had complained on all sides of disgraceful treatment last time we were there. We were alleged to have said that any settler would have shown us more hospitality. There was no truth in this, and the propagation of such a lie could only be for the purpose of discrediting us. However, the people soon thawed, and ended by making our stay as comfortable as they knew how.

A launch took us down river to Corumba, where to our great embarrassment we were hailed as heroes. The Brazilians were full of admiration for anyone who would willingly court a meeting with *bugres*—as they called the savages—and it was impossible to convince them that we had caught no more than a glimpse of any during the whole trip.

Five of the six peons died from the effects of the journey. The sixth—the man I had goaded on at the point of the knife—came to me the following year and asked to accompany me again. He was voluble about what he called our 'English stamina', and harboured no ill-feelings towards me. On the contrary, he followed me about with every sign of devotion.

The upshot of the exploration was that both Commissions agreed to proceed in the following year to the source of the Verde under my guidance, while a third Brazilian party ascended the river verifying its course to corroborate my maps. After that we would jointly erect the marks to record it permanently as a frontier point.

*Lost Trails, Lost Cities.* By Brian Fawcett. Funk & Wagnalls Company, 1953.

# AUSTRALIA
# AND THE PACIFIC

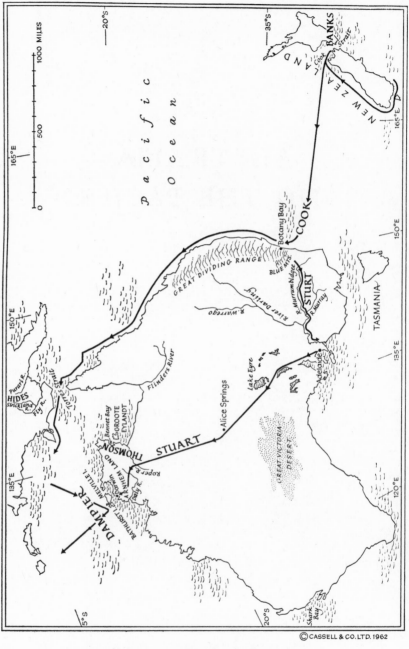

1000 MILES

500

0

165°E

20°S

35°S

165°E

*Pacific Ocean*

NEW ZEALAND

Cook Strait

BANKS

COOK

Botany Bay

150°E

GREAT DIVIDING RANGE

BLUE MTS

R. Murrumbidgee

R. Murray

STURT

R. Murray

TASMANIA

135°E

R. Warrego

River Darling

150°E

Torres Strait

Purari R.

HIDES

Strickland

Fly R.

Flinders River

Lake Eyre

Alice Springs

Adelaide

Bennet Bay

GROOTE EYLANDT

THOMSON

STUART

GREAT VICTORIA DESERT

120°E

135°E

ARNHEM LAND

Roper R.

Daly R.

Darwin

MELVILLE I.

BATHURST I.

DAMPIER

Shark Bay

5°S

20°S

# AUSTRALIA

# Ferdinand Magellan
## 1470-1521

MAGELLAN (Fernão de Magalhães), the inspirer and leader of the first circumnavigation of the world (1519–22) in its most critical stages, was a Portuguese who eventually transferred to the service of Spain. The precise circumstances of this transfer and its relation to his plans for a world voyage are not clear. He had served in the Spice Islands (the Moluccas) in 1509–12, and it is probable that it was then he first conceived the idea. But his plans were founded upon contemporary ideas regarding the distribution of land and water on the globe, and his was not the first voyage that sought a water passage through America into the Pacific. (There are no sound reasons for supposing that he was aware of the existence of the Straits of Magellan before his great voyage.) After passing through the Straits he followed a course across the Pacific on which by chance he sighted no land save a few insignificant islets until his landfall on the Ladrones. Magellan was killed while involved in a tribal clash in Mactan in the Philippines. His flagship the *Victoria*, however, after a hazardous voyage under the command of Sebastian del Cano, eventually completed the circumnavigation, reaching Spain in 1522. The best account of the voyage, from which the following passage is extracted, was written by the Italian pilot Antonio Pigafetta. It is evidence of the rapid *tempo* of the discoveries that thirty years after Columbus's landfall in the West Indies the Pacific Ocean should have been crossed and the first world voyage completed. Within those thirty years a 'New World' had indeed come into being.

★    ★    ★

After going to fifty-two degrees latitude south, we found on the day of the Eleven Thousand Virgins a strait, the cape of which we called the Cape of the Eleven Thousand Virgins,[1] on account of this great miracle. This strait is a hundred and ten leagues, that is, four hundred and forty miles in length and half a league, more or less, in width.

[1] Now known by the abbreviated form of C. Virjines.

It issues in another sea called the Mar Pacifico (the Pacific Ocean), and is surrounded by very high mountains covered with snow. In this place it was not possible to anchor because no bottom was found, but moorings of twenty-five or thirty fathoms length were carried ashore. But for the captain-general, we should not have found this strait, for everyone thought and said that it was land-locked. But the captain-general, who knew where to navigate for a very tortuous strait, as he had seen it on a chart in the Treasury of the King of Portugal, which had been made by that very excellent man, Martin of Bohemia,[1] sent on before two ships, the *St. Anthony* and the *Conception*, to see what was within the cape of the bay. And we with the other two ships, the flagship called *Trinity* and the other the *Victoria*,[2] remained waiting for them within the bay.

That night there was a great storm which lasted till the next day at midday, and during which we were forced to weigh the anchors and let the ships go hither and thither about the bay. The other two ships met with such a head wind that they could not weather a cape which the bay made almost at its extremity; wishing to come to us, they were near being driven into shoal water. But on approaching the extremity of the bay, and thinking themselves lost, they saw a small mouth, or rather not a mouth but a small promontory and, as though abandoning hope, threw themselves at it so that perforce they discovered the strait. Seeing that it was not a promontory but a strait in the land they went further on and found a bay, then going still further they found another strait and another bay larger than the first two. Rejoicing greatly, they immediately returned to report it to the captain-general. Amongst us we thought that they had perished, first because of the great storm, next because two days had passed without our seeing them, and also because of certain smokes made by two of their men to advise us. While in this suspense we saw the two ships under all sail, with ensigns spread, coming towards us; these, when near us, suddenly discharged many cannon.

[1] It is not now thought that any such chart was made by Martin Behaim.
[2] The *Victoria* was the sole vessel to complete the first circumnavigation of the world.

Then, together, thanking God and the Virgin Mary, we went to seek further. . . .

Wednesday, the twenty-eighth of November, 1520, we came forth out of the said strait, and entered into the Pacific sea. We passed three months and twenty days without obtaining any provisions, eating biscuit or rather powdered, biscuit riddled with the worms that had devoured the good, and stinking from the urine of rats. We drank water that was yellow and putrifying for many days. We also ate the ox hides which were above the main-yard to prevent it from breaking the shrouds: they were very hard on account of sun, rain, and wind, and we left them for four or five days in the sea, and then put them a short time above the embers, and ate them thus; also very often the sawdust of wood. Rats were sold for half-a-ducat each, and even then they could not be got. But above all the other evils, this was the worst; the gums, upper and lower, of some grew so much that they were unable to eat, and so died. To this disease[1] nineteen men succumbed, also the giant, and an Indian from the county of Verzin.[2] Twenty-five or thirty were sick in the arms, legs or elsewhere, so that few remained fit. By the grace of God, I had no sickness.

During those three months and twenty days, we ran about four thousand miles in the open sea through this Mar Pacifico. It is well named Pacific, for during this time we met with no storm, and saw no land except two small uninhabited islands in which we found only birds and trees. We named them the Unfortunate Islands; they are distant two hundred leagues from one another, and we found no bottom near them. There we saw many sharks. The first isle is in fifteen degrees of south latitude, and the other island is in nine degrees. Each day we ran fifty, sixty or seventy leagues, by estimation. And if our Lord and his blessed Mother had not given us such good weather we should all have died of hunger in this very vast sea. I believe of a certainty that no one will ever again make such a voyage.

If, when we had issued from this strait, we had sailed continuously

[1] i.e., scurvy.
[2] The 'giant' was a Patagonian. Verzin was a district of south-east Brazil.

westwards, we should have circumnavigated the world without finding any land[1] except the Cape of the Eleven Thousand Virgins, which is the eastern Cape of the strait in the ocean sea, with Cape Desire to the west in the Pacific sea. These two capes are exactly in fifty-two degrees of south latitude. . . .

About seventy leagues on this course, and in 12° latitude and 146° longitude, on Wednesday, the 6th March, we discovered a small island to the north-west, and two others to the south-west. One of these islands was larger and higher than the other two. The captain-general wished to touch at the largest to get fresh supplies but it was not possible because the people of these islands boarded the ships and robbed us in one way or another so that it was impossible to guard against them. Whilst we were striking the sails to go ashore, they stole with much address and diligence the small skiff, which was made fast to the poop of the flagship, so annoying the captain-general that he landed forty armed men, burned forty or fifty houses and many small boats, killed seven men and recovered the skiff. We set sail at once, following the same course. Before we went ashore some of our sick men begged us that if we killed man or woman, that we should bring them their entrails, so that they would be cured immediately. . . .

All these people live according to their will, for they have no lords; they go naked, and some of them wear beards, and have black hair down to the waist. They wear small hats of palm leaves after the fashion of the Albanians. The people are as tall as us, and well made; they do not worship. When they are born they are white, later they become brown, and have their teeth black and red; this they consider beautiful. The women also go naked, except that they cover their nature with a thin bark, pliable like paper, which grows between the tree and the bark of the palm. They are beautiful, delicate, and whiter than the men, and have their hair loose and flowing, very black and long, down to the earth. They do not go to work in the fields, but remain at home weaving cloth, baskets and other things necessary in the house from palm leaves. They eat *cochi*, *battate*[2]

[1] This is quite correct.            [2] Coconuts

[sweet potato], birds, figs a palm long, sugar-cane, flying fish and other things. The women annoint their bodies and their hair with oil of *cocho* and *giongioli* [sesame]. Their houses are all built of wood, covered with planks, with fig leaves six feet in length, with floors and windows. Rooms and beds are all furnished with beautiful palm mats. They sleep on palm straw which is soft and fine. These people have no arms, but use sticks, pointed with fish bone at the end. They are poor, but ingenious, and great thieves, for which reason we called these three islands the Islands of the Thieves.[1] Their sport is to go to sea with their women in their little boats. They are like the *fuseleres*, but narrower. Some black, or white, others are red. On the opposite side to the sail, they have a large pointed piece of wood with poles across it which rest on the water in order to sail more securely.[2] The sails are of palm leaves sewed together, and made like a lateen sail. For rudders they have boards like hearth shovels with poles at the top and there is no difference between the poop and the prow in these boats, and they bound like dolphins from wave to wave. These thieves thought, according to the signs they made, that there were no other men in the world but themselves.

Saturday, the 16th of March, 1521, we arrived at dawn off a high land, three hundred leagues distant from the Ladrones. This isle is named Zamal.[3] The next day the captain-general wished to land at another uninhabited island near the first, to be more secure and to obtain water, also to repose there for a few days. He pitched two tents on shore for the sick, and had a sow killed for them.

[1] i.e., the Ladrone Islands, now the Southern Marianas Is.
[2] Pigafetta is describing the catamaran.
[3] The island of Samar in the Philippines.

*The First Voyage Round the World by Magellan.* Trsl. from accounts of Pigafetta. Ed. by C. R. Markham. Hakluyt Soc. ser. 1, v. 52, 1874. Trsl. revised from the original Italian.

# William Dampier
## 1652-1715

THE coasts of Australia were sighted by Dutch navigators in the early years of the seventeenth century, on voyages into the Gulf of Carpentaria. The western coasts were later charted by other Dutch captains and in 1642 Tasman established the insularity of the continent and discovered Van Diemen's Land (Tasmania). Little more was done until the discovery of the eastern coast by Captain James Cook in 1770. In the interval, however, the north and west coasts were visited by William Dampier. Dampier was a remarkable character whose merits were not immediately recognized. The *Dictionary of National Biography* describes him as 'pirate; captain, R.N., and hydrographer'.

In 1683, he embarked on a buccaneering vessel and after some extraordinary adventures found himself four years later on the northern coasts of New Holland (Australia), probably off Bathurst or Melville Islands. He was a keen, if disillusioned, observer of the natives—they were no 'gentle savages' in his eyes—and recorded what he saw in vigorous, picturesque prose.

On the strength of these experiences, he succeeded in persuading the Admiralty to put him in charge of the first scientific expedition to leave British shores (1698) and on this voyage he visited the coast of Western Australia in the region of Shark Bay.

★ ★ ★

The 4th day of January, 1688, we fell in with the Land of New Holland [Australia] in the Lat. of 16° 15′ having, as I said before, made our course due south from the shoal that we past by the 31st day of December. We ran in close by it, and finding no convenient anchoring because it lies open to the N.W., we ran along shore to the eastward, steering N.E. for so the land lies. We steered thus about twelve leagues and then came to a point of land from whence the land trends east and southerly for ten or twelve leagues, but how afterwards I know not. About three leagues to the eastward of this point there is a pretty deep bay, with abundance of islands in it and a very good place to anchor in or to hale ashore. About a league to the eastward of that point we anchored January the 5th, 1688, two miles from the shore, in twenty-nine fathoms, good hard sand, and clean ground.

New Holland is a very large tract of land. It is not yet determined whether it is an island or a main continent[1]; but I am certain that it joins neither to Asia, Africa, nor America. This part of it that we saw is all low, even land, with sandy banks against the sea; only the points are rocky, and so are some of the islands in this bay.

The land is of a dry sandy soil, destitute of water, except you make wells, yet producing divers sorts of trees, but the woods are not thick nor the trees very big. Most of the trees that we saw are Dragon trees, as we supposed, and these too are the largest trees of any there. They are about the bigness of our large apple trees and about the same heighth, and the rind is blackish and somewhat rough. The leaves are of a dark colour; the gum distils out of the knots or cracks that are in the bodies of the trees. We compared it with some Gum Dragon, or Dragon's Blood that was aboard, and it was of the same colour and taste. The other sorts of trees were not known by any of us. There was pretty long grass growing under the trees, but it was very thin. We saw no trees that bore fruit or berries.

We saw no sort of animal nor any track of beast, but once; and that seemed to be the tread of a beast as big as a great mastiff-dog.[2] Here are a few small land birds, but none bigger than a blackbird and but few sea-fowls. Neither is the sea very plentifully stored with fish, unless you reckon the manatee and turtle as such. Of these creatures there is plenty, but they are extraordinary shy, though the inhabitants cannot trouble them much, having neither boats nor iron.

The inhabitants of this country are the miserablest people in the world. The Hodmadods of Monomatapa,[3] though a nasty people, yet for wealth are gentlemen to these who have no houses and skin garments, sheep, poultry, and fruits of the earth, ostrich eggs, etc.,

1 The Dutch, however, had proved that Australia was not joined to any other continent.
2 Probably the kangaroo.
3 The Hottentots of south-east Africa.

as the Hodmadods have. And setting aside their humane shape, they differ but little from brutes. They are tall, strait-bodied and thin with small, long limbs. They have great heads, round foreheads and great brows. Their eyelids are always half closed to keep the flies out of their eyes, they being so troublesome here that no fanning will keep them from coming to one's face; and without the assistance of both hands to keep them off, they will creep into one's nostrils, and mouth too, if the lips are not shut very close; so that from their infancy being thus annoyed with these insects, they do never open their eyes as other people. And therefore they cannot see far unless they hold up their heads as if they were looking at somewhat over them.

They have great bottle noses, pretty full lips and wide mouths. The two fore-teeth of their upper jaw are wanting in all of them, men and women, old and young, whether they draw them out, I know not; neither have they any beards. They are long visaged and of a very unpleasing aspect, having no one graceful feature in their faces. Their hair is black, short and curled, like that of the Negroes, and not long and lank like the common Indians. The colour of their skins, both of their faces and the rest of their body, is coal black, like that of the Negroes of Guinea.

They have no sort of clothes, but a piece of the rind of a tree tied like a girdle about their waists and a handful of long grass, or three or four small green boughs full of leaves, thrust under their girdle to cover their nakedness.

They have no houses but lie in the open air without any covering, the earth being their bed and the heaven their canopy. Whether they cohabit one man to one woman or promiscuously, I know not; but they do live in companies, twenty or thirty men, women, and children together. Their only food is a small sort of fish which they get by making wares [weirs] of stone across little coves or branches of the sea; every tide bringing in the small fish, and there leaving them for a prey to these people who constantly attend there to search for them at low water. This small fry I take to be the top of their fishery. They have no instruments to catch great fish should they come, and such seldom stay to be left behind at low water. Nor could we catch any fish with our hooks and lines all the while we lay there. In other places at low water, they seek the cockles, muscles and periwinkles. Of these shellfish there are fewer still, so that their chiefest dependance is upon what the sea leaves in their wares which, be it much or little, they gather up and march to the places of their abode. There the old people that are not able to stir abroad by reason of their age, and the tender infants, wait their return; and what Providence has bestowed on them they presently broil on the coals and eat it in common. Sometimes they get as many fish as makes them a plentiful banquet; and at other times they scarce get every one a taste. But be it little or much that they get, every one has his part, as well the young and tender, the old and feeble, who are not able to go abroad, as the strong and lusty. When they have eaten they lie down till the next low water, and then all that are able march out, be it night or day, rain or shine, 'tis all one; they must attend the wares, or else they must fast, for the earth affords them no food at all. There is neither herb, root, pulse nor any sort of grain for them to eat, that we saw; not any sort of bird or beast that they can catch, having no instruments wherewithal to do so.

I did not perceive that they did worship anything. These poor creatures have a sort of weapon to defend their ware or fight with their enemies, if they have any that will interfere with their poor fishery. They did at first endeavour with the weapons to frighten us who, lying ashore, deterred them from one of their fishing-places. Some of them had wooden swords, others had a sort of lances. The sword is a piece of wood shaped somewhat like a cutlass.[1] The lance is a long strait pole sharp at one end and hardened afterwards by heat. I saw no iron nor any other sort of metal; therefore it is probable they use stone-hatchets, as some Indians in America do, described in Chap. IV.

How they get their fire I know not; but probably as Indians do, out of wood, I have seen the Indians of Bon-Airy do it, and have myself tried the experiment. They take a flat piece of wood that is pretty soft and make a small dent in one side of it then they take another hard round stick, about the bigness of one's little finger and, sharpening it at one end like a pencil, they put that sharp end in the hole or dent of the flat soft piece and then, rubbing or twirling the

[1] Probably a boomerang.

hard piece between the palms of their hands, they drill the soft piece till it smokes and at last takes fire.

These people speak somewhat through the throat, but we could not understand one word that they said. We anchored, as I said before, January the 5th, and seeing men walking on the shore, we presently sent a canoe to get some acquaintance with them, for we were in hopes to get some provision among them. But the inhabitants, seeing our boat coming, run away and hid themselves. We searched afterwards three days in hopes to find their houses, but found none; yet we saw many places where they had made fires. At last, being out of hopes to find their habitations, we searched no farther, but left a great many toys ashore in such places where we thought that they would come. In all our search we found no water but old wells on the sandy bays.

At last we went over to the islands and there we found a great many of the natives. I do believe there were forty on one island, men, women, and children. The men at our first coming ashore threatened us with their lances and swords, but they were frighted by firing one gun which we fired purposely to scare them. The island was so small that they could not hide themselves, but they were much disordered at our landing, especially the women and children, for we went directly to their camp. The lustiest of the women, snatching up their infants, ran away howling, and the little children run after squeaking and bawling; but the men stood still. Some of the women, and such people as could not go from us, lay still by a fire, making a doleful noise, as if we had been coming to devour them, but when they saw we did not intend to harm them they were pretty quiet and the rest that fled from us at our first coming returned again. This, their place of dwelling, was only a fire with a few boughs before it, set up on that side the winds was of.

'A New Voyage Round the World.' By Captain William Dampier. 6th ed. 1717. In *Dampier's Voyages*, ed. by J. Masefield. Unicorn Press, 1906. Vol. I.

# James Cook
## 1728-1779

AFTER Dampier's voyages, the next Englishman to contribute to knowledge of Australia was Captain James Cook. In one voyage (1769–72) he solved the main outstanding problems of the character of the Australian continent. Sailing south from Tahiti in 1770, he proved to most people's satisfaction that no vast southern continent extended into temperate latitudes; that New Zealand was a relatively small isolated island group, and that the eastern coastline of Australia had no relation to the island groups discovered by sixteenth-century Spaniards in the south-west Pacific. He also confirmed the separation of New Guinea from Australia, proved by the forgotten voyage of L. Vaez de Torres. Australia thus emerged as an island of continental proportions, related rather to the island-world of South-Eastern Asia than to the hypothetical Antarctic continent of the theorists. On two subsequent voyages Cook, besides making important contributions to the geography of the Pacific Ocean, demonstrated conclusively that if an Antarctic continent existed, it probably scarcely extended north of the parallel of 70° south latitude. In the space of ten years, Cook proved himself the outstanding navigator and hydrographer in the history of exploration. In the following extract his discovery of Botany Bay is described.

*　　*　　*

[28 April 1770]. . . . At daylight in the morning we discovered a bay[1] which appeard to be tollerably well sheltered from all winds into which I resolved to go with the ship and with this view sent the master in the pinnace to sound the entrance while we kept turning up with the ship haveing the wind right out. At noon the entrance bore NNW distance one mile.

Sunday 29th. In the pm winds southerly clear weather with which we stood into the bay and anchor'd under the south shore two mile within the entrence in six fathoms water, the south point bearing

[1] Botany Bay.

SE and the north point East. Saw as we came in on both points of
the bay several of the natives and a few hutts, men, women and
children on the south shore abreast of the ship, to which place I went
in the boats in hopes of speaking with them accompanied by Mr.
Banks, Dr. Solander and Tupia; as we approached the shore they all
made off except two men who seemed resolved to oppose our
landing. As soon as I saw this I ordered the boats to lay upon their
oars in order to speake to them but this was to little purpose for
neither us nor Tupia could understand one word they said. We
then threw them some nails, beeds, etc., a shore which they took up
and seem'd not ill pleased in so much that I thout (thought) they
beckon'd to us to come a shore; but in this we were mistaken,
for as soon as we put the boat in they again came to oppose us
upon which I fired a musket between the two which had no other
effect than to make them retire back where bundles of thier darts lay,
and one of them took up a stone and threw at us which caused my
fireing a second musquet load with small shott, and altho some of the
shott struck the man, yet it had no other effect than to make him lay
hold of a shield or target to defend himself. Emmidiatly after this
we landed which we had no sooner done than they throw'd two
darts at us. This obliged me to fire a third shott soon after which
they both made off, but not in such haste but what we might have
taken one, but Mr. Banks being of opinion that the darts were
poisoned made me cautious how I advanced into the woods. We
found here a few small hutts made of the bark of trees in one of which
were four or five small children with whome we left some strings of
beeds, etc. A quantity of darts lay about the hutts; these we took
away with us. Three canoes lay upon the beach, the worst I think I
ever saw; they were about twelve or fourteen feet long made of
one peice of the bark of a tree drawn or tied up at each end
and the middle kept open by means of peices of sticks by way of
thwarts.

After searching for fresh water without success except a little in a
small hole dug in the sand, we embarqued and went over to the
north point of the bay where in coming in we saw several people,
but when we now landed there were no body to be seen. We found
here some fresh water which came trinkling down and stood in

pools among the rocks; but as this was troblesome to come at I sent a party of men a shore in the morning to the place where we first landed to dig holes in the sand, by which means and a small stream they found fresh water sufficient to water the ship. The strings of beeds etc. we had left with the children last night were found laying in the hut this morning; probably the natives were afraid to take them away. After breakfast we sent some empty casks a shore and a party of men to cut wood and I went my self in the pinnance to sound and explore the bay in the doing of which I saw several of the natives, but they all fled at my approach. I landed in two places one of which the people had but just left, as there were small fires and fresh muscles broiling upon them—here likewise lay vast heaps of the largest oyster shells I ever saw.

Monday 30th. As soon as the wooders and waterers were come on board to dinner ten or twelve of the natives came to the watering place and took away their canoes that lay there but did not offer to touch any one of our casks that had been left ashore, and in the afternoon sixteen to eighteen of them came boldly up to within a hundred yards of our people at the watering place and there made a stand. Mr. Hicks who was the officer ashore did all in his power to entice them to him by offering them presents etc. but it was to no purpose; all they seem'd to want was for us to be gone. After staying a short time they went away. They were all arm'd with darts and wooden swords,[1] the darts have each four prongs and pointed with fish bones; those we have seen seem to be intended more for striking fish than offensive weapons, neither are they poisoned as we at first thought. After I had returnd from sounding the bay I went to a cove on the north side where in three or four hauls with the saine [seine] we caught above three hundred pounds weight of fish which I caused to be equally divided among the ship's company. In the am I went in the pinnance to sound and explore the north side of the bay where I neither met with inhabitants or any thing remarkable. Mr. Green took the Suns Meridion altitude a little within the south entrence of the bay which gave the latitude 34° 0′ S.

[1] Throwing sticks.

Tuesday 1st [May]. Gentle breezes northerly. In the pm ten of the natives again viseted the watering place. I being on board at this time went emmidiatly ashore, but before I got there they were going away; I follow'd them alone and unarm'd some distance along the shore, but they would not stop until they got farther off than I choose to trust my self; these were arm'd in the same manner as those that came yesterday. In the evening I sent some hands to haul the saine (seine) but they caught but a very few fish. A little after sun rise I found the variation to be 11° 3′ East. Last night Torby Sutherland seaman departed this life and in the am his body was buried a shore at the watering place which occasioned my calling the south point of this bay after his name. This morning a party of us went ashore to some hutts not far from the watering place where some of the natives are daly (daily) seen; here we left several articles such as cloth, looking-glasses, combs, beeds, nails, etc. After this we made an excursion into the country which we found deversified with woods, lawns and marshes; the woods are free from under wood of every kind and the trees are at such a distance from one a nother that the whole country or at least great part of it might be cultivated without being oblig'd to cut down a single tree; we found the soil every where except in the marshes to be a light white sand and produceth a quantity of good grass which grows in little tufts about as big as one can hold in one's hand and pretty close to one another; in this manner the surface of the ground is coated in the woods between the trees. Dr. Solander had a bad [?bare] sight of a small animal some thing like a rabbit and we found the dung of an animal which must feed upon grass and which we judged could not be less than a deer [kangaroo], we also saw the track of a dog or some such like animal [probably a dingo]. We met with some hutts and places where the natives had been and at our first seting out one of them was seen, the others I suppose had fled upon our approach.

saw some trees that had been cut down by the natives with some sort of a blunt instrument and several trees that were barked, the bark of which had been cut by the same instrument; in many of the trees, especially the palms, were cut steps about three or four feet asunder for the conveniency of climeing them. We found two sorts of gum one sort of which is like Gum Dragon and is the same as I suppose Tasman took for gum lac; it is extracted from the largest tree in the woods [Eucalyptus trees].

*The Journals of Captain James Cook, R.N.* Vol. I. 'The voyage of the *Endeavour,* 1768–71'; edited by J. C. Beaglehole. (Hakluyt Soc.) Cambridge, 1955. (Spelling slightly modernized).

# Joseph Banks
## 1743-1820

SIR JOSEPH BANKS was the leader of what would now be regarded as the scientific staff on Cook's first voyage of discovery. This party was equipped and maintained at his own expense. His Journal is an invaluable complement to Cook's records. Banks was a typical eighteenth-century 'natural philosopher', with a special interest in botany, and he showed marked sympathy with, and understanding of, the cultures of native peoples. Later as President of the Royal Society he was able to promote scientific exploration in many parts of the world and to exercise powerful influence on the young British settlement at Botany Bay which was to develop into the Commonwealth of Australia. There is no doubt that this voyage with Cook was of the greatest importance in the formation of Banks's outlook. In similar fashion it was George Forster's experiences on Cook's second voyage which stimulated the imagination of the young Alexander von Humboldt, afterwards acknowledged as the 'founder of modern geography'. If Cook had achieved nothing else than the stirring of the imagination of Humboldt and Banks his contribution to science would still have been of incalculable value. The two brief extracts describe Banks's impressions of New Zealand.

★    ★    ★

17th Jan. 1770. This morn I was awaked by the singing of the birds ashore from whence we were distant not a quarter of a mile; the numbers of them were certainly very great, who seem'd to strain their throats with emulation; perhaps their voices were certainly the most melodious wild music I have ever heard, almost imitating small bells, but with the most tunable silver sound imaginable to which may be the distance was no small addition; on inquiring of our people I was told that they had observed them ever since we have been here and that they begin to sing at about one or two in the morn and continue till sunrise, after which they are silent all day like our nightingales.[1] . . .

[1] The bell-bird (*Anthorris melanura*).

25th Jan. Dr. Solander and myself (who have now nearly exhausted all the plants in our neighbourhood) went today to search for mosses and small things in which we had great success gathering several very remarkable ones. In the evening we went out in the pinnance and fell in with a large family of Indians who have now began to disperse themselves as I believe is their custom into the different creeks and coves where fish is most plentiful, a few only remaining in the *heppah* or town to which they all fly in times of danger; these people came a good way to meet us at a place where we were shooting shags, and invited us to the place where the rest of them were twenty or thirty in number, men, women, children, dogs, etc; we went and were received with all possible demonstrations of friendship if the numberless hugs and kisses we got from both sexes and old and young in return for our ribbons and beads may be accounted such; they also sold and gave us a great many fish with which we went home well pleased with our new acquaintance.

26th Jan. Went today to take another view of our new Straits,[1] the westernmost end of which the captain was not quite sure of; we found however a hill in a tolerable convenient situation upon which we got and saw the strait quite open and four or five leagues wide; we then erected a small monument of stone[2] such as five stout men could do in half an hour, and laid in it musquet balls, beads, shot etc., that if perchance any Europeans should find and pull it down, they will be sure it is not Indian workmanship; this done we returned to our dinners of shags and fish which we had shot and caught in coming and were dressed by the boat's crew; in the place we had appointed to dine in was a family of Indians who as usual behaved with much friendship and civility to us, showing us water etc., from whence we went to the town from whence Indians came on the 19th which was in this arm of the bay; here we were received as usual, everybody seemed glad to see us and conducted us through the whole works. The town was much like the other,

1 The *Endeavour* was off the extreme north-east coast of South Island, in 41° lat. S.
2 Placed by Dr. Beaglehole near Cape Koamaru, South Island. The Strait which Cook and Banks saw is Cook Strait, separating North Island and South Island.

situated upon an island or rock so steep in all parts that it was almost in danger of our necks that we climbed up to it; like the other it had also only one fighting stage; it contained maybe from eighty to a hundred houses about as many as the other. Just as we were going away our friends took so great a fancy to our merchandise that they filled out boat full of dried fish for which they took nails, ribbons, paper, etc.

27th Jan. Indians came on board in the morn and traded a little, afterwards the Dr. and myself went ashore but could find no plants at all; we have, I believe, got all that are in our neighbourhood, though the immense thickness of the woods which are almost rendered impassable by climbing plants entangling every way has not a little retarded us.

*Sir Joseph Banks in New Zealand from his Journal.* Edited by W. P. Morell. Reed, Wellington, 1958.

# Charles Sturt
## 1795-1869

THE exploration of interior Australia was inaugurated when in 1813 Gregory Blaxland traversed the barrier of the Blue Mountains which shut in the settlement of Sydney on the west. Progress depended upon the activities of the cattle and sheep ranchers in search of new grazing, themselves influenced by the succession of good and bad seasons, the rivalries of the young States, the fluctuating hopes of establishing new settlements in the tropical north, and after 1851 the lure of gold. Intermingled with these were motives of scientific inquiry and the sheer love of adventure. Charles Sturt, in many respects the most distinguished of these early pioneers, was actuated by these latter motives combined with a strong sense of duty. After a preliminary journey in 1828 when he reached the upper waters of the Darling river, he set out by boat down the Murrumbidgee to its junction with a fine river which he named the Murray. It is this journey which is described in the extract below. Continuing downstream he passed another junction, with what he correctly supposed to be the Darling, and eventually reached the sea. On a subsequent expedition he penetrated towards the centre of the continent, north-west of Lake Eyre.

★    ★    ★

It was with considerable apprehension that I observed the river [Murray river] to be shoaling fast, more especially as a huge sand-bank, a little below us, and on the same side on which the natives had gathered, projected nearly a third-way across the channel. To this sand-bank they ran with tumultuous uproar, and covered it over in a dense mass. Some of the chiefs advanced to the water to be nearer their victims, and turned from time to time to direct their followers. With every pacific disposition and an extreme reluctance to take away life, I foresaw that it would be impossible any longer to avoid an engagement, yet with such fearful numbers against us I was doubtful of the result. The spectacle we had witnessed had been one of the most appalling kind, and sufficient to shake the firmness of most men; but at that trying moment my little band preserved their temper and coolness, and if any thing could be gleaned from their countenances, it was that they had determined on an obstinate resistance. I now explained to them that their only chance of escape depended, or would depend, on their firmness. I desired that after the first volley had been fired, M'Leay and three of the men would attend to the defence of the boat with bayonets only, while I, Hopkinson, and Harris would keep up the fire as being more used to it. I ordered, however, that no shot was to be fired until after I had discharged both my barrels. I then delivered their arms to the men, which had as yet been kept in the place appropriated for them, and at the same time some rounds of loose cartridge. The men assured me they would follow my instructions, and thus prepared, having already lowered the sail, we drifted onwards with the current. As we neared the sand-bank, I stood up and made signs to the natives to desist; but without success. I took up my gun, therefore, and cocking it, had already brought it down to a level. A few seconds more would have closed the life of the nearest of the savages. The distance was too trifling for me to doubt the fatal effects of the discharge, for I was determined to take deadly aim in hopes that the fall of one man might save the lives of many. But at the very moment when my hand was on the trigger and my eye was along the barrel, my purpose was checked by M'Leay who called to me that another party of blacks had made their appearance upon the left bank of the river. Turning round, I observed four men at the top of their speed. The foremost of them, as soon as he got ahead of the boat, threw himself from a considerable height into the water. He struggled across the channel to the sand-bank, and in an incredibly short space of time stood in front of the savage against whom my aim had been directed. Seizing him by the throat, he pushed him backwards, and forcing all who were in the water upon the bank, he trod its margin with a vehemence and an agitation that were exceedingly striking. At one moment pointing to the boat, at another shaking his clenched hand in the face of the most forward, and stamping with passion on the sand; his voice that was at first distinct and clear was lost in hoarse murmurs. Two of the four natives remained on the left bank of the river, but the third followed his leader (who proved to be the remarkable savage I have previously noticed) to the scene of action. The reader will imagine our feelings on this occasion: it is impossible to describe them. We were so wholly lost in interest at the scene that was passing that the boat was allowed to drift at pleasure. For my own part I was overwhelmed with astonishment, and in truth stunned and confused; so singular, so unexpected, and so strikingly providential had been our escape.

We were again roused to action by the boat suddenly striking upon a shoal which reached from one side of the river to the other. To jump out and push her into deeper water was but the work of a moment with the men, and it was just as she floated again that our attention was withdrawn to a new and beautiful stream coming apparently from the north.[1] The great body of the natives having posted themselves on the narrow tongue of land formed by the two rivers, the bold savage who had so unhesitatingly interfered on our account was still in hot dispute with them, and I really feared his generous warmth would have brought down upon him the vengence of the tribes. I hesitated, therefore, whether or not to go to his assistance. It appeared, however, both to M'Leay and myself, that the tone of the natives had moderated, and the old and young men having listened to the remonstrances of our friend, the middle-aged warriors were alone holding out against him. A party of about seventy blacks were upon the right bank of the newly discovered river, and I thought that by landing among them, we should make a diversion in favour of our late guest; and in this I succeeded. If even they had still meditated violence, they would have to swim a good broad junction, and that, probably, would cool them, or we at least should have the advantage of position. I therefore ran the boat ashore, and landed with M'Leay amidst the smaller party of natives, wholly unarmed, and having directed the men to keep at a little distance from the bank. Fortunately, what I anticipated was brought about by the stratagem to which I had had recourse. The blacks no sooner observed that we had landed, than curiosity took place of anger. All wrangling ceased, and they came swimming over to us like a parcel of seals. Thus, in less than a quarter of an hour from the moment when it appeared that all human intervention was at an

[1] The Darling river.

end, and we were on the point of commencing a bloody fray which, independently of its own disastrous consequences, would have blasted the success of the expedition, we were peacefully surrounded by the hundreds who had so lately threatened us with destruction; nor was it until after we had returned to the boat and had surveyed the multitude upon the sloping bank above us that we became fully aware of the extent of our danger, and of the almost miraculous intervention of Providence in our favour. There could not have been less than six hundred natives upon that blackened sward. But this was not the only occasion upon which the merciful superintendance of that Providence to which we had humbly committed ourselves was strikingly manifested. If these pages fail to convey entertainment or information, sufficient may at least be gleaned from them to furnish matter for serious reflection; but to those who have been placed in situations of danger where human ingenuity availed them not, and where human foresight was baffled, I feel persuaded that these remarks are unnecessary.

It was my first care to call for our friend and to express to him, as well as I could, how much we stood indebted to him, at the same time that I made him a suitable present; but to the chiefs of the tribes I positively refused all gifts, notwithstanding their earnest solicitations. We next prepared to examine the new river and, turning the boat's head towards it, endeavoured to pull up the stream. Our larboard oars touched the right bank, and the current was too strong for us to conquer it with a pair only; we were, therefore, obliged to put a second upon her, a movement that excited the astonishment and admiration of the natives. One old woman seemed in absolute extasy, to whom M'Leay threw an old tin kettle in recompense for the amusement she afforded us.

As soon as we got above the entrance of the new river, we found easier pulling, and proceeded up it for some miles, accompanied by the once more noisy multitude. The river preserved a breadth of one hundred yards and a depth of rather more than twelve feet. Its banks were sloping and grassy, and were overhung by trees of magnificent size. Indeed, its appearance was so different from the water-worn banks of the sister stream that the men exclaimed, on entering it, that we had got into an English river. Its appearance certainly almost justified the expression, for the greenness of its banks was as new to us as the size of its timber. Its waters, though sweet, were turbid, and had a taste of vegetable decay as well as a slight tinge of green. Our progress was watched by the natives with evident anxiety. They kept abreast of us, and talked incessantly. At length, however, our course was checked by a net that stretched right across the stream. I say checked, because it would have been unfair to have passed over it with the chance of disappointing the numbers who apparently depended on it for subsistence that day. The moment was one of intense interest to me. As the men rested upon their oars, awaiting my further orders, a crowd of thoughts rushed upon me. The various conjectures I had formed of the course and importance of the Darling passed across my mind. Were they indeed realized? An irresistible conviction impressed me that we were now sailing on the bosom of that very stream from whose banks I had been twice forced to retire. I directed the Union Jack to be hoisted, and giving way to our satisfaction, we all stood up in the boat and gave three distinct cheers. It was an English feeling, an ebullition, an overflow, which I am ready to admit that our circumstances and situation will alone excuse. The eye of every native had been fixed upon that noble flag, at all times a beautiful object, and to them a novel one, as it waved over us in the heart of a desert. They had until that moment been particularly loquacious, but the sight of that flag and the sound of our voices hushed the tumult, and while they were still lost in astonishment, the boat's head was speedily turned, the sails were sheeted home, both wind and current were in our favour, and we vanished from them with a rapidity that surprised even ourselves, and which precluded every hope of the most adventurous among them to keep up with us.

Arrived once more at the junction of the two rivers, and un- molested in our occupations, we had leisure to examine it more closely. Not having as yet given a name to our first discovery, when we re-entered its capacious channel on this occasion, I laid it down as the Murray River, in compliment to the distinguished officer, Sir George Murray, who then presided over the colonial department, not only in compliance with the known wishes of his Excellency

General Darling, but also in accordance with my own feelings as a soldier.

*Two Expeditions into the Interior of Southern Australia.* By Charles Sturt. 2 vols. 1834.

# John M'Doual Stuart
## 1815-1866

IN the mid-nineteenth century there was keen rivalry between Victoria and South Australia for the first crossing of the continent, partly allied with the search for good cattle country and partly with the wish to control an important line of communication. In 1860, Richard O'Hara Burke and John Wills from Victoria reached the tidal waters of the Flinders River, Gulf of Carpentaria, but died on the return journey through mismanagement and ill fortune.

Meanwhile from South Australia, Stuart, an experienced bushman, was working in the general direction pioneered by Sturt, which was approximately followed later by the overland telegraph line and the transcontinental highway. Despite difficulties and hardships, Stuart persisted with great determination, his efforts being crowned with success on his third attempt. In 1862 he reached the northern coast east of Port Darwin, as described below. Like many of his contemporaries, Stuart was excessively optimistic about the future of much of the country he traversed.

★ ★ ★

Friday, 9th May, Nash Spring.[1] Sent King and Nash with the horses that carried the water bags back to the depot, while I and the other two, at twenty minutes to eight o'clock a.m., proceeded on a bearing of 290°, following one of the native tracks running in that direction. At about a mile they became invisible; for that distance I observed that a line of trees was marked down each side of the track by cutting a small piece of bark from off the gum-trees with a tomahawk. This I had never seen natives do before; the marks are very old. At eighteen miles and a half struck another track (the trees cut in the same way) crossing our course; followed it, bearing 10° east of north, and at about two miles came on a native well with moisture in it. Followed the valley on the same course, but seeing

[1] Nash Spring was about forty miles south of Daly Waters, Northern Territory. It was named after a member of the expedition, as was Thring Creek later.

no more appearance of water, I again changed to my original course and, at a quarter to four o'clock, finding that I was again entering the dense forest and scrub, I camped at a good place for feed for the horses, but no water. The whole of the day's journey has been through a wooded country, in some places very thick, but in most open; it is composed of gums, hedge-trees, and some new trees—the gums predominating; there were also a few patches of lancewood scrub. For the first eighteen miles the soil was light and sandy with spinifex and a little grass mixed. At the end of eighteen miles I again got into the grass country with occasionally a little spinifex. Wind, south-east. Cold during the night and morning.

Saturday, 10th May. The Forest. Started at five minutes to seven o'clock a.m. (same course, 290°). Almost immediately encountered a dense forest of tall mulga with an immense quantity of dead wood lying on the ground. It was with the greatest difficulty that the horses could be made to move through it. At a mile it became a little more open, which continued for six miles. At seven miles I thought, from the appearance of the country, that it was dipping towards the north-north-west; I therefore changed my course to north-west, and in less than a mile again entered a dense forest of tall mulga, thicker than I had yet been into. Continued pushing, tearing, and winding into it for three miles. The further I went the denser it became. I saw that it was hopeless to continue any further. We were travelling full speed, and making little more than a mile an hour throughout the ten miles gone over today. The country is a red light soil, and covered with abundance of grass, but completely dried up. No rain seems to have fallen here for a length of time. We have not seen a bird, nor heard the chirrup of any to disturb the gloomy silence of the dark and dismal forest—thus plainly indicating the absence of water in and about this country. I therefore retraced my steps towards Nash Spring; passed our last night's camp, and continued on till sundown, one of the horses being completely knocked up. Camped without water. Wind, south-east.

Sunday, 11th May, The Forest. This morning the horse that was so bad last night was found dead, which put us in a very awkward position—without a pack-horse. We had to leave behind the pack-saddle, bags, and all other things we could not carry with us on our riding-horses. Proceeded to Nash Spring, which we reached after two o'clock p.m., with another of the horses completely knocked up. It was with difficulty that he reached it. I suppose the days being so extremely hot, and the feed so dry that there is little nourishment in it, is the cause of this, as they were horses that had been out with me on my last year's journey, and had suffered from want of water a longer time than on this occasion. I am nearly in a fix with a long journey before me, the horses unable to do more than two nights without water, and the water-bags losing half their contents in one day's journey. To make the Victoria[1] through the country I have just passed into would be impossible. I must now endeavour to find a country to the northward and make the Roper. I am very vexed about the water-bags turning out so badly, as I was placing great dependence on them for carrying me through. I must try and push through the best way possible. Wind, south-east. . . .

Thursday, 24th July, Thring Creek. Entering the Marsh. Started at 7.40, course north. I have taken this course in order to make the sea coast, which I suppose to be distant about eight miles and a half, as soon as possible; by this I hope to avoid the marsh. I shall travel along the beach to the north of the Adelaide. I did not inform any of the party, except Thring and Auld, that I was so near to the sea, as I wished to give them a surprise on reaching it. Proceeded through a light soil, slightly elevated, with a little ironstone on the surface, the volcanic rock cropping out occasionally; also some flats of black alluvial soil. The timber much smaller and more like scrub, showing that we are nearing the sea. At eight miles and a half came upon a broad valley of black alluvial soil, covered with long grass; from this I can hear the wash of the sea. On the other side of the valley, which is rather more than a quarter of a mile wide, is growing a line of thick heavy bushes, very dense, showing that to be the boundary of the beach. Crossed the valley, and entered the scrub, which was a complete network of vines. Stopped the horses to clear a way, whilst I advanced a few yards on to the beach, and was gratified and delighted to behold the water of the Indian Ocean in

[1] This W.N.W. course would have taken him to sea in Joseph Bonaparte Gulf, about $2\frac{1}{2}°$ south of the point he finally reached.

Van Diemen Gulf, before the party with the horses knew anything of its proximity. Thring, who rode in advance of me, called out, 'The Sea!' which so took them all by surprise, and they were so astonished, that he had to repeat the call before they fully understood what was meant. Then they immediately gave three long and hearty cheers. The beach is covered with a soft blue mud. It being ebb tide, I could see some distance; found it would be impossible for me to take the horses along it; I therefore kept them where I had halted them, and allowed half the party to come on to the beach and gratify themselves by a sight of the sea, while the other half remained to watch the horses until their return. I dipped my feet, and washed my face and hands in the sea, as I promised the late Governor Sir Richard McDonnell I would do if I reached it. The mud has nearly covered all the shells; we got a few, however. I could see no seaweed. There is a point of land some distance off, bearing 70°. After all the party had had some time on the beach, at which they were much pleased and gratified, they collected a few shells; I returned to the valley, where I had my initials (J.M.D.S.) cut on a large tree, as I did not intend to put up my flag until I arrived at the mouth of the Adelaide. Proceeded on a course of 302° along the valley; at one mile and a half, coming upon a small creek with running water, and the valley being covered with beautiful green grass, I have camped to give the horses the benefit of it. Thus have I, through the instrumentality of Divine Providence, been led to accomplish the great object of the expedition, and take the whole party safely as witnesses to the fact, and through one of the finest countries man could wish to behold—good to the coast, and with a stream of running water within half a mile of the sea. From New-castle Water to the sea-beach, the main body of the horses have been only one night without water, and then got it within the next day. If this country is settled, it will be one of the finest Colonies under the Crown, suitable for the growth of any and everything—what a splendid country for producing cotton! Judging from the number of the pathways from the water to the beach, across the valley, the natives must be very numerous; we have not seen any, although we have passed many of their recent tracks and encampments. The cabbage and fan palm-trees have been very plentiful during today's journey down to this valley. This creek I named 'Charles Creek', after the eldest son of John Chambers, Esq., it is one by which some large bodies of springs discharge their surplus water into Van Diemen Gulf; its banks are of soft mud, and boggy. Wind, south. Latitude 12° 13′ 30″.

The Journals of John McDouall Stuart, 1858–1862. Edited from Mr. Stuart's MS. by William Hardman. London, 1864.

# Jack Gordon Hides
## 1906-1936

THE coast line of New Guinea was charted by Portuguese, Dutch and British navigators from the sixteenth century onwards, but the exploration of its difficult and mountainous interior has largely been carried out since the closing decades of the last century. Between the two wars, officers of the Papuan administration made some remarkable journeys in the mountainous country separating Papua and the mandated territory of north-east New Guinea, revealing densely populated areas whose existence had hitherto been unsuspected. Among these officers was J. G. Hides, who, with a party of native police, opened up the Wen country, a mountainous area between the headwaters of the Strickland and Purari rivers, May 1935.

★     ★     ★

Morning came with a cloudless sky, and the sun over the mountains in the east to make the heavy dew sparkle in the grass of the park. With hungry stomachs life seemed hard indeed. Three men, carrying unstrung bows and bundles of arrows, came in to lead us as we prepared to move off. I asked them again for food, but they explained that we would get it at some place farther on. I knew that they were up to something, but we had nothing else to do but follow them.

We crossed a grass basin covered with snow-white balsam and heliotrope stock—a pretty sight—and followed the guides to some small limestone pinnacles two to three miles distant from the park where we had rested for the night. Through a gap in these pinnacles, and extending south-eastwards, we could see another valley system, a tableland of hollows and mounds, all covered with grass and cultivations. The three natives pointed to it, and called the country the Wen.[1]

A large crowd of men began to appear at our rear. Some of them trailed their bows behind them. Whenever they saw us look back,

[1] Part of the elevated plateau between the headwaters of the Purari and Strickland rivers.

they would drop their weapons and stand with arms akimbo.
Others carried their arms covered with green pandanus leaves, or
hidden in bundles of sugar-cane.

A terrific din of yodelling was going on all the time, in front as
well as in the rear; but apart from watching the men carefully, we
made no sign.

Climbing to the top of the gap, where one track led up both ways
of the saddle, and the other down into the south-east, we found
about twenty unarmed men ready to receive us. Their friendliness
was overdone—obviously forced—but I did all I could to show that
we neither feared them nor anything they could do. I took photographs of them, and explained that our way was down the valley
of the Wen; they in turn told me that they were of the Injigale
people, and the place where we now stood was called Bangalbe. I
knew what they were up to, and I wanted to ask them why they
wanted to kill us, and to explain that our rifles were not things to be
despised; but some of those smirking, self-possessed faces would
have taken a lot of convincing.

While all this was going on, a man appeared on the saddle about
twenty yards away above us, and with an impatient, plain gesture
told the unarmed natives with us that they were to move the
patrol on down the track. With that he disappeared down a side-
track, and the men to whom we had been talking now nervously
urged us to be on our way. The yodelling on the by-tracks had
ceased, and we were told there would be no guides, that the peo ⸱
were going back. This was an obvious lie; how cheaply they took
us! I turned to Sergeant Orai standing by me. His beard was black
and fuzzy, his uniform torn and dirty with a hundred and fifty
days of breaking across as many miles of mountains, and in the
haggard and worn face of this great Papuan was a grim coolness. I
did not speak to him, but he uttered my thoughts.

'It is here that we find it, Taubada,' he said.

I ordered all the police to load their carbines, and getting the
carriers bunched closely together, we went down into the timber
following the track south-eastwards. Of the four police in front,
two watched the right-hand side of the track and two the left side.

We had not gone more than two hundred yards when a terrific

din of yodelling arose on all sides of us, and the whole line was attacked. It all happened with remarkable suddenness, but every man was ready for them, and Borege was the only one to take an arrow. I fired in front of me and at the back of me, at men not fifteen feet away, rushing with short stabbing spears. The poor carriers got new strength; they yelled and screamed and threw their steel tomahawks at the attacking natives. To give some idea of how these people regarded us, and how closely they attacked, Constable Badua, rushed at close quarters by spearmen, started swinging his rifle instead of firing. He was pulled to the ground, a man with a battle-axe on top of him; and had I not heard Badua's call for help, and seen the incident, he would have been killed by two other natives assisting his assailant. I shot one of them as I rushed to Badua's assistance and, pulling his assailant off him, after hitting him with the butt of my rifle, allowed him to run off. The struggle was over by then; it had only lasted about fifteen seconds. The thunder of the rifles had brought silence in the country around us, and we walked out of the timber into cultivations again.

Our attackers came to meet us with presents of food. They stood and offered the bunches of bananas and bundles of spinach; but the food was thrown back at them, and I explained that we did not take presents from people who tried to murder us; and further, that when we were ready for the food, we would take it. They stood like down-hearted schoolboys, and for all their treachery, my heart went out to them. So that when a little later about twenty venerable old men met us, and with great difficulty and care explained by gestures that this was not the section that had attacked us, I pretended to believe their story. At the same time I told them that we would now take the food we wanted.

Their answering gestures could have been read as: 'Go to it, old man.'

We killed two pigs in a pen nearby, dug what potatoes we wanted, and then handed the old men axes, which they all smilingly accepted. Then with large fires going, and food cooking, we gorged ourselves to contentment.

The attitude of these people was extraordinary. Within an hour or so of the attack, fully three hundred men, all of them genuinely friendly, were sitting around the party; and it would have been indelicate, I thought, to have even suggested to them that only a short time before we had been fighting with them. They seemed to treat a fight like a football match. They could be treacherous, but they could also be gentlemen.

That night we slept contentedly in one of their parks, with the natives sleeping in the farmhouses within a hundred yards of the camp, and the next morning at daylight we were on our way following a good road down the western side of the Wen plateau. I could see the contour drains cutting across every acre of country. At first I believed that they were for irrigation, but now I could see that they were to prevent erosion of the soil, for in many places in this Wen country I could see sections of the drains supported with timber to keep the soil in place.

We now had plenty of guides, and as we proceeded on hundreds of men came to join our party from all points, all of them unarmed, and those not carrying presents of food were walking uprightly and with their arms folded. It was all so pleasant; women could be seen in the green potato fields, and little boys ran with the party. How we wished it would continue always. There was no hooting or yodelling now, no derisive laughter to follow stumbling police and carriers: the people were genuinely friendly, courteous and respectful. And our party were equally courteous and respectful, and considerate of the smallest detail. Not even a potato leaf was taken without the asking, no road was followed without invitation, and presents of steel were exchanged for food. As we rested at one point, I heard Sergeant Orai addressing his police and carriers.

'You must forget the fight,' he said. 'You must remember that this is not your mother's country, that it belongs to these people; and you must not forget to treat these people as you were treated yourselves when the Government first came to your village.'

It was the finest thing I had ever heard from a native, and it showed the great feeling of common brotherhood that has come into the minds of these Papuans.

*Papuan Wonderland.* By J. G. Hides. Archer House, Inc., 1936.

# Donald Thomson
## 1901-

ARNHEM LAND, the region of northern Australia immediately west
of the Gulf of Carpentaria, has little to offer the settler, and its
aboriginal inhabitants were formerly reputed to be particularly
hostile to white men. After clashes between the natives and the
authorities, Thomson, a trained anthropologist, offered to establish
contact with the natives and to study their problems. Despite much
opposition, he was allowed in 1935 to enter the country and after
many adventures returned with the first scientific account of these
remarkable people. The extract describes the conclusion of his
journey along the east coast opposite Groote Eylandt, from Roper
River northwards to Bennet Bay, after all but one of his native
companions had deserted him. Thomson later saw arduous service in
the Pacific and has recently returned from an important anthropological expedition to central and western Australia.

★   ★   ★

The struggle of these days, the effort to keep going and to keep the
boy from giving up, will live with me for a long time. I remember
how on this and the succeeding two days we dared not look far
ahead at a distant landmark; the effort that we knew would be
needed to reach it seemed more than we could stand. Instead, we fixed
our eyes on a tree or something on the beach and concentrated only
on reaching that. My Journal of that day [16 June 1935], written
at the Minnie, reads:

'For the last few miles I was so tired and in such pain that I felt
half anaesthetic to the touch of the sand. I had great blisters on the
soles of both feet—the one on the left much worse than the one on
the right. These had burst and were giving me serious pain, and I
found that the blisters were packed full with sand. Cleaned them
out by removing the skin and tied my feet with some old rag I
had had for cleaning the gun. Lay down aching and very cold.

'The boy made a half-hearted attempt to find a crossing, then we
huddled under the lee of a great rock and made a little fire; we were

far too spent to do much foraging for firewood. The boy had told me that the river[1] was knee deep, now he reported that the tide was not low enough. I woke him again later—but the tide had turned and was then running in; it was too late to cross. A day lost; all this day's effort seemed to be in vain. Had to sleep. Cold, stormy, overcast night with high wind; breakers booming all night.

'June 17th. Am writing this after the worst day yet. The boy announced that we could not cross here but that we had better go up and around the Minnie. Tide high now and rising. The boy also says that he believes that there is a tributary on the south of the Minnie that winds for a long way westwards. Painful to stand on my feet, much less to walk. Struck native tracks and followed them south-west through sand-hills and found good water near a tributary creek about a mile back from the mouth. Decided that we could cross here, and we settled down to wait all day for the tide to fall. Today, the last two or three teaspoonfuls of sugar that I had kept are finished; did not use it yesterday but held it over. Cooked a damper and tried to make a raft—at least the boy did; I could give little help as I can only walk with difficulty. Shot a Bar-shouldered Dove and had a few mouthfuls each—our only fresh meat for the day—and a little bacon. Went to inspect the mouth of the river. At the mouth saw a crocodile just slide into the water as we got there and it seemed the last straw. . . . Decided to push on up the river and try to get over. We laboured along a native pad over terrible country for what was probably only two or two and a half miles, and then climbed a tree and saw that after all the river ran south more and more and broadened into a wide maze of mangroves. Decided, to the boy's disgust, to return to the mouth and try to cross that way. He says it is dangerous; the alternative—miles of travel by night to cross the Minnie or get around it—to me, barefooted and scarcely able to walk, impossible.' We decided to wait till nightfall, when the tide would be low. Tiger (my Kangaroo dog) very emaciated and coat staring, but still game. . . . If we get over tonight I shall be more free with the cartridges.

The hours of waiting seemed an eternity. The boy collected a bundle of dry branches and lashed them together with strips of bark.

[1] The Minnie, the last river to be crossed before reaching Bennet Bay.

The tide fell very slowly. It was late at night, the moon obscured by clouds, and bitterly cold. Just as we were ready a shadow seemed to pass in the water; we waited, but in the dark depths there was nothing to be seen. After a little while we went on. Pluckily, the boy made a crossing first, reached a sandbank and stuck a fish spear there; then, with the aid of the rough raft on which I laid my swag, I crossed to the sandbank. With my stiff and swollen leg I was not much use for swimming. The boy made another journey and this time Tiger swam too.

We landed on the outer fringe of a dense tangle of mangroves, muddy underneath, with high roots like stilts and of an impenetrable blackness. We climbed on top of this tangle of roots and groped our way through fetid ooze and a confusion of roots. When we reached the other side the boy was exhausted and his teeth were chattering violently. We walked across the open plain on the fringe of the mangroves to the edge of a strip of scrub, made a fire, and lay down.

Before daylight in the morning—the seventh day of the journey to Bennet Bay—we were away again, making north. We returned to the beach and the going was not at all bad. Ordinarily it would have been reckoned easy walking, but we were very weak from long travel and from want of food and rest. My greatest trouble that day was to keep the boy going; he wanted to give up and lie down. He asked me to leave him to die. Always in my mind and spurring me on was the worry lest Kapiu, the Torres Straits islander in charge of the boat, might become anxious and I was afraid that he might then sail for Groote Eylandt, where there was a wireless set, to ask for help. This would have meant defeat for me, a disaster far worse than anything that could have happened on the journey.

I cannot describe adequately that journey. We were both by this time in a desperate state; the pain of the sand on our now skinned and lacerated feet and swollen legs brought a feeling of numbness and of intense cold. There was about us a vast space that seemed suddenly to have closed in like a material, substantial thing. It was as if at each step we had to force our way through a solid nothingness. So had the sense of unreality become fantastic.

The boy had long since abandoned his blanket. I tore mine up now to make bandages for my feet; but these filled with sand which added to the pain of the wounds and after many attempts had to be abandoned. After a while, we did not talk much. Our pace was reduced to little more than a crawl. The boy insisted on lying down at frequent intervals, but for me these halts only made matters worse. Before the day was out we had some difficulty in getting on to our feet after a rest, and the pain of walking was intensified by each halt. We walked as close to the water's edge as possible, for the sand was harder there and progress less painful. But it was an intense effort even to move up the width of the beach. Early that morning I noticed what appeared to be a dead turtle at the water's edge, so shrunken and emaciated that it seemed at first to have been long dead. It proved to be a small green turtle, thrown up on the beach in the storms of the past week, injured too badly to regain the water but still alive. It provided us with a little meat which we needed badly, very pale in colour for it had little blood; almost like fish. A little later in the morning we saw turtle tracks across the beach and found a nest of fresh eggs. We dug these out, broke the soft parchment-like shells, and greedily swallowed some of them raw. The remainder we carried.

Early in the day we came abreast of Bickerton Island which lies between Groote Eylandt and Cape Barrow at the head of Bennet Bay. But by night-fall, after a full day's walk, we had made such little progress that we were still miles from Cape Barrow. This was the worst day of the journey. The boy lay down at frequent intervals and when I tried to get him on to his feet he begged me to leave him behind. I knew that we could not now be far from Bennet Bay. If I could find water we could live for several days on the turtle eggs. During the day we saw native tracks, still fresh. They were still moving northward, but the tracks were obviously recent and indicated that the natives had passed since the storm and therefore that they were not far ahead of us. Towards nightfall we reached an old camping place which my companion remembered having touched previously in a boat that put in for water.

We found two lagoons in both of which there were water lilies, and close to one of these lagoons we made camp. The water lilies meant food in emergency, for the seed capsules and the rootstock form an important part of the diet of the natives. But the boy was now too spent and too cold to swim for them. Here we boiled the last morsel of bacon that we had cherished, carefully conserving the liquid in which it had been boiled in order to cook the pieces of turtle meat that we had carried since morning. This, with as many turtle eggs as we could eat, made the best meal that we had had since leaving the vessel. Another cold night followed.

On the following morning, June 19, we were much refreshed. But the boy was very weak and I was now suffering so much pain from my feet and legs that I could stand only with difficulty. It was impossible for us to carry our loads if we were to make any progress. Before leaving camp we dug a hole and buried most of the remaining turtle eggs to preserve them in case of need. My remaining possessions, a sheet of canvas and the tomahawk, we also abandoned, placing them in a tree close to where we had slept. We were now a little to the south of Cape Barrow, and leaving the beach here, we turned west and set a course for the north of Bennet Bay where the *St. Nicholas* should be waiting for us. We knew that she should not be far off or, failing the boat, we should find a native camp. But although we again started early, we made little progress and after several hours we had covered only a short distance. During the morning we saw smoke and evidence of recent fires and we burned what dry vegetation we could, hoping to attract the attention of hunting parties that might be about. Much of the skin had now gone from the soles of my feet. Stones, sticks and sharp grass stems made the journey a painful ordeal. I sat down and again bandaged my feet to protect them with the remaining rags of blanket. But during the morning we had to wade through a wide, shallow swamp area, and the clumsy bandages dragged so that I could scarcely lift my feet and they had to be abandoned.

Early in the afternoon we came out on a grassy plain and thence emerged on a salt pan. In the distance a green wall of mangroves marked the vicinity of salt water. A little later we sighted what appeared to be a group of natives. But this was no mirage or vision that mocked at us. The natives proved to be men of the Nunguboiyu tribe, members of the group whose tracks we had been crossing from time to time during the past week, then always moving in a northerly direction. I remember the sight of those figures and how they affected us as if it were yesterday: the sight of other human beings. Only eight days had elapsed, but there are occasions when time cannot be measured. A mist shimmered before me, a dry lump rose in my throat and I had to swallow hard. We could not relax at once. I know that I could not talk. There was the need to retain control and to present outwardly only a mask of indifference. I remember our formal greeting. It was as if they were old friends from whom we had been parted only a few hours. I know that I must have seemed unfriendly, even callous, for I could not trust myself to speak.

'Arnhem Land: explorations among an unknown people.' By Donald F. Thomson. *Geogr. Jn.* 112 (1948).

# POLAR REGIONS

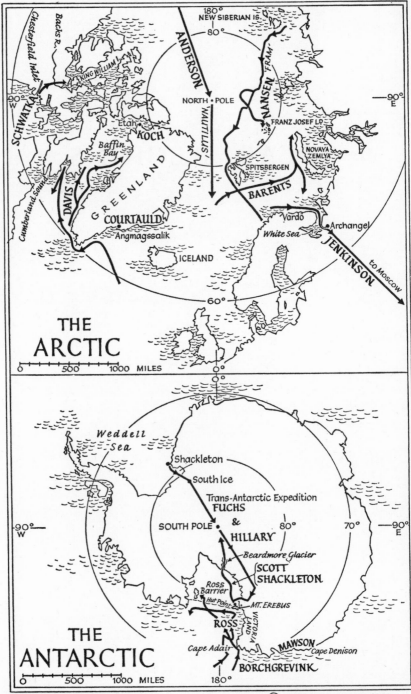

THE
ARCTIC

0       500       1000   MILES

THE
ANTARCTIC

0       500       1000   MILES

# John Davis
## 1550-1605

THE search for a north-west passage to Cathay received a check after Frobisher's disastrous voyage of 1578. The attempt to penetrate by the north-east, though it had almost incidentally resulted in a profitable trade with Russia, proved equally discouraging. In 1584 therefore a newly-formed North-West Company initiated a series of important voyages led by John Davis of Sandridge in Devon, a competent, precise man regarded by many as the outstanding English navigator and hydrographer of his day. In the years 1585 to 1587, Davis performed three voyages in the waters west of Greenland. On the first he examined the south-west coast of Greenland (which he called the Coast of Desolation) and striking north-westwards discovered Cumberland Sound in Baffin Island, which he concluded, correctly, was not the hoped-for passage. The next year he inspected another inlet, Exeter Sound further to the north. Finally in 1587, a remarkably open year, he sailed as far as 73° N. and then pushed to the westwards, but was turned back by ice. Though Davis failed, like many after him, to find the long-sought passage, he pioneered the route followed by his successors. The following summary of his work, extracted from his *Worldes hydrographical discription* (London, 1595) contains also the earliest detailed description of the Greenland Eskimo.

*     *     *

In my first voyage not experienced of the nature of those climates, and having no direction either by chart, globe, or other certaine relation in what altitude that passage was to be searched, I shaped a northerly course, and so sought the same towards the south, and in that my northerly course I fell upon the shore which in ancient time was called Groenland, five hundred leagues distant from the Durseys, west-north west northerly, the land being very high and full of mightie mountaines all covered with snowe, no views of wood, grasse, or earth to be seene, and the shore two leagues off into the sea so full of yce as that no shipping could by any meanes come near the same. The lothsome view of the shore, and irksome noyse of the yce was such, that it bred strange conceites among us, so that we supposed the place to be wast and voyd of any sensible or vegitable creatures, whereupon I called the same Desolation; so coasting this shore towards the south in the latitude of sixtie degrees, I found it to trend towards the west; I still followed the leading therof in the same height, and after fiftie or sixtie leagues it fayled and lay directly north, which I still followed, and in thirtie leagues sayling upon the West side of this coast, by me named Desolation, we were past al the yce and found many greene and pleasant isles bordering upon the shore, but the mountaines of the maine were still covered with great quantities of snow.[1] I brought my ship among those isles, and there mored to refresh ourselves in our weary travell, in the latitude of sixtie-foure degrees or there about. The people of the countrey having espyed our shippes came downe unto us in their canoas, and holding up their right hand to the sunne and crying 'Uliaout', would strike their breasts: we doing the like the people came aboard our shippes, men of good stature, unbearded, small eyed and of tractable conditions, by whome as signes would permit, we understood that towards the north and west there was a great sea, and using the people with kindenes in giving them nayles and knives which of all things they most desired, we departed, and finding the sea free from yce, supposing ourselves to be past al daunger, we shaped our course west-north-west, thinking thereby to passe for China, but in the latitude of sixtie-sixe degrees wee fell with another shore, and there found another passage of twenty leagues broad directly west into the same,[2] which we supposed to be our hoped straight; we entered into the same thirtie or fortie leagues, finding it neither to wyden nor straighten; then considering that the yeere was spent (for this was in the end of August) not knowing the length of the straight and dangers thereof, we tooke it our best course to returne with notice of our good successe for this small time of search.

And so returning in a sharpe fret of Westerley windes, the 29th of September, we arrived at Dartmouth. And acquainting master

[1] Davis was now off south-west Greenland.
[2] Cumberland Sound, Baffin Land.

Secretarie with the rest of the honourable and worshipfull adventurers of all our proceedings, I was appointed againe the seconde yere to search the bottome of this straight, because by all likelihood it was the place and passage by us laboured for.

In this second attempt the marchants of Exeter and other places of the West became adventurers in the action, so that being sufficiently furnished for six moneths, and having direction to search these straights untill we found the same to fall into another sea upon the west side of this part of America, we should againe returne; for then it was not to be doubted but shipping with trade might safely be conveied to China and the parts of Asia. We departed from Dartmouth, and arriving unto the south part of the Coast of Desolation, coasted the same upon his west shore to the latitude of sixtie-sixe degrees, and there ancored among the isles bordering upon the same, where we refreshed ourselves; the people of this place came likewise unto us, by whom I understood through their signes that towards the north the sea was large.

At this place the chiefe ship whereupon I trusted, called the *Mermayd of Dartmouth,* found many occasions of discontentment, and being unwilling to proceed, shee there forsook me. Then considering how I had given my faith and most constant promise to my worshipfull good friend master William Sanderson, who of all men was the greatest adventurer in that action, and tooke such care for the performance thereof, that he hath to my knowledge at one time disbursed as much money as any five others whatsoever out of his owne purse, when some of the companie have been slacke in giving in their adventure. And also knowing that I should loose the favor of M. Secretarie Walsingham if I should shrink from his direction; in one small barke of thirty tunnes whereof M. Sanderson was owner, alone without farther comfort or company I proceeded on my voyage, and arriving at these straights followed the same eighty leagues[1] untill I came among many islands, where the water did ebbe and flowe six fadome up right, and where there had bene great trade of people to make traine.[2] But by such things as there we found wee knew that they were not Christians of Europe that had used that trade; in fine, by searching with our boat we found small

[1] Davis was now in Baffin Bay.    [2] Train Oil.

hope to passe any farther that way, and therefore retourning agayne recovered the sea and coasted the shore towards the south, and in so doing (for it was too late to search towards the north) we found another great inlet neere forty leagues broad, where the water entered in with violent swiftnesse, this we also thought might be a passage; for no doubt the north partes of America are all islands by ought that I could perceive therein; but because I was alone in a small barke of thirtie tunnes, and the yeere spent, I entred not into the same, for it was now the seventh of September, but coasting the shore towardes the south wee saw an incredible number of birds; having divers fishermen aboord our barke they all concluded that there was a great skull of fish, we being unprovided of fishing furniture with a long spike nayle made a hooke, and fastening the same to one of our sounding lines, before the bait was changed we tooke more than fortie great cods, the fish swimming so abundantly thicke about our barke as is incredible to bee reported, of which with a small portion of salt that we had, we preserved some thirtie couple, or thereabouts, and so returned for England.

And having reported to M. Secretarie Walsingham the whole successe of this attempt, he commanded me to present unto the most honourable Lord high Treasurour of England some part of that fish, which when his Lordship saw, and heard at large the relation of this second attempt, I received favourable countenance from his honour, advising me to prosecute the action of which his Lordship conceived a very good opinion.

The next yere, although divers of the adventurers fell from the action, as all the Westerne marchants, and most of those in London; yet some of the adventurers, both honourable and worshipfull, continued their willing favour and charge, so that by this meanes the next yere two shippes were appointed for the fishing and one pinnesse for the discoverie.

Departing from Dartmouth, through God's mercifull favour, I arrived at the place of fishing, and there according to my direction I left the two ships to follow that busines, taking their faithfull promise not to depart untill my returne unto them, which should be in the fine of August, and so in the barke I proceeded for the discoverie; but after my departure in sixteene dayes the two shippes had finished their voyage, and so presently departed for England, without regard of their promise; myselfe not distrusting any such hard measure proceeded for the discoverie, and followed my course in the free and open sea betweene north and north-west to the latitude of 67°, and there I might see America west from me, and Desolation (Greenland) east; then when I saw the land of both sides I began to distrust it would proove but a gulfe; notwithstanding, desirous to know the full certainty I proceeded, and in 68 degrees the passage enlarged, so that I could not see the Westerne shore; thus I continued to the latitude of 73° in a great sea, free from yce, coasting the westerne shore of Desolation. The people came continually rowing out unto me in their canoes, twenty, forty, and one hundred at a time, and would give me fishes dryed, salmon, salmon peale, cod, caplin, lumpe, stonebase, and such like, besides divers kinds of birds, as partridge, fesant, guis, sea-birds and other kindes of flesh.

I still laboured by signes to know from them what they knew of any sea towards the north; they still made signes of a great sea as we understood them, then I departed from that coast thinking to discover the north parts of America.

And after I had sayled towards the west forty leagues, I fel upon a great banke of yce: the winde being north and blew much, not seeing any shore west from me, neither was there any yce towards the north, but a great sea, free, large, very salt and blew, and of an unsearcheable depth. So coasting towards the south I came to the place where I left the ships to fish, but found them not. Then being forsaken and left in this distresse, referring myselfe to the mercifull providence of God, I shaped my course for England, and unhoped for of any, God alone releeving me, I arrived at Dartmouth.

By this last discovery it seemed most manifest that the passage was free and without impediment towards the north;[1] but by reason of the Spanish fleet [The Armada], and unfortunate time of M. Secretarie's death, the voyage was omitted and never sithins attempted.

The cause why I use this particular relation of all my proceedings for this discovery, is to stay this objection—Why hath not Davis discovered this passage being thrise that wayes imploied?

[1] This is in fact a channel to the Arctic Ocean.

How far I proceeded and in what forme this discovery lieth, doth appeare upon the globe which M. Sanderson to his very great charge hath published, for the which he deserveth great favour and commendations. Made by master Emery Mulineux[1], a man wel qualited, of a good judgement and very experte in many excellent practices in myselfe being the onely meane with master Sanderson to imploy master Mulineux therein, whereby he is now growne to a most exquisite perfection.

[1] Emery Molyneux was the maker of the first English globe, 1592.

*The Voyages and Works of John Davis the Navigator.* Ed. by A. H. Markham. Hakluyt Soc. 1st ser. vol. 59, 1880.

# Willem Barentszoon
## died 1597

THE Dutch were later more successful in the search for the north-
east passage than the English, and their main effort was concentrated in the three voyages of Willem Barentszoon (known to
English writers as William Barents) who was financed by Amster-
dam merchants in the years 1594 to 1596. The Dutch, profiting from
English reports of the bad ice conditions in Vaigach Strait south of
Novaya Zemlya, proposed to strike further north. In 1596 Barents,
after examining the coasts of Spitsbergen, made a landfall on the
west coast of Novaya Zemlya and succeeded in rounding its northern
extremity. Ice conditions, however, obliged him to abandon the
attempt and to winter ashore. Their vessel having been crushed by
the ice, they built two boats and, weakened by scurvy, began the
long trip homewards. The survivors of this remarkable trial eventually made the coast of Lapland, where they were warmly received
by a Russian ship, and eventually reached Vardö. Gerrit de Veer's
simple account of Barents's death described below is one of the most
moving passages in the literature of exploration. There was an
interesting sequel. Nearly three hundred years later, the winter
quarters were found and many relics removed to Holland. Among
the books and manuscripts recovered were translations of a Spanish
manual of navigation, a Portuguese history of China and the
narrative of the English Arctic expedition of Pet and Jackson,
1580.

*    *    *

The 16th of June [1597] we set sail again, and got to the Islands of
Orange with a south wind, which are thirty-two miles distant from
Point Desire;[1] there we went on land with two small barrels and a
kettle, to melt snow and put the water into the barrels, as also to
seek for birds and eggs to make meat for our sick men; and being
there we made fire with such wood as we found there, and melted
the snow, but found no birds. But three of our men went over the

[1] On the west coast of Spitsbergen.

ice to the other island, and got three birds, and as we came back again, our master (which was one of the three) fell into the ice, where he was in great danger of his life, for in that place there ran a great stream; but by God's help he got out again and came to us, and there dried himself by the fire that we had made.

At this fire we dressed the birds, and carried them to the boat to our sick men, and filled our two runlets with water that held about two gallons apiece; which done, we put to the sea again with a south-east wind and nasty mizzling weather, whereby we were all damp and wet, for we had no shelter in our open boats and sailed west and west-by-south until off the Ice Point.

And being there, both our boats lying hard by each other, the skipper called to William Barents to know how he did, and William Barents made answer and said 'Fine, mate. I still hope to be able to run before we get to Wardhuus.'[1] Then he spake to me and said 'Gerrit, if we be near Ice Point, lift me up again. I must view it once more.' At this time we had sailed from the Islands of Orange to Ice Point about twenty miles, and then the wind was westerly, and we made our boats fast to a great piece of ice, and there ate somewhat; but the weather was still fouler and fouler, so that we were once again enclosed with ice and forced to stay there.

The 17th of June in the morning, when we had broken our fast, the ice came so frighteningly upon us that it made our hair stand upright upon our heads, it was so fearful to behold; by which means we could not save our boats, so that we thought verily that it was a foreshowing of our last end. For we drove away so hard with the ice, and were so sore pressed between a flake of ice that we thought verily the boats would burst into a hundred pieces, which made us look pitifully one upon the other, for now 'good advice was dear', and every minute of an hour we saw death before our eyes. At last, being in this discomfort and necessity, it was said, 'If we could take hold with a rope upon the fast ice, we might therewith draw the boat up and so get out of the great drift of ice.'

[1] Vardö, northern Norway.

But as this counsel was good, yet it was so full of danger that it was the hazard of his life that should take upon him to do it; yet without doing it, was it most certain it would cost us all our lives. This counsel (as I said) was good, but no man durst hang the bell about the cat's neck, fearing to be drowned; yet necessity required to have it done, and the most danger made us choose the least.

So that being in that perplexity and as 'A drowned calf may safely be risked', I, being the lightest of all our company, took on me to carry a rope upon the fast ice. And so, creeping from one piece of driving ice to another, by God's help got to the fast ice, where I made a rope fast to a high hummock, and they that were in the boat drew it thereby unto the said fast ice, and then one man alone could draw more than all of them could have done before. And when we had gotten thither, in all haste we took our sick men out and laid them upon the ice, laying clothes and other things under them for them to rest on, and then took all our goods out of the boats, and so drew them upon the ice, whereby for that time we were delivered from that great danger, making account that we had escaped out of death's jaws, as it was most true. . . .

The 20th of June it was indifferent weather, the wind west, and when the sun was in the south-east Claes Adrianson began to be extreme sick, whereby we perceived that he would not live long, and the bo'sun came into our boat and told us in what case he was, and that he would not long continue alive; whereupon William Barents spake and said, 'I think I shall not live long after him'; and yet we did not judge William Barents to be so sick, for we sat talking one with another and spake of many things, and he read in my little chart which I had made touching my voyage, and we had some talk on it. At last he laid away the chart and spake unto me, saying, 'Gerrit, give me some drink.' He had no sooner drunk but he was taken with so sudden a qualm that he turned his eyes in his head and died presently, and we had no time to call the master out of the other boat to speak unto him. And so he died shortly before Claes Adrianson. The death of William Barents put us in no small discomfort, as being the chief guide and only pilot on whom we reposed ourselves; but we could not strive against God, and therefore we must of force be content.

*The Three Voyages of William Barents to the Arctic Regions, 1594-96.* By Gerrit de Veer. 2nd Ed. by Koolemans Beyren. Hakluyt Soc. 1st Ser., v. 54, 1876.

# James Clark Ross
## 1800-1862

AFTER the voyages in Antarctic waters of Captain James Cook and the Russian Admiral Thaddeus Bellingshausen, European activities in the far south were carried on largely by whalers and sealers. The identity of the first navigator to sight any part of the actual mainland of Antarctica has been hotly debated; a good case can be advanced for the British Naval officer, Edward Bransfield who sighted the Graham Land peninsula in 1819. British commercial skippers continued to make discoveries, which helped to inaugurate a period of more intense activity which saw the expeditions of Dumont d'Urville from France and Lieutenant Wilkes from the United States. However, it was a British expedition—Captain James Ross with the *Erebus* and *Terror*, 1839-41, which made the decisive advance. In the course of a remarkable cruise primarily designed to make magnetic observations, Ross sighted Victoria Land, and discovered, as he records below, two most unsuspected features—the two volcanic peaks, which he named Mt. Erebus and Mt. Terror, and the even more intriguing phenomenon, the great Ross Ice Barrier. Ross later attempted to penetrate further south without success. It was across the Ross Barrier that the South Pole was reached some seventy years later. The *Erebus* and *Terror* were lost eventually in Sir John Franklin's Arctic disaster.

\* \* \*

[Jan. 27, 1841]. At between two and three miles distant from the land,[1] the soundings were regular, in thirty-eight to forty-one fathoms, on a bed of fine sand and black stones, and probably good anchorage might be found near the shore with southerly winds. A high cliff of ice projects into the sea from the south and south-west sides, rendering it there quite inaccessible, and a dangerous reef of rocks extends from its southern cape at least four or five miles, with apparently a deep water passage between them and the cape; several

---

[1] Franklin Island, Ross Sea.

icebergs of moderate size were aground on the banks to the northward and westward of the island. At midnight the bearings of eight
separate islands are given in the log of the *Erebus*; but as these
afterwards proved to be the summits of mountains, at a great
distance, belonging to the mainland, they do not appear upon the
chart as islands. With a favourable breeze, and very clear weather,
we stood to the southward, close to some land which had been
in sight since the preceding noon, and which we then called the
'High Island'; it proved to be a mountain,[1] twelve thousand four
hundred feet of elevation above the level of the sea, emitting flame
and smoke in great profusion; at first the smoke appeared like snow-
drift, but as we drew nearer its true character became manifest.

The discovery of an active volcano in so high a southern latitude
cannot but be esteemed a circumstance of high geological importance and interest, and contribute to throw some further light on the
physical construction of our globe. I named it 'Mount Erebus', and
an extinct volcano to the eastward, little inferior in height, being by
measurement ten thousand nine hundred feet high, was called
'Mount Terror'.

A small, high, round island, which had been in sight all the
morning, was named 'Beaufort Island', in compliment to Captain
Francis Beaufort of the Royal Navy, Hydrographer to the Admiralty, who was not only mainly instrumental in promoting the
sending forth our expedition, but afforded me much assistance
during its equipment by his opinion and advice; and it is very
gratifying to me to pay this tribute of respect and gratitude to him
for the many acts of kindness and personal friendship I have received
at his hands. At 4 p.m. we were in lat. 76° 6' S., long. 168° 11' E.
The magnetic dip 88° 27' S., and the variation 95° 31' E. We were
therefore considerably to the southward of the magnetic pole,
without any appearance of being able to approach it on account
of the land-ice, at a short distance to the westward, uniting with the
western point of the 'High Island' which, however, afterwards
proved to be part of the mainland, and of which Mount Erebus
forms the most conspicuous object. As we approached the land under

---

[1] Mount Erebus, on Ross Island.

all studding-sails, we perceived a low white line extending from its eastern extreme point as far as the eye could discern to the eastward.[1] It presented an extraordinary appearance, gradually increasing in height as we got nearer to it, and proving at length to be a perpendicular cliff of ice, between one hundred and fifty and two hundred feet above the level of the sea, perfectly flat and level at the top, and without any fissures or promontories on its even seaward face. What was beyond it we could not imagine; for being much higher than our mast-head, we could not see anything except the summit of a lofty range of mountains extending to the southward as far as the seventy-ninth degree of latitude. These mountains, being the southernmost land hitherto discovered, I felt great satisfaction in naming after Captain Sir William Edward Parry, R.N.

Whether 'Parry Mountains' again take an easterly trending, and form the base to which this extraordinary mass of ice is attached, must be left for future navigators to determine. If there be land to the southward it must be very remote, or of much less elevation than any other part of the coast we have seen, or it would have appeared above the barrier. Meeting with such an obstruction was a great disappointment to us all, for we had already, in expectation, passed far beyond the eightieth degree, and had even appointed a rendezvous there in case of the ships accidentally separating. It was, however, an obstruction of such a character as to leave no doubt upon my mind as to our future proceedings, for we might with equal chance of success try to sail through the cliffs of Dover, as penetrate such a mass. When within three or four miles of this most remarkable object, we altered our course to the eastward for the purpose of determining its extent, and not without the hope that it might still lead us much further to the southward. The whole coast here from the western extreme point now presented a similar vertical cliff of ice, about two or three hundred feet high. The eastern cape at the foot of Mount Terror was named after my friend and colleague Commander Francis Rawdon Moira Crozier, of the *Terror*, to whose zeal and cordial co-operation is mainly to be ascribed, under God's blessing, the happiness as well as success of the expedition[2]: At

[1] The edge of the Ross Ice Shelf.
[2] Cape Crozier is the eastern extremity of Ross Island.

4 p.m. Mount Erebus was observed to emit smoke and flame in unusual quantities, producing a most grand spectacle. A volume of dense smoke was projected at each successive jet with great force, in a vertical column, to the height of between fifteen hundred and two thousand feet above the mouth of the crater, when condensing first at its upper part, it descended in mist or snow and gradually dispersed, to be succeeded by another splendid exhibition of the same kind in about half an hour afterwards, although the intervals between the eruptions were by no means regular. The diameter of the columns of smoke was between two and three hundred feet, as near as we could measure it; whenever the smoke cleared away the bright red flame that filled the mouth of the crater was clearly perceptible; and some of the officers believed they could see streams of lava pouring down its sides until lost beneath the snow which descended from a few hundred feet below the crater, and projected its perpendicular icy cliff several miles into the ocean. Mount Terror was much more free from snow, especially on its eastern side where were numerous little conical crater-like hillocks, each of which had probably been, at some period, an active volcano; two very conspicuous hills of this kind were observed close to Cape Crozier. The land upon which Mount Erebus and Terror stand comprised between Cape Crozier and Cape Bird had the appearance of an island from our present position; but the fixed ice, not admitting of our getting to the westward of Cape Bird, prevented our ascertaining whether it was so or not at this time.

The day was remarkably fine, and favoured by a fresh north-westerly breeze we made good progress to the E.S.E., close along the lofty perpendicular cliffs of the icy barrier. It is impossible to conceive a more solid-looking mass of ice; not the smallest appearance of any rent or fissure could we discover throughout its whole extent, and the intensely bright sky beyond it but too plainly indicated the great distance to which it reached to the southward. Many small fragments lay at the foot of the cliffs, broken away by the force of the waves, which dashed their spray high up the face of them.

Having sailed along this curious wall of ice in perfectly clear water, a distance of upwards of one hundred miles, by noon

we found it still stretching to an indefinite extent in an E.S.E.
direction.

*A Voyage of Discovery and Research in the Southern and Antarctic
Regions, 1839–43.* By Sir James Clark Ross, R.N. 2 vols, 1847.
Vol. I.

# Frederick Schwatka
## 1849-1892

THE first conclusive evidence of the fate of the Franklin expedition was found in 1854 by Dr. John Rae when he came upon the relics of a party of thirty men near the mouth of Back's Fish River. It was then clear that the ships had been abandoned in the Victoria Channel and that these men had died from exhaustion and scurvy on a march southwards. Interest in the Arctic then moved in general to Greenland and the Arctic islands, and finally to the North Pole, but the Franklin epic still cast a romantic glamour over the Arctic. It was used by the American newspaper owner, James Gordon Bennett, to publicize Lieut. Schwatka's expedition of 1878 on another search for relics. This journey is also of interest as an early example of the trend towards the adoption of Eskimo techniques of travel. Schwatka, who had not been born when the Franklin disaster occurred, established a base at Winchester Inlet in the north-west of Hudson Bay and travelled overland to Back's Fish River, and northwards into King William Island. The incident described below took place on the east coast of Adelaide Peninsula. It is related by W. H. Gilder, second in command.

*    *    *

From this point onward our march was attended with the most profitable results. On the evening of the 4th of June (1878) we met a young man named Adlekok who, during the previous summer had found a new cairn erected by white men near Pfeffer River, which had never been seen by any other Innuits. Nearby were three graves and a tent place in which he found a pair of wire-gauze snow-goggles, which we bought from him. This information seemed of sufficient importance to be followed up immediately before any other natives should find and rob the cairn. Consequently the next day Lieutenant Schwatka and I took a light sled, with Toolooah to drive and Adlekok as guide, and visited the spot. We took a day's rations with us, to use in case we did not get back that night, and started with a head wind and storm that confined our view to the immediate vicinity of the sledge. Our guide however, took us through this trackless waste of smooth ice, a distance of over twenty-five miles, without deviation from the direct line, with no land-marks or sun to steer by; but on he went with the unerring instinct of a dog until we struck the land at the western banks of Pfeffer River. Arrived at the cairn we found it as he said, 'a white man's cairn' unmistakably, but before proceeding to take it down we examined it carefully and found scratched on a clay stone with the point of a sharp instrument,

$$\boxed{\begin{array}{c} \text{MAY} \\ \text{H XII} \\ 1869 \end{array}}$$

and on the opposite side,

$$\boxed{\begin{array}{c} \text{ETERNAL HONOR TO THE DISCOVER-} \\ \text{ERS OF THE NORTH WE-} \end{array}}$$

and knew it to be the cairn erected by our countryman, Captain Hall, over the bones of two of Franklin's men which he speaks of having found here. A portion of the inscription was lost by the breaking off of a piece of the stone on which it was written. We did not take down the monument, but after making a hasty sketch, returned to camp, having travelled over fifty miles in ten hours.

At this camp we found another interesting relic, in a pine board that seems to have been part of the head of a bunk or other per-manent fixture, and has the initials 'L. F.' in brass tacks upon it. This was picked up on the west coast of Adelaide Peninsula, near where the ship went down that drifted through Victoria Strait, and may serve to identify that vessel, thus proving a most interesting and valuable relic. At the next camp, which was our last stopping-place on the mainland, we met an old woman named Tooktoocheer, widow of Pooyetah, who was among the first to visit the boat place we saw a few days ago. We were somewhat disappointed in her as a witness, for she was so old that her memory was at fault, and she would wander about to different places and relate circumstances without explanation. Her son, who was present at the interview, was a lad of about twelve years when he visited the boat place with his parents, and retained a vivid recollection of the place. His testimony, therefore, proved to be what we had hoped of his mother's. All the time he was talking the old woman sat nodding approval as the circumstances he was relating were recalled to her memory. His name is Ogzeuck-keuwock, and he is an *aruketko*, or medicine-man, in his tribe. The recollection of the boat place was somewhat impressed upon his mind by the explosion of a can of powder with which he and another lad were playing after the articles were found there. The effects of the explosion came near proving fatal at the time, and when I met him during the fall on King William Land, he told me he had never entirely recovered from the shock.

I give the interview with Tooktoocheer and her son as I recorded it in my note-book at the time, so that each reader may draw his own conclusions. Some of the statements will undoubtedly appear strange, but in the main they are perfectly intelligible and exceedingly interesting. Tooktoocheer said she was from Okbil-legeok (Pelly Bay of the charts), a portion of the Netchillik country. She is the widow of Pooyetah, spoken of by Sir John Ross and Captain Hall. She appeared to be about seventy years old, and was an object of high esteem by her people, as was evinced in the care that was bestowed upon her comfort. She said she had never seen any of Franklin's men alive, but saw six skeletons on the mainland and two on the island. This she pointed out on the southern coast near ninety-five degrees west longitude. There were no graves at either place. Her husband was with her at the time, and seven other Innuits. This was when she was at the boat place west of Richardson Point (in Adelaide Peninsula). In fact, she seemed to have the two places somewhat mixed up in her mind, and Ogzeuck-keuwock took up the thread of the narrative here. In answer to a question which we asked his mother, he said he saw books at the boat place in a tin case, about two feet long and a foot square, which was fastened, and they broke it open. The case was full. Written and printed books were shown him, and he said they were like the printed ones. Among the books he found what was probably the needle of a compass or other magnetic instrument, because he said when it touched any iron it stuck fast. The boat was right side up, and the tin case in the boat. Outside the boat he saw a number of skulls. He forgot how many, but said there were more than four. He also saw bones from legs and arms that appeared to have been sawed off. Inside the boat was a box filled with bones; the box was about the same size as the one with the books in it.

He said the appearance of the bones led the Innuits to the opinion that the white men had been eating each other.[1] What little flesh was still on the bones was very fresh; one body had all the flesh on. The hair was light; it looked like a long body. He saw a number of wire snow-goggles, and alongside the body with flesh on it was a pair of gold spectacles. (He picked out the kind of metal from several that were shown him). He saw more than one or two pairs of such spectacles, but forgot how many. When asked how long the bodies appeared to have been dead when he saw them, he said they had probably died during the winter previous to the summer he saw them. In the boat he saw canvas and four sticks (a tent or sail), saw a number of watches, open-faced; a few were gold but most were silver. They are all lost now. They were given to the children to play with and have been broken up and lost. One body—the one with flesh on—had a gold chain fastened to gold ear-rings, and a gold hunting-case watch with engine-turned engraving attached to the chain, and hanging down about the waist. He said when he pulled the chain it pulled the head up by the ears. This body also had a gold ring on the ring finger of the right hand. It was taken off and has since been lost by the children in the same way that the other things were lost. His reason for thinking that they had been eating each other was because the bones were cut with a knife or saw. They found one big saw and one small one in the boat; also a large red tin case of smoking tobacco and some pipes. There was no cairn there. The bones are now covered up with sand and sea-weed, as they were lying just at high-water mark. Some of the books were taken home for the children to play with, and finally torn and

[1] Dr. John Ray had also come to this conclusion, which was hotly disputed.

lost, and others lay around among the rocks until carried away by the wind and lost or buried beneath the sand.

His statement in reference to one of the deceased wearing a watch by a chain attached to his ears appears strange, but I give the statement as he made it. The chain may in some way have become attached to the ears or, ridiculous as the story sounds, there may have been some eccentric person in the party who wore his watch in that way, and if such should prove to be the case, this would certainly identify him beyond doubt. While the old woman sat in our igloo giving her statement or trying to recollect the circumstances, I succeeded in getting a good portrait sketch of her, which attracted considerable interest among the natives, and Ogzeuck-keu-wock, who towards the latter part of the interview had begun to exhibit symptoms of impatience, turned quickly around as soon as he had finished, and asked to have his portrait taken also, in which I accommodated him, much to his gratification.

*Schwatka's Search; Sledging in the Arctic in Quest of the Franklin Records.* By W. H. Gilder, 1881.

# Fridtjof Nansen
## 1861-1930

AMONG Nansen's claims to fame was his revolutionary advance in Polar travel. Generally speaking, Arctic travellers had depended upon the supplies they carried. Their equipment was usually that of contemporary navies, and procedure was moulded by naval discipline and custom. Sledging parties struggled along rather like a boat's crew in a rough sea. Nansen adapted native appliances and methods to scientific purpose. Ski and dog teams enabled the explorers to travel at speed in relative comfort, rations were scientifically designed and parties lived 'off the land' (or sea). By mastering Eskimo techniques, explorers survived in conditions previously considered impossible. Nansen, also having carefully appreciated all relevant factors, was prepared to take 'considered risks'.

When the relics of the *Jeannette*, which sank off the New Siberian Islands, were found on the coast of south-west Greenland, Nansen planned to turn what had previously been the final obstacle to the attainment of the North Pole, i.e., the 'pack ice', to advantage by putting the specially constructed *Fram* into the pack off the New Siberian Islands and drifting across the Polar basin. At the most advantageous moment, he proposed to set out from the *Fram* for the Pole. His plans worked out almost precisely as he foresaw (the drift began in September 1893), but he and his companions were finally beaten by the pack. However he established a 'furthest north', (86° 14' N.), as he relates below, and on the astonishing return journey to Franz Josef Land gave a triumphant demonstration of the efficacy of his technique when applied by resolute men.

*　　*　　*

Friday, April 5th [1895]. Began our march at three yesterday morning. The ice, however, was bad, with lanes and ridges, so that our progress was but little. These lanes with rubble thrown up on each side are our despair. It is like driving over a tract of rocks, and delays us terribly. First I must go on ahead to find a way, and then get my sledge through; then, perhaps, by way of a change, one falls into the water; yesterday I fell through twice. If I work hard in finding a way and guiding my sledge over rough places, Johansen is no better off, with his two sledges to look after. It is a tough job to get even one of them over the rubble, to say nothing of the ridges; but he is a plucky fellow, and no mistake, and never gives in. Yesterday he fell into the water again in crossing a lane, and got wet up to his knees. I had gone over on my snow-shoes shortly before, and did not notice that the ice was weak. He came afterwards without snow-shoes walking beside one of the sledges, when suddenly the ice gave and he fell through. Happily he managed to catch hold of the sledge, and the dogs, which did not stop, pulled him up again. These baths are not an unmixed pleasure now that there is no possibility of drying or changing one's clothes, and one must wear a chain mail of ice until they thaw and dry on the body, which takes some time in this temperature. I took an observation for longitude and a magnetic observation yesterday morning, and have spent the whole forenoon today in calculation (inside the bag) to find out our exact position. I find our latitude yesterday was 86° 2·8′ N. This is very little, but what can we do when the ice is what it is? And these dogs cannot work harder than they do, poor things. I sigh for the sledge-dogs from the Olenek daily now. The longitude for yesterday was 98° 47′ 15″, variation 44·4°.

I begin to think more and more that we ought to turn back before the time we originally fixed. It is probably three hundred and fifty miles or so to Petermann's Land[1] (in point of fact it was about four hundred and fifty miles to Cape Fligely); but it will probably take us all we know to get over them. The question resolves itself into this: Ought we not, at any rate, to reach 87° N.? But I doubt whether we can manage it, if the ice does not improve.

Saturday, April 6th. Two a.m. — 11·4 Fahr. (−24·2° C.). The ice grew worse and worse. Yesterday it brought me to the verge of despair, and when we stopped this morning I had almost decided to turn back. I will go on one day longer, however, to see if the ice is

[1] Franz Josef Land.

really as bad farther northwards as it appears to be from the ridge, thirty feet in height, where we are encamped. We hardly made four miles yesterday. Lanes, ridges, and endless rough ice, it looks like an endless moraine of ice-blocks; and this continual lifting of the sledges over every irregularity is enough to tire out giants. Curious this rubble-ice. For the most part it is not so very massive, and seems as if it had been forced up somewhat recently, for it is incompletely covered with thin, loose snow, through which one falls suddenly up to one's middle. And thus it extends mile after mile northwards, while every now and then there are old floes, with mounds that have been rounded off by the action of the sun in the summer—often very massive ice.

I am rapidly coming to the conclusion that we are not doing any good here. We shall not be able to get much farther north, and it will be slow work indeed if there be much more of this sort of ice towards Franz Josef Land. On the other hand, we should be able to make much better use of our time there, if we should have any over. 8.30 p.m. −29.2° Fahr. (−34° C.).

Monday, April 8th. No, the ice grew worse and worse, and we got no way. Ridge after ridge and nothing but rubble to travel over. We made a start at two o'clock or so this morning and kept at it as long as we could, lifting the sledges all the time; but it grew too bad at last. I went on a good way ahead on snow-shoes, but saw no reasonable prospect of advance, and from the highest hummocks only the same kind of ice was to be seen. It was a veritable chaos of ice-blocks, stretching as far as the horizon. There is not much sense in keeping on longer; we are sacrificing valuable time and doing little. If there be much more such ice between here and Franz Josef Land, we shall, indeed, want all the time we have.

I therefore determined to stop, and shape our course for Cape Fligely.

On this northernmost camping-ground we indulged in a banquet, consisting of lobscouse, bread-and-butter, dry chocolate, stewed 'tytlebær', or red whortleberries, and our hot whey drink, and then, with a delightful and unfamiliar feeling of repletion, crept into the dear bag, our best friend. I took a meridian observation yesterday, by which I see that we should be in latitude 86° 10′ north, or there-

abouts. This morning I took an observation for longitude. At 8.30
a.m. −25·6° Fahr. (−32° C.).'

Tuesday, April 9th. Yesterday's was our first march homewards.
We expected the same impracticable ice but, to our amazement, had
not gone far before we came on tolerably good ground which
improved steadily and, with only a few stoppages, we kept at it till
this morning. We came upon ridges, to be sure, but they always
allowed themselves to be negotiated pretty easily, and we did well.
Started yesterday about two in the afternoon, and kept going till
one this morning.

Thursday, April 11th. Better and better. Found nothing but
beautiful level tracts of ice yesterday with a few ridges which were
easy to get over, and some lanes with young ice on which gave us
rather more trouble. They ran, however, about in our direction
(our course is now the magnetic S. 22° W., or about the true
W.S.W.), and we could go alongside them. At last, however, we
had to make a crossing, and accomplished it successfully, although
the ice bent under us and our sledges more than was desirable.
Late in the afternoon we came across a channel which we proposed
to cross in the same way. We reached the other side with the first
sledge safely enough, but not so with the other. Hardly had the
leaders of the team got out to the dangerous place where the ice was
thinnest and where some water was on the surface, when they
stopped and warily dipped their paws in the water. Then through
went one of them, splashing and struggling to get out. The ice
began to sink under the weight of the other dogs and the sledge,
and the water came flowing up. I dragged dogs and sledge back as
quickly as possible, and succeeded in driving them all on to the firm
ice again in safety. We tried once again at another place, I running
over first on snow-shoes and calling to the dogs, and Johansen
pushing behind, but the result was no better than the first time, as
'Suggen' fell in, and we had to go back. Only after a long detour,
and very much fagged, did we finally succeed in getting the two last
sledges over. We were lucky in finding a good camping-place,
and had the warmest night and the most comfortable (I might
almost say cosy) morning—spent, be it said, in repairs—that we
have had on the trip. I think we did the longest day's march

yesterday that we have yet achieved: about fifteen miles. Two in the afternoon, — 17·6° Fahr.

[Franz Josef Land was not sighted until July 12th].

*Farthest North; a voyage of exploration of the ship* Fram, *1893–6.*
By Fridtjof Nansen. 2 vols. Constable, 1879. Vol. 2.

# Carsten Borchgrevink
## 1864-1934

IN the closing decades of the nineteenth century, interest in the
Antarctic was again aroused by European scientists, and plans for
international co-operation were concerted. In this revival an important part was played by a remarkable and courageous Norwegian,
C. Borchgrevink. After some experience in a whaler and fired by the
spirit of scientific inquiry, he initiated single-handed an Antarctic
expedition, for which he secured the powerful support of the force-
ful newspaper proprietor, Sir George Newnes. In 1898, his party was
the first to winter on the Antarctic Continent, and later was the first
to advance some distance southwards on the Ross Barrier. Borchgrevink was unlucky not to find a more convenient spot for his base,
but his expedition set the pattern for subsequent Antarctic expeditions. The character of his achievement was adequately recognized
only with the award of the Patron's Medal of the Royal Geographical Society in 1934. He describes below one of his abortive attempts
to find a way up to the Polar plateau.

*       *       *

[April 1899.] We observed great movement in the ice-pack in
Robertson Bay during the middle of April. On the 22nd I resolved
to attempt my first penetration into Robertson Bay on the ice which
then, though young, was already about two and a half feet thick.
I took with me Mr. Fougner, Mr. Bernacchi,[1] and the Finn Savio,
provision for twenty days, twenty sledge-dogs, and one small
collapsible boat. We left Camp Ridley[2] at 11 a.m., and proceeded
in the pack until darkness began to set in. The pack along the cliffs
was rather small, and the ice which bound the floes together rather
thin, so we had to proceed with great caution, and when I at last
decided to camp on a small beach at the foot of the perpendicular
wall of Victoria Land, we had great difficulty in reaching that little
place. The beach or slope where we pitched our camp was not thirty

[1] L. C. Bernacchi later served as physicist on Scott's *Discovery* expedition,
1901–3.
[2] At Cape Adare.

yards at the widest part; it was some four feet above water, and had a crescent formed with the concave side some fifteen chains in length. From the perpendicular wall of Victoria Land a kind of gravel rush had taken place, and formed a deep slope from the walls of the rocks down to the beach, with a slope of from sixty to seventy degrees, rising to a height of about thirty feet. Above us the perpendicular wall rose to about five hundred feet at places overhanging the little beach, which seemed completely isolated from everywhere, except by way of the bay. Shortly after landing a southerly wind rose, which continued to increase in force until it became a violent gale. We had pitched the silk tent, and my companions took their sleep whilst I kept watch. At 7 p.m. I had to wake them as the ice began to break up. It was not a moment too early; it just gave us time enough to save our provisions by carrying them on to the top of the gravel slope, where drift snow and ice had formed a sort of gallery, about six feet broad, immediately on to the mountain wall. The drift snow had also formed a kind of fence at the outside of this gallery to the height of about four feet. In the six-foot groove between this fence and the perpendicular wall of Victoria Land we pitched our tent, but before doing so we had an arduous task. We hauled away, suffering intensely from the cold, our fingers dying as we hung to the ropes while pulling provisions and travelling gear up to our limited accommodation. The huge breakers washed over the beach and sent spray about us; it froze immediately, and soon land and men were covered with a sheet of ice. Although everyone realized the awkward position, all worked calmly. On Monday night, the 23rd, the bay was completely free from ice and was perfectly calm. I then sent Mr. Fougner and the Finn Savio towards Camp Ridley in the small collapsible boat, and with emergency rations sufficient for a few days. However, shortly after leaving us, and having gone out of our sight, they met with heavy ice drifting rapidly into the bay which, as mentioned, it had left during the gale. Mr. Bernacchi and myself, who soon afterwards noticed the floating ice masses, were naturally very anxious about them, ignorant as we were of their fate in the little canvas boat. We ourselves were without any craft whatever to take us away from our temporary place of refuge. For two days we remained in ignorance of Mr.

Fougner's and the Finn's fate, but in the evening of the 25th both of them appeared on a very steep ice swell, which descended from the perpendicular wall of Victoria Land. By help of a small axe and an alpenstock they cut footholds in the ice and then slowly approached us. I soon discovered that they were in a pretty weak condition, and while Mr. Bernacchi started to cook some food for them, I began to cut steps in the steep ice-slope to meet them. At night we were again all safe on our little camping-place. However, Mr. Fougner and the Finn had spent two days and nights under the shelter of the canvas boat, and thought they had discovered a possible place, or the only possible place, for an ascent to the ridge of Victoria Land some five thousand feet above us. But the first five hundred feet would necessarily involve great risk in the ascent. On the 27th I decided to attempt the ascent. We started in the following order: the Finn Savio, Mr. Fougner, Mr. Bernacchi, and then myself, roped together. We had to cut footholds in the ice. By following in the steps by which Mr. Fougner and the Finn had reached us, we were enabled to attain the place where these two had camped under the small boat, and saw. the spot likely to offer the only chance of escape. It was a kind of rough groove in the perpendicular cliff, partly covered with ice and snow. After having had a good feed of seal-beef we began the ascent. Some of our poor sledge-dogs which had ventured along with us on the slope howled melancholy notes as they saw us ascend. Three of them had already perished by losing their foothold coming round the icy slope, and one was precipitated into the abyss below when we were some two hundred feet up in the groove. Cautiously and slowly we climbed upwards, while the lesser slope some four hundred feet above us seemed always to grow further away as we slowly ascended towards it. All the night through we continued to climb, while the cold increased as we got up in the heights. By way of the ridge we were enabled to proceed towards Camp Ridley, where great anxiety had prevailed already on the day when the ice broke up, as they knew of no place where we could possibly have camped at the time.

*First on the Antarctic Continent; the British Antarctic Expedition, 1898–1900.* Newnes, 1901.

# Robert Falcon Scott
## 1868-1912

IN the revival óf Antarctic exploration during the last decade of the nineteenth century, Britain, mainly in the person of Sir Clements Markham (President R.G.S. 1893-1905) played a leading part. The first large-scale British expedition (*Discovery* 1901-4) was the result of his persistent badgering of government, and it was led by the man he had picked for this command, Robert Falcon Scott, a naval officer with a scientific background. Six years later, spurred on by Ernest Shackleton's success (see page 330), Scott organized a second expedition with a comprehensive plan of scientific investigation, but inevitably involved in the 'race for the Pole'. The tragic story of this expedition has often been retold; many factors contributed to the disaster—an unaccountable error in organization of the final dash, scurvy on the return sledging journey, and sheer bad luck with the weather at the crisis. Scott and his party reached the Pole on 18th January 1912, to find themselves forestalled by the Norwegian, Roald Amundsen, as recounted below. The expedition, however, was redeemed by the fortitude of their end and by the importance of its contribution to science.

★    ★    ★

Friday, January 12th. Camp 64. T. −17·5°. Lat. 88° 57'. Another heavy march with snow getting softer all the time. Sun very bright, calm at start; first two hours terribly slow. Lunch, 4¾ hours, 5·6 miles geo.; Sight Lat. 88° 52'. Afternoon, 4 hours, 5·1 miles—total 10·7.

In the afternoon we seemed to be going better; clouds spread over from the west with light chill wind and for a few brief minutes we tasted the delight of having the sledge following free. Alas! in a few minutes it was worse than ever, in spite of the sun's eclipse. However, the short experience was salutary. I had got to fear that we were weakening badly in our pulling; those few minutes showed me that we only want a good surface to get along as merrily as of old. With the surface as it is one gets horribly sick of the monotony and

325

can easily imagine oneself getting played out, were it not that at the lunch and night camps one so quickly forgets all one's troubles and bucks up for a fresh effort. It is an effort to keep up the double figures, but if we can do so for another four marches we ought to get through. It is going to be a close thing.

At camping tonight everyone was chilled and we guessed a cold snap, but to our surprise the actual temperature was higher than last night, when we could dawdle in the sun. It is most unaccountable why we should suddenly feel the cold in this manner; partly the exhaustion of the march, but partly some damp quality in the air, I think. Little Bowers is wonderful; in spite of my protest he would take sights after we had camped tonight, after marching in the soft snow all day where we have been comparatively restful on ski.

Night position—Lat. 88° 57' 25" S.; Long. 160° 21' E.; Var. 179° 49' W. Minimum T. −23·5°.

Only sixty-three miles (geo.) from the Pole tonight. We ought to do the trick, but oh! for a better surface. It is quite evident this is a comparatively windless area. The sastrugi[1] are few and far between, and all soft. I should imagine occasional blizzards sweep up from the S.E., but none with violence. We have deep tracks in the snow, which is soft as deep as you like to dig down.

Saturday, January 13th. Lunch Height 10,390. Barometer low! lunch Lat. 89° 3' 18". Started on some soft snow, very heavy dragging and went slow. We could have supposed nothing but that such conditions would last from now onward, but to our surprise, after two hours we came on a sea of sastrugi, all lying from S. to E., predominant E.S.E. Have had a cold little wind from S.E. and S.S.E., where the sky is overcast. Have done 5·6 miles and are now over the 89th parallel.

Night camp 65.—Height 10,270. T. −22·5°, Minimum −23·5°. Lat. 89° 9' S. very nearly. We started very well in the afternoon. Thought we were going to make a real good march, but after the first two hours surface crystals became as sandy as ever. Still we did 5·6 miles geo., giving over eleven for the day. Well, another day with double figures and a bit over. The chance holds.

It looks as though we were descending slightly; sastrugi remain as

[1] Small ridges of hard snow.

326

in forenoon. It is wearisome work this tugging and straining to advance a light sledge. Still, we get along. I did manage to get my thoughts off the work for a time today, which is very restful. We should be in a poor way without our ski, though Bowers manages to struggle through the soft snow without tiring his short legs.

Only fifty-one miles from the Pole tonight. If we don't get to it we shall be d . . . d close. There is a little southerly breeze tonight; I devoutly hope it may increase in force. The alternation of soft snow and sastrugi seem to suggest that the coastal mountains are not so very far away.

Sunday, January 14th. Camp 66. Lunch T. −18°, Night T. −15°. Sun showing mistily through overcast sky all day. Bright southerly wind with very low drift. In consequence the surface was a little better, and we came along very steadily 6·3 miles in the morning and 5·5 in the afternoon, but the steering was awfully difficult and trying; very often I could see nothing, and Bowers on my shoulders directed me. Under such circumstances it is an immense help to be pulling on ski. Tonight it is looking very thick. The sun can barely be distinguished, the temperature has risen and there are serious indications of a blizzard. I trust they will not come to anything; there are practically no signs of heavy wind here, so that even if it blows a little we may be able to march. Meanwhile we are less than forty miles from the Pole.

Again we noticed the cold; at lunch today (Obs: Lat. 89° 20′ 53″ S.) all our feet were cold, but this was mainly due to the bald state of our finnesko. I put some grease under the bare skin and found it made all the difference. Oates seems to be feeling the cold and fatigue more than the rest of us, but we are all very fit. It is a critical time, but we ought to pull through. The barometer has fallen very considerably and we cannot tell whether due to ascent of plateau or change of weather. Oh! for a few fine days! So close it seems and only the weather to baulk us.

Monday, January 15th. Lunch camp, Height 9,950. Last depot. During the night the air cleared entirely and the sun shone in a perfectly clear sky. The light wind had dropped and the temperature fallen to −25°, minimum −27°. I guessed this meant a hard pull, and guessed right. The surface was terrible, but for 4¾ hours yielded

6 miles (geo.). We were all pretty well done at camping, and here we leave our last depot—only four days' food and a sundry or two. The load is now very light, but I fear that the friction will not be greatly reduced.

Night, January 15th. Height 9,920. T. $-25°$. The sledge came surprisingly lightly after lunch—something from loss of weight, something, I think, from stowage, and, most of all perhaps, as a result of tea. Anyhow we made a capital afternoon march of 6·3 miles, bringing the total for the day to over twelve (12·3). The sastrugi again very confused, but mostly S.E. quadrant; the heaviest now almost east, so that the sledge continually bumps over ridges. The wind is from the W.N.W. chiefly, but the weather remains fine and there are no sastrugi from that direction.

Camp 67. Lunch obs: Lat. 98° 26′ 57″; Lat. dead reckoning, 89° 33′ 15″ S.; Long. 160° 56′ 45″ E.; Var. 179° E.

It is wonderful to think that two long marches would land us at the Pole. We left our depot today with nine days' provisions, so that it ought to be a certain thing now, and the only appalling possibility the sight of the Norwegian flag forestalling ours. Little Bowers continues his indefatigable efforts to get good sights, and it is wonderful how he works them up in his sleeping-bag in our congested tent. (Minimum for night $-27·5°$.) Only twenty-seven miles from the Pole. We ought to do it now.

Tuesday, January 16th. Camp 68. Height 9,760. T. $-2·35°$. The worst has happened, or nearly the worst. Noon sight showed us in Lat. 89° 42′ S., and we started off in high spirits in the afternoon, feeling that tomorrow would see us at our destination. About the second hour of the march Bowers's sharp eyes detected what he thought was a cairn; he was uneasy about it, but argued that it must be sastrugus. Half an hour later he detected a black speck ahead. Soon we knew that this could not be a natural snow feature. We marched on, found that it was a black flag tied to a sledge bearer; nearby the remains of a camp; sledge tracks and ski tracks going and coming and the clear trace of dogs' paws—many dogs. This told us the whole story. The Norwegians have forestalled us and are first at the Pole. It is a terrible disappointment, and I am very sorry for my loyal companions. Many thoughts come and much discussion have we had.

Tomorrow we must march on to the Pole and then hasten home with all the speed we can compass. All the day-dreams must go; it will be a wearisome return. We are descending in altitude—certainly also the Norwegians found an easy way up.

Wednesday, January 17th. Camp 69. T. −22° at start. Night −21°. The Pole. Yes, but under very different circumstances from those expected. We have had a horrible day—add to our disappointment a head wind 4 to 5, with a temperature −22°, and companions labouring on with cold feet and hands.

We started at 7.30, none of us having slept much after the shock of our discovery. We followed the Norwegian sledge tracks for some way; as far as we make out there are only two men.[1] In about three miles we passed two small cairns. Then the weather overcast, and the tracks being increasingly drifted up and obviously going too far to the West, we decided to make straight for the Pole according to our calculations. At 12.30 Evans had such cold hands we camped for lunch—an excellent 'week-end one'. We had marched 7·4 miles. Lat. sight gave 89° 53′ 37″. We started out and did six and a half miles due south. Tonight little Bowers is laying himself out to get sights in terrible difficult circumstances; the wind is blowing hard, T. −21°, and there is that curious damp, cold feeling in the air which chills one to the bone in no time. We have been descending again, I think, but there looks to be a rise ahead; otherwise there is very little that is different from the awful monotony of past days. Great God! this is an awful place and terrible enough for us to have laboured to it without the reward of priority. Well, it is something to have got here, and the wind may be our friend tomorrow. We have had a fat Polar hoosh in spite of our chagrin, and feel comfortable inside—added a small stick of chocolate and the queer taste of a cigarette brought by Wilson. Now for the run home and a desperate struggle. I wonder if we can do it.

*Scott's Last Expedition. Vol. I. The Journals of Capt. R. F. Scott, R.N.,* arranged by L. Huxley. Smith, Elder, 1913.

[1] Amundsen had in fact four companions.

# Ernest Henry Shackleton
## 1874-1922

ERNEST SHACKLETON, an officer of the mercantile marine, had his first experiences of Antarctic travel with Scott's *Discovery* expedition. These experiences had not been happy, for he had broken down on the return southern journey, and had been sent home. However to a man of Shackleton's temperament, this was a challenge rather than a defeat. In the face of considerable discouragement he organized the Imperial Antarctic Expedition of 1907-9, and entered whole-heartedly into the 'race for the Pole'. Working from Scott's old base at Hut Point, he pioneered a route up the Beardmore Glacier (subsequently followed by Scott in 1911) to the Polar plateau, and made a determined but hazardous dash southwards, which only fell short of its objective by ninety-seven miles. The return journey was also touch and go, but as his subsequent career showed, Shackleton always rose to the occasion in the field. Perhaps the greatest contributory factor to his achievements was his companions' firm conviction that the 'Boss would never let them down'.

★     ★     ★

February 25th [1909]. We turned out at 4 a.m. for an early start, as we are in danger of being left if we do not push ahead rapidly and reach the ship.[1] On going into the tent for breakfast I found Marshall suffering from paralysis of the stomach and renewed dysentery, and while we were eating, a blizzard came up. We secured everything as the Bluff showed masses of ragged cloud, and I was of opinion that it was going to blow hard. I did not think Marshall fit to travel through the blizzard. During the afternoon, as we were lying in the bags the weather cleared somewhat, though it still blew hard. If Marshall is not better tonight I must leave him with Adams and push on, for time is going on, and the ship may leave on March 1, according to orders, if the Sound is not clear of ice. I went over through

[1] The *Nimrod*, which was to wait for them in McMurdo Sound until February 28th.

the blizzard to Marshall's tent. He is in a bad way still, but thinks that he could travel tomorrow.

February 27th (1 a.m.). The blizzard was over at midnight, and we got up at 1 a.m. had breakfast at 2, and made a start at 4. At 9.30 a.m. we had lunch, at 3 p.m. tea, at 7 p.m. hoosh [stew], and then marched till 11 p.m. Had another hoosh, and turned in at 1 a.m. We did twenty-four miles. Marshall suffered greatly but stuck to the march. He never complains.

March 5th. Although we did not turn in until 1 a.m. on the 27th, we were up again at 4 a.m. and after a good hoosh, we got under way at 6 a.m. and marched until 1 p.m. Marshall was unable to haul, his dysentery increasing, and he got worse in the afternoon after lunch. At 4 p.m. I decided to pitch camp, leave Marshall under Adam's charge, and push ahead with Wild, taking one day's provisions and leaving the balance for the two men at the camp. I hoped to pick up a relief party at the ship. We dumped everything off the sledge except a prismatic compass, our sleeping-bags and food for one day, and at 4.30 p.m. Wild and I started, and marched till 9 p.m. Then we had a hoosh, and marched until 2 a.m. of the 28th, over a very hard surface. We stopped for one hour and a half off the north-east end of White Island, getting no sleep, and marched till 11 a.m., by which time our food was finished. We kept flashing the heliograph in the hope of attracting attention from Observation Hill, where I thought that a party would be on the look-out, but there was no return flash. The only thing to do was to push ahead, although we were by this time very tired. At 2.30 p.m. we sighted open water ahead, the ice having evidently broken out four miles south of Cape Armitage, and an hour and a half later a blizzard wind started to blow, and the weather got very thick. We thought once that we saw a party coming over to meet us, and our sledge seemed to grow lighter for a few minutes, but the 'party' turned out to be a group of penguins at the ice-edge. The weather was so thick that we could not see any distance ahead, and we arrived at the ice-edge suddenly. The ice was swaying up and down and there was grave risk of our being carried out. I decided to abandon the sledge as I felt sure that we would get assistance at once when we reached the hut, and time was becoming important. It was necessary that we should get food and shelter speedily. Wild's feet were giving him a great deal of trouble. In the thick weather we could not risk making Pram Point, and I decided to follow another route seven miles round by the other side of Castle Rock. We clambered over crevasses and snow slopes and after what seemed an almost interminable struggle reached Castle Rock from whence I could see that there was open water all round the north. It was indeed a different home-coming from what we had expected. Out on the Barrier and up on the plateau our thoughts had often turned to the day when we would get back to the comfort and plenty of the winter quarters, but we had never imagined fighting our way to the back-door, so to speak, in such a cheerless fashion. We reached the top of Ski Slope at 7.45 p.m., and from there we could see the hut and the bay. There was no sign of the ship, and no smoke or other evidence of life at the hut. We hurried on to the hut, our minds busy with gloomy possibilities, and found not a man there. There was a letter stating that the Northern Party had reached the Magnetic Pole, and that all the parties had been picked up except ours. The letter added that the ship would be sheltering under Glacier Tongue until February 26th. It was now February 28th, and it was with very keen anxiety in our minds that we proceeded to search for food. If the ship was gone, our plight, and that of the two men left out on the Barrier, was a very serious one.

We improvised a cooking-vessel, found oil and a Primus lamp, and had a good feed of biscuit, onions and plum pudding, which were amongst the stores left at the hut. We were utterly weary, but we had no sleeping-gear, our bags having been left with the sledge, and the temperature was very low. We found a piece of roofing felt which we wrapped round us, and then we sat up all night, the darkness being relieved only when we occasionally lighted the lamp in order to secure a little warmth. We tried to burn the magnetic hut in the hope of attracting attention from the ship, but we were not able to get it alight. We tried, too, to tie the Union Jack to Vince's cross on the hill, but we were so played out that our cold fingers could not manage the knots. It was a bad night for us, and we were glad indeed when the light came again. Then we managed to get a little warmer, and at 9 a.m. we got the magnetic hut alight, and put up the flag. All our fears vanished when in the distance we saw the ship, miraged up. We signalled with the heliograph, and at 11 a.m. on March 1st we were on board the *Nimrod* and once more safe amongst friends. I will not attempt to describe our feelings. Every one was glad to see us, and keen to know what we had done. They had given us up for lost, and a search-party had been going to start that day in the hope of finding some trace of us. I found that every member of the expedition was well, that the plans had worked out satisfactorily, and that the work laid down had been carried out. The ship had brought nothing but good news from the outside world. It seemed as though a great load had been lifted from my shoulders.

The first thing was to bring in Adams and Marshall, and I ordered out a relief-party at once. I had a good feed of bacon and fried bread, and started at 2.30 p.m. from the Barrier edge with Mackay, Mawson and McGillan, leaving Wild on the *Nimrod*. We marched until 10 p.m., had dinner and turned in for a short sleep. We were up again at 2 a.m. the next morning (March 2nd), and travelled until 1 p.m., when we reached the camp where I had left the two men. Marshall was better, the rest having done him a lot of good, and he was able to march and pull. After lunch we started back again, and marched until 8 p.m. in fine weather. We were under way again at 4 a.m. the next morning, had lunch at noon, and reached the ice-edge at 3 p.m. There was no sign of the ship, and the sea was freezing over. We waited until 5 p.m., and then found that it was possible to strike land at Pram Point. The weather was coming on bad, clouding up from the south-east, and Marshall was suffering from renewed dysentery, the result of the heavy marching. We therefore abandoned one tent and one sledge at the ice-edge, taking on only the sleeping-bags and the specimens. We climbed up by Crater Hill, leaving everything but the sleeping-bags, for the weather was getting worse, and at 9.35 p.m. commenced to slide down towards Hut Point. We reached the winter quarters at 9.50, and Marshall was put to bed. Mackay and I lighted a carbide flare on the hill by Vince's cross, and after dinner all hands turned in except Mackay and myself. A short time after Mackay saw the ship appear. It was now blowing a hard blizzard, but Mackintosh had seen our flare from a distance of nine miles. Adams and I went on board the *Nimrod*, and Adams, after surviving all the dangers of the interior of the Antarctic continent, was nearly lost within sight of safety. He slipped at the ice-edge, owing to the fact that he was wearing new finnesko [sealskin boots], and he only just saved himself from going over. He managed to hang on until he was rescued by a party from the ship. A boat went back for Marshall and the others, and we were all safe on board at 1 a.m. on March 4th.

*The Heart of the Antarctic* (1907–9). By E. H. Shackleton. 2 vols. Heinemann, 1909.

# Douglas Mawson
## 1882-1958

MAWSON first went to the Antarctic as one of Shackleton's scientists in 1907. With Edgeworth David he had reached the South Magnetic Pole. Mawson was more interested in the scientific than the spectacular value of such work; foreseeing the interest which Australia must take in the Antarctic, he organized in 1912 an Australian expedition with an elaborate scientific programme. Parties were landed at points west of the Ross Sea. Mawson himself worked from Cape Denison in King George Vth Land. He began the astonishing journey eastwards over the ice cap, to which the following extract relates, accompanied by B. E. S. Ninnis, a soldier, and Dr. Xavier Mertz, a Swiss mountaineer. In its course Ninnis with sledge and dogs was lost in a crevasse and shortly afterwards Mertz died of exhaustion. Alone and with little food, Mawson struggled on through an extraordinary series of crises, and finally reached Cape Denison again, where the party had to spend another winter until relieved by Captain J. K. Davis in the *Aurora*. The half sledge which Mawson drew is now in the House of the Royal Geographical Society. He maintained his Antarctic interests throughout his life, directing exploration and research on behalf of the Commonwealth Government.

\*     \*     \*

When I got away at 8 a.m. I found that the pulling was easier than it had been on the previous day. Nevertheless I covered only two miles and had to consider myself fortunate in not winding up the whole story then and there. This is what happened, following the account in my diary.

'Going up a long, fairly steep slope, deeply covered with soft snow, broke through lid of crevasse but caught myself at thighs, got out, turned fifty yards to the north, then attempted to cross trend of crevasse, there being no indication of it; a few moments later found myself dangling fourteen feet below on end of rope in crevasse—sledge creeping to mouth—had time to say to myself, "so this is the end," expecting the sledge every moment to crash on my head and all to go to the unseen bottom—then thought of the food uneaten on the sledge; but as the sledge pulled up without letting me down, thought of Providence giving me another chance.' The chance was very small considering my weak condition. The width of the crevasse was about six feet, so I hung freely in space, turning slowly round.

A great effort brought a knot in the rope within my grasp and, after a moment's rest, I was able to draw myself up and reach another and, at length, hauled myself on to the overhanging snow-lid into which the rope had cut. Then, when I was carefully climbing out on to the surface, a further section of the lid gave way, precipitating me once more to the full length of the rope.

Exhausted, weak and chilled (for my hands were bare and pounds of snow had got inside my clothing) I hung with the firm conviction that all was over except the passing. Below was a black chasm; it would be but the work of a moment to slip from the harness, then all the pain and toil would be over. It was a rare situation, a rare temptation—a chance to quit small things for great—to pass from the petty exploration of a planet to the contemplation of vaster worlds beyond. But there was all eternity for the last and, at its longest, the present would be but short. I felt better for the thought.

My strength was fast ebbing; in a few minutes it would be too late. It was the occasion for a supreme attempt. New power seemed to come as I addressed myself to one last tremendous effort. The struggle occupied some time, but by a miracle I rose slowly to the surface. This time I emerged feet first, still holding on to the rope, and pushed myself out, extended at full length, on the snow—on solid ground. Then came the reaction, and I could do nothing for quite an hour.

The tent was erected in slow stages and I then had a little food. And then an idea presented itself which greatly improved my prospects. It was to construct a ladder from alpine rope; one end of which was to be secured to the bow of the sledge and the other carried over my left shoulder and loosely attached to the sledge harness. Thus, if I fell into a crevasse again, it would be easy for me, even though weakened by starvation, to scramble out again by the ladder, provided the sledge was not also engulfed.

Notwithstanding the possibilities of the rope-ladder, I could not sleep properly at all; my nerves had been so over-taxed. All night considerable wind and drift continued.

On the 19th it was overcast and light snow was falling. I resolved 'to go ahead and leave the rest to Providence.'

As they wallowed through the deep snow my feet and legs kept breaking through into space. Then I went right under, but the sledge was held back and the ladder 'proved trumps'. A few minutes later I was down again, but I emerged again without much exertion, half-smothered with snow. Faintness overcame me and I stopped to camp, though only a short distance had been covered.

All around was a leaden glare, the snow-clouds 'coralling' me in. The sun had not shown up for some days and I was eager to see it once more, not only that it might show up the landscape but for its cheerful influence and life-giving energy. A few days previously my condition had been improving, but now it was going back.

During the night of the 18th loud booming noises, sharp cracks and muffled growls issued from the neighbouring crevasses and kept waking me up. At times one could feel a vibration accompanying the growling sounds, and I concluded that the ice was in rapid motion.

The sun at last appeared on the 19th, and I was off by 8.30 a.m. The whole surface was a network of crevasses, some very wide. Along one after another of these I dragged the sledge until a spot was reached where the snow-bridge looked to be firm. Here I plunged across, risking the consequences.

After three hours' marching nothing serious had happened and I found myself on safer ground with a 'pimply' surface visible ahead, close under the slopes of the highlands. Once on this I became over-reliant, and in consequence sank several times into narrow fissures.

At 1 p.m. the Mertz Glacier was at last crossed and I had reached the rising hills on its western side. Overlooking the camp, five hundred feet above the glacier, were beetling, crevassed crags, but I could trace out a good road, free from pitfalls, leading to the plateau, at an elevation of three thousand feet.

To lighten my load for the climb I threw away alpine rope,

finnesko crampons, sundry pairs of worn crampons and socks, while I rubbed a composition on the sledge-runners which prevented them from sticking to wet snow.

January 20th was a wretched day; overcast, with wind and light drift. In desperation I got away at 2 p.m. in a wind which proved to be of considerable assistance. I could see nothing of my surroundings; one thing was certain, and that was that the ascent had commenced and every foot took me upward. The day's work amounted to about two and a half miles.

On the 21st the sun shone brightly and there was a good following wind. Through deep snow I zigzagged up for three miles before deciding to camp.

Wind and drift prevailed early on the 22nd but fell away towards noon, and I was then favoured with a glorious sunny day. Away to the north was a splendid view of the open sea; it looked so beautiful and friendly that I longed to be down near it. Six miles had been covered during the day, but I felt very weak towards the end on account of the heavy pulling.

During the early hours of the 23rd the sun was visible, but about 8 a.m. the clouds sagged low, the wind rose and everything became blotted out in a swirl of driving snow.

I wandered on through it for several hours, the sledge capsizing at times owing to the strength of the wind. It was not possible to keep an accurate course, for even the wind changed direction as the day wore on. Underfoot there was soft snow which I found comfortable for my sore feet, but which made the sledge drag heavily at times.

When camp was pitched at 4 p.m. I reckoned that the distance covered in a straight line had been three and a half miles.

Erecting the tent single-handed in the high wind was a task which required much patience and some skill. The poles were erected first and then the tent was gathered up in the proper form and taken to the windward side of the legs where it was weighted down. The flounce on the windward side was got into position and piled up with snow blocks. Other blocks of snow had previously been placed in a ring round the legs in readiness to be tumbled on to the rest of the flounce when the tent was quickly slipped over the apex of the poles.

In very windy weather it was often as much as two hours after halting before I would be cosy within the shelter of the tent.

High wind and dense driving snow persisted throughout the 24th and I made five and a half miles, sitting on the sledge most of the time with the sail up.

The blizzard continued on the 25th, but after the trying experience of the previous two days, I did not feel well enough to go on. Outside, the snow fell in 'torrents', piled up round the tent and pressed in until it was no bigger than a coffin, of which it reminded me.

I passed most of the day doctoring myself, attending to raw and inflamed places. Tufts of my beard and hair came out, and the snowy floor of the tent was strewn with it at every camp.

'January 26th. I went on again in dense, driving snow. There was no need of the sail. The wind, which was behind, caught the sledge and bundled it along so that, though over a soft surface of snow, the travelling was rapid. The snow was in large, rounded grains, and beat on the tent like hail. Altogether nine miles were covered.

'January 27th. Blizzard-bound again. The previous day's exertions were too much for me to undertake the same again without a long rest.

'January 28th. In the morning the wind had moderated very much but the sky remained overcast and snow continued to fall. It was a long job digging the tent out. Soon after the start the sun gleamed and the weather improved. The three-thousand-foot crest of the plateau had been crossed and I was bearing down rapidly on Commonwealth Bay,[1] the vicinity of which showed up as a darker patch on the clouds of the north-west horizon.

'The evening was fine and I really began to feel that Winter Quarters were approaching. To increase my excitement Madigan Nunatak came into view for a time in the clear, evening light. Distance covered, over eight miles.'

The calm of the previous evening was broken again, and I started on the morning of January 29th in considerable drift and a fairly strong wind. After going five miles I had miraculous good fortune.

[1] The expedition's main base was on Cape Denison, Commonwealth Bay, in King George V Land.

I was travelling along on an even down grade and was wondering how long the two pounds of food which remained would last, when something dark loomed through the drift a short distance away to the right. All sorts of possibilities fled through my mind as I headed the sledge for it. The unexpected happened—it was a cairn of snow erected by McLean, Hodgeman and Hurley, who had been out searching for us. On the top of the mound was a bag of food, left on the chance that it might be picked up, while in a tin was a note stating the bearing and distance of the mound from Aladdin's Cave (E. 30° S., distance twenty-three miles), that the ship had arrived at the hut and was waiting, that Amundsen had reached the Pole, and that Scott was remaining another year in Antarctica.

It was rather a singular fact that the search party only left this mound at eight o'clock on the morning of that very day (January 29th). It was about 2 p.m. when I found it. Thus, during the night of the 28th, our camps had been only about five miles apart.

[The *Aurora* however had sailed, and Mawson was obliged to remain at Cape Denison until relieved in December.]

*The Home of the Blizzard; the Australasian Antarctic Expedition, 1911–14.* By Sir Douglas Mawson. Heinemann, 1915. Vol. I.

# Lauge Koch
## 1892–

THE exploration of Greenland, which received an impetus with Nansen's crossing of the ice-cap, has been carried on mainly by Danish and British travellers. Among the Danes Lauge Koch is prominent. As cartographer and geologist he first accompanied Knud Rasmussen in 1917 on an important expedition which mapped the great fiords of northern Greenland as far as De Long Fiord. The season, however, was a bad one; there was heavy snow in May and·June, which impeded travel, and the game upon which they depended for supplies was scarce. On the return journey the party was in dire straights. Three days before the following account by Koch opens, Rasmussen and an Eskimo had left the others to press on to Etah for succour. After Dr. Wulff's death, Koch and his Eskimo companions continued slowly on, and were rescued at the last moment by a relief party from Etah.

★    ★    ★

Another good day of travelling—short distances, much rest, much meat. Although Wulff complained about his heart the whole time, and about his stomach and his terrible weakness, he made constant botanical observations which indicated that his memory and his sense of observation were as yet surprisingly fresh, in sharp contrast to his exhausted body. When his fingers were too stiff for him to write, he dictated to me that which he wished to put down. On the whole it enlivened him considerably to speak about the plants he found on the way. His botanical interests were as alive as ever and his keenness to add to his results unchanged. Now and then the hope seemed to awake that, in spite of all, he would be able to manage, and this always stimulated him greatly. And why not hope for the best? In two days we had shot and eaten nine hares, we four men! We saved nothing, partly because we were yet too exhausted to carry anything, partly because there was no indication that game would decrease further ahead. On the contrary, we were going towards the real reindeer district!

But the next day was to be quite different from the two previous days. All night we had sleet, and during the day constant showers. This prevented us from seeing the hares. Furthermore, we came into quite a different type of country, with deep, stony cloughs, poor in vegetation. After four hours of strenuous marching we decided to leave the border-zone of the inland-ice and go towards the sea— towards the land with a more even terrain, more fertile ground, and richer in game.

As usual we started by noonday. In the afternoon Bosun shot a young hare which we ate raw; otherwise we saw no game that day.

On the top of every mountain slope we passed we had to wait for Wulff, often for a long time, although it was to the interest of us all to get quickly ahead to better hunting-grounds. Thus it was that in twelve hours we had covered a distance of hardly eight kilometres. Wulff had several times during the day been quite unbalanced, very irritable, and occasionally not quite clear. During the day he had often declared that it was better to die—'this walk was worse than death.'

Again we had snow-showers during the night. Several times I awoke and noticed that Wulff's sleep was very restless, and that he was constantly chewing tobacco—a practice which, in spite of our warnings, he indulged in excessively of late.

After twelve hours of rest we went on again. None of us spoke much, but I noticed at once that peace had settled on Wulff's thoughts. I was therefore highly surprised when, after three hours, he suddenly stopped and said, 'Now I can go no further because of my heart. Will you find a place for me where I can lie down?— preferably near to a lake where I can get something to drink, and where you will be able to find me if you get game in the immediate future.'

I had the definite impression that this was the result of a man's ripe and well-considered reflection. It would be of no avail to attempt to dissuade him. We had just sat down by a lake near a large clough which would be easy to recognize, but to gain time and yet another chance to save his life, I pointed to a lake some two kilometres further ahead. He agreed to my choice and we went together towards it; once more to encourage him I mentioned how com-

paratively near we were to people, and how slight were the difficulties yet before us compared with those we had already overcome.

'Yes,' said Wulff, 'To think of giving up after having gone
through so much and surmounted so many difficulties as we already
have! No, rather make yet another attempt! But,' he added, 'for
all that, this is walking to one's own funeral.'

I at once told the Eskimoes that Wulff had altered his decision,
so we set our course away from the lake again.

The snow had ceased to fall, there was some wind from the north,
and still some fog lay across the land. The Eskimoes parted company
to hunt each in his direction; two hours later Bosun returned with
fresh excrements of reindeer. As Wulff had again remained some
way behind, I went up on a mountain crag to look out for game.
He had sat down, but as soon as he sighted me he called up to me:
'All right, you go down into the clough; I am coming soon.'

This we did. At the bottom of the clough the hunters had lost the
tracks of the reindeer, so we all sat down, chewing willow-roots
whilst we waited.

As Wulff came down to us the first thing he said was, 'Well dear
comrades, here I will rest; I think there will be shelter by the great
stone on the other side of the river.'

He spoke quite calmly, and no emotion was noticeable. As I made
another attempt to coax him to continue, he replied definitely and
shortly: 'No, I cannot continue; there is an end to it now! Just do me
the service to write a few letters for me, and let the Eskimoes boil
some water so that I can get a little warmth in my body whilst I
dictate the letters.' Then he rose and walked up to the big stone which
he had selected; and here he had laid down when I reached the spot.

In vain I considered what I could do to help Wulff, and in vain
did I discuss the situation with the Eskimoes, who were gripped
uncannily by his last decision. But we were absolutely powerless
when he himself gave up and refused to go on. To remain in the
big clough void of game would be certain death for us all.

My own position was not much different from Wulff's. I also was
weak and my life depended entirely upon the hunt of the Eskimoes;
I myself had no strength to hunt. If both Wulff and I remained in
the clough there would be two instead of one to relieve, in case the

luck of the hunt should turn; and if this did not soon happen the Eskimoes' strength also would probably run out, and help would fail. In that case it would mean not merely catastrophe for us all, but the dearly-bought results of our expedition would be lost, as nobody would be able to find us in this clough. There was nothing for it; we who had as yet not given in must continue without Wulff; that was the only chance for the four of us. Further, Wulff was quite clear as to the position and its hopeless seriousness. Inukitsoq and Bosun had hunted incessantly since we had arrived on land; they had shirked no exertion—often they had gone out again when we were camping, and faithfully had they brought to us whatever booty they caught. And so far this had been comparatively plenty. But what was the good of it all when Wulff would no longer eat the only thing we could procure—boiled hare? And now he himself had preferred to remain lying here.

As soon as the water was boiled and he had drunk himself warm, he dictated a letter to Knud Rasmussen—a detailed letter which set out his Last Will. After that he himself wrote a letter to his parents and his daughter. Occasionally I noticed some emotion, but he was absolutely calm.

When he had finished the letter he lit his pipe and dictated to me a botanical survey of the vegetation in Inglefield Land. This was the last thing he did. We then lay speaking for a while, and whilst we were discussing a probable rescue he said, 'I suppose if I remain perfectly quiet I can live for another couple of days, and if during the next few days you can shoot a reindeer I shall, of course be glad of relief. But it is no earthly good coming back with hare-bones. If several days should elapse and you then meet with people, it is probable that only oatmeal gruel and port wine can save me.'

He then inquired how long I myself thought I could last. I replied that without hunting I supposed I had the strength to walk for yet another day, whilst the Eskimoes probably could keep up for a couple of days.

By now we had remained with Wulff for a good couple of hours, and as the Eskimoes were impatient to continue the interrupted hunting I made ready to break up. Although the situation in itself was a sad one, I did not at the moment feel very touched at the departure: I myself was too weak, and I had a feeling of walking to meet my own death.

Wulff remained quiet as we went; his last words to us were, 'Well, I will finally wish for you personally that you may reach your goal. When you meet difficulties, remember that now it is you that must save our results. May good fortune follow you. And now farewell!'

*Greenland by the Polar Sea.* By Knud Rasmussen. Heinemann, 1921. Trsl. from the Danish by A. and R. Kenney.

# Augustine Courtauld
## 1904-1959

AFTER the First World War, it was realized in Britain that with the development of air transport the Arctic regions would become of considerable importance, since the most direct routes between Western Europe and North America would lie across them. Greenland especially would occupy a strategic position. H. G. Watkins, a young Cambridge man, therefore organized the British Arctic Air Route Expedition, 1930–2. This was joined by Augustine Courtauld, also a Cambridge man. A base was established at Angmagssalik on the east coast of Greenland. Journeys were made inland, one party voyaged round to Prins Christians Land by kayak, and others crossed the ice-cap to the west coast. One subject on which it was clearly essential to obtain data was the meteorological conditions on the ice-cap: a meteorological station was accordingly set up about fifty miles inland. It became clear that the station would be completely isolated in winter. Courtauld, however, volunteered to occupy it alone to carry out continuous observations through the winter months. Extracts from his diary of this unique achievement (6th Dec. to 5th May) follow. The Press made much of this incident; perhaps the least perturbed of all was Courtauld himself, completely confident in 'Gino' Watkins's leadership.

\*　　　\*　　　\*

December 6th, Saturday. Today broke fine so it was time for them to go. I got up at 3.30 and cooked their breakfast. By ten they were ready. I took a photo and then with a 'Damma, damma, damma' they were away down the trail. Although there was a feeble sun, it was bitterly cold and I did not watch them long. Coming out again an hour later I could just see them as a speck in the distance. Now I am quite alone. Not a dog or even a mosquito for company. However it is very comfortable, or will be when I have cleared up the mess a bit. The great problem at the moment is to get my things dry. My sleeping-bag is full of ice and all my clothes except what I have got on are the same. Still my pipe tastes just as ever and the igloo is warm, so really there is nothing to complain of unless it be the curse of having to go out every three hours into the cold wind to observe the weather.

December 7th, Sunday. Fine and cold (56° below). Up at 7 a.m. for the first observation. Breakfast about 10.30. Lunch 2.30. Supper 7.30. With a certain amount of tidying up in between. Left little finger painful and swollen, also both big toes.

December 8th, Monday. Cold clear day again. Sun did not rise and I suppose will not until the middle of next month. Got on with drying clothes in intervals between met. observations which happen at 7, 10, 1, 4, 7, and 10.

December 9th, Tuesday. Nothing of note today except that I changed my underclothes as I had had itching for the last night or two. Found a good many bugs, much to my disgust, so put my clothes out in the snow in the pious hope that the cold will kill them. This is what comes of lending one's sleeping-bag to Eskimoes.

December 10th, Wednesday. Did some tidying up. Lamp lit first time today instead of taking four hours as it did yesterday. No more signs of bugs.

December 11th, Thursday. Toes hurting, also fingers. Took an observation of Aldebaran to find how much the clock has gone wrong in the last three months. Reading *Forsyte Saga*, Vol. II— V.G. Even better than Vol. I. Opened pea-flour and marge today. Found jam made out of cocoa V.G., much better than drinking it, and agree in this respect with G.K.C. Filled paraffin cans (4 gallons).

December 12th, Friday. Windy day with drifting snow. House went down to 35° but primus put it to 60° again. Stopped up ventilation hole to try and keep in heat at night. Entrance to tunnel blocked up when I went out for 10 p.m. obs. Had to dig my way out. This weather won't help the others getting back. Filled pemmican bag, 1½ lb.

December 13th, Saturday. Strong N.W. wind blowing snow so that one could hardly see to get out to the instruments. A blizzard in fact. Entrance to tunnel completely stopped up and had to dig myself out for every observation. Played a game of chess this evening and then bandaged toes. Both seem quite dead but are going.

December 14th, Sunday. Dug out the entrance this morning, but the wind shifted to S.E. and filled it up again. V. warm, temperature went up to plus 5°. Found I am only smoking 1·7 oz. a week. Tobacco should last at this rate seventeen weeks. Reading *Black Arrow, Friendly Arctic, Isaak* (Walton). All V.G. What I shall do when I have finished all the books God knows. Made out a list for a chap's dinner when I get home.

December 16th, Tuesday. Still this warm wind blowing stronger than ever. Had a job to get out of house this morning. Found I was digging up into a vast snow drift, so had to make a hole vertically upwards, and after some time burrowing managed to scramble out. Got lost getting to the instruments at seven o'clock, for the drift was too thick. Tonight unbandaged toes. Unpleasant sight. Left toe-nail came off. Other will soon, I expect.

December 27th, Saturday. North-east wind has drifted up the whole place again. Did a certain amount of digging today and yesterday, but toes hurt too much to stay out more than a few minutes at a time. It is now just three weeks since the others left. Had an awful fright early this morning. Just getting to sleep again after 7 a.m. obs. when there was a soft rumbling close to my head which increased and ended in a dull crash. It flashed across my mind as it began that the weight of snow was too much and the whole house was going to come in on me. However nothing happened so I concluded that the tunnel had fallen in and that I should have a job to get out as the spade would be buried. However that was not so and I think that some of the blocks in the wall of the house have given way and fallen in but it is impossible to find out until a lot of snow has been removed from the top. Hope nothing further happens tonight.

January 4th, Sunday. A frightful day. There was a gale blowing when I woke up this morning and of course the tunnel was snowed up. Managed to dig myself out and came back with clothes full of snow which got over everything. One piece dropped inside the lamp and broke the mantle. Dug out again at eleven o'clock, 1 and 2.30. Each time the entrance was blocked right up and snow drifting in about as fast as I could dig. By this time (2.30) the back of the tunnel was so full of snow caused by digging out the entrance that I could scarcely wriggle up it. At 2 the drift at the entrance was deeper than my height and I had some difficulty in getting out even when I had dug away the snow. At 3.30 I found I could no longer get the snow back from the entrance. The tunnel was too full already and the wind was still increasing. It is blowing a full gale blizzard, and outside one can hardly see one's spade, and one's face gets covered up directly. So, as I cannot get out, I shall have to stay in and the met. will have to go hang till the wind drops. Then I shall have to find some way of getting out. Hope the air keeps breathable and that the roof doesn't collapse. If (a) doesn't or (b) does my end should be peaceful enough, and I have four slabs of chocolate to eat during it. Anyhow it won't be attended by the fuss and frills one's pegging out at home would.

January 5th, Monday. Came to the conclusion this morning that it was impossible to dig out the tunnel, so dug out the entrance of the starboard snow house and cut a hole in the roof. Luckily it did not fall in and so I was able to get out. THANK GOD.

The gale which rose again this morning calmed down by evening and so all is once more peaceful.

February 1st, Sunday. After the south-east gale had finished—this gale blew so hard that I had to walk or rather stagger backwards to get to the observations—it started again from north-west. In the meantime the paraffin has nearly run out in the house, and I cannot dig the other tin out while these gales are blowing. Tried digging but did not locate it. Of course the hole fills up directly one stops digging. The fact is I am not sure of its exact position now that everything is drifted up with snow. Changed clothes tonight for the original inhabited ones, but the inmates have been done down by leaving them out in the cold. Just finished *Vanity Fair*. Like it well. There is something very satisfying in reading perfect English whatever the story and have now started de Quincey's *Opium Eater* which seems very long-winded and pedantic, but again it is well worth reading for its style.

I wonder when, if ever, I shall get away from here. Not that I am bored, but I notice that my legs are getting very thin, partly from want of exercise and partly from lack of fresh food I suppose. If I have to sledge back it will be pretty rotten unless the going is good enough to ride, These gales are nerve-racking things. I am daily expecting the house to fall in, for both the side snow houses have partly done so. I wish there could be some decent weather. Whenever the sun is out and it is clear it is about 50° below zero, and the rest of the time it blows blizzards so that one can see or do nothing on account of the drift.

February 14th, Saturday. Have now been ten weeks alone. Weather this week has been damnable. First of all too cold to do any digging (90 degrees of frost) so that I am running short of rations because the others are buried about ten feet under snow. Then I left the opening of the snow-house roof unstopped one night and it came on to blow from the south-east and filled it up completely. With great difficulty I got it a bit clear and stopped it coming in from that direction, when last night it went back to the north-west and filled it up again. Now impossible to get out without letting all the snow down into the tunnel, which is so small now that I can only just wriggle through it. Only one more day's food after today. Still blowing.

April 26th. Just six months since we left the Base and started on sledge rations. Been here alone twenty weeks. Everything running out. Using last candle. V. little paraffin. What I shall do for drinking water I don't know. Only two more biscuits. In four days I officially run out of food but have a reserve, Thank God, of pemmican and marge. Smoking tea as I have no fuel to cook it with.

May 6th, Wednesday. Written on sledge returning to the Base.

Yesterday was the greatest day in my life. All Monday I kept on wondering what it was that May 5th should be famous for. I could not think of anybody's birthday or any event so I decided it must be that the relief was going to arrive. Yesterday (May 5th) the primus gave its last gasp as I was melting water for the morning meal. I was lying in my bag after this so-called meal of a bit of pemmican and margarine and had just decided that I should have to start and walk back on June 1st if I could get out, when suddenly there was an appalling noise like a bus going by followed by a confused yelling noise. I nearly jumped out of my skin. Was it the house falling in at last? A second later I realized the truth. It was somebody, some real human voice, calling down the ventilator. It was a wonderful moment. I could not think what to do or say. I yelled back some stuttering remarks that seemed quite futile for the occasion. 'Hooray,' they shouted. 'Are you all right?' 'Yes, thank God you've come. I am perfectly fit.' 'Thank God,' they said. It was Gino and Freddie;[1] they were as relieved as I was. The whole world seemed turned inside out. At one moment I was lying in the dark wondering how ever I was going to see anybody again or ever get home, and the next home was in sight. It was bright sunshine they said outside and they had reached by navigation a place about two miles away where they had camped and from which they had gone out on skis to find the Station. They told of many happenings. Apparently Jamie, Martin and Quintin[2] had been up in March but had failed to find the Station, so directly they got back Gino, Freddie and John Rymill started off equipped with the best navigation gear and had reached me in fifteen days from the Base. They said the going was excellent and that I should be able to ride the whole way back. This was an incredible relief to hear, for with my weakened condition I could never have walked or skied it.

[1] H. G. Watkins and F. Spencer Chapman.
[2] J. M. Scott, Martin Lindsay and Quintin Riley.

Courtauld's diary was published in J. M. Scott's: *Portrait of an Ice-cap with Human Figures.* Chatto and Windus, 1953.

# *Vivian Fuchs*
## 1908–

AFTER World War II, Antarctic research progressed with ever-increasing momentum. There was the conviction that scientific knowledge of the world was incomplete while a considerable and peculiar portion of its surface remained uninvestigated. Economic motives diminished in importance except perhaps as regards the Antarctic's role in the oceanic and atmospheric circulation of the world and its consequent influence on fisheries and crops. There was also its potential value in the air routes of the future. Scientific interest was immensely stimulated by the programme of the International Geophysical Year, 1957–8. The continent remained also a challenge to the spirit of adventure, as the region where man could best engage the forces of nature at their severest and most relentless. Developments during the war in many directions, perhaps most decisive in forms of transport, were applied on a huge scale. One major journey remained unachieved, though Shackleton had planned it in 1914, the crossing of the continent *via* the South Pole. This was accomplished by Sir Vivian Fuchs, in collaboration with Sir Edmund Hillary, in 1957–8, when his party crossed from the Weddell Sea to the Ross Sea. Though he relied on mechanized transport (Sno-cats), Fuchs also took dog teams in case of emergency. A scientific programme, considerable in the circumstances, was carried out. The extract describes the journey from Shackleton Base on the Weddell Sea towards the South Pole.

*　　*　　*

(27 December 1957.) At last, just before nine o'clock, the break-down party pulled into camp,[1] having cured the trouble by fitting a new Weasel radiator. Setting off at twenty past ten that night, we were in trouble again when George's 'Wrack and Ruin' lost power and was only able to crawl. Roy Homard soon cured this, and we had travelled fifteen miles by a quarter to four in the morning, when

[1] The party had left South Ice, their depot in the Weddell Sea sector on Christmas Eve. The South Pole was distant 555 miles.

we stopped at the fifty-five-mile cairn. So developed the picture of events which were to be our lot throughout almost the entire journey—long hours slowly grinding over hard sastrugi, or through deep soft snow, frequent minor troubles with one or other of the vehicles, time spent every three hours in taking meteorological and gravity observations, and the periodic boring of holes for seismic shooting; camping, eating, vehicle maintenance and sleeping had all to be fitted into what hours remained. As a result there was generally very little time for sleep, and at the end of the journey I am sure we all considered the outstanding hardship to have been lack of rest.

On 29th December we reached the cairn marking a hundred miles from South Ice, where we found Ken and Jon with the dog teams, and Geoffrey and Hannes with 'Haywire'. The cairn stood in a hollow running east-west to join another deep, curious-looking depression which appeared to extend almost north-south. Unfortunately we had no time to investigate, but Geoffrey's gravimeter indicated a sudden shallowing of the ice, and we thought that the surface disturbances were probably due to this. Our position at this time, as observed by David Stratton, was 83° 33′ S. 29° 02′ W., and the approximate altitude 5,800 feet.

General vehicle maintenance, carried out every two hundred miles, was now due, and in addition a number of sledge tow bars, which had been broken by the heavy going, had to be electrically welded. We therefore knew that our stop was bound to be longer than usual, and this had the advantage of allowing the dogs to get well ahead again. The increasing altitude was making the Sno-cats overheat as they hauled their six-ton pay loads in second and third gears. I therefore took the opportunity of replacing the four-bladed fan on 'Rock 'n Roll' with another having six blades.

31st December was a day of beautiful clear weather, but not a good day for us. Troubles came one after another: first the welding of the two bars proved to be a much longer job than we had expected, then there were difficulties with two of the Weasels, and when we were finally about to start, at seven in the evening, Hal's rammsonde became stuck three metres down, and we had to dig a pit to that depth before we could recover it. By half past eight we had moved off, but did not get very far, for first George Lowe broke a sledge runner, and then Allan's Weasel 'Rumble' broke a track and had to be abandoned as no replacement was being carried. Fortunately we had left the Muskeg tractor at the last camp site only six miles back. It had been the first vehicle to be dropped, according to our plan to abandon them when the consumption of fuel had sufficiently lightened the loads. Now we could go back and pick it up to replace 'Rumble'. As the result of these troubles we camped where we were, but I again sent Hannes and Geoffrey on with 'Haywire' to get into position for another seismic shot. At midnight I made the rounds, giving everyone a tot of brandy with which to see in the New Year.

On New Year's Day conditions were so good that we hoped to cover fifty miles, but the surface was too soft for the Muskeg which was towing two heavy sledges, and it could not travel faster than two to five m.p.h. Everyone had a soft spot for 'Hopalong' because it had gone so far and so well with a heavy load, and had given no trouble. When first we had left it, we had all been sad, then delighted when it had joined us again, but there was no place for sentiment where the efficiency of the party was concerned, and having no Muskeg spares, it had to be the next to go. In the circumstances we had been working it as hard as possible, to save extra load on the Weasels, which would have to travel further.

To speed our progress, the second sledge was taken from 'Hopalong' and put as a third behind the 'County of Kent', which seemed to take it easily. 'Hopalong' could now keep up five m.p.h. in third gear, which was reasonable, for it had never been in top gear for the entire 530 miles from Shackleton. In all we covered thirty-nine miles that day, the last nine over increasingly severe sastrugi, which in the end so separated the vehicles that we were forced to camp to let them assemble. This worsening surface was the beginning of our most continuously bad area and next day, 2nd January, I wrote:

'Another thirty miles today, but what a labour! All vehicles in first and second gear all the way over the most corrugated fields of continuous sastrugi. The strain on vehicles and sledges is prodigious; particularly I worry about the gear-boxes, for these constant hours of heavy work in low gear are bound to tell on them. Already

'Rock 'n Roll's' lay-shaft is very much noisier than it was. One bright spot is that the six-bladed fan now maintains the engines at 160° even with the radiator doors half shut.

With the dog tracks still extending ahead of us, there was no need for navigation, and Geoffrey and Hannes continued ahead, followed by the two Weasels and the Muskeg, which were slower than the 'cats' over the murderous sastrugi. It was impossible to go round the high ice-hard ridges, for they formed a great field that extended out of sight in all directions. The best that could be done was for each driver to judge the course for his own particular type of vehicle, and often we found ourselves scattered a mile or two apart, working and weaving our way among the ridges four and five feet high. Sometimes, when there was no easier way, vehicles and sledges had very deliberately to be driven at a speed of half a mile an hour or less over vertical drops. Wending our way, twisting and turning, sometimes at right angles to the course, we tried to keep within reasonable distance of the dog sledge tracks which preserved a fairly steady line and prevented us from making too much extra mileage. When the snow cairns were visible (usually at a distance of about two miles) they were an excellent guide, for we could work steadily towards them. Even the trail of the dog teams wandered considerably and here and there the tracks in the snow revealed the upsetting of a sledge, or where two ski tracks ended abruptly against a ridge we knew that someone had come to grief.

Over this terrain the Sno-cats handled much better than the Weasels, for their articulated tracks conformed more easily to the surface and their great power, and five forward gears, gave easier control. Yet the drivers had their own problems, because the second or third sledges tended to swing more freely and, linked with a wire tow, would catch up and ram the 'cat' or the sledge ahead. The Weasels, on the other hand, did not roll but pitched heavily. Climbing to the top of a sharp-topped ridge, they would tilt up and up, then suddenly dip violently forward, followed by the plunging 2½-ton sledge. Some drivers had the added irritation of towing a dog sledge behind the main load and this, being narrow, would yaw from side to side, often turning over and having to be righted by a fuming passenger. And yet we had good reason for taking these additional sledges. Should the vehicles break down, making it necessary for us to walk the remainder of the distance, we had to have something that we could manhaul.

Mile after mile this trial of tempers and equipment continued— would it ever stop, we wondered? By now we had expected to be well up on the polar plateau, experiencing relatively easy going instead of these endless sastrugi stretching at right angles to our path. The winds, it seemed, must blow perpetually from the east, scouring and grooving the surface year after year.

As the day progressed, David Stratton and I first found Allan Rogers with a steel tow bar that had caught in a snow ridge and been bent right back beneath the sledge. This was unscrewed and replaced with a wire tow. Then, further on, we found Geoffrey and Hannes together with Hal and George. The seismic spread was ready, but it was essential to wait until the last of the vehicles had ceased to roll, for the extremely delicate instruments would record their vibrations even at a distance of a mile or two. While they were waiting, Hal had decided to drive his rammsonde into the bottom of the pit that had been prepared for the explosive charge. There it had again become jammed in a hard layer of ice several metres down, and a new pit had to be dug before the seismic shot could be fired. When this had been done, we pushed on again to catch up the dog teams, and found them encamped after we had covered thirty miles in the day.

That night I was able to speak to Hillary, who said that he was expecting to arrive at the Pole the following day. For him that would be the 4th January, as he was on the other side of the date line.

*The Crossing of Antarctica: the Commonwealth Trans-Antarctic Expedition, 1955–8.* By Sir Vivian Fuchs and Sir Edmund Hillary. Little, Brown & Company, 1959.

# William R. Anderson
## 1921-

THE possibilities of the submarine as an intrument of Polar exploration had been tested with little success by Sir Hubert Wilkins in
1931. Its value for this purpose was triumphantly vindicated by
Commander W. R. Anderson, United States Navy, in the nuclear-
powered submarine *Nautilus* in 1958, when he navigated under
the central Arctic basin and the North Pole to the North Atlantic
Ocean. This achievement also vindicated modern methods of 'blind'
navigation. The voyage threw much light upon the configuration of
the ocean bottom, and was also notable for demonstrating the
practicability of an underwater North-West Passage.

* * *

Saturday morning, August 2nd, found 116 people running along at
four hundred feet at cruising speed on course 000 true, just about
forty-four hours short of culminating the most thrilling and adventurous cruise any sailor ever embarked upon. Overhead the ice was
almost solid and incredibly rough, projecting downward as much as
sixty-five feet from the surface, but averaging ten to fifteen feet
thick. It would be less than honest to say that one can submarine
under it with total abandon.

At first Frank Adams and I stood 'watch and watch', which meant
that one of us was up and about at all times. When my co-skipper
took over I could turn in for a few hours of sleep, knowing that the
ship was in experienced and capable hands.

As we plunged deeper under the pack I thought, Where is the
point of no return? Here? A hundred miles from here? A day's
journey away? At the Pole itself, perhaps? Frankly, I did not know.
But I had computed it to be at the 'Pole of Inaccessibility', the
geographic centre of the ice pack, about four hundred miles below
the true Pole. But who cared? We were safe, warm, and comfortable in our home beneath the sea.

Morale was high and excitement at fever pitch. Once we had
reached deep water beneath the pack, all hands felt that from then

on out it was a run for 'home'. Although our ship's log read eighteen knots, Chief Machinist's Mate Stuart Nelson, who by then was nicknamed 'Stop Leak', scampered forward from the engine room to ask if the engineers couldn't make 'just a couple more going-home turns'. I ordered twenty knots. The whole ship seemed to purr along contentedly.

'Boy, this is the way to explore,' remarked Robert N. Jarvis, Hospitalman First Class. Pipe in hand, a cup of coffee beside him, he took his ease between atmosphere analyses. 'Pinging up and down and all around at twenty knots, fresh air all day long, a warm boat, I'd hate to walk across these ice fields up there to the Pole the way Admiral Peary did it.'

Though most of us considered the North Pole a desirable objective, our primary mission was to cross from the Pacific Ocean to the Atlantic Ocean, blazing a new north-west passage. Actually, from the standpoint of compass performance, it might have been preferable to avoid the Pole, to ease around it at lower latitude. However, the route across the Pole was the shortest and fastest. Besides, who could resist the temptation to cross the North Pole when it was so close at hand?

Dr. Lyon remained glued to his sonar equipment hour after hour, watching the recording pens trace the contour of the underside of the ice. His new instruments displayed the ice in far greater detail, and with much greater accuracy, than the machines we had used in 1957. In fact, it was at this point that we discovered that the ice pack was far thicker than we had estimated in 1957, and that pressure ridges (ice forced downward when two massive floes press against one another) projected down to 100 or 125 feet. As we sped along, Dr. Lyon's instruments collected in each hour more precise data on the ice and the Arctic Basin floor than have been assembled in all history. When he finally left the ship, he had accumulated two trunkfuls of data.

And what of peaks rising abruptly from the uncharted ocean floor? Our detection equipment kept a sharp 'eye' on these obstacles. We found several. At latitude 76° 22′ north, in a region where there are no charted soundings, our fathometer, which had been running along fairly steadily at about 2,100 fathoms, suddenly spiked up to 1,500 fathoms, and then, to my concern, to less than 500.

I camped alongside the fathometer for several hours, intently watching the rugged terrain as it unfolded beneath us. I saw incredibly steep cliffs—undersea ranges—rise thousands of feet above the ocean floor. Several times I ordered speed slackened, then resumed, as a promontory levelled off or descended as rapidly as it had risen. The shape of these undersea mountains appeared phenomenally rugged, and as grotesque as the craters of the moon.

[August 3] When we crossed the Pole, of course, no bells would ring, nor would we feel a bump. Only our instruments could tell us how close we had come. Since we had made the decision to cross the Pole, we were determined to hit it precisely on the nose. Along with Navigator Shep Jenks and his assistant, Chief Petty Officer Lyle B. Rayl, I had stationed myself in the Attack Centre, and although we were almost as far north as man can go on this planet, we were literally sweating over the charts and electronic position-indicators, making minute, half-degree adjustments at the helm.

The hour by *Nautilus* clocks, which were still set on Seattle time, was 1900 or seven o'clock in the evening. Our nuclear engine, which up to then had pushed *Nautilus* more than 124,000 miles, was purring smoothly. Our electronic log, or speedometer needle, was hovering about twenty knots, the depth gauge needle about four hundred feet. Our sensitive sonar indicated that the endless polar ice pack was running between eight and eighty feet thick. Above the ice, we imagined, the polar wind was howling across its trackless, barren stamping ground, grinding massive floes one upon the other.

By then we had been under ice for sixty-two hours. Obviously, it was not possible to take the usual fix on heavenly bodies to determine our position, so we were navigating primarily by dead reckoning. This means that we were spacing our speed and course on the chart and plotting our position every half-hour or so, accordingly. Our bottom soundings, sometimes useful in submerged navigating, did not help, of course, in this uncharted, unsounded area. Our precision fathometer had indicated differences of as much as eight thousand feet at those rare points where soundings were made, so we could not rely on it. Our only check on our navigating was the inertial navigator. At the exact moment we crossed the Pole, we knew, the instrument would give a positive indication. Tom Curtis moved closer to his dials and scopes as we drew near.

A mile south of the Pole, I told Jenks to inform me when we were four-tenths of a mile from the Pole as indicated by the electronic log. The mileage indicator was moving rapidly. It was only a matter of seconds. *Nautilus* crewmen had gathered in the Attack Centre and the Crew's Mess.

On Jenks's mark, I stepped up to the mike of the ship's public-address system: 'All hands—this is the Captain speaking. . . . In a few moments *Nautilus* will realize a goal long a dream of mankind— the attainment by ship of the North Geographic Pole. With continued Godspeed, in less than two days we will record an even more significant historic first: the completion of a rapid transpolar voyage from the Pacific to the Atlantic Ocean.

'The distance to the Pole is now precisely four-tenths of a mile. As we approach, let us pause in silence dedicated with our thanks for the blessings that have been ours during this remarkable voyage—our prayers for lasting world peace, and in solemn tribute to those who have preceeded us, whether in victory or defeat.'

The juke box was shut off, and at that moment a hush literally fell over the ship. The only sound to be heard was the steady staccato of pinging from our sonars steadily watching the bottom, the ice, and the dark waters ahead.

I glanced again at the distance indicator, and gave a brief count-down to the crew. 'Stand by. 10 . . . 8 . . . 6 . . . 4 . . . 3 . . . 2 . . . 1. MARK! August 3, 1958. Time, 2315 (11.15 p.m. Eastern Daylight Saving Time). For the United States and the United States Navy, the North Pole.' I could hear cheers in the Crew's Mess.

I looked anxiously at Tom Curtis. He was smiling. The inertial navigator had switched precisely as expected, positively confirming that we had crossed the exact North Pole. Curtis sang out: 'As a matter of fact, Captain, you might say we came so close we pierced the Pole.'

I stood for a moment in silence, awe-struck at what *Nautilus* had achieved. She had blazed a new submerged north-west passage, vastly decreasing the sea-travel time for nuclear submarines from the Pacific to the Atlantic, one that could be used even if the Panama Canal were closed. When and if nuclear-powered cargo submarines are built, the new route would cut 4,900 miles and thirteen days off the route from Japan to Europe. *Nautilus* had opened a new era, completely conquered the vast, inhospitable Arctic. Our instruments were, for the first time, compiling an accurate and broad picture of the Arctic Basin and its approaches. *Nautilus*'s achievement was dramatic proof of United States leadership in at least one important branch of science; and it would soon rank alongside or above the Russian sputnik in the minds of millions. Lastly, for the first time in history a ship had actually reached the North Pole. And never had so many men—116—been gathered at the Pole at one time.

I was proud of what *Nautilus* had done, yet I felt no sense of personal triumph or achievement. That we had reached the Pole was the work and support of many people. My reaction, frankly, was an overwhelming feeling of relief that after months and months of preparation and two unsuccessful probes we had finally made it.

Precisely at the Pole, for the record, I made note of some statistics which may or may not prove useful. The water temperature was 32·4 degrees Fahrenheit. The depth of the sea was 13,410 feet, exactly 1,927 feet deeper than reported by Ivan Papanin, a Russian who landed there, he claims, in an aeroplane in 1937. (In 1909 Admiral Peary had found the depth 'greater than 9,000 feet'.) At the exact Pole our ice detectors noted a pressure ridge extending twenty-five feet down.

*Nautilus 90 North*. By Commdr. William R. Anderson, U.S.N. World Publishing Company, 1959.